All God's People

dsmith@heritageseminary.net

ALL GOD'S PEOPLE

A Theology of the Church

DAVID L. SMITH

Wipf & Stock
PUBLISHERS
Eugene, Oregon

Wipf and Stock Publishers
199 West 8th Avenue, Suite 3
Eugene, Oregon 97401

All God's People
A Theology of the Church
By Smith, David L.
Copyright©1996 by Smith, David L.
ISBN: 1-59244-538-1
Publication date 2/6/2004
Previously published by Victor Books, 1996

To John, Richard, and Kathryn,
with the prayer that the church will
come to mean as much to them
as it does to me.

CONTENTS

PREFACE

No institution on earth is more important than the church. Conceived in the mind of God before the foundation of the earth, founded by Christ during His earthly ministry, and animated by the power of the Holy Spirit, the church is a vital part of the salvation of human beings. No statement is more true than "no salvation outside of the church," though we may not interpret it in quite the same way as the one who originally coined it. That a great many Christians—especially evangelical Christians—do not share this high view of the church is a tragedy of epic proportions which has led to a weakening of the cause of Christ in this world.

If the kingdom of God in this world is to prosper, then the church must prosper. If the church is to prosper, then Christians must have a deeper appreciation of it. My aim in writing this volume is to aid in this whole process. Only through a more penetrating perception of what the church is all about may one achieve the necessary esteem for it.

I have attempted to write the book as simply and straightforwardly as possible. It is aimed at a broad audience ranging from the knowledgeable lay leader to the seminarian. It is as complete as I could make it in the space allowed. It is as inclusive as I could make it, given biblical constraints. But it is also my own theological position without apology.

8

I am grateful to all those theologians down through the centuries who have preceded me in thinking about the church. While I do not agree with everything all of them have written, their labors have contributed enormously to our knowledge of the monumental importance of this divinely initiated institution through the ages. Even the writings of those not held to be "orthodox" have helped to give a right perspective to our thinking.

As always, I would extend my gratitude to my colleagues at Providence College and Seminary for their affirmation of my endeavors. And without the support of my wife and her willingness to do without my attention for large blocks of time, I could not have completed this work.

Underlying all, I thank my Heavenly Father who has given me a love for His Son through whose Spirit I have been established as a member of the body of Christ and so have been engrafted as one of God's own people.

David L. Smith
January 1995

INTRODUCTION

The church has played a major role in the history of North America. It is difficult to imagine Maryland and Quebec without the Roman Catholics; or the Atlantic Provinces of Canada, the American South, and Rhode Island without the Baptists; or Western Canada and the Midwestern United States without the Lutherans and Mennonites; or Ontario and Virginia without the Anglicans (Episcopalians). The list could go on and on. The church has exerted a major influence on the shape and direction of both Canada and the United States, from the drafting of the First Amendment to the American Constitution through lobbying by the nonestablished churches to the naming of Canada as a "Dominion" through the suggestion of a Baptist founding father who had been studying Psalm 72.

In recent years, however, the church has been struggling. Those frequenting churches on a regular basis have been decreasing in number. Today only about 40 percent of the American population can be found in church on a given Sunday (and not the same 40 percent each Sunday)[1] and only 35 percent of Canadians (down from 67 percent forty years ago!).[2] Most denominations, furthermore, are suffering staggering losses of members, and the few that are making numerical gains are not keeping up with the percentage increase in population.[3] Trends would also indicate that massive numbers of people who attend

11

churches are not joining them, preferring to keep their options open to shift from one congregation to another.[4]

While there are undoubtedly many factors involved in this monumental change in the church's situation, one may be isolated from among them. Christian people are either ignorant of, or misunderstand, what the church is about. They have become disconnected from the foundations of the faith. A proper understanding of the nature of the church as God intended it to be should effect changes in the attitudes of Christian people and how they practice their faith (both as individuals and corporately). It should serve to reconnect and reroot them in the vital underpinning of Christian faith and practice. This book sets out to give people such a necessary comprehension.

The book is divided into three basic sections, which evidence the author's methodology. While each section can stand on its own as a separate and independent theology, with the exception of the biblical theology all draw on the others. Thus, there is also an interconnectedness. The first section, "A Historical Theology of the Church," surveys the history of the theology of the church, beginning with the early church, the formative years for all Christian theology. Chapter 2 looks at the Medieval period, as thinking became more formalized and set. Chapter 3 examines the revolution in thinking as the Reformers attempted to reestablish New Testament concepts of the church in daily practice. Chapter 4 considers the evolution and diversification of Protestant thinking in regard to the nature of the church, and the fifth chapter brings us into contemporary thinking by Christian theologians of many stripes.

The second section, "A Biblical Theology of the Church," is divided into three chapters. Chapter 6 reviews the Old Testament theology of the people of God, examining what relationship the Hebrew people of that time might have to the church. Chapter 7 scrutinizes the theology of the Gospels in regard to the people of God—dealing especially with Jesus' views of the church—and the eighth chapter analyzes the Apostolic sense of the people of God, which is the heart of an evangelical theology of the church.

12

The third section is "A Systematic Theology of the Church," and seeks both to systematize the biblical theology and synthesize it with the social sciences, philosophy, and psychology (but always under the supreme authority of the Scriptures), to present us with a sweeping view of the church as both God and humanity are related to it. Chapter 9 reflects upon the origin of the church in the mind of God and in physical reality. The nature of the church is the content of chapter 10; how does one define the church, and should it be seen as local or universal in its scope? Chapter 11 examines the mission of the church, namely, the carrying out of the Great Commission through evangelism, education, worship, and good works. The ministry of the church is the focus of the twelfth chapter, looking at *charismata*, ordination, the place of women in leadership roles, and church governance. Is there a form of governance which may be categorized as *the biblical* pattern? Chapter 13, which deals with membership in the church, ponders the role of baptism as initiation and the significance of the Lord's Supper to continuing fellowship. The final chapter considers church unity; various possible types of unity are examined with a view to the possibility of reconciling the present state of the church with the New Testament depiction: is ecumenism a viable answer to this problem?

If theology cannot be practically applied, it is not worth very much. The conclusion, therefore, is "A Practical Theology of the Church," seeking to take what has been learned and relate it both redemptively and functionally to the present situation in which we find ourselves.

PART 1

A Historical Theology
of the Church

CHAPTER ONE

The Church of the
Patristic Period

No faith has had such a meteoric growth as Christianity. Beginning as a tiny sect of a despised religion in an obscure outpost of the Roman Empire, within six centuries it had become the official religion of that empire and included in its membership the vast majority of the population. How did the Christian church view itself during this early era of its existence? To what degree was it influenced by the society around it, and to what degree did it influence that society? These are some of the questions considered in this chapter.

THE FIRST CENTURY: CREATING THE CONTEXT

The first century A.D. may be seen as the period of gestation, birth, and early infancy of the church. During this period events occurred and directions were taken which would lay the foundations of the church. Changes would occur over time, but the general form and concept were set.

The New Testament Church[1]

While it may be cogently argued that the church had its beginnings in the mind of Jesus (see chap. 7), one may also date its birth from the Pentecost immediately following His resurrection. The risen Lord had commanded His followers not to leave Jerusalem, but to wait there for God's promise to be fulfilled, namely, the baptism of the Holy Spirit (Acts 1:4-5). On the Day

17

of Pentecost, an occasion where "God-fearing Jews from every nation under heaven" (Acts 2:5) were visiting Jerusalem, the Spirit descended visibly and audibly. The disciples "were filled with the Holy Spirit and began to speak in other tongues as the Spirit enabled them" (2:4). Both local and Diaspora Jews were drawn to the place where all of this was happening. Peter took advantage of the situation to make an impassioned speech on Jesus' teaching, ministry, and passion, concluding that "God has made this Jesus, whom you crucified, both Lord and Christ" (2:36). When the convicted group asked what response was appropriate, Peter exhorted them to "repent and be baptized, every one of you, in the name of Jesus Christ" (2:38). Some 3,000 followed Peter's advice. They were baptized. The church had been born!

The Jerusalem Connection. This early church in Jerusalem multiplied rapidly under the direction and witness of the disciples. Undoubtedly, many of their converts were members of devout groups who had long awaited the coming of the kingdom of God. Many may have belonged to radical Jewish groups (such as the Zealots), but a number of the priests became believers (Acts 6:7). Nonetheless, the fledgling church enjoyed a good reputation in the community at large. Led by the Twelve under the supervision of James the Just, the early believers attended the temple services regularly, and in every aspect of life gave the appearance of being devout Jews who observed Hebrew customs and the law.

One group was adamantly opposed. The Sadducees, who had included the chief priests and temple rulers, hated these upstarts who focused on the resurrection of their Leader (indubitably because the Sadducees denied any possibility of resurrection in either the present or future). "Attempts were made to repress them . . . but they refused to be intimidated and persisted in proclaiming Jesus, crucified by men but raised to life by God, as Israel's true Messiah."[2]

The opportunity for an intense persecution came with the appearance of Stephen, a Hellenistic Jew and Christian, who was an able and aggressive apologist for the new faith. The frustration of the Jewish leaders with his zealous defense of the faith led them to do away with him. His martyrdom was the start of an intense persecution led by Saul of Tarsus. Yet such oppression simply served to spread the Christian cause for, wherever they went, the believers evangelized those about them. Consequently, the church spread throughout Judea, into Samaria, and on into Syria, Phoenicia, and Cyprus. Ultimately, the persecutor himself was converted (Acts 9) and became a most effective missionary.

Even with the spread of Christianity into Gentile centers, and with the increasing number of Gentiles flooding into the church, Jerusalem remained the most important center of the faith. Doctrinal tensions—such as the relationship of Jewish religious observances to Christian practice—were discussed and resolved at Jerusalem (Acts 15:1-35). The Gentile churches, furthermore, contributed regularly to the maintenance of believers in the Jerusalem church (1 Cor. 16:1-5).

As Gentile Christianity became more powerful, tensions increasingly developed with Jerusalem over the observance of the Old Testament law. The Jerusalem church saw no difficulty in practicing both their newfound faith and their former faith simultaneously. James the Just (Jesus' half brother), who functioned as overseer of the Jerusalem church (though Scripture never accords him that title), enjoyed an amazing reputation for holiness in the community at large. Eusebius of Caesarea tells us that "he was in the habit of entering the temple alone, and was often found upon his bended knees, and interceding for the forgiveness of the people; so that his knees became as hard as camels', in consequence of his habitual supplication and kneeling before God."[3] Tradition has it that, following the arrest of Paul and his extradition to Rome, the Sanhedrin got together (about A.D. 61) and, in the absence of a Roman governor, condemned James; he was then executed by stoning and clubbing to death.[4]

In A.D. 66, spurred on by Roman atrocities and corruption, the Jews rebelled against the Empire. Nero sent Vespasian to put down the revolt. Jerusalem was strongly fortified and, alone among the communities in Judea, managed to hold out against the legions. The death of Nero led to a temporary suspension of hostilities, but with the ascension of Vespasian to the throne, the war was renewed under his son Titus. The city was entered in August of 70, and within a month, all resistance in Jerusalem was ended. The temple and much of the city was razed.

With the destruction of Jerusalem, the influence of the church there quickly faded. With the exception of a very few, most believers had fled to Transjordan, Syria, and Egypt. Some were absorbed into the Pauline church; others maintained their practice of combining Jewish and Christian practices; still others moved into a more Jewish-oriented style, viewing Jesus as essentially a second Moses, and completely rejecting Paul as an apostle of Christ. This last group were known as Ebionites (from the Hebrew *ha'ebyonim*, "the poor"). They continued on until the seventh century, when they were overwhelmed by Islam.[5]

The church continued in Galilee under the leadership of relatives of Jesus (children of his half brother Judas) through the end of the first century. The Emperor Domitian had been persecuting Jews and Christians alike in an effort to bring the line of David to extinction. He had Jesus' family brought before him for questioning. Upon learning, however, that they were poor farm folk, and that Christ's kingdom was not of this world, he "commanded them to be dismissed, and by a decree ordered the persecution to cease. Thus delivered, they ruled the churches, both as witnesses and relatives of the Lord . . . even to the times of Trajan."[6]

The Diaspora Model. During the persecution led by Saul of Tarsus against Christianity, believers fled in many different directions and—like the Jews of the exilic and postexilic periods—were dispersed throughout the region. But wherever they went they evangelized, and new churches were planted in a number of Gentile centers. One of these was Antioch of Syria, capital of the Roman province of Syria, with a very cosmopolitan population and a reputation for religious syncretism.[7]

Barnabas seems to have played a major role in the organization of the Antioch church, along with Paul. From early in its history, this church had a large proportion of Gentile members. Inevitably, tensions arose between the Gentiles and those Jewish believers who insisted on obedience to the Old Testament law. Even though this particular problem was resolved (see Acts 15:1-35), conflicts between Jewish believers (largely from the church at Jerusalem) and the Gentile churches continued, and a division between the two groups was created and steadily widened.

About the same time as the church at Antioch was in formation, a number of other Christian communities were undoubtedly being established. A church evidently existed in Damascus prior to Paul's conversion (Acts 9:1-19). There was a church in Rome at a fairly early date (possibly founded by Diaspora Jews who had been converted to Christ). Beyond that, nothing can be said with certainty.[8]

The only sure information from the early life of the church in areas outside of Palestine is that in Acts and the Epistles concerning the missionary work of Paul. In three successive journeys to Asia Minor and Greece, he and his missionary partners established churches in a number of places, including Cyprus, Antioch of Pisidia, Lystra, Iconium, Philippi, Thessalonica, Berea, Corinth, and Ephesus. No doubt converts from these churches visited and evangelized cities in their surrounding area.

Observations. Whoever founded the early churches, by the conclusion of the first Christian century they were to be found everywhere throughout the Roman Empire. Nor were they by any means uniform in their doctrinal emphases. While all communities agreed on the lordship of Christ, they agreed on very little else. And these varying communities, having received from the Jews a gift of hatred for heretics, frequently clashed with much rhetoric over opposing doctrinal positions. Each group was striving to be *the* "orthodox" church.

The Witness of Clement of Rome

One of the church fathers who lived in the immediate post-apostolic era was Clement (ca. 30–ca. 100), whom Eusebius calls the third bishop of Rome.[9] If Eusebius' account is correct, he lived during the reign of Domitian, and wrote toward the close of the first Christian century.[10]

Clement's Epistle to the Corinthians (known generally as 1 Clement because of a spurious second epistle) sought to respond to events in the Corinthian church more calamitous than those of Paul's day. There was dissension in that church.

21

Presbyters who had been appointed by the apostles were being unlawfully rejected. A spirit of insurrection pervaded the church.[11] While the epistle does not give a systematic ecclesiology, it does present us with some implications of interest.

Ray Petry suggests that this epistle, written under the aegis of the church at Rome, demonstrates that even at this early date "Roman Christian officialdom was beginning to inject into its fraternal exchanges a tone of . . . patronizing unction." They were particularly concerned because the schism at Corinth endangered "regularity in worship and the ordered church life so cherished at old Rome."[12]

The Unity of the Church. Practically from the beginning of his letter, Clement appealed to the Corinthians to maintain unity by inveighing against schism.

> By reason of the sudden and repeated calamities and reverses which are befalling us, brethren, we consider that we have been somewhat tardy in giving heed to the matters of dispute that have arisen among you, dearly beloved, and to the detestable and unholy sedition [the Greek may also be rendered "schism"], so alien and strange to the elect of God, which a few headstrong and self-willed persons have kindled to such a pitch of madness that your name, once revered and renowned and lovely in the sight of all men, hath been greatly reviled.[13]

Clement reminded them of their past when, being filled with the Holy Spirit, they found every disloyalty and division appalling. He suggested that the cause of the trouble in their ranks was a prideful falling away from the Lord. "Hence come jealousy and envy, strife and sedition, persecution and tumult, war and captivity . . . each goeth after the lusts of his evil heart."[14]

On the Role of Liberty. In an effort to heal the split in the Corinthian church and restore those who had been wrongfully dismissed, Clement made an observation on the role of the presbyters, linking them to the apostles.

> They appointed the aforesaid persons, and afterwards they provided a continuance, that if these should fall asleep, other ap-

proved men should succeed to their ministration. Those therefore who were appointed by them, or afterward by other men of repute with the consent of the whole church, and have ministered unblamably to the flock of Christ . . . these men we consider to have been unjustly thrust out from their ministration. For it will be no light sin for us, if we thrust out those who have offered the gifts of the bishop's office unblamably and holily.[15]

The bishops—appointed either by the apostles personally or by others at their direction and with full church consent—served "the flock of Christ" as shepherds without reproach and in all holiness. To oust them from their office would be a grievous sin against the Christ in whose name they served.

Clement concluded his epistle by admonishing the church to cease "from this foolish dissension" and "render obedience unto the things written by us through the Holy Spirit" and "be speedily at peace."[16] In Clement's view, what he was writing to them was inspired by the Spirit of God. The Corinthians should realize this, stop their infighting, obey the injunctions of the Roman church, and make peace.

Conclusions. Little was as important in the early church—whether apostolic or immediately post-apostolic—as its unity. Schism was regarded as a vile sin. One may also see a glimpse of the bishops' being appointed for life, as long as they lived and served without reproach.

During this period the church was still charismatic, that is, led by the Holy Spirit. As the first Christian century drew to a close, however, a formalization was in process which would become increasingly apparent during the century following.

Ignatius of Antioch

Some interpreters view Ignatius as a contemporary of the Apostle John.[17] Certainly, he lived at a date not much later than the apostles; for he was martyred in A.D. 115. While awaiting death, he wrote seven epistles which have been preserved for us. In these epistles, the word *ekklēsia* is used thirty-nine times. Ignatius sought to facilitate the unity and growth of the church by increasing the power of a bishop to a place above the elders and deacons, making him in effect both the ruler of the church and a rallying point for it. Everything that Ignatius wrote about the church centered on the bishop's vital role in it.

Against Schism. Like his forebears in the faith, Ignatius was concerned about the unity of the church. Harmony involved submission to the bishop; by so doing the church's members were in accord with the Father and the Son.

> So then it becometh you to run in harmony with the mind of the bishop. . . . For your honourable presbytery, which is worthy of God, is attuned to the bishop, even as its strings to a lyre. Therefore in your concord and harmonious love Jesus Christ is sung. And do ye, each and all, form yourselves into a chorus, that being harmonious in concord and taking the key note of God ye may in unison sing with one voice through Jesus Christ unto the Father, that He may both hear you and acknowledge by your good deeds to be members of His Son. It is therefore profitable for you to be in blameless unity, that ye may be partakers of God always.[18]

In his Letter to the Smyrnaeans, Ignatius made much the same point, exhorting church members in that center to "shun divisions, as the beginning of evils," and instead, "follow your bishop, as Jesus Christ followed the Father."[19]

Following the bishop was also a hedge against the development of heresy, a condition which also threatened the fabric of church solidarity. He praised the Ephesians for their appropriate conduct, "for that you live according to the truth, and that no heresy hath a home among you; nay, ye do not so much as listen to any one, if he speak of aught else save concerning Jesus Christ in truth."[20] In a typically apostolic analogy, he reminded his readers that, "as ye are stones of a temple, which were prepared beforehand for a building of God the Father."[21] They could not give themselves over to heresy; for that would destroy the oneness of the spiritual building into which they had been fashioned.

On Church Officers. While Clement had declared in his Epistle to the Corinthians that the bishops were not to be removed from office, but were appointed for life, he had never suggested that they were in a position far above the rest of the church. Indeed, Clement makes little differentiation between presbyters and bishops. Ignatius, however, advocated a carefully organized hierarchy culminating in the "monepiscopate"[22] (i.e., the supreme authority of a single bishop over all other bishops, presbyters, and other church officers).

Ignatius' emphasis on the supremacy of the bishop is clearly seen in his Letter to the Magnesians. Ignatius compared the officers of the existing church to a heavenly pattern: "the bishop presiding after the likeness of God, and the presbyters after the likeness of the council of the Apostles, with the deacons . . . [who have] been entrusted with the diaconate of Jesus Christ."[23]

Ignatius also affirmed the supremacy of the bishop by insisting that baptism and communion were valid only where sanctioned by the bishop. For Ignatius, mediating the ordinances evidently had become the sole province of the bishop. Ignatius declared to the Smyrnaeans that, "it is not lawful apart from the bishop either to baptize or to hold a love-feast; but whatever he shall approve, this is well-pleasing also to God; that everything which ye do may be sure and valid."[24]

Conclusions. Ignatius took the church one step farther than Clement of Rome in its organizational pattern. The bishop had become the ruler of the church, one step above the presbyters, and the sole dispenser of the ordinances. He was responsible only to God. At the same time, emphasis was still placed on the local congregation. As Earl Radmacher aptly notes, "The individual congregation, subject to the bishop and the presbytery, is a copy of the church universal which is led by Christ and the apostles."[25]

Polycarp

Polycarp (b. ca. 70) was a contemporary of Ignatius of Antioch (indeed, one of the latter's letters is addressed to him), and is spoken of by tradition as a disciple of the Apostle John. He was martyred about A.D. 155 or 156. About two or three decades earlier, the church at Philippi had asked Polycarp to write them a letter containing words of exhortation.

Among other matters, Polycarp spoke to the Philippian believers about the role of presbyters, deacons, and widows.

Polycarp's teaching on widows followed that of the Apostle Paul. In 1 Timothy 5, Paul assigned widows a semiofficial role in the church, insisting that they were to be women with a deep and balanced faith in Christ who were given to regular prayer. Similarly, Polycarp taught that widows were expected to abstain "from all calumny, evil speaking, false witness, love of money, and every evil thing, knowing that they are God's altar, and that all sacrifices are carefully inspected, and nothing escapeth Him of either their thoughts or intents."[26]

As in his instructions for widows, Polycarp crafted his instructions for deacons on the basis of Paul's teaching (1 Tim. 3:8-13). They were to be above reproach; for they served not just human beings but Christ. Like their precursors in the office they could not be "calumniators, [nor] double-tongues, [nor] lovers of money," but rather "temperate in all things, compassionate, diligent, walking according to the truth of the Lord who became a minister (deacon) of all."[27]

Presbyters were to exhibit a pastoral concern for God's people. In regard to this office, Polycarp was more explicit than Paul had been in 1 Timothy 3:1-7.

> And the presbyters also must be compassionate, merciful towards all men, turning back the sheep that are gone astray, visiting all the infirm, not neglecting a widow or an orphan or a poor man: but providing always for that which is honorable in the sight of God and of men, abstaining from all anger, respect of persons, unrighteous judgment, being far from all love of money, not quick to believe anything against any man, not hasty in judgment, knowing that we are all debtors of sin.[28]

Furthermore, the presbyters were to be persons of wisdom and discernment in regard to doctrinal concerns, maintaining a separation "from the false brethren and from them that bear the name of the Lord in hypocrisy, who lead foolish men astray."[29]

As an example of what a presbyter should *not* be, Polycarp cited one of their own number, a man named Valens. He and his wife were evidently a latter-day Ananias and Sapphira; they were guilty of abusing the presbyter's office for material gain, and of perverting the truth. Their end, should they not repent, would be "as one of the Gentiles who know not the judgment of the Lord."[30]

Conclusions. While Polycarp did not exhibit the sense of formal organization found in Ignatius of Antioch, one must not conclude that he was not of a similar mind. His epistle was not intended for the same purposes. However, he clearly stood in the apostolic tradition in maintaining the high quality of character for those holding ecclesiastical office.

The Ministry in the Didachē

The *Didachē* is a church manual written by some branch of the primitive Christian community, probably early in the second century. It purports to be "The Teaching of the Twelve Apostles" (the common English title for it). The book is divided into two sections: the first, which may or may not be of Christian origin, is a moral treatise contrasting the paths of righteousness and unrighteousness, of life and death; the second part deals with ecclesiastical rites and orders.

Concerning Baptism. The *Didachē* introduces what some call "clinical baptism"—the use of affusion (sprinkling)—when immersion is impossible for one reason or another. Baptism was always to be "in the name of the Father and of the Son and of the Holy Spirit." The manual's first expectation was immersion in flowing water; failing that, in still water; while the water should be cold, warm was permissible. "But if thou hast neither, then pour water on the head thrice. . . ." Both the one being baptized and the one baptizing should fast for a day or two prior to the observance of the ordinance.[31]

Concerning the Lord's Supper. No one should be permitted to partake of the Eucharist who had not been baptized. Proper observance required a prayer before the cup and one before the bread (the manual seems to have reversed the order of 1 Corinthians 11). The prayer for the cup went as follows:

27

We give Thee thanks, O our Father, for the holy vine of Thy son David, which Thou madest known unto us through Thy Son Jesus; Thine is the glory for ever and ever.

With regard to the bread, it went:

We give Thee thanks, O our Father, for the life and knowledge which Thou didst make known unto us through Thy Son Jesus; Thine is the glory for ever and ever. As this broken bread was scattered upon the mountains and being gathered together became one, so may Thy Church be gathered together from the ends of the earth into Thy kingdom; for Thine is the glory and the power through Jesus Christ for ever and ever.[32]

At the conclusion of the Supper, a prayer of thanksgiving was to be offered. It included a supplication for the church, "to deliver it from evil and to perfect it in Thy love; and gather it together from the four winds—even the Church which Thou hast sanctified—into Thy kingdom which Thou hast prepared for it."[33]

Regarding Teachers. Consonant with general practice in the primitive community, itinerant teachers were to be welcomed. But a watchful eye and a discerning ear were to be maintained: "if the teacher himself be perverted and teach a different doctrine to the destruction thereof, hear him not; but if to the increase of righteousness and the knowledge of the Lord, receive him as the Lord."[34]

Concerning Apostles and Prophets. The manual appears to view apostles in the secondary New Testament sense of the word, that is, as delegates or messengers of another local church. It seems to regard—at least, in this context—apostles and prophets as synonymous.

In the spirit of hospitality, apostles were to be "received as of the Lord." But they should not overstay their welcome. One night's lodging was standard and, if need be, a second; "but if he abide three days, he is a false prophet." Nor would a true prophet ask for money: "and whosoever shall say in the Spirit, give me silver or anything else, ye shall not listen to him; but if he tell you to give on behalf of others that are in want, let no man judge him.''[35]

Should an itinerant wish to settle down and work in a particular assembly, he "is worthy of his food." Permanently situated prophets were to receive the firstfruits of the congregation; "for they are your chief-priests."

> If thou makest bread, take the firstfruit and give according to the commandment. In like manner, when thou openest a jar of wine or oil, take the firstfruit and give to the prophets; yea and of money and raiment and every possession take the firstfruit, as shall seem good to thee and give according to the commandment.[36]

What "the commandment" was, is not specified. The author may have been referring to Paul's exhortation in 1 Corinthians 16:1-2. Or, more probably (for there is a somewhat Hebraic orientation evident in the composition), he may have had in mind the firstfruits commandment of Exodus 23:19 or even possibly the tithes commandment of Numbers 18:21.

Regarding the Lord's Day. The manual sets forth a regimen for the primitive community to follow. The Eucharist was to be observed on the Lord's Day. Before its observance, however, a prayer of confession was required, "that your sacrifice may be pure." Anyone at odds with his or her fellow believer could not partake of the ordinance, or even join the assembly "until they have been reconciled, that your sacrifice may not be defiled.''[37]

Regarding Church Offices. The manual shows itself more akin to the apostolic orders than to those of the early fathers such as Ignatius. There appears to be an equality of position and a shared, democratic rule.

> Appoint for yourselves therefore bishops and deacons worthy of the Lord, men who are meek and not lovers of money, and true and approved; for unto you they also perform the service of the prophets and teachers. Therefore despise them not; for they are your honorable men along with the prophets and teachers.[38]

Conclusions. It is hard to believe that the *Didachē* is as chronologically advanced as most scholars would have us believe; for it demonstrates evidences of being much more primitive than the writings of Ignatius or Polycarp. The structure of church governance appears to be more charismatic and less formal than that of Ignatius' day. And the instructions regarding itinerants and the services of the church are much more rudimentary and less sophisticated. If one does place its time of writing in the early second century, then our conclusions must be that, at this point, there were great differences between local assemblies in observance and polity both.

The Shepherd of Hermas

The Shepherd of Hermas is the longest of the writings of the early church fathers. The hero is one Hermas, who receives a series of visions, mandates, and allegorical parables from a divine teacher, the Shepherd. The work seems to have been written in Rome some time prior to the mid-second century. It was quoted as Scripture (or at least, as quasi-canonical) by Irenaeus, Clement of Alexandria, Origen, and Tertullian. But the Muratorian Canon (A.D. 180) rejected it as inspired, although commending it for personal and private edification.[39]

The author's main problem appears to be a lack of commitment on the part of some of the members of the church. He was particularly concerned with post-baptismal sin (i.e., sin after conversion). If one were to sin after baptism, could one be forgiven?

Stones of a Building. In his third vision, Hermas was transported out into the countryside where he was shown a great tower under construction. Men were dragging stones to the site; some were from the depths of the ocean, and others were from the dry land.

> The stones that were dragged from the deep they placed in every case, just as they were, into the building, for they had been shaped and they fitted in their joining with the other stones; and they adhered so closely one with another that their joining could not possibly be detected; and the building of the tower appeared as if it were built of one stone.[40]

While all the stones from the ocean were usable, only some brought from dry land were fit. Some were cast a short distance from the tower; others were broken apart and thrown away.

Hermas' guide explained to him that the tower was the church. It was being constructed by God's angels. The stones that fit so beautifully together "are the apostles and bishops and teachers and deacons, who walked after the holiness of God, and exercised their office . . . in purity and sanctity for the elect of God."[41] Those stones from the bottom of the sea represented the martyrs. Those from the dry land which were brought and used were "those the Lord hath approved because they walked in the uprightness of the Lord, and rightly performed His commandments." Those stones cast close to the tower were sinners who desired to repent; "they will be useful for the building, if they repent." But the ones broken in pieces and thrown away from the tower represented those who "received the faith in hypocrisy, and . . . have not salvation, for they are not useful for the building by reason of their wickedness."[42] These stones had no hope of ever being used in the building (i.e., of ever being saved and added to the church).

Sin and Baptism. In the fourth mandate, Hermas was instructed regarding sin and repentance. " 'I have heard, Sir,' say I, 'from certain teachers, that there is no other repentance, save that which took place when we went down into the water and obtained remission of our former sins.' He saith to me, 'Thou has well heard; for so it is.' "[43] Hermas' guide allowed that after baptism one more repentance would be permitted; but the person who sinned following that forgiveness would find it hard to repent, and "he shall live with difficulty."[44]

Conclusions. Like his contemporaries, Hermas was jealous for the unity of the church. That the church is one while being many is illustrated by the analogy of the stones for the tower. In this, Hermas was paralleling the analogy of 1 Peter 2:5. He went beyond the Apostle Peter, however, by making salvation more a matter of works than of faith.

This same rigorism is seen in his view of baptism and sin. While some might repent of sin once after baptism, to do so more than once would be difficult if not well-nigh impossible.

It may be that he was employing hyperbole in an effort to force
his readers to see the need for utter devotion to Jesus Christ,
but it is more likely that he should be taken at face value.

Irenaeus of Lyons

Irenaeus was born in Asia Minor about A.D. 130 and spent his
Christian training as a disciple of Polycarp. He was sent to Gaul
as a presbyter and was appointed Bishop of Lyons in 177. He is
best known for his apologetic work against Gnosticism. Two of
his major writings have survived the years: *Against Heresies*
and *Proof of the Apostolic Preaching*. In the course of developing his arguments against the gnostic heresy, he had much to
say about the church.

The Nature of the Church. When one examines Irenaeus' views
on the church, it would seem that in his battle against heresy he
collected the foundational orthodox theological truths of his day
and superimposed his own outline upon them. Like his contemporaries he saw the church as the new Israel, the sublime body of
Christ, and the mother of believers. It was, furthermore, the special realm of God's Spirit; one could achieve fellowship with the
Lord through the church alone. "Where the Church is, there is
the Spirit of God; and where the Spirit of God is, there is the
Church and all grace; and the Spirit is the truth."[45]
The church, according to Irenaeus, is the sole reserve of
God's truth. The proof of this lies in the apostolic succession;
the knowledge of the apostles has been handed down from
bishop to bishop.

> It would take too long in a volume such as this to list the succes-
> sion of all the churches, [and] we will indicate only those of the
> greatest and most ancient church of Rome, recognized by all and
> founded and established by the two most glorious apostles,
> Peter and Paul. This church has the tradition handed down to us
> through successions of bishops. . . . For it is necessary that every
> church, that is, persons who are faithful everywhere to the tradi-
> tion which has been handed down from the apostles which has
> been conserved by those who are everywhere, agree with this
> church on account of its more powerful origin.[46]

Consequently, believers should be quick to obey the presbyters of the church, who are entrusted as guardians of the truth because they stand in the apostolic succession of the episcopacy. They should be equally swift to shun as heretics those who depart from the apostolic succession and so are schismatics.[47]

On the Lord's Supper. Irenaeus saw the Lord's Supper as an offering to God, seeing it as a fulfillment of Malachi 1:11. The bread and cup, along with other offerings from the congregation, were rendered to God as a "thank-offering" and were seen as *oblationes*. The bishop or presbyter received the elements as gifts and offered them to God with the *eucharista*, or prayer of thanksgiving, as a "sacrifice."[48]

Irenaeus conceived of the presentation of the bread and cup in a twofold fashion: they were a memorial of the gifts of creation as well as of the salvific sufferings of Jesus. Such a view was not inconsistent with the priesthood of every believer; for the Eucharist was a congregational thankoffering rather than a priestly oblation.[49]

Conclusions. Irenaeus' views of the church and the Lord's Supper varied only slightly from his predecessors in the faith. But they did provide seeds which were supplemented by certain successors and ultimately grew into the doctrine of papal infallibility and the sacrifice of the mass.

Clement of Alexandria

Clement was born Titus Flavius Clemens about A.D. 150, the son of pagan parents. His native city was Athens and there he began his education. How and when he became a Christian is unknown, but following his conversion he traveled to southern Italy, Syria, and Palestine to imbibe learning from the best known Christian teachers. Ultimately, he arrived in Alexandria, where he became the pupil and assistant to Pantaenus and, about the year 200, succeeded him as head of the Alexandrian school of catechumens. Shortly thereafter, a persecution under Septimus Severus forced him into exile, where he died about 215.[50]

The Unity of the Church. Clement held fast to the unity of the
church, declaring that there was but a single church just as
there is only one Father, one Word, and one Holy Spirit. He
referred to the church universal as a virgin mother who feeds
her offspring with the holy milk of God's Word.[51]

> The universal Father is one, and one the universal Word; and
> the Holy Spirit is one and the same everywhere, and one is the
> only virgin mother. I love to call her the Church. This mother,
> when alone, had not milk, because alone she was not a woman.
> But she is once virgin and mother—pure as a virgin, loving as a
> mother. And calling her children to her, she nurses them with
> holy milk, viz., with the Word for childhood.[52]

The unity of the true church, Clement maintained, was vastly
different from the heretical sects. The true church, he avowed, is
one, something acknowledged by all the disparate groups within
it. In it are enrolled those people who, according to God's purposes, are righteous. What is more, the unity of the church is
modeled on the unity of God. The church is joined to God, and it
is this joint heritage that false teachers seek to sunder into numerous sects.[53] Indeed, nothing is more important, alleged Clement,
than the unity of the church: "But the preeminence of the
Church, as the principle of union, is, in this surpassing all things
else, and having nothing like or equal to itself."[54]

Church Officers. Clement's view of the offices of the church was
somewhat like that of Ignatius in that he believed the earthly
reality to be a pattern of the heavenly ideal. But Clement differed from Ignatius in identifying the angelic host as the pattern
for the church rather than the Trinity.

> According to my opinion, the grades here in the Church, of
> bishops, presbyters, deacons, are imitations of the angelic glory,
> and of that economy which, the Scriptures say, awaits those who,
> following the footsteps of the apostles, have lived in perfection of
> righteousness according to the Gospel. For these taken up in the
> clouds, the apostle writes, will first minister [as deacons], then be
> classed in the presbyterate, by promotion in glory (for glory differs
> from glory) till they grow into "a perfect man."[55]

To attempt to describe in detail the hierarchical order of angels is novel to theology at this point.

The Ordinances. While Clement was more concerned with the concept of the Logos than any other theological matter, he nonetheless had instructions on the ordinances for his flock. "In fact, Logos and *mysterion* are the two poles around which his christology and ecclesiology move."[56]

Baptism, for Clement, was the pathway to perfection and illumination; in receiving the ordinance, the faithful imitate Christ.

> The same also takes place in our case, whose exemplar Christ became. Being baptized, we are illuminated; illuminated, we become sons; being made sons, we are made perfect; being made perfect, we are made immortal. . . . This work is variously called grace, and illumination, and perfection, and washing: washing, by which we cleanse away our sins; grace, by which the penalties accruing to transgressions are remitted; and illumination, by which that holy light of salvation is beheld, that is, by which we see God clearly. Now we call that perfect which wants nothing. For what is yet wanting to him who knows God?[57]

One may go further, based on evidence from his *Stromata* (3.12), and assert that Clement had a very biblical view of baptism as a sign of spiritual rebirth. He declared that the Lord "wishes us to be converted and to become as children acknowledging Him who is truly our Father, regenerated by water; and this is a different begetting than that in creation."

Like the Apostle John, Clement used the antithesis of darkness and light. Those who do not know Christ live in darkness, but who are baptized have been cleansed of the sins which cloud the light of the Divine Spirit; having the eye of the Spirit free, they are full of light. This light is the illumination of knowledge, bestowed on the believer by the Holy Spirit, a process which commences at baptism.[58]

This process of illuminating knowledge, Clement maintained, is continued in the Eucharist.

> Elsewhere the Lord, in the Gospel according to John, brought this out by symbols when He said: "Eat ye my flesh, and drink my blood"; describing distinctly by metaphor the drinkable

35

properties of faith and the promise, by means of which the Church, like a human being consisting of many members is refreshed and grows, is welded together and compacted of both.[59]

Clement compared Christ's flesh to the Holy Spirit who is the Creator of flesh, and His blood to the Word, "for as rich blood the Word has been infused into life." The two together represent "the Lord, the food of babes—the Lord, who is Spirit and Word."[60]

Baptism, then, regenerates humans and turns them into babes in Christ. The Lord's Supper serves to join them into a single body (albeit with many members) in Jesus Christ. There they are taught and nourished, and grow into Christian perfection.

A Summary

The Christian literature of the second century evinces a continuing of the process of formalization begun in the closing decades of the previous century. Unity was still paramount in the minds of the writers, but an important aspect of it had now become submission of all believers and officers in the church to a single bishop. Ignatius saw the bishop's role as patterned on the rule of God. At the same time, there is no evidence of a move toward a monarchical episcopate in Rome.

The church's observance of the ordinances slowly began to shift. For the first time affusion is mentioned along with immersion, although it is not the preferred mode. And a narrowness may be noticed in regard to the Christian life (and sin) which cannot be found in Scripture. There appears to have been a harshness developing which placed a greater emphasis on works than on faith.

THE THIRD CENTURY: INCREASING SACRAMENTALISM

The evolution of formal church organization would continue in the third century. So would the increasing emphasis on penitential and atoning works. There would also be a shifting of views on the ordinances, which would become more and more sacramental in their scope.

36

Tertullian

Tertullian was born in Carthage (North Africa) about A.D. 150, but was not converted to Christianity until about forty years of age. He quickly became a capable apologist for his new faith and a leading theologian in the North African (Catholic) church. About 207, however, he left his church to espouse Montanism, perhaps as a protest against an ever encroaching hierarchy which was lax in dealing with sin. Tertullian was a prolific author both before and during his Montanist period; as a result, he is a valuable source of information on the customs and theology of his time.[61]

On the Church. During his Catholic phase, Tertullian's concept of the church was not greatly different from that of his predecessors. "We are a body, knit together by the bond of piety, by unity of discipline and by the contract of hope."[62] There is but one church in the world, just as there is one Lord, one hope, and one baptism. That church is the bride of Christ and the mother of all true believers. It is, he insisted, the unique residence of the Spirit, the sole holder of apostolic revelation, and its teaching is validated by an unbroken succession of bishops.[63]

In 207, however, with his move to the Montanists, Tertullian's views underwent a radical shift. Instead of the visible, hierarchical church, he held to a charismatic society whose essential nature is Spirit. Authority is vested not in a hierarchy or even a clergy, but in those who are filled with the Holy Spirit.[64]

On Baptism. Tertullian was convinced that baptism was necessary to salvation: "Happy is our sacrament of water, in that, by washing away the sins of our early blindness, we are set free and admitted into eternal life!"[65] Because there is only one baptism—that being effected in the true church—baptism performed or received by heretics is invalid. Only the bishop may authorize baptism, asserted Tertullian, although his power can be delegated to presbyters and deacons, and even on occasion to laypeople. But the latter must be with caution; for the laity must not seek to assume for themselves the specific tasks of bishops. Imitation of the episcopal office is the mother of division.[66]

Baptism might be administered to children, but Tertullian preferred that they should wait until they should be of an age of discernment. The ordinance may never be repeated, except in the case of heretics, whose baptism in such a state is invalid. The effects of the ordinance include the remission of sins, regeneration, liberation from death, and the gift of the Holy Spirit.[67]

On the Eucharist. Tertullian taught that the Lord's body and blood in the Supper are just as real as the waters of baptism. Just as in baptism one's body is washed in water to cleanse the soul, so in Communion "the flesh feeds on Christ's body and blood so that the soul may be filled with God."[68]

Conclusions. Tertullian's ecclesiology was little different from that of his contemporaries. While there were some changes in his doctrine of the church because of his move to Montanism and his desire to return to a charismatic rather than an episcopal polity, his views on most church-related practices had changed little from his earlier days as a Catholic.

Origen of Alexandria

Origen (ca. 185–ca. 254) was born to believing parents. His father, Leonidas, was martyred in the persecution by Septimus Severus in 202. Origen, still in his teens, began to teach literature and philosophy to provide support for himself and his family. Because of the persecution there was a dearth of catechists for new converts, and Bishop Demetrius of Alexandria asked Origen — then eighteen — to take on that responsibility (which he did with great zeal).[69]

Disagreements with the bishops of Alexandria forced Origen to leave that city. He took up residence in Caesarea, Palestine, where he established a school much like the one he had operated in Alexandria. There he spent some two decades in writing and teaching theology. He was a prolific author, with about 8,000 titles to his credit, only a handful of which have survived.[70]

In spite of Origen's having been condemned as a heretic by a council at Constantinople in 543 (a course of action endorsed by Pope Vigilius and all of the patriarchs of Orthodoxy), he had much to say about the church which is worth our consideration.

On the Church. Origen viewed the church both as the "assembly of Christian people" and the mystical body of Christ. The Logos is the principle of the church's life, residing in the latter as the soul indwells the body:[71] "we say that the holy Scriptures declare the body of Christ, animated by the Son of God, to be the whole Church of God, and the members of this body — considered as a whole — to consist of those who are believers."[72] Nor can any individual member of the body do anything apart from the Word (Logos).

Origen, long before Augustine, declared the church to be the city of God on earth, coexisting with the secular state. It is, therefore, a "state within a state," but through the indwelling Logos, it will overcome the secular state.[73]

> But our belief is, that the Word shall prevail over the entire rational creation, and change every soul into His own perfection; in which state every one, by the mere exercise of his power, will choose what he desires, and obtain what he chooses . . . we hold that in the mind there is no evil so strong that it may not be overcome by the Supreme Word and God.[74]

On the Ordinances. Origen held to a sacramental view of baptism *(ex opere operato)* believing the rite to be efficacious in and of itself. He argued that every person comes into this world "tainted with the stain of iniquity and sin . . . if there were nothing in infants that required remission and called for lenient treatment, the grace of baptism would seem unnecessary."[75] He claimed that infant baptism was a tradition received by the church from the apostles: "For those who have been entrusted with the secrets of the divine mysteries, knew very well that all are tainted with the stain of original sin, which must be washed off by water and the Spirit."[76]

While Origen many times acknowledged that there is really only one forgiveness of sins — in the waters of baptism — he nonetheless alleged that there are a variety of ways to receive remission of sins committed after observance of the rite. These included: martyrdom, almsgiving, forgiving one who sins

39

against us, converting a sinner, charity, and works of penance after the confession of sins (with great sorrow) before a priest.[77]

Origen also exhibited a sacramental view of the Lord's Supper. He stated: "But we give thanks to the Creator of all, and, along with thanksgiving and prayer for the blessings we have received, we also eat the bread presented to us; and this bread becomes by prayer a sacred body, which sanctifies those who sincerely partake of it."[78] He seemed, further, to hold an almost transubstantial view of the bread for, in his *Homilies on Exodus* (13.3), he observed that those who are present at the Sacrament take great care when receiving the bread that not a crumb fall to the ground. To allow such a thing to happen would be a crime of great magnitude.

Like his teacher, Clement of Alexandria, Origen saw the elements of the Eucharist in a second sense—as representative of the Word of God which nourishes the communicant. He noted in his *Commentary on Matthew* (85) that that bread which the Word of God (i.e., Second Person of the Trinity) owns as His body is the Word which feeds the soul, and that drink which He acknowledges as His blood is the Word which permeates those who drink it. While he did occasionally express that the literal interpretation of the Eucharist was one commonly held by the church, he allowed that it was the idea of the simple mind; a symbolic interpretation was more valued by God and more likely to be held by the learned believer.[79]

Conclusions. Origen's thought, however heretical it may have been in areas other than ecclesiology, seems to have made substantial impact on Roman Catholicism. For the first time, the church decidedly moves away from the simple *sensus literalis* of Scripture in regard to the ordinances of the church in favor of a much more sacramental view. An additional sacrament also began to emerge, namely, the rite of penance (albeit in a somewhat rudimentary manner).

Cyprian of Carthage

Caecilius Cyprianus Thascius was born in Carthage between 200 and 210 to a wealthy and sophisticated pagan family. He won great acclaim in his native city as a rhetorician. At about 40 years of age he was converted to Christianity. In 248 he was popularly acclaimed as bishop of Carthage.

In 250 there was a severe persecution under the reign of the Emperor Decius. Cyprian left Carthage and went into hiding, but continued to direct the affairs of his diocese. By 251 he had returned to his church. But he was then compelled to resolve the problem of those who had lapsed from the faith during the persecution and had offered pagan sacrifices as required by the Empire. Many of these people had repented and sought re-admission to the church. Cyprian was inclined to permit their reinstatement. He faced great opposition, however, from many who had remained faithful. A synod of sixty African bishops supported his view, and he excommunicated those who opposed him.

He was involved in a second controversy over the baptism of heretics. In North Africa and Asia Minor it was usual to require those who had been baptized by heretics to be rebaptized before being admitted to the orthodox church. The church at Rome, however, recognized the validity of heretic baptism. Cyprian upheld the African position, despite opposition from Pope Stephen.

In a persecution under Valerian, Stephen died in 257. Cyprian was banished the same year and in 258 was beheaded, a martyr for the faith.

On the Church. Cyprian's ecclesiology dominated the West until the time of Augustine. His doctrine was undergirded by the assumption that the Catholic Church was a unity. This unity was spoken of by the Old Testament, was handed down by Christ through the apostles, was the object of His high-priestly prayer, and was proclaimed by the Apostle Paul. It was part and parcel of God's very nature and being. The church's unity, he asserted, was guaranteed by the episcopacy, the divinely initiated principle of unity throughout the church. The bishops are representative of the apostles, not only in an unbroken succession, but by having been ordained to office by Christ Himself. Furthermore, the episcopacy itself is one and indivisible; each bishop in his diocese is a microcosm of the church.[80]

In his *Epistles* 33.1, Cyprian traced episcopal leadership back to Jesus' statement to Peter in Matthew 16:18.

Our Lord, whose commandment we must fear and obey, establishes the honorable rank of bishop and the constitution of His Church when in the gospel He speaks and says to Peter: "I say to thee: Thou art Peter and upon this rock I will build my Church and the gates of hell shall not prevail against it. And I will give to thee the keys of the kingdom of heaven. . . ." Thence have come down to us in course of time and by due succession the ordained office of the bishop and the constitution of the Church, forasmuch as the Church is founded upon the bishops and every act of the Church is subject to these rulers.[81]

On the Primacy of Rome. Cyprian believed that each bishop answered only to God, and to no other human being. "So long as the bond of friendship is maintained and the sacred unity of the Catholic Church is preserved, each bishop is master of his own conduct, conscious that he must one day render an account of himself to the Lord (*Epist.* 55.21)."[82] In his dispute with Pope Stephen, he made it clear that Peter had claimed no primacy among the apostles. Consequently, he would brook no interference in his diocese from anyone outside; for "to each shepherd has been assigned one portion of the flock to direct and govern and render hereafter an account of his ministry to the Lord (*Epist.* 59.14)."[83] He did, elsewhere, speak of Rome as "the leading Church," but its primacy was one of honor, not of governance.[84]

Cyprian's thought was of a federated council of bishops where all were equal. Each bishop possessed a certain autonomy, although it behooved him to pay heed to the advice of brother bishops, and to submit to the decisions of an episcopal synod. He practiced what he preached. To reach difficult decisions, he would convene a council of bishops and follow its direction.[85]

On Baptism. Cyprian's position on baptism was somewhat ambiguous. A convert is regenerated, he believed, through washing with water, and it is on this occasion that the Holy Spirit descends. He was explicit that "the Spirit is received in baptism, and when they have been baptized and have obtained the Holy Spirit converts draw near to drink the Lord's cup."[86] Infants, too, according to their capacity, may receive the Holy

Spirit upon baptism (Cyprian differed from Tertullian, who did not like infant baptism). Even those who are clinically baptized because of illness, will receive the Holy Spirit as readily as those who have received an episcopal laying on of hands. On other occasions, Cyprian attributed the gift of the Spirit to the imposition of the bishop's hands along with the making of the sign of the cross. Historian J.N.D. Kelly observes, however, that "Cyprian must count as a conservative who resisted the fashionable tendency to recognize two distinct rites, and endeavored rather to hold them together as two different aspects of Christian initiation."[87]

Like Tertullian, Cyprian held that there was a higher, more important and efficacious baptism, namely, in blood (i.e., martyrdom). Comparing the two baptisms — water and blood — he declared: "This [martyrdom] is a baptism greater in grace, more sublime in power, more precious in honor, a baptism which the angels administer, a baptism in which God and His Anointed One rejoice, a baptism after which one sins no more, a baptism which completes our growth in faith, a baptism which at our departure from this world unites us at once to God."[88]

On Penance. Cyprian taught that public penance required three steps: (1) confession, (2) satisfaction (depending on the seriousness of the sin), and (3) reconciliation following its completion. "I entreat you, beloved brethren, that each one should confess his own sin, while he who has sinned is still in this world, while his confession may be received, while the satisfaction and the remission made by the priests are pleasing to the Lord (*De lapsis* 28; *Epist.* 16.2)."[89] In this way, those who have committed sin following their baptism may find forgiveness, and whatever the gravity of their deed, it will be mitigated; for God is willing to save all whom He has redeemed at such high cost.[90]

On the Lord's Supper. Cyprian was the first of the church fathers to formulate a theory of the Lord's Supper along the lines of a sacrifice. He used expressions such as "sacrifice," "oblation," and even "the dominical victim." His ideas, however, reached their fullest demonstration in *Epistle* 63, where he countered the teaching of the Aquarians, a heretical sect which celebrated the Eucharist with water instead of wine. His theme was that the Supper should as closely as possible reproduce Jesus Christ's activities and intentions on that occasion. On the celebration of the ordinance the priest takes on the role representing Christ; "he fulfills the role of Christ when he imitates what He did, and only then does he offer a true, complete sacrifice in the Church to the Father when he begins to offer it after the pattern of Christ's offering."[91] He talked of offering this sacrifice on behalf of people in need and the dead, thus demonstrating that he saw the Communion as having some objective efficacy.[92]

Cyprian also seems to have held a representative view of the Atonement. When Christ was crucified on our behalf, all we were with Him; for He was bearing our sins. He wrote in his *Epistles* 63.13 that, in the bread, "as many grains, collected, and ground, and mixed together into one mass, make one bread, so in Christ, who is the heavenly bread, we may know, that there is one body, with which our number is joined and united." Likewise, with the cup, when the water is blended with the wine, the people become one with Christ, and the congregation of believers is connected and fused with Him on whom they believe.[93]

Conclusions. Cyprian was a conservative who followed essentially in the footsteps of those Fathers who had gone before him. He was prone to emphasize infant baptism more than his predecessor Tertullian, believing that infants would be possessed by the Holy Spirit, and so should be baptized as quickly after birth as possible. He differed from the Roman church on the matter of penance, holding that God would forgive a penitent who made confession—including those who had lapsed from the faith. He differed again from his Roman brethren on the baptism of heretics, favoring their rebaptism (on the grounds that a heretical baptism was an invalid reception of the sacrament). Cyprian saw the Eucharist in terms of a sacrifice; when the priest celebrated the ordinance, he represented Christ and made a true sacrifice on the altar. In Christ's sacrifice, all believers were one with Him on the cross in being offered to God.

THE FOURTH AND FIFTH CENTURIES:
AN INCREASING DIVISION

In the period between the Councils of Nicaea and Chalcedon (A.D. 325–451) particularly, and throughout the fourth and fifth centuries in general, one may note an ever-increasing gap between East and West in the development of ecclesiology. Teaching in the Greek church on the doctrine of the church remained essentially static, while in the Latin church it flourished. One reason may be that ecclesiology was not the burning issue in the East that it was in the West. In Rome, there was a progressive attempt to have Peter's chair accepted by all Christendom not only as first in honor (which it already was) but also as having jurisdiction by divine ordinance (which it lacked, especially in the East). Thus, the East hesitated to acknowledge Rome as the seat of infallibility in doctrine or primacy in rule, while West demanded that the whole church recognize its authority.

The Alexandrian Fathers

The Alexandrian school established by Origen continued on even after his ouster. It was headed by men such as Heraclas, Dionysius the Great, Theognostus, and Pierius. From this school issued many leading scholars. Some stayed in Alexandria, but others moved to Caesarea, Antioch, and other centers where they were active in theological discussion and church leadership.

Athanasius. Athanasius was one of the outstanding Alexandrian bishops. Born in 295 in Alexandria, he was made at an early age a part of the household of Bishop Alexander (of Alexandria), and was given a fine classical and Christian education. In 319 he was ordained a deacon and, shortly afterward, was appointed Alexander's secretary. It was in this capacity that he attended and participated in the debates of the Council of Nicaea, where the opponents of Arius (led by Alexander) were victorious. Three years later, on Alexander's death, Athanasius succeeded him as bishop.

Athanasius proclaimed the church as the mystical body of

Christ. His view rested upon his doctrine of the deification of the believer in Christ. In Christ believers are united with God and are made His children by adoption. Because they have been mystically united with the Son of God, they are able to participate with Him in His death, resurrection, and immortality. In his argument against the Arians, Athanasius used one of their favorite verses—John 17:21—against them. They claimed that the unity of believers with Christ and His Father was one of resemblance alone. Not so, responded Athanasius. Believers are not only united by like nature, "but through participation in the same Christ we all become one body, possessing the Lord in ourselves."[94]

Athanasius believed that, in order to be authentic, baptism must rest on a solid, orthodox Christian faith. Arian baptism was invalid, for example, not because it failed to use the required Trinitarian formula, but because the Arian faith was defective. In his *Discourse Against the Arians* (42), he observed that not only the Arians were at fault in this regard. "There are many other heresies, too, which use the words only, but not in a right sense, as I have said, nor with sound faith, and in consequence the water which they administer is unprofitable, as deficient in piety, so that he who is sprinkled by them is rather polluted by irreligion than redeemed. . . ." The necessary course of action, should any of the followers of heresies desire to unite with the orthodox church, was to be rebaptized.[95]

There is strong evidence that Athanasius held to a very literal view of the eucharistic body and blood of Christ. In a segment of his sermon "To the Newly Baptized" preserved by Eutychius of Constantinople, he declared that

> as long as the invocation and prayers have not begun, there is only bread and wine. But after the great and wonderful prayers have been pronounced, then the bread becomes the body of Our Lord Jesus Christ, and the wine becomes His blood. . . . After the great prayers and the holy invocations have been pronounced, the Word descends into the bread and the wine, and the body of the Word is.[96]

Didymus the Blind. Born in 313, Didymus lost his eyesight at the age of four. In spite of his handicap he gained a superb education without ever attending school or learning to read. He acquired so outstanding a reputation for learning that Athanasius chose him to head the Alexandrian school for catechumens. He was its last teacher; for it closed shortly after his death. Among his best-known pupils were Jerome and Rufinus. Unlike many of his contemporaries, Didymus remained aloof from the theological controversies of his day.

Much of Didymus' work was devoted to an explication of the Person and work of the Holy Spirit. He was convinced that the believer is transformed in baptism by the Spirit. The Spirit is the fullness, the apex, of all God's gifts to humankind. In his *De Spiritu Sancto* (9), Didymus asserted, "It is impossible for anyone to acquire the grace of God if he have not the Holy Ghost: in Whom we prove that all the gifts of God consist."

This same Holy Spirit disseminates the various graces throughout Christ's church: "He founded His Church upon the rivers, making it, through His divine legislation, capable of receiving the Holy Ghost, from Whom, as from their fountainhead, the different graces flow as fountains of living water."[97] And it is this same Spirit by whose power the church has become Mother of all; for her children are born out of her virginal womb into the baptistery. In his *De Trinitate* (2.13), Didymus noted that "the baptismal pool of the Trinity is a workshop for the salvation of all those who believe. It frees from the serpent sting all those who are washed therein, and, remaining a virgin, becomes the mother of all through the Holy Ghost." It is not surprising, then, to learn that elsewhere he called the church both the bride of Christ (*De Trinitate* 2.6.23) and our Mother (*In Proverbia* 1624C).[98]

Didymus was a precursor of Augustine in respect to his views on baptism. He believed that original sin was taken care of by Jesus in His own baptism in the Jordan River. All of Adam's progeny have inherited this sin through the sexual intercourse of their parents. Because Jesus was born of a virgin, He is the one human exception.[99]

Cyril of Alexandria. Cyril, a nephew of the Alexandrian patriarch Theophilus, was elected to succeed his uncle on the former's death in 412. He served as patriarch until his own death in 444.

Teaching on the mystical body of Christ reached its fullest thought in the East with Cyril. Like Athanasius, he interpreted the idea of Christ's prayer to the Father that His disciples might be one with Father and Son as implying a real union: "If we are all one body with one another in Christ—not only with one another, but with Him who comes to us in His flesh—how can we help being one, all of us, both with one another and with Christ? Christ is the bond of unity inasmuch as He is one and the same, God and man."[100]

While Cyril, a prolific author, had little to contribute to the theology of the church as such, he did strongly support and reinforce Mariology. Like members of the Alexandrian school before him, he insisted that Mary must be termed the Mother of God if indeed it was God who was born into this world and later was crucified in the Person of Jesus Christ.

> But forasmuch as the Holy Virgin brought forth after the flesh God personally united to flesh, for this reason we say of her that she is "the Mother of God" (Θεοτοκος), not as though the nature of the Word had its beginning of being born from the flesh, for He was "in the beginning" . . . but, as we said before, because having personally united man's nature to Himself, He vouchsafed also to be born in the flesh, of her womb.[101]

Such a doctrine he considered to be the height of orthodox belief.

Conclusions. In the Alexandrian Fathers following Origen, a somewhat static view of ecclesiology emerges. In regard to the sacraments, Athanasius rightly held that baptism must be undergirded by a sound, biblical faith. But his view of the Lord's Supper was very near to transubstantiation, namely, that the bread and cup quite literally became the body and blood of Christ following the prayer of consecration. Didymus rightly taught that the Holy Spirit both founded and empowers the church through the graces He disseminates. s43the other hand, he taught the transmission of original sin (guilt) through sexual intercourse and its resultant procreation. Cyril promoted and affirmed the idea of Mary as "Mother of God" (rather than as "Mother of Christ").

The Antiochene Fathers

The school of the church at Antioch took a much more literal approach to theology than did the Alexandrians. Their exegetes emphatically rejected the allegorical method, using instead a historical-grammatical style of interpretation of Scripture. The Bible, they asserted, must be interpreted in a manner consistent with its original meaning. The foremost representatives of the Antiochene school included Diodore of Tarsus (d. 394), Theodore of Mopsuestia (d. 428), and John Chrysostom (d. 407). Nestorius was also from this school; when he was condemned as a heretic, its influence diminished substantially.[102]

Theodore of Mopsuestia. Theodore, a pupil of Diodore of Tarsus, was born in Antioch and studied rhetoric and literature under the famous philosopher Libanius, in whose school he struck up a lifelong friendship with John Chrysostom. About 383 he was ordained a priest, and in 392 was appointed Bishop of Mopsuestia in Cilicia. He died in 428 after attaining wide recognition as an orthodox scholar, but he was condemned as a heretic by the Council of Constantinople in 553.[103]

Theodore spoke of the body of Christ without any direct reference to the church as such. Christ's body was that union of believers created through baptism and the working of the Spirit of God.[104]

Like many of his contemporaries, Theodore held to a literal view of the Lord's Supper, denying vigorously that it was only symbolic. In his *Catechetical Homilies* (5) he wrote:

> It is with justice, therefore, that when He gave the bread He did not say: "This is the symbol of my body," but: "This is My body": likewise when He gave the cup He did not say: "This is the symbol of My blood," but: "This is my blood," because He wished us to look upon the [elements] after their reception of grace and the coming of the Spirit, not according to their nature but to receive them as they are the body and blood of Our Lord.[105]

He went even further to declare that, though the communicant takes only a small portion of the elements, he nonetheless receives all of the Lord in that portion: "Although He comes to us after having divided Himself, all of Him is nevertheless in every portion, and is near to all of us . . . in order that we may hold Him and embrace Him with all our might, and make manifest our love to Him" (*Cat. Hom.* 6).[106]

Theodore believed that penance was a necessary prerequisite to the Eucharist, especially for those who had fallen into grave sin after their baptism. He taught his pupils that there was a difference between "involuntary" and "great" sins. They would find forgiveness for the former in the Communion, if they were truly repentant. "If we do good works with diligence and turn away from evil works and truly repent of the sins that come to us, we will undoubtedly obtain the gift of the remission of sins in our reception of the holy Sacrament" (*Cat. Hom.* 117-18).[107] The latter category of sins, however, made reception of the Eucharist impossible, unless these sins were confessed in secret to a priest: "[Penitence] is the medicine for sins, which was established by God and delivered to the priests of the Church, who in making use of it with diligence, will heal the afflictions of men." Furthermore, ". . . God greatly cares for us, gave us penitence and showed us the medicine of repentance, and established some men, who are the priests, as physicians of sins, so that, if we receive in this world through them, healing and forgiveness of sins, we shall be delivered from the judgment to come" (*Cat. Hom.* 120-23).[108] When sinners repented they were reinstated into the fellowship with the same confidence they had previously enjoyed; for they were fully forgiven.

John Chrysostom. John was born in Antioch in 347 and educated initially by a devout Christian mother, Anthusa. He was also, like Theodore of Mopsuestia, a pupil of Diodore of Tarsus. In 380 he was made a deacon and, in 386, a presbyter. The following year he was appointed Patriarch of Constantinople. He was later called "Chrysostom" ("Golden-mouthed") because of his eloquence, and he filled his church to overflowing whenever he spoke. Because of his preaching against the lax morality of the Empress, he was deposed and banished, dying in exile in 407. He is the sole member of the Antiochene school whose orthodoxy has never been disputed.[109]

Chrysostom's ecclesiology was not new. He declared that the

church is a bride won by Christ at the cost of His own blood. Its striking attribute is unity. It coheres through mutual love. The church is universal in its scope, and is imperishable and unchanging, the backbone and foundation of the truth.[110]

In the Greek tradition, John held that baptism is efficacious only through the power of the Holy Spirit. Under His aegis, the believer is sealed in much the same way as the Jew is sealed to God in circumcision. Moreover, as the believer is baptized, he is assimilated into Christ and, emerging from the water, is fully regenerated and clothed with justice and holiness.[111]

Like his contemporary, Theodore of Mopsuestia, John was a fervent advocate of the real presence of Christ in the Eucharist. "When the priest stands before the Table, holding up his hands to heaven, and invokes the Holy Spirit to come and touch the elements . . . the Spirit gives his grace . . . he descends . . . he touches the elements . . . the sacrifice of the lamb [is] completed" (*De coemetrio et cruce* 3). It is this *Epiclesis* (statement of consecration) which causes the change in the elements.

> The priest stands, fulfilling the original pattern, and speaks those words; but the power and grace come from God. "This is my body," he says. This statement transforms the oblations . . . the statement, "This is my body," uttered once, makes complete the sacrifice at every table in the churches from that time until now, and even till Christ's coming (*De proditione Judae* 1.6).[112]

He went even further in his *Homilies on John* (46): "Not only ought we to see the Lord: we ought to take him in our hands, eat him, put our teeth into his flesh, and unite ourselves with him in closest union."[113]

John was typical of his day in the elevation of the clergy above the laity. The office of the priest, he asserted, though an earthly task, "ranks among the heavenly things," for it was created "by the Paraclete himself." Indeed, the priests "imitate the actions of angels." Christians must remember that earthly rulers have power only to bind the body, but "what priests do on earth God confirms on high: the Lord ratifies the decision of his servants."[114]

While John devoutly believed in penance and confession of

51

sins, he did not teach the necessity of confession to a priest. Rather, the sinner should privately and directly seek God's forgiveness: "Confess to God without ceasing! I do not lead you into the circle of your fellow servants, and I do not force you to reveal your sins to men. Unfold your conscience to God alone . . . and ask for help from Him" (*Homilia contra Anomeas* 5). In fact, Chrysostom noted that a priest could forgive sins only twice—in baptism and in extreme unction (*De sacerdotio* 3.6).[115]

Conclusions. The Antiochene Fathers espoused a view of ecclesiology—especially of the ordinances—similar to that of other Greek Fathers of the time. Unity was still a priority. Baptism was first and foremost a work of the Holy Spirit. The Eucharist was held in highest esteem with a view approaching transubstantiation. A confession of sins was deemed important prior to partaking. With some, penance was heading toward sacramentalization. The common view of the priesthood was similar to the latter Roman Catholic view, with the priest possessing divinely bestowed powers not enjoyed by the laity.

A Summary

Clement of Alexandria stressed the unity of the church; he held the idea of one catholic church dating back to the apostles. Nothing in the world is as important as the church, and nothing in the church is as important as its unity. That unity is created through the Lord's Supper. While baptism recreates or regenerates the individual, the Eucharist joins individuals into a single, united body.

Origen saw the church as the mystical body of Christ, indwelt and impelled by the Logos. He held a sacramental view of baptism, which washed away the taint of original sin. He favored infant baptism and claimed that it was passed down from the apostles. While Origen accepted the literal view of the Eucharist as the prevailing one in the church, he endorsed a symbolic interpretation thereof as being higher in nature. He also suggested that works of penance after a confession of failure to a priest could mitigate sin.

The Alexandrian school were proponents of a traditional

view of the church, which moved away from the *sensus literalis of Scripture*: a transubstantial view of the Eucharist, the transmission of original guilt through human procreation, and the idea of Mary as "Mother of God." The Antiochene Fathers, while more literal in their exegetical endeavors, followed a similar line. Theodore of Mopsuestia propounded the separation of clergy and laity; John Chrysostom, while stressing the need for penance, made it a matter between the sinner and God; a human intermediary was unnecessary.

Jerome

Jerome (ca. 345–420) was one of the leading theologians in the Western church of the fourth and fifth centuries. In 405 he completed the Vulgate Bible, which was eventually accepted as the authorized version of the Latin church.[116]

On the Church. Because he served as secretary to Pope Damasus (366–384), who was a strong promoter of the theory of Roman primacy, it should not be surprising to discover that Jerome was of a like mind. In his *Epistles* 15 to Damasus, he wrote:

> I follow no one as supreme leader except Christ only; hence I attach myself in communion with your Beatitude, that is, with the see of Peter. I know that the Church is built upon this rock. Whoever eats a [passover] lamb outside this house, is profane. Anyone who is not in Noah's ark will perish when the flood prevails.[117]

On the Clergy. Jerome admitted that, in New Testament times, there had been no difference between presbyters and bishops, and that the church had been governed by the presbyters as a body. Through Satan's schemes, however, division entered the body of Christ, and so "it was decreed in the whole Church that one of the presbyters should be chosen to preside over the others, and that the whole responsibility for the Church should devolve on him, so that the seeds of schism should be removed."[118]

Jerome had a very high view of the clergy—and especially of the episcopacy. They were, he contended, "the successors of the Apostles, who with holy words consecrate the body of Christ, and who make us Christians." They possess the keys of the kingdom of heaven, and they "guard the chastity of the bride of Christ."[119]

But Jerome suffered no delusions about the clergy. Character, not rank, counted before Christ. "Not all bishops are bishops indeed. You consider Peter; mark Judas as well. . . . For it is not ecclesiastical rank that makes a man a Christian."[120]

On Baptism. Jerome acknowledged that, in many churches, it was held that the Holy Spirit descended upon a believer following baptism when the bishop laid hands on him. Such a practice, he confessed, was "more by way of honoring the episcopate than from any compulsory law." Indeed, "if necessity so be, we know that even laymen may, and frequently do, baptize . . . for it will hardly be said that we must believe that the eunuch whom Philip baptized lacked the Holy Spirit."[121]

Jerome did not sanction heretic baptism as valid. Arians, for example, could not receive the Holy Spirit, even if a bishop consecrated them with the laying on of hands. "How then can he receive the Holy Ghost from the Church, who has not yet obtained remission of sins?"[122]

On the Eucharist. Jerome was not in full accord on the Eucharist with his Greek Christian contemporaries, most of whom were conversionists. Rather, he favored a symbolic view of the Eucharist. The elements were a "type" of Christ just as the Passover was a "type" of His sacrifice on the cross. In his *Commentary on Ephesians* 1.7, he averred that

> the blood and flesh of Christ are to be understood in two ways. There is that spiritual and divine flesh and blood, of which he himself said: "My flesh is really food, and my blood is really drink"; and, "unless you eat my flesh and drink my blood, you will not have eternal life." There is also the flesh which was crucified, and the blood which was poured out under the soldier's spear. A corresponding distinction is to be understood, in the case of his saints, between the flesh which is to "see the salvation of God," and the flesh and blood which "cannot possess the Kingdom of God."[123]

Conclusions. Jerome believed in the primacy of the church of Rome, although there is no evidence that he held the Bishop of Rome to be the head of the church. He held that the clergy — and particularly the bishops, as the successors of the apostles — were responsible for the care of the church. While he did not believe in the necessity of a separate confirmation (apart from baptism) for the reception of the Holy Spirit, he did contribute toward its evolution by affirming it as a means of episcopal honor. The Holy Spirit, however, would descend only on one who possessed Christ as a result of valid baptism, and therefore, heretics could not receive the Spirit; for they did not possess Christ. Jerome did not side with those colleagues who held a conversionist (transubstantial) view of the Eucharist. He saw the elements as only a "type" of Christ.

Ambrose of Milan

Born in 339 to a patrician Roman family, Ambrose received a traditional education for one of his class, and was then appointed governor of a northern province, residing in Milan, Italy. In 374, upon the death of the Arian bishop of the city, Ambrose was acclaimed bishop, even though he had not been baptized. This obstacle was quickly overcome, and he was speedily moved up through the ranks of church leadership until he was placed in the highest position.[124]

Ambrose exerted substantial influence upon Augustine and baptized him in 387. His writings were mainly pastoral and practical. We shall examine his views on the sacraments, especially baptism and the Lord's Supper.

On Baptism. Ambrose held that the power of baptism is derived from the Godhead, particularly the Holy Spirit.[125] Nor is baptism valid unless the believer has been baptized according to the Trinitarian formula: "unless he is baptized in the Name of the Father, and of the Son, and of the Holy Spirit, he cannot receive remission of sins nor gain the gift of spiritual grace."[126] Furthermore, baptism is necessary to the forgiveness of sins: "The water, then, is that in which the flesh is dipped, that all carnal sin may be washed away. All wickedness is there buried . . . guilt is swallowed up and error done away."[127]

55

While chrismation (confirmation) was still closely related to baptism, Ambrose saw it as a separate sacrament, which occurred through the anointing with oil and laying on of hands.

> After this [baptism], you went up to the priest, consider what followed. Was it not that of which David speaks: "Like the ointment upon the head, which went down to the beard, even Aaron's beard"? . . . Consider now why this is done . . . that we, too, may become a chosen race, priestly and precious, for we are all anointed with spiritual grace for a share in the kingdom of God and in the priesthood."[128]

On the Lord's Supper. Ambrose received from Greek theology the idea of the conversion of the elements into the body and blood of Christ. According to Ambrose's idea of conversion, the bread and wine become the body and blood of Christ following the words of consecration: "Before the blessing of the heavenly words another nature is spoken of, after the consecration the Body is signified. He Himself speaks of His blood. Before the consecration, it has another name, after it is called Blood. And you say, Amen, that is, It is true."[129]

Conclusions. Ambrose differed little from his contemporaries in regard to baptism and confirmation. He did introduce a variation into the eucharistic views of the Latin church by affirming the Greek idea of the conversion of the elements. While this view was not strongly held by his contemporaries (as will be seen with Augustine), it was adopted in the Middle Ages by the Roman church and, as transubstantiation, became dogma.

Augustine of Hippo

Aurelius Augustinus (354–430) was born and lived all but five years of his life in Roman North Africa. He was taught the Christian faith from earliest childhood by his devout mother Monica, but was repelled by what he considered the barbarism of the Old Testament, and so converted to Manicheism, a dualistic heresy which disavowed the Old Testament and encouraged both asceticism and devotion to Christ. After nine years of practicing this approach to religion, he became disillusioned with its truth claims and went to Rome where he dabbled in many philosophies. In 384, Augustine was appointed imperial rhetorician at Milan, where he came under the influence of the local bishop, Ambrose, and neoplatonic philosophy. Both led him back to the orthodox faith. In 387, he was baptized, and following his mother's death in 388, returned to North Africa, where he founded a monastic community at Tagaste. In 391 he was inducted into the priesthood at Hippo, and five years later, was appointed bishop, in which position he spent his remaining years. He died in 430 as the Arian Vandals besieged his city.[130]

On the Church. Augustine did much writing on ecclesiology because of his ongoing battle against the Donatists, a schismatic North African group who had refused to recognize Caecilian as the legitimate bishop of Carthage because he had been consecrated by a bishop who had apostatized by giving up Scriptures to be burned during the persecution of Diocletian. The Catholics argued that ordination (or any other sacrament) did not depend for its efficacy on the character of the dispenser.

Augustine held that the church is Christ's domain, His mystical body and His bride. He is the Head of the church, and "the husband-wife relationship is the same as that between the head and the body, the husband being 'the head of the wife.' "[131] Augustine pictured the church with Christ its Head as the third mode of His existence (the other two being as eternal Word and as God-man). "There are many Christians, but only one Christ. The Christians themselves along with their Head, because He has ascended to heaven, form one Christ . . . we who are many are a unity in Him."[132]

The life-giving basis of this mystical body is the Holy Spirit, who may be received only in and through the church. Because the Holy Spirit—being God—is pure love, therefore the life-principle of the church may be said to be love. It is this love which forms the many members into one and creates a unity with its Head. Through faith men and women become one with Christ, and the church in hope looks ahead to the consummation of the age and its full salvation. Thus, the church is the fellowship of all who are joined together with one another and with Christ in faith, hope, and love.[133]

From his conception of the church as a fellowship of love came Augustine's teaching on the church's unity. Because they are members of one body, believers must be a unity. Such unity also necessitates unity of doctrine, and any failure in doctrinal unity involves heresy. Even more important, however, is the unity of love. Those who do not love their fellow-believers and their Lord are not true members of the church, but rather are schismatics. It was such a disdain for believers, Augustine argued, that made the Donatists schismatic; they were tearing the church asunder.[134]

The church, Augustine averred, is not only one, but catholic in its scope. In arguing against the Donatist bishop Honoratus, who claimed that his was the only true church, Augustine countered that he found it peculiar that "Christ should lose His inheritance, which is spread over the whole world, and should suddenly be found surviving only in the Africans, and not in all of them." On the other hand, "the Catholic Church exists indeed in Africa" and throughout all the world, but "the party of Donatus does not exist in all those places in which the writings of the apostles, their discourse, and their actions have been current."[135]

On Baptism. Augustine strongly believed that baptism is requisite to salvation (for human beings can be redeemed only within the church which may be entered only through baptism).[136]

Because the guilt of original sin had been passed on from Adam and Eve to all of their posterity,[137] its taint was so great that even the newly born were affected by it. Only through (infant) baptism could complete and immediate cleansing be accomplished. Infants, furthermore, declared Augustine, "believe by means of other people, even as they have derived those sins which are remitted them in baptism from other people,"[138] and thereby they attain salvation. Augustine wrote much of this in the context of a diatribe against the Pelagians, who held that infants are born innocent and free from any effects of original sin.[139]

In spite of his view on the necessity of infant baptism, Augustine did not view the sacrament as efficacious apart from a life of faith. To the contrary, he held that "we all know that if one baptized in infancy does not believe when he comes to years of discretion . . . then he will have no profit from the gift he received as a baby."[140]

Unlike Cyprian, Augustine believed that even heretic baptism was efficacious; "when they [heretics] return within the pale of the Church, and are converted through repentance, it is never given to them a second time, and so it is ruled that it could never have been lost."[141] When asked why Cyprian had required rebaptism of heretics converting to Catholicism, Augustine responded that his predecessor in the faith had not had the full illumination the church presently possessed. But he noted that Cyprian had always allowed "that he should thankfully receive any one that could be found with a fuller revelation of the truth."[142]

On Penance. Augustine saw penance as a threefold concern. There was, first, the repentance which preceded baptism; because of it, all sins were remitted in the water of baptism. There was, secondly, penance accomplished through fasting and prayer, wherein believers might obtain the remission of venial sins. Thirdly, there was penance of a formal character for sins of a serious nature committed after one's baptism. The church had the power to remit these because Jesus had given to it the power of binding and loosing (Matt. 16:18-19).[143] All who are a part of the church and continue in it, however, will be saved regardless of their moral character, the flaws of which would be removed by "suffering a punishment of fire, lasting for a time proportionate to the magnitude of their crimes and misdeeds, but they shall not be punished with everlasting fire."[144]

On the Eucharist. Augustine's doctrine of the Lord's Supper is not easy to analyze. But the overall evidence would suggest that he was a realist rather than a conversionist. In writing on the Eucharist, he noted that "a sacrifice therefore is the visible sacrament of an invisible sacrifice; that is, it is a sacred sign. . . . What is commonly called a sacrifice is the *sign* of a sacrifice."[145]

In his *On the Doctrine of Christ* 3.24, he determined that

if a command seems to order something immoral or criminal, or to forbid what is useful or beneficial, then it is figurative. "Un-

59

less," he says, "you eat the flesh, and drink the blood, of the Son of Man, you will not have life in yourselves." This seems to order crime or immorality: therefore it is figurative.[146]

Just as the life received by the communicant in the Supper is a spiritual gift, so the eating and drinking must be seen as occurring in a spiritual sense, as well.

Although it was a sign, Augustine saw the Eucharist in terms of a sacrifice. It was the crowning sacrifice to which all the Old Testament sacrifices pointed. But "instead of all those sacrifices and oblations His body is offered, and is distributed to the participants."[147] Christ is both the Priest and the Sacrifice. But because the members of the church are a part of His mystical body, they are offered up with Him. "The whole redeemed community . . . is the universal sacrifice offered to God through the great high priest, Who offered Himself in His passion for us, so that we might be the body of so great a Head."[148]

Conclusions. Augustine keenly promoted the Western view of the church. It is the mystical body of Christ, the Catholic and only true church. The Holy Spirit Himself, through His being as love, shapes the many members of the church into a single body, of which Jesus Christ is the Head.

Entry into the church occurred through baptism. Augustine's view of inherited original sin (as guilt) was so intense that he promoted infant baptism as a means of mitigating it. Babies could have faith (albeit through others) and so could receive the Holy Spirit. Since baptism was efficacious regardless of its dispenser, even heretic baptism was valid. Thus, Augustine promoted the Roman view of baptism over against that of Cyprian of Carthage.

One's standing in Christ was maintained through penance. Augustine was a strong advocate of that rite. Not only would it prepare a person for baptism, but it would also ameliorate sins committed after baptism. Those guilty of venial sins could fast and pray to avoid purgatory, while those guilty of more serious sins needed formal penance. Yet at the same time, all baptized would be saved regardless of the quality of their lives, although some would have to pass through a period of purgatory.

Union in Christ took place through the Eucharist. Like

Jerome, Augustine saw the Eucharist as symbolic, although he held to a "real presence" view. It was a spiritual sign of a spiritual sacrifice offered by Christ (as the church—body and Head) to God for the sins of humankind.

Though Augustine has always been regarded as the premier theologian of the church, many of his teachings did not endure the test of time. Calamitous events in the Western Empire— occurring even as Augustine's life and career ended—were to precipitate changes to what he held as truth.

1.1 A Summary of Patristic Ecclesiology

Father	Church Unity	Nature	Ministry	Sacraments
Clement of Rome	Schism the result of falling away from God.	———	To oust an overseer is a grievous sin against Christ.	———
Ignatius of Antioch	Division is the beginning of evil.	———	Required obedience to bishop. Bishop over presbyters reflects a divine pattern.	Baptism and the Lord's Supper may be given only by the bishop.
Didachē	———	———	Itinerant teachers to be welcomed if they teach true doctrine.	Introduction of "clinical" baptism. Only those baptized may take the Eucharist.
Irenaeus of Lyons	———	Church the new Israel; body of Christ; mother of believers; and the sole reserve of God's truth.	———	Eucharist a sacrifice to God, a priestly oblation.
Clement of Alexandria	One church as there is one God. Unity of church modeled on unity of God.	———	Grades of clergy; bishop, presbyters, deacons—all based on heavenly model.	Baptism washes away sin. Eucharist joins believers into one body.

Tertullian	Church is one, knit together by piety and discipline.	Church is bride of Christ; mother of believers; sole holder of apostolic revelation.	Desired a return to charismatic offices of ministry.	Baptism necessary to salvation; not for children. Eucharist real flesh and blood of Christ.
Cyprian of Carthage	Unity guaranteed by an episcopacy in the apostolic succession.	————	Bishop is the ruler of the church	Held to baptismal regeneration. Eucharist an oblation. Penance is the path to post-baptismal forgiveness.
John Chrysostom	The church coheres through mutual love.	The church is universal, unchanging foundation for all truth.	The office of priest is created by the Holy Spirit, who confirms priest's work.	Held to real presence of Christ in Lord's Supper. Epiclesis makes elements a real sacrifice. Forgiveness of sin is possible only in baptism and extreme unction.
Jerome	The pope is the rock of unity.	————	Bishops established over presbyters to prevent schism.	Holy Spirit descends upon believer at baptism. Held symbolic view of Eucharist.
Augustine of Hippo	Love creates the unity of the church with Christ as its Head. Because they are members.	The church's relation to Christ is analogous to wife's relation to her husband.	————	Baptism prerequisite to salvation. Infant baptism washes away original sin. All baptism is efficacious. Held to real presence of Christ in Lord's Supper.

THEOLOGY AFTER AUGUSTINE

The period following Augustine was one of political and social turmoil in the West as it fell prey to the barbarian invasions, particularly by Arians who were not friendly to Roman Christianity. It was during this period, however, that people looked to the church—and especially to the papacy—for stability and order. As a result, the popes made great strides toward establishing papal supremacy throughout Western Christendom. In the East, on the other hand, little had changed, including Greek ecclesiology. Life and thought continued much as they had in the previous century.

Gregory the Great

Born in Rome about 550 to a wealthy patrician family who had already supplied two popes to the Christian cause, Gregory received a superb education and entered the civil service. In 574, however, he sold his property and used the proceeds to establish six monasteries in Sicily, retaining his home on the Caelian Hill as a monastery for himself and some friends. There he lived as a simple monk. Five years later he was appointed by the pope as seventh deacon of the Christian community in Rome, responsible for administering welfare. In 590 Gregory became pope.[149]

On the Church. Gregory viewed the church differently than Augustine. For Gregory, the church was not only the body of which Christ is the Head; it was also a door by which people might come to God. "She is both in this world and beyond this world, a pathway between the two."[150] The church was not only Christ's body in a mystical sense, but in a physical one, as well; for it was composed of human beings.[151]

While Augustine believed that church and state did not cooperate in the process of salvation, Gregory—perhaps out of necessity—did not share this perception. He had been an administrator for both church and state, and felt that the church's function (among others) was to mold and guide a basically profane world. One historian comments that, in this regard, "Gregory's conception of the Papacy's directive role, its duties in the secular world, was far more closely in keeping with medieval thinking than Augustine's ideal of an otherworldly Church."[152]

OBSERVATIONS ON THE PATRISTIC PERIOD

The 600 or so years from the beginning of the New Testament church to the end of the reign of Gregory the Great saw major changes in the church and its doctrine. The church began as a united fellowship but in a few years theological tensions had developed between different groups within it, and an effective split took place between the Jewish and Gentile congregations, although a mutual support system and fellowship still existed. Within less than a century heretical groups were disturbing the peace of the church (groups such as the Ebionites and Gnostics).

With the death of the first generation of Christians, it was impossible to appeal to them for definitive words on problems which arose in matters of polity and doctrine. As a consequence, traditions evolved which seem to have been somewhat out of accord with straightforward biblical teaching. Some of these concerned matters of ecclesiastical polity, more involved the sacraments.

As the first century drew to a close great emphasis was being placed on the church's unity. The church's polity was still essentially charismatic, but a process of institutionalization was under way. During the second century this process was furthered by a separation of clergy from laity. Ignatius of Antioch declared that the leadership functions of the church were patterned after those of heaven; the bishop was patterned upon God Himself and was to be the sole mediator of the ordinances. We must conclude, however, because of evidence presented in the *Didachē*, that the various churches did not all follow the same pattern, for that work—likely dated toward the end of the first century, although with earlier sources included[153]—is much more primitive and charismatic in its organizational structures.

Changes in the observance of the ordinances became more pronounced in each century. Immersion was evidently no longer the sole mode for baptism. Affusion (or pouring) and then sprinkling were added as acceptable modes. A rigorism which cannot be found in the biblical teaching was developing in regard to sin in the Christian life. Baptism was efficacious in the washing away of sins to the point of the ordinance's administration, but not beyond. As a result, penance was introduced to ameliorate post-baptismal sins. While public penance was initially the desired mode, by the end of the fourth century it had been largely forsaken in the East, and in the West was continued with less and less rigor. Under Gregory the Great it became a sacrament.

The Eucharist evolved into a sacrament as well. The Alexandrians saw the Lord's Supper as a symbolic rite. But in the West, Cyril and Augustine saw the elements as figurative. John Chrysostom was an Eastern exception, speaking of a transelementation of the bread and cup into the body and blood of Christ.

Toward the latter part of the second century a gap began to develop between the churches of the Eastern Empire and those of the West, which became increasingly obvious. One area of increasing divergence had to do with the matter of episcopal primacy. Ignatius had opened the door by making the bishop head of the local church as Christ is Head of the church universal. Irenaeus took this view a step further by seeing the bishop as a direct successor of the apostles and therefore custodian of God's truth. He further attributed to Rome a special preeminence throughout the church by virtue of its founding by Peter and Paul. Tertullian promoted Irenaeus' view (although he was of a decidedly different—and opposite—opinion after becoming a Montanist). By the fourth century, Cyprian was maintaining that the bishops represented not just the apostles, but Christ Himself, and possessed the power to forgive sins. Because the bishops were necessary to the saving grace mediated by the church, outside of the church no one might be saved.

The bishops of Rome adopted these views and vigorously promoted them. The primacy of the papacy was greatly advanced in the West when Gregory I was forced by the barbarian invasions to take on a secular leadership role in addition to his spiritual one. In the East, meanwhile, the bishops resisted such a view of Roman primacy, acknowledging that see to be first in honor, but otherwise on a par with all of the others. While the Eastern Orthodox Church was to change very little in the coming Middle Ages, Roman Catholicism would continue to evolve into varying mutations of the ecclesiology held by the apostolic church.

CHAPTER TWO

The Medieval Church

While the Middle Ages were a time of great upheaval and change for the church, the theologians of this period had only a few elements to add to the evolution of ecclesiology. The two concepts that did come to the fore were the primacy of Rome and the identification of the church with the kingdom of God.[1] It was also during this time that the present system of sacraments in the Roman Catholic Church was completed and the number set at seven (by the Council of Florence in 1439).

Our focus on the Middle Ages will be entirely on the Roman Catholic Church. Ecclesiology in Eastern Orthodoxy changed very little from the fifth century onward. The West, however, continued to develop its views of the church and the sacraments.

THE PRE-SCHOLASTIC PERIOD

The beginning of the Middle Ages marked a progression from the old ways and ideas to new ones in almost every sphere of life. The *pax Romana* collapsed under assaults from the European barbarians and then from the Saracens and Moors. In this tremendous turmoil, the Roman Church was the vehicle by which the endowment of the old culture and society was conserved and mediated to the new.[2]

Events in the Western church had little impact on the Eastern church. The Eastern Empire persisted until almost the close of the Medieval period, and—in regard to its church doctrine and polity—changed not at all. In the West, however, the church was forced to evangelize and disciple the Germanic tribes, who received the Christian faith with almost no protest.[3]

> In this period we do not notice any real development of dogma. The church in the main fortified and defended her dogmatic structure. Augustine had prepared the way for the medieval conception of Christianity. His ideas, though often misunderstood and misinterpreted, controlled the theology of the church. The task of theologians, then, was chiefly to gather together the doctrinal materials acquired, to sift them, to preserve them.[4]

Most of the theological work accomplished in this era was a systematizing and interpreting of the church fathers, and especially of Augustine.

The Controversy over the Eucharist

The variation in views of the Lord's Supper between Ambrose of Milan and Augustine of Hippo created some tensions in European worship practices. The older Gallic and Spanish liturgies demonstrated the Ambrosian influence, expressing the concept of the conversion of the elements through priestly consecration. The Roman liturgy, however, showed the symbolic eucharistic concepts of Augustine. By the end of the eighth century, the Roman liturgy had infiltrated worship practices among the Franks, and it became increasingly apparent that, for the sake of the church's unity, the doctrine of the Lord's Supper should proceed in one direction or the other.[5]

Although theologians, for the most part, held to the symbolical view of Augustine, the common people were more inclined toward the realism of Ambrose. The people of ninth-century Europe were rather pious folk who possessed a very unrefined faith in the miraculous; they had no difficulty believing that the bread and wine of the Eucharist were somehow changed into the very body and blood of the Lord.[6]

A major controversy over the nature of the Lord's Supper developed in the ninth century as the result of a book entitled *On the Body and Blood of the Lord*, written in 831 by Paschasius Radbertus, a monk of the abbey at Corbie, France, and published in 844. In it, he asserted that the bread and wine of the Eucharist are in actuality the body and blood of Christ, the very flesh conceived by the Virgin Mary, crucified at Calvary, and resurrected three days later; the blood is the same fluid that coursed from His wounded side. While this flesh and blood do not appear to be so, the believer by ingesting the bread and wine is feeding on and nourished by the Lord.[7]

It was not long before criticism of Radbertus' stand surfaced. Rhabanus Maurus, Archbishop of Mainz and the most prolific writer of the Carolingian era, reemphasized the Augustinian position. He maintained that the bread and wine are signs of Christ's body and blood, and not His actual flesh, as Radbertus suggested. The latter idea was odious. "Rhabanus did not deny that as a result of the consecration a change does take place, but he felt that bread and wine become Christ's body and blood 'mystically' or 'sacramentally.' "[8]

Ratramnus, also a monk of Corbie, attacked Radbertus' ideas in a work of the same name, *On the Body and Blood of the Lord*. He attempted to respond to two concerns: first, does the Eucharist hold a mystery which can be discerned with the eyes of faith alone; and, are the bread and cup indistinguishable from the body and blood of the earthly Jesus when they are transmuted. He rejected the identification of the elements with Jesus' literal body and blood, holding that in the Eucharist they do not change their nature. There is a change, it is true; but it is spiritual and symbolic. What the believer ingests at the rite is neither simply the flesh of Christ nor simply bread and wine, but something more sublime. Thus, Ratramnus could respond positively to the question of whether the Supper holds a mystery which can be discerned with the eyes of faith alone.[9]

Other than a clear understanding of the two viewpoints, nothing was settled by this controversy. No dynamic definitions were forthcoming from Rome. But the die had been cast; for public opinion—and even many church leaders—favored Radbertus' views.

During the next two centuries the Radbertian concept gained ground. In 1050, Berengar of Tours, one of the foremost theologians and scholars of his day, wrote a letter to another leading theologian, Lanfranc, a monk of Bec, berating him for advocating the Radbertian theory of the Lord's Supper; Berengar alleged that it was unreasonable, unbiblical, and contrary to the teaching of the great fathers such as Jerome and Augustine. He insisted that the elements are merely emblematic of Christ's body and blood. When they are consecrated, they receive a spiritual power which is grasped by faith. But Christ is not present in literal bodily form.[10]

Berengar was opposed not only by Lanfranc, but also by Hugo of Longres, Durandus of Troanne, and Guitmund of Aversa. They had him condemned at Rome and Vercelli in 1050 without a hearing. A series of further trials led to his exile to an ascetic and solitary life on the island of St. Come, near Tours, where he died in 1088. His opponents went beyond Radbertus in their views. Lanfranc avowed that the elements become the literal flesh of Christ for believer and unbeliever alike. Guitmund of Aversa declared that the entire body of Christ is in every segment of the bread. By the early twelfth century, Hildebert of Lavardin, the Archbishop of Tours, was using in sermons the term *transubstantiation*. Radbertus' theory had become the *de facto* doctrine of the church.

The Fight for Papal Supremacy

One of the major developments of ecclesiology which came during the pre-Scholastic period of the Middle Ages was the embellishment of the papal office. The lofty place occupied by the papacy during this period can be traced to several factors. Traditions created in the Patristic period were foundational. The decline of imperial power in the West, coupled with the barbarian invasions, liberated the popes from Byzantine control. Successful papal missions to Britain, France, and the Germanic states enhanced papal influence. The support of the Carolingian monarchs provided additional power. And political disintegration in Europe during the ninth and tenth centuries gave impetus to papal claims of a center of unity with divinely bestowed powers.[11] The personal power and abilities of several individual popes also contributed greatly to the attempt to establish papal supremacy in the West.

Nicholas II. Nicholas II (1059–1061), elected with the aid of the reforming monk Hildebrand (later Gregory VII), made a major

69

contribution to papal power by establishing the College of Cardinals as the electoral body responsible for the selection of future popes. In this way he helped to free the papacy from the control of the Holy Roman Emperor. His "Papal Election Decree" dictated that:

> On the death of a pontiff of the universal Roman church, first, the cardinal bishops, with the most diligent consideration, shall elect a successor; then they shall call in the other cardinal clergy [to ratify their decision], and finally the rest of the clergy and the people shall express their consent to the new election.[12]

The candidate should preferably come from the church in Rome but, failing someone suitable, might be chosen from another church. Should wicked people by force of arms prevent the enthronement of the pope elect, he should nonetheless exercise all governing functions, including control of revenues. And should someone be elected or enthroned by methods contrary to Nicholas' decree (e.g., as the result of rebellion), he should "be expelled from the holy church of God and . . . be subjected to perpetual anathema as Antichrist and . . . be deposed without appeal from every ecclesiastical rank which he may have held formerly."[13]

Nicholas also took steps to strengthen the role of the papal legate. Through the latter's work the power of Rome could influence more thoroughly all of Europe.[14]

Gregory VII. Gregory VII (1073–1085) was a former Benedictine monk named Hildebrand. Born about 1021, he had received a good education and, after taking holy orders, had become associated with the Cluniac reform movement. A close friend of Bishop Bruno of Toul, he had the opportunity for meaningful reform efforts when the latter became Pope Leo IX and appointed him to the Curia. Hildebrand was the power behind the throne of succeeding popes, especially that of Nicholas II (see above) and his successor Alexander II.

When Alexander died, Hildebrand was acclaimed by the people of Rome and elected by the College of Cardinals as Pope Gregory VII. He determined to enforce priestly celibacy as a way of liberating the church from the world. In 1074 he forbade future clerical marriages, and ordered married priests to abandon their wives or give up reciting the mass. The result was that "legal wives became harlots, and legitimate children, bastards."[15]

Gregory was determined that no civil power should control the church, but rather that the church should exercise control over the civil authority. As a result, he fought long and hard against lay investiture, a practice whereby civil rulers — generally lay persons — gave priests and bishops their symbols of office. In the *Dictatus Papae*, written by Gregory or under his authority, he decreed "that all princes shall kiss the foot of the pope alone," and "that he has the power to depose emperors." Moreover, "his decree can be annulled by no one, and that he can annul the decree of anyone." Furthermore, "by his command or permission subjects may accuse their rulers," and "he has the power to absolve subjects from their oath of fidelity to wicked rulers."[16]

Gregory had the opportunity to test his decree against Henry IV, the Holy Roman emperor, who attempted to reject papal authority. The first round of the conflict was won by the pope and ended with Henry standing barefoot in the snow for three days at Canossa, Italy, in 1077 until Gregory revoked his excommunication and gave him absolution. The second round was won by Henry, who invaded Italy and appointed an antipope, Wibert. Gregory died in exile at Salerno.

Innocent III. Under Innocent III (1198–1216), the medieval papacy reached its highest point of power. The scion of Roman patricians, he was both a theologian and a lawyer. He rose to the College of Cardinals and, in the papal service, showed great skill in a variety of religious and civil arenas.

As pope, Innocent was successful in dominating the kings of England and France. In 1205, he appointed Stephen Langton Archbishop of Canterbury. King John refused to accept the appointment and so, in 1208, Innocent placed the English realm under an interdict, resulting in the church's denial of the sacraments to any person. When John retaliated by seizing church properties, the pope excommunicated him in 1209 and, in 1212, declared the English throne vacant. He also invited the French to invade England, which forced John to accept Langton

71

as Archbishop, return seized property, and even ask Innocent to become his overlord.

When Philip Augustus of France divorced his wife (with the approval of a council of French bishops), she appealed to Innocent, who ordered her restoration. The king refused, and France was placed under an interdict and, after a long conflict, the queen was reinstated.

Innocent's crowning achievement was the Fourth Lateran Council of 1215. Here, the power of the pope and his clergy over secular society was affirmed and a multitude of reforms enacted. We shall discuss its significance separately, below.

Conclusions. The efforts of the papacy to wrest control of church affairs out of the hands of laypeople, particularly European monarchs and noblemen, enjoyed some limited success. By the end of the first Christian millennium, the major nations of Europe had come to accept the pope as supreme in matters pertaining to the church. But the papacy was not as successful in its campaign to control these monarchs. Successful over the short term, papal power reached its zenith in the early thirteenth century, but went into a decline which led to the captivity of the popes at Avignon, France, for almost a century.

At the same time, these efforts were not all in vain. Theologically, great strides were made in achieving the goal of primacy in the Christian church. Such dogma as papal infallibility rested on the foundations built by these popes and their successors.

The Fourth Lateran Council

The Fourth Lateran Council, also known as "the Great Council," was the crown of medieval papal legislation. Most Roman Catholic scholars hold it to be the most important council other than Trent. Called by Innocent III in April of 1213, it assembled in November of 1215, and was attended by some 400 archbishops and bishops, almost all of whom were Roman Catholics.[17]

In addition to proclaiming a new crusade against Islam, the council promulgated seventy canons. Several of these were ecclesiological.

Canon I not only affirmed the Creed of the church, but also the church's unity. "There is one Universal Church of the faithful, outside of which there is absolutely no salvation."[18] The unity of the church is demonstrated both by the sacraments and by their celebration by a priest who stands in the apostolic succession.

The same canon also decreed that Jesus Christ is both priest and sacrifice to God for sinful human beings. His body and blood "are truly contained in the sacrament of the altar under the forms of bread and wine; the bread being changed (transubstantiatis) by divine power into the body; and the wine into the blood."[19] Nor might the Eucharist be rightfully administered by anyone who had not been ordained into the Christ-founded apostolic succession.

According to the same canon, baptism was to be executed in water, according to the Trinitarian formula, and "duly conferred on children and adults in the form prescribed by the Church by anyone whatsoever, leads to salvation."[20] If one should sin after baptism, one might be restored by true repentance.

Canon 21 required that all church members must, after reaching an age of discretion, confess all of their sins on an annual basis to their parish priest, and perform faithfully the tasks of penance assigned them. They must also receive the Lord's Supper at least once a year at Easter. "Otherwise they shall be cut off from the Church (excommunicated) during life and deprived of Christian burial in death."[21] Priests, for their part, were cautioned against revealing the confidences of the confessional; the breaching of that trust would be punished by lifelong confinement to a monastery and deposition from the sacerdotal office.

Conclusions. The pre-Scholastic period of the church's history accomplished little new ecclesiologically. In regard to the sacraments, the period served to reaffirm and further dogmatize what was already in place. The Eucharistic Controversy narrowed the ways of interpreting the Lord's Supper to one only— transubstantiation—and this was dogmatized by the Fourth Lateran Council.

The effort to promote papal supremacy was given impetus by several of the stronger popes. While not very successful politically, it was reasonably so doctrinally, though its end result was

73

not achieved for several centuries when, at Vatican I, the dogma of papal infallibility was decreed.

The Scholastic Period

The term *Scholasticism* was derived from the Greek *scholē*, signifying a place of learning. While "Scholastic" was applied to instructors in the court of Charlemagne, it did not really become meaningful on a broad scale until the tenth century or so, when theologians began trying to justify faith by reason. They treated theology from a philosophical rather than a biblical viewpoint.[22]

Hugo of Saint Victor

Hugo (or Hugh) of St. Victor (ca. 1096–1141) was a pious Augustinian Platonist who became director of the school of the Canons of Saint Victor in Paris. His *Summa of the Sentences* was as highly thought of as Peter Lombard's own. And he had much more to say about the church.

Hugo saw two states in the church—the rulers and the ruled—a restatement of the teachings of Cyprian. The right side of the church is made up of the clergy, and the left side of the laity. The former administers those things pertaining to spiritual life, and the latter administers those things which pertain to the temporal life. Each of the sides is governed by a ruler—the clergy by the pope, and the laity by a king. The nature of the church harmonizes fully with this concept. In the order of ranking in the church, the archbishops and four patriarchs are over the bishops, while over them all is the pope, who is responsible to God alone. There was no doubt in Hugo's mind that the spiritual power was superior to the secular.[23]

Hugo's view of the relationship of church and state was an approximation of that of Gregory VII. It may be summed up in four statements:

1. The clergy are related to the laity as a government to its subjects.
2. This exalted position of the clergy is explained by their authority to dispense the sacraments.

3. The clergy is a graded organism, whose summit is the pope.
4. The secular power is by divine right subject to the spiritual.[24]

In regard to the sacraments, Hugo was typical of his day. His was probably the clearest definition of a sacrament in medieval times, "a corporeal or material element, openly [and] sensibly presented, representing by similitude and signifying by institution, and containing by consecration, some invisible and spiritual grace."[25] For example, once consecrated, the waters of baptism carry spiritual grace. He held that confirmation was superior to baptism because the former imparted the Holy Spirit whereas the latter simply cured the disease of sin.[26]

Thomas Aquinas

Thomas Aquinas (ca. 1225–1274), known as "the Angelic Doctor," was born into a noble family (he was a nephew to the Holy Roman Emperor, Frederick Barbarossa). He was educated at Monte Cassino and the University of Naples, and was a student of Albert Magnus in Cologne. Thomas' two great works were the *Summa Theologiae* (an effort to synthesize faith and reason into a totality of truth) and the *Summa Contra Gentiles* (an apologetic against Islam to train missionaries). The former was a systematic theology which made him the premier theologian of Roman Catholicism.[27]

On the Church. Thomas saw the church in a metaphorical sense as Christ's mystical body. He used Paul's description of it in likeness to a human body with the different parts under the co-ordination of the head (1 Cor. 12). Just as the head of the body is the center of order, perfection, and power, so Christ is Head of the church. The analogy should not be pressed too far, however; for "the members of an organism are all together at one given period of time, whereas the members of the mystical body are dispersed throughout the ages . . . from the beginning of the world until its end."[28]

He held the institutional church to be "a society of saints" and a congregation of Christians to which every believer belonged. It is not a perfect society; for it includes unrepentant sinners as well as the absolved. But perfection is its goal, which will be attained in heaven rather than on earth.[29]

Thomas had a high view of the papal position. Because of Pauline-Petrine-Roman primacy, the pope has plenitude of power in the spiritual realm. Indeed, he is the final authority in all matters of faith and practice. And he alone has the authority to call, convene, and close a general council. His power exceeds that of any council. At the same time, Thomas denied the pope secular authority, except as that authority had spiritual aspects.[30]

On the Eucharist. Thomas taught that Christ's promise to His followers to give them His body to eat and His blood to drink was fulfilled "in the sensible sign of the accidents of bread and wine, instituted to give grace, not, as in the case of the other sacraments, by the power of the Holy Ghost in them, but by containing the very body and blood of Christ Himself."[31] Because Christ used unleavened wheaten bread at the Last Supper and wine mixed with water, these are the fitting and required materials for the church to use in the Eucharist. By the priest's words of consecration, the substance of the bread is transformed into the substance of the body of Christ, and the substance of the wine into the substance of His blood. This transformation is known as transubstantiation. "If that term is understood, all else that will be said about the sacrament will have nothing of the vague or indistinct about it; if the content of that term is believed, the whole truth of the Eucharist is known."[32]

Since one is what one eats, in the partaking of the elements of the Supper one becomes united with Christ. Such an idea helps to explain the unity of the mystical body; since all who partake of the elements are one with Christ, all are one with each other, as well.

On Baptism. Thomas saw baptism as "a sensible sign instituted by Christ to give the first sanctifying grace which is the birth of a man to the life of God."[33] The water of baptism (after its consecration) is tantamount to the life of God; for, "in the instant of the baptism of Christ [by John the Baptist], plain, ordinary water was consecrated by this contact with God."[34]

Thomas was indifferent to the mode. It really makes little

difference, he averred, whether the water is poured upon a person's head or if the head is put under the water. "The limitation of the process to a 'pouring' of water in the Latin church is not a matter of validity, but of lawfulness; it must be done this way under pain of sin for the minister, but not under pain of nullity for the sacrament."[35]

In baptism the soul is purified from all sin, regardless of one's age. Through this sacrament the likeness of God—lost at the Fall—is indelibly stamped on the one who receives it. And yet, for all this, baptism is incomplete by itself; for it produces only a spiritual child. More is needed if one is to become spiritually mature.

On Confirmation. The fullness of life, Thomas declared, occurs with the coming of the Holy Spirit and His grace, signified by the olive oil of the chrism of confirmation. In this sacrament the spiritual child becomes a spiritual adult. "Just as infancy and adolescence are ordained to full manhood in the natural order, so Baptism is ordered to Confirmation in the supernatural order; Confirmation is as necessary to the supernatural order as manhood is in the natural."[36] Only those signed with the sign of the cross may possess a full and mature understanding of God.

William of Ockham

William of Ockham (ca. 1290–ca. 1349) was born in the village of Ockham, in Surrey, England. About the age of 19 he entered the Franciscan order and began a study of theology at Oxford, culminating with the degree of Master in the *Sentences* of Peter Lombard. William was noted for his new form of nominalist philosophy which rejected the existence of "universals" and argued only "particulars" have real existence. He stressed that God could be known only by faith and not by reason, and that His will is supreme. In these areas he was a forerunner of Reformation theology.[37]

On the Church. In regard to his teaching on the church, William was atypical of his time. He asserted that Christ—not the pope—is the Head of the church. And he suggested that laypeople ought to have a greater measure of authority through participation in general (or, ecumenical) councils. His book *On the Power of Emperors and Pontiffs* (written 1346–1347) was quite critical of the papacy.

William was adamant that the authority underlying the church is the Scriptures. They take precedence over all else. "Human authority," he declared, "is by no means to be relied upon in those things which pertain to the faith, because our faith is above the human intellect." Consequently, no pope or church can by declarations alter anything whatsoever in biblical truth.[38]

Nor did William allow that papal authority should extend into the temporal realm. Since Christ had forbidden Peter and the apostles to exercise power over Gentile kings and emperors, such power is also forbidden to Peter's successors in Rome. He quoted both Peter Lombard and Bernard of Clairvaux, who, in giving advice to popes, warned them not to get "involved in any sort of mundane business at all," for Christ had appointed them to spiritual concerns.[39]

> If, therefore, the pope, except in case of necessity, intervenes in temporals, he is considered to put his sickle into another's harvest, unless he has received authority over such matters from the emperor or someone else. And indeed what he does in such matters is not valid, since "those things that are done by a judge are null and void if they do not belong to his office."[40]

William also denied that the pope necessarily had supreme authority to convoke a general council. If it is well known that a pope is a notorious heretic, then "anyone . . . ought to exhort other catholics to assemble a general council." There was a descending order for such a task: first, prelates and canon lawyers, followed by kings and princes, and lastly laypeople; "even catholic women, if they know the pope to be a heretic and the electors negligent in regard to the election of a supreme pontiff, ought . . . to urge catholics to convene in a general council." He further commended the attendance of women at such a council, "if they can further the common good thereby."[41]

On the Sacraments. William was atypical of his age in regard to the sacraments, as well. His view of the Lord's Supper was really one of consubstantiation rather than transubstantiation, for he taught that the substance of the bread and cup, not merely the accidents, remains along with the substance of Christ's flesh and blood. While he felt that transubstantiation could be defended neither on the basis of logic nor the Bible, like several of his Nominalist colleagues, he accepted the doctrine because of the authority of the Roman Church.[42] In fact, William declared, "This is my faith, since it is the Catholic faith; for whatever the Roman Church believes, this alone and not anything else do I believe, either explicitly or implicitly."[43]

2.1 Medieval Views of the Lord's Supper

Realistic Views	Literal Views
Rhabanus Maurus: Bread and wine are signs of the Lord's body and blood, not His actual flesh.	**Paschasius Radbertus:** Bread and wine are the very flesh and blood of Jesus, conceived by Mary, crucified, and raised.
Ratramnus of Corbie: The bread and wine do not change their nature. Any change is spiritual and symbolic.	**Lanfranc of Bec:** The elements become the literal body and blood of Christ for believers and unbelievers alike.
Berengar of Tours: The elements are emblematic of Christ's body and blood. When consecrated, they receive spiritual power grasped only by faith.	**Thomas Aquinas:** The bread and wine become the body and blood of Christ by transubstantiation. By partaking of the elements, one becomes united with Christ.
John Wycliffe: Rejected transubstantiation as contrary to Scripture and as tantamount to paganism. Christ is spiritually present in the elements.	**William of Ockham:** Held to consubstantiation rather than transubstantiation, but accepted the latter because of Christ's authority.

Observations on the Scholastic Era

Little formal doctrine on the church per se was produced by the Schoolmen. It was not high on their list of priorities. With the exception of the doctrine of papal primacy, which they expanded and developed substantially, they relied, for the most part, on Augustine's ecclesiology, with refinements here and there.

One area in which there was considerable movement, though, was the related realm of the sacraments. Since the early church had produced no set dogma, the Scholastic theologians worked hard at formalizing a doctrine of the sacraments. They did for that doctrine what the church fathers had done for the doctrines of theology and Christology.[44]

Scholasticism came to understand the sacraments as God's means of infusing humans with justifying grace. Baptism cleanses from sin and regenerates; confirmation matures the spiritual life by imparting the Holy Spirit; the Eucharist nourishes the spiritual life; penance restores it when it is lost through post-baptismal sin; holy orders generate the needed rulers of the church. While not all of the Schoolmen were united in their views of the sacraments, all accepted the magisterial dogma because of their acceptance of the church's authority. The writings of dissidents, such as Ockham, however, influenced both Renaissance and Reformation theologians, who were much more strident in their objections.

THE RENAISSANCE THEOLOGIANS

The Renaissance, which began mid-fourteenth century in Europe, may be regarded as a bridge from the medieval to the modern era.[45] It began in Italy with a rebirth of interest in the classical literature (including the Bible) in their original languages. It blossomed as it spread throughout Europe into a reexamination of every aspect of human endeavor. While many of those participating in this revolution were spiritual pagans, large numbers were dedicated Christian believers who were seeking to serve God more adequately by getting back past ecclesiastical tradition to church principles clearly dictated in the Scriptures.

John Wycliffe

John Wycliffe (ca. 1330–1384) overlapped the end of the Middle Ages and the commencement of the Renaissance. A leading philosopher at Oxford University, he was invited to serve at the royal court of England. While there, he offended the church by affirming the Crown's right to confiscate the property of corrupt clergy. He was condemned by the pope in 1377, but was protected by politically powerful friends.[46]

On the Church. One of Wycliffe's books, *The Church and Her Members*, set forth his ecclesiology. The Bride of Christ, he taught, is tripartite.

> The first part is in bliss with Christ, the head of the Church, and contains angels and blessed men who are now in heaven. The second part of the Church are saints in purgatory: these commit no additional sins, but purge their old sins. . . . The third part of the Church is composed of true men that are living on earth, who shall afterwards be among the saved in heaven and who live here the lives of Christian men. The first part is called the victorious, the second is called the sleeping, and the third is called the fighting Church; and these three together make up the Church.[47]

Wycliffe was a firm believer in predestination. The church is the company of those predestined to salvation. While a person cannot surely know whether he is a part of that elect company or not, "in proportion as a man may hope that he shall be saved in bliss, so he should suppose that he is a limb of holy Church; and thus he should love holy Church and worship it as his mother."[48]

Wycliffe's strong belief in predestination led him to take up a position that directly challenged papal authority. "No pope that lives," Wycliffe asserted, "knows whether he is a member of the Church or whether he is a limb of the devil, destined to be damned with Lucifer."[49] Consequently, many Roman Catholics who strive for the pope are, in fact, striving for the devil and not for the Christian faith. "The true vicar of Christ should be the poorest man of all, and the meekest of all men, and the man of most labor in Christ's Church."[50] But Wycliffe knew of no cardinals who fit that picture. To say that Christ needs a vicar on earth is to "deny Christ's power and place this devil above Christ."[51]

For Wycliffe, the one authority on earth for the believer is not a pope but the Bible. As a consequence, tradition, ecclesial infallibility, and the like are worthless, as is anything else which has no foundation in the Scriptures.

On the Sacraments. In his tract, *On the Eucharist*, Wycliffe rejected transubstantiation as the meaning of the Lord's Supper. It was contrary, he argued, both to logic and to Scripture. Indeed, belief in such a view was tantamount to—if not worse than—pagan superstition.[52] His own view was one of spiritual presence; Christ was spiritually present in the elements of the Eucharist.

John Hus

John Hus (ca. 1372–1415), a Czech nationalist, was ordained a priest in 1400. Much of his time was spent as a professor at the Charles University in Prague, and as rector and preacher in Bethlehem Chapel near the university. An avid but critical disciple of John Wycliffe's teachings, he emphasized the authority of Scripture in the church and taught that neither popes nor cardinals should establish any doctrine contrary to the Bible, nor should any Christian obey an order from them which was wrong.[53]

Hus was involved in numerous struggles with the church. In 1414 he traveled to the Council of Constance to explain his views, but even though he was under a safe-conduct from the Holy Roman Emperor, he was arrested, tried for heresy, and condemned to the stake without a hearing. His death, in 1415, resulted in his Bohemian countrymen founding the Hussite church, which persisted until its destruction by the Hapsburgs in 1620.[54]

Hus' teaching on the church was contained in his work *On the Church*, much of which was drawn from the writings of John Wycliffe. Hus taught that the church is the complete body of all those who from eternity have been predestined to salvation. Only Christ is Head of the church, and no visible sign can make one a member of it. All church institutions are human inventions and so are not valid.[55]

Hus had no more use for the papacy than did Wycliffe. His view of the pope was that, "even though all men were to call him holy and most holy, if his acts be contrary to Christ he is not holy, whether or not he is called so."[56] That he holds the highest office in Roman Catholicism does not make him holy, as one can see from the example of Judas Iscariot. Indeed, "the saints affirm that the worthier the office the greater the damnation of the incumbent if he be sinful."[57]

Desiderius Erasmus

Erasmus (ca. 1466–1536) was probably the most influential of all Renaissance scholars. While he was best known for his edition of the Greek New Testament, he was also a knowledgeable theologian, writing such works as *The Handbook of the Militant Christian* (1503), *In Praise of Folly* (1511), *Familiar Colloquies* (1518), and *Free Will* (1524).

Because Erasmus was not a systematic theologian, his ecclesiology must be culled from his various writings. One must also keep in mind his context. He was critical of Rome while being a committed Roman Catholic. He was caught in the crossfire between Rome and Lutheranism while not wishing to take the side of either (although he was frequently accused by one side of supporting the other!). He desired above all else the unity and peace of the church.

In a note to Franciscan Conrad Pellican, who later left the Roman Church, he reiterated his strong belief that the Church of Rome was the one true church. In his work *On Free Will*, he restated his conviction.

> Granting that the Spirit of Christ could have let his people fall into error on some secondary point, with no immediate repercussions for the salvation of men, how can you admit that He left His Church in error for 1300 years, and that from among this crowd of holy men, He could not find one to whom He should show what we late-comers pretend constitutes the very depth of the whole Evangelical doctrine?[58]

Erasmus held the church to be the body of Christ. He defined this body as "a certain congregation of all men throughout the whole world who agree in the faith of the Gospel, who worship one God the Father, who put their whole confidence in His Son, and who are guided by the same Spirit of Him."[59] At the same time, he refused to say that he believed "in" the church; for "we must believe in God alone," whereas the church consists of human beings.[60]

In regard to the sacraments, Erasmus appears to have had some doubts about the notion of *ex opere operato*. He declared that "in the Church . . . there is forgiveness of sins by baptism . . ." but also observed that "entrance to the Church is faith, without which baptism is of no avail."[61] As far as Mass (Eucharist) went, he asserted that "those problems relating to the quality of the Mass, the *ex opere operato* and the *ex opere operantis* elements, ought to be laid aside until a general council has made a pronouncement concerning them. . . ."[62] He had no problem with calling Holy Communion a "sacrifice," for that was the term used by the early Fathers. He did admit, however, that "Christ having once died, will die no more," although "this one sacrifice is renewed daily in symbolic rites, whereby we receive new grace as from an inexhaustible font."[63] Any commands regarding other spiritual observances, if not found in Scripture, argued Erasmus, are to be taken as advice rather than dictates: dialogue, persuasion, and prayer are fine, but persons should in no way be forced into a religion which they find repellent.[64]

Conclusions. While the Renaissance theologians—as typified by those mentioned above—did not go as far in their criticisms of Rome or in their demands for reform as those who followed them, they may rightly be termed "the forerunners of the Reformation." It may be true that none of them grasped the idea of justification by faith—an idea that would soon become the center of Reformation theology: but they did demand a return to the biblical roots for doctrine, and they averred that only what was biblical was required in faith and practice. And many of them (e.g., Wycliffe and Hus) espoused the priesthood of all believers. These principles were foundational to the Reformation.

SUMMARY AND OBSERVATIONS

The Middle Ages were a time of change and development in Roman Catholic ecclesiology. While no new doctrines were propounded, substantial effort was expended in preserving and systematizing patristic (especially Augustinian) teachings on the church.

One area in which movement took place during the pre-scholastic period (ninth to twelfth centuries) was in the sacraments. By the ninth century a division had occurred between the theologians, who followed the symbolic view of the Eucharist held by Augustine, and the common people who embraced the realistic (literal) concept espoused by Ambrose. After two centuries of wrangling, the latter view, known as *transubstantiation*, prevailed. In 1215, the Fourth Lateran Council made transubstantiation official dogma. The sacraments of baptism and penance were also dogmatized.

During this same time, successive popes emphasized the supremacy of the papacy over the Christian world. Though their efforts were not a political success, the papacy was accorded the premier spiritual place in the Western world.

The Scholastic theologians continued the effort at regularizing the teachings on the sacraments. They taught that baptism regenerates and transforms sinners; they are spiritually fed by the body and blood of Christ; they receive the Holy Spirit in confirmation; penance restores the sinner who has fallen; holy orders (ordination) supplies the church with needed leaders. Even though Scholastic theologians did not all agree on what the sacraments signified, they all accepted them as set forth by the magisterium because of their submission to the church's authority.

Some of the latter Schoolmen strongly influenced the views of Renaissance thinkers, who have been seen as the precursors of the Reformation. They favored a return to the biblical basis for doctrine (as over against church tradition). Many of them supported a noncoercive faith and the priesthood of believers. They questioned the efficacy of the sacraments apart from faith on the part of the recipient. And they held that only the elect were members of the true church visible and invisible.

While these theologians did not go as far as some who would come after them, the principles they advocated and the biblical practices they modeled set the stage for the Protestant Reformation and exerted a strong influence on its proponents.

CHAPTER THREE

The Church in the Reformation Era

While the Reformation may be seen as a religious revolution which attempted to return to the purity and simplicity of New Testament Christianity, its causes were many and varied. They included economic, political, and intellectual factors. But diverse as they were, they combined to produce a situation which profoundly affected the common conceptions of the church and its ministry. The direction taken in ecclesiological thinking varied according to the Reformation group being examined.

LUTHERAN ECCLESIOLOGY

The Protestant Reformation began in Germany on the eve of All Saints' Day, 1517, when Martin Luther (1483–1546), an Augustinian monk and professor of biblical studies at the University of Wittenberg, proclaimed a debate on the sale of indulgences by the Roman Catholic Church. This he did by posting his arguments in *95 Theses* on the Wittenberg church door.

The attack on the sale of indulgences was also an attack on papal authority; for the pope claimed the power "to shut the gates of hell and open the door to paradise." Luther was ultimately excommunicated by the pope (1520) and outlawed by Emperor Charles V (1521). But his dramatic stand against both the church and the state on spiritual concerns had even more dramatic results. Luther's protestations motivated similar protests and reform efforts all across Europe.[1]

Luther's expulsion by Rome caused him to found a new

church. He put forth its basic principles in 1530 at the Diet of Augsburg. Further writings and creeds by Luther and other theologians contributed to the shaping and definition of what came to be called the Lutheran church.

Martin Luther

In examining Luther's teaching on the church, we must keep in mind his education and vocation as a Roman Catholic monk and theologian. It was never his intention to separate from the Roman Church; he was interested only in moving back toward its biblical and patristic roots. His excommunication undoubtedly caused him anger and hurt, and led him to a stronger reaction against the doctrine of Rome than otherwise would have been. Influences of these things may be found in his teachings on the church, its ministry, and the sacraments.

The Church. Luther's views must be divided into two time periods: his pre-Reformation and his post-Reformation days. Prior to the Reformation he viewed the pope as *an* authority, although he never considered him as *the* supreme authority. In a treatise in 1520 against Leipzig Friar Augustine Alveld (who had attacked him), he declared that "Christendom, which alone is the true Church, may not and cannot have an earthly head. It may be ruled by no one on earth, neither bishop nor pope. Here only Christ in heaven is the head and he rules alone."[2] Nonetheless, his conclusion was:

> Since we see that the pope has full authority over all our bishops, and he has not arrived at this power without God's providence . . . I do not want anyone to oppose the pope. . . . I shall accept whatever the pope establishes and does, on condition that I judge it first on the basis of Holy Scripture. For my part he must remain under Christ and let himself be judged by Holy Scripture.[3]

By 1521, however, in a tract against the attacks of Jerome Emser of Leipzig, he declared that the pope was undeniably shown to be the apostle of Satan.[4] By this time, Luther would concede meaningful authority in the church only to Scripture and to the Christ it revealed. No head but Christ was needed! Luther's post-Reformation definition of the church was

> an assembly of all people on earth who believe in Christ, as we pray in the Creed, "I believe in the Holy Spirit, the communion of saints." This community or assembly means all those who live in true faith, hope, and love. Thus, the essence, life, and nature of Christendom is not a physical assembly, but an assembly of hearts in one faith.[5]

He noted that the distinction between the New Testament church and the church of his day was that of a fellowship as over against an organization. The early Christians were a brotherhood, not an institution.[6]

Luther referred to this community of believers as the "invisible church." In so terming it, he was not inferring that the church was something ethereal, but that it was the true inner vital relationship believers enjoy with Christ and with one another. The invisible church includes all true Christians throughout all time and from every part of the globe.[7] "*Ecclesia* . . . should mean the holy Christian people, not only of the days of the apostles, who are long since dead, but to the end of the world, so that there is always a holy Christian people on earth, in whom Christ lives, works, and rules."[8]

A "visible church" (i.e., an institutional body or organization), however, is necessary so that believers might carry out the Lord's work. Luther asserted that "the Church must appear in the world. But it can only appear in a mask, a veil, a shell, or some kind of clothes which a man can grasp, otherwise it can never be found."[9] Apart from faith, the visible church is only a human organization. But through faith, it is the vehicle by which God approaches and apprehends human beings, a channel of His saving grace. Unlike the invisible church, the visible church is subject to human flaws and may fall into error but God can and does use it nonetheless.[10] It is possible, though, for a visible church to apostatize and no longer be the true church, but an institution of Satan, who loves to counterfeit the things of God. Luther saw the Roman Catholic Church as a sterling example of this transition (although he did include the Eastern Orthodox, Hussites, and Reformed as true churches!).

Luther designated the visible church by the German term *Gemeinde*, meaning a religious community or congregation. It included both saved and unsaved alike. Membership in the community, therefore, is not limited to those who have faith. No human being can ever be sure who is elect and who is not. The Luther scholar Altman Swihart observes, "Luther has been accused of making the Christian religion individualistic, but this is far from true. For him it was unthinkable that anyone having a personal relationship with Christ would deliberately choose to be outside the visible church."[11] He was very clear that there is no salvation outside of the church, visible or invisible.

Church Polity. Because the church must exist as an empirical historical entity, some form of structure is necessary. Since a charismatically endowed leadership is a relic of the earliest church, and since the preaching of the Word and the administration of the sacraments are two functions vital to a church's very constitution, some provision must be made for officers to conduct these activities while not interfering with the priesthood of all believers.[12]

Luther asserted that each congregation is responsible for selecting and calling its own pastoral leadership. Indeed, "no bishop should institute anyone without the election, will, and call of the congregation. Rather, he should confirm the one whom the congregation chose and called."[13] Moreover, no ecclesiastical government of any kind has the right to supersede the will of the congregation.

In order to be a pastor (upon the call of the congregation), one must simply function as one. No ordination or other special rite is required. When the community, the body of Christ, calls a person, it is really Christ who is calling. While ordination may be accepted, Luther avowed, it should not be seen as a sacrament; for it confers no grace. It is merely an induction by the congregation into the pastoral office and a public affirmation of the minister's vocation. Luther felt that the vocation of a pastor was not different in any way from that of a farmer or some other "secular" occupation.[14]

Baptism. Luther maintained that God deals with people in two ways: outwardly, first, through the proclaimed Word and through physical signs such as the sacraments; and second, inwardly through the Holy Spirit and faith (including the gifting by the Spirit). But Luther firmly believed that the outward part must precede the inward.[15]

He rejected the Roman Catholic concept of seven sacraments, accepting only two—baptism and the Lord's Supper. Baptism is the means of becoming a part of Christ (including His body, the church), and of entering the new life. Baptism constitutes an "admission to all divine blessings."[16]

Baptism, wrote Luther, "means to plunge something completely into the water, so that the water covers it." While it was customary in his time not to immerse infants but only to pour some baptismal water upon them, "nevertheless the former is what should be done." The significance of the rite demands immersion. "For baptism . . . signifies that the old man and the sinful birth of flesh and blood are to be wholly drowned by the grace of God."[17]

Luther taught, moreover, that baptism is an external sign by which the people of Christ are separated from all other persons. The sign consists of thrusting people into the water and drawing them out again, in the name of the Triune God. Baptism signifies a blissful dying to sin and a resurrection by God's grace, so that the old self, born in sin, is done away with and a new self, begotten in grace, arises. One's sins are drowned in baptism, and instead of sin, righteousness issues forth.[18]

In spite of his emphasis on the new birth as a result of baptism, Luther stressed that the sacrament's meaning could not be fully completed until physical death. Sin never ceases in one's life until death terminates both. "Therefore the life of a Christian, from baptism to the grave, is nothing else than the beginning of a blessed death."[19]

While baptism cleanses one from one's sins and guilt, sin nonetheless remains at work in that person's life. The sacrament is the sign of a beginning of growth into purity and innocence, a process to be completed in the next life. It is also a sign that God has allied Himself to the believer and is pouring out His grace and His Holy Spirit in order to prepare the believer for that Last Day. Baptism is also a pledge on the part of the believer to continue in the new life and the battle against sin.[20]

Unlike Roman Catholic teaching that the sacrament is *ex opere operato*, Luther proclaimed that baptism is empty apart from faith. Faith simply means that one resolutely believes Christ.[21] Without faith, the one baptized will fall increasingly deeper into sin and despair. He asserted: "if anyone has fallen into sin, he should all the more remember his baptism, how God has here made a covenant with him to forgive all his sins, if only he will fight against them even until death. Upon this truth, upon this alliance with God, a man must joyfully dare to rely."[22]

The Lord's Supper. Just as he had done in his teaching on baptism, Luther divided his concerns on the Lord's Supper into three sections: the sacrament itself, its significance, and the faith which must accompany it.

The sacrament, or external sign, consists of bread and wine. In the initial days of the Reformation, Luther maintained that Communion "in one kind" was sufficient for the laity; as long as the people could see the priest consume both bread and wine, they did not have to partake of the latter.[23] It was not long, however, before he had changed his position, condemning Rome for withholding the wine from the laity, and accusing Roman Catholicism of "acting impiously and contrary to the act, example, and institution of Christ."[24]

The significance of the sacrament is the fellowship of all the saints; hence, its common name communion (from the Latin *communio*, "fellowship"). In the sacrament believers are incorporated into Christ's spiritual body and so become one with Him and with one another. "To receive this sacrament in bread and wine, then, is nothing else than to receive a sure sign of this fellowship and incorporation with Christ and all saints."[25]

Luther's position on the nature of the Lord's Supper differed only slightly from the Roman Catholic Church's view of transubstantiation. He declared that Christ "gave his true natural flesh in the bread, and his natural true blood in the wine," but rather than the elements turning into the body and blood of Christ, "his flesh [was] under the bread, his blood under the wine,"[26] a position which came to be known as *consubstantiation*. In a tract against the Swiss Reformed Church, which taught a symbolic view of the elements, Luther vehemently

91

avowed, "Christ gives his body to eat when he distributes the bread. On this we take our stand, and we also believe and teach that in the Supper we eat and take to ourselves Christ's body truly and physically."[27]

Everything accomplished in the sacrament depends on faith. It can benefit only one who believes in Christ's atonement and intercession. It blesses one when one remembers Christ and so is "strengthened in faith" and "made ardent in love."[28]

Conclusions. Martin Luther was strongly influenced in his theology by both Augustine of Hippo and the nominalist philosophy advanced by William of Ockham and Duns Scotus. But his personal pilgrimage — which reached its high point in the discovery of the importance of faith — greatly modified his doctrinal views in a direction away from the traditional Roman Catholicism of his day.[29] In many respects we can see his thinking on the church as a backward leap to the positions of the early church fathers.

Because of his excommunication from Rome he was forced to adopt a concept of the church that differed from the traditional concept of the church. Yes, there is but one church; that church, however, is invisible and stretches across all ages to embrace all persons who have by faith committed themselves to Jesus Christ.

Because of his conflicts with the Roman Catholic hierarchy, Luther posited church authority in each local body of Christ. Nor did he make any distinction between clergy and laity. No class differentiations exist in Christ. Priests are a necessity because of the need for order and structure in the visible church. Being a pastor is no different a vocation nor more important than being an artisan or farmer.

The sacraments retained much of the Roman Catholic views. But they were reduced from seven to the two found in Scripture. And they were pronounced efficacious only in the presence of faith. Luther agreed that one entered the kingdom of God by baptism, but only when faith accompanied baptism. By the same token, the Lord's Supper was a participation in the body of Christ in a very literal way, but only when eaten in faith. Faith was the underlying factor in all of Luther's doctrinal teaching.

Philip Melancthon

Philip Melancthon (1497–1560) was a contemporary of Luther and an early supporter of his reform movement. A teacher of Greek, first at Tübingen and then at Wittenberg, he came in contact with Luther in 1518 and publicly defended him at the Leipzig Disputations the following year. In 1521 Melancthon published *Loci Communes*, the first book to describe clearly the teachings of the German Reformation. He was also the author of the *Augsburg Confession* (1530), which is still the doctrinal standard of Lutheranism worldwide. Upon Luther's death he became the guiding light of the German movement.[30]

The Church. Melancthon's teaching on the church followed Luther's. There is only one true church, but that church is inclusive of all believers who have been justified by faith in Christ and who have received the sacraments as instituted by the Gospel. Melancthon observed, however, that "it is not necessary for the true unity of the Christian church that ceremonies, instituted by men, should be observed uniformly in all places."[31]

He defined the church as "nothing else than the assembly of all believers and saints." Because it exists in an empirical earthly form, the church will always have hypocrites and evildoers mixed in with it. Thus, the church contains both a kingdom of Christ and a kingdom of Satan.[32]

Matters of Polity. From Melancthon's definition of the church flow a number of inferences regarding clergy and their position. The power of bishops to wield temporal authority is not divinely bestowed and has no connection whatsoever with the Gospel. Rather, it is the ministry of the bishop to proclaim the Gospel, absolve from sin, rule on doctrine, condemn that which is counter to the Gospel, and bar from the believing community those who live wicked lives. In the event that this office is used to do those things contrary to the Gospel, parish ministers and churches do not have to obey the bishop.[33]

In the same way, any regulations a bishop should make which cannot be substantiated by Scripture need not be obeyed. Such rules would include feast days, observance of the cult of saints, or even prohibition of clerical marriages.

The Sacraments. Melancthon's Roman Catholic rootage was clearly demonstrated in regard to the sacraments. He taught that baptism is basic to salvation. Consequently, even children should be baptized, "for in Baptism they are committed to God and become acceptable to him."[34]

In the Lord's Supper, declared Melancthon, the literal body and blood of Jesus are really present "under the form of bread and wine [consubstantiation] and are there distributed and received."[35] Against his detractors, he insisted that Lutherans had not abolished the Mass (Eucharist) but had restored it to its rightful place and had liberated it from a multitude of abuses. "Thus the Mass is preserved among us in its proper use, the use which was formerly observed in the church and which can be proved by St. Paul's statement in 1 Cor. 11:20ff. and by many statements of the fathers."[36] Toward the latter part of his career, however, he backed away from Luther's position somewhat, affirming the spiritual presence of Christ in the Supper, but denying His bodily ubiquity.[37] At the same time, Melancthon asserted that, apart from accompanying faith on the part of their recipient, the sacraments were invalid.

Conclusions. While Melancthon's doctrine approximated Luther's own in most cases, there was one area of distinction in regard to the teaching on the church. Here, the two men started at opposite poles. While Luther began with the idea of the invisible church, manifested on earth by the visible church which contains the saved and unsaved together, Melancthon started with the idea that there is and always has been a true and visible church which must of necessity exist with a commingling of false believers and wicked persons. Only those who are true believers, however, are genuine members of the true church. Thus, with Melancthon we have the concept of a church within a church, a congregation of believers as a part of the greater community of believers and unbelievers alike.

SOME OBSERVATIONS ON THE GERMAN REFORMATION

Luther revolutionized German ecclesiology almost single-handedly. His insistence on the necessity of *sola fide* (faith alone) and *sola Scriptura* (Scripture alone) was a major turning point in European spiritual life. His work meant a return to a simpler Christian practice much more like that of the Patristic church.

Unfortunately, Luther's desire for a state or territorial church undid much of what he had taught. As Penrose St. Amant has observed, "Luther's dilemma, which he never really resolved, was that he wanted a confessional church made up of people who exercised personal faith and a territorial church consisting of everyone, including infants, in a given area."[38] Problems in the church which could not be easily resolved at the local level moved him away from congregationalism. Instead of a bishop, he created the office of superintendent, filled by the Elector of Saxony who, in turn, appointed "visitors" (including Luther and his theologians) to oversee liturgical practices and doctrines. And so the stage was set for a German state church.[39]

Melancthon set Luther's ideas in a systematic, concrete form. "Luther created a new church; Melancthon established a theology in harmony with it."[40] His doctrinal emphases, though not always easily received by his colleagues, set the direction of the German Reformation movement for centuries to come.

THE REFORMED ECCLESIOLOGY

That aspect of Reformation thought known as Reformed theology began in Switzerland about the same time as—and separately from—the German Reformation of Martin Luther. Because Switzerland was a federation of autonomous cantons, each area made its own decision through its own democratically elected government as to what religion it would embrace. And we find three different kinds of Reformation theology developing: In the southern, French-speaking cantons, led by the city of Geneva, the theology of John Calvin came to the fore. In the northern, German-speaking cantons, led by the city of Zurich, the theology of Ulrich Zwingli held sway. Zurich also saw the birth of the theology of the radical reformers known as the Anabaptists. The theologies of Calvin and Zwingli are included in the term "Reformed theology."

Ulrich Zwingli

Ulrich (or Huldreich) Zwingli was born on New Year's Day 1484 in the Swiss alpine village of Wildhaus. Two factors

95

shaped his early life and its direction: Swiss patriotism and Erasmian humanism. In one of his early writings he describes himself as "a Swiss professing Christ among the Swiss."[41] Educated at Basel, Bern, and Vienna, he became vicar of Glarus, where he learned Greek and studied Patristics. In 1518 he was appointed people's priest of the Great Minster in Zurich. It was there, as he lectured on the New Testament, that he began to effect reforms, working hand in hand with the Zurich city council.[42]

Zwingli's reforms were challenged from two opposing directions. The Roman Catholic bishop of Constance felt that he had gone too far and attempted to stop him; Zwingli bested him in two public debates in 1523. Zwingli was also challenged by former colleagues Conrad Grebel and Felix Mantz (whose followers became known as Anabaptists), who felt that he had not gone far enough toward New Testament Christianity; against them Zwingli and the Zurich city council unleashed a bitter persecution, martyring Mantz by drowning in 1527.[43]

In 1529 Zwingli met with Luther at Marburg in an effort to unify the Reformation, but the two could not agree on the nature of the elements in the Lord's Supper, and so the movement remained divided. In 1531 the Roman Catholic cantons of Switzerland sent an army against Zurich. Zwingli accompanied the Protestant forces as chaplain and was killed at the battle of Kappel.[44]

The Church. Zwingli's views on ecclesiology were shaped by his reactions against Roman Catholicism and Anabaptism as much as anything else. In reaction against the former, he rejected all idea of hierarchy. Christ and Christ alone is the head and foundation of the church. All believers are given the keys to the kingdom, which may be defined as the authority to proclaim the Gospel. Against the latter, he opposed a distinct separation of church and state, positing the two in a mutual partnership serving the kingdom of God.

Zwingli, like his fellow reformers, saw the church both as invisible and visible. The invisible church is composed of all those people throughout the world and throughout time "who are founded and built up in one faith upon the Lord Jesus Christ." In his latter ministry, Zwingli further defined his view of the invisible and universal church as the totality of the elect of all ages.[45] By contrast, the visible church is found in the local congregations. Not all who comprise this visible expression of the true, invisible church are saved, for some are reprobates. Even Judas Iscariot belonged to this church.[46]

Because he was very much concerned with the social and political implications of the Reformation, Zwingli tended to blur the distinction between the church and the state. In his eyes the magistrate, every bit as much as the minister, was a servant of Christ. Reformation scholar Timothy George aptly observes:

> Zwingli's involvement in political and economic affairs was directed toward a reformation of the whole community, of the entire life of society. Church and state were related as soul and body, distinct yet necessarily conjoined and interdependent. More than any other reformer, Zwingli reacted against the clerical supremacy of the medieval church. . . . Zwingli believed that the Bible taught (Ex. 14:16) that priests were to be subordinate to the magistrates.[47]

Thus, the church and state were inextricably intertwined, both being servants of God. But the former, in Zwingli's mind, was to be subservient to the latter.

Baptism. Zwingli defined a sacrament as "nothing else than an initiatory ceremony or pledging . . . [whereby] the person initiated is bound to perform for the office, order, or institution to which he has devoted himself what the institution or office demands."[48] The sacraments should not be considered as *ex opere operato*; they do not purify or transform in and of themselves.

Zwingli used baptism as an example to show that it was faith alone — wholly apart from the sacraments — that purified the believer. When adults are baptized, they are asked whether they have trusted Christ for salvation. Only after responding affirmatively are they baptized. Thus, faith is present before the sacrament is dispensed, and is not bestowed by it. One must realize, therefore, that "a sacrament is a sign of a sacred thing, *i.e.*, of a grace that has been given."[49] Against Roman Catholicism, he categorically rejected the power of baptism to remove original sin. He did not see original sin in a universal condemnatory light, but rather as a defect which has a devastating effect on all humanity. Nor could baptism be an instrument of regeneration; for that was accomplished by Christ's atoning death on Calvary.[50]

Zwingli also disputed the Roman Catholic doctrine that infants who died unbaptized went to Limbo. He held that the children of Christian parents were elect because their parents were under the covenant of grace; thus it did not really matter whether they had been baptized or not.[51]

Prior to the Anabaptist crisis, Zwingli believed that children should not be baptized, but only those who had been instructed and had reached an age of sensibility. He shared this view with many of his colleagues, including Erasmus, Gullame Farel, Johannes Oecolampadius, and Balthasar Hubmaier. But in late 1524 he wrote a series of articles repudiating that view and defending infant baptism as the sign of the New Israel, the church, somewhat analogous to circumcision in the old Israel. Secondly, Christian baptism has its basis in John's baptism rather than in Matthew 28; since Jesus had been both circumcised and baptized, it was a sign that the two rites were equal in value (albeit under different dispensations). Thirdly, while the New Testament does not specifically allude to infant baptism, such a practice may be inferred from several passages (such as Luke 18:15-17).[52]

Even more importantly, Zwingli retained infant baptism as a political weapon against the Anabaptists, who refused to have their babies christened. In 1526 he persuaded the Zurich council to require a baptismal register in each parish. Those citizens who refused to have their infants baptized would be expelled. Thus, baptism became an instrument of political conformity—a goal Zwingli believed in passionately.[53]

The Lord's Supper. In accordance with his definition of a sacrament, Zwingli saw the Lord's Supper as a memorial feast which reminds participants of their redemption by Christ's sacrifice on Calvary. Following the work of a Dutch Protestant named Honius, who argued that the Latin word *est* in the words of the Supper's institution meant *significat*, Zwingli determined that the bread and cup serve only as a sign of the body and blood of the Savior. Faith in Christ's sacrifice as confessed by participating believers is the spiritual eating and drinking of His body and blood.[54] Zwingli asserted:

> I believe that in the holy Eucharist . . . the true body of Christ is present by the contemplation of faith. . . . But that the body of Christ in essence and really, *i.e.*, the natural body itself, is either present in the supper or masticated with our mouth and teeth . . . we not only deny, but constantly maintain to be an error, contrary to the Word of God.[55]

Thus, he rejected the Roman Catholic concept of transubstantiation and the Lutheran idea of consubstantiation, both of which held that the elements are literally changed into Christ's flesh and blood.

Conclusions. Zwingli's life was a myriad of contradictions and intrigues. He was unquestionably given over to the service of Jesus Christ, but he was also given to cruel invective and brutality against those he considered enemies. He also seemed to place political stability and success above faithfulness to the Scriptures, as evidenced by his abrupt reversal in the matter of believer's baptism. At the same time, he was more faithful to the principle of *sola Scriptura* than was Luther, and was just as strong as the latter in his emphasis on faith as the ground of the Christian life. While his productive theological years were cut short by his death in battle, his views influenced Calvin and other Reformed theologians probably much more than they realized.

John Calvin

John Calvin (1509–1564) was the major figure of the French and French-Swiss Reformations, even though he was a "second generation" reformer, coming on the scene more than a decade after Luther and Zwingli began their movements. He is perhaps the greatest theologian of the Christian faith after Augustine of Hippo. Educated at Orléans, Bourges, and Paris, Calvin was a keen and conscientious scholar who did much more to systematize Reformation theology than either Luther or

Zwingli. His magnum opus was *The Institutes of the Christian Religion*, first published in 1536 and constantly revised throughout his lifetime.

For Calvin, the church was all important after God Himself. Out of the four books of his *Institutes*, the entire fourth book is devoted to ecclesiology.

On the Church. Calvin defined the church as "all the elect from the beginning of the world . . . the whole multitude of men spread over the earth who profess to worship one God and Christ."[56] It is, moreover, a community of believers: "the saints are gathered into the society of Christ on the principle that whatever benefits God confers upon them, they should in turn share with one another."[57]

As a compendium of all the elect, the church is invisible in its form, but it is revealed in the visible church, which is comprised of those who profess Christ, have been initiated into Him by baptism, and attest their mutual unity by partaking in the Lord's Supper and by agreeing in God's Word. Even though the visible church may contain many hypocrites, because the invisible church is visible to God alone, believers are commanded to revere it and keep communion with it.[58]

In order that believers might not be deceived by some group calling itself a church when it was not, Calvin listed a number of "marks" to serve as tests of verification for the true church. These included:

1. "In Word and sacrament it has the order approved by the Lord."[59]
2. God is One.
3. Christ is God and the Son of God.
4. Our salvation rests in God's mercy.[60]

Such marks do not imply, stressed Calvin, that all churches must agree completely on everything. Some articles of doctrine are essential; others may be disputed without fracturing the unity of the faith.

On Church Polity. Although Christ alone rules over the church, because He is not among us in visible presence, He has ordained the ministry of human beings to declare His will. Indeed, "this human ministry which God uses to govern the church is the chief sinew by which believers are held together in one body."[61]

Calvin borrowed from Martin Bucer, the chief reformer of Strasbourg, the idea of a fourfold division of church office: pastor, teacher, presbyter, and deacon. Interestingly, he held the office of pastor to be of supreme importance, asserting that "neither the light and heat of the sun, nor food and drink, are so necessary to nourish and sustain the present life as the apostolic and pastoral office is necessary to preserve the church on earth."[62] He had nothing to say about the teaching office of the church, tending to merge it into the pastoral office. Although he acknowledged that Ephesians 4:11 referred to other offices — apostles, prophets, evangelists — Calvin believed them to be temporary in nature, now and again revived "as the need of the times demands."[63]

Presbyters come in two kinds, Calvin averred. There are those who are engaged in the ministry of the Word (i.e., pastors). But there are also those who are called to administrative tasks. "Governors were . . . elders chosen from among the people, who were charged with the censure of morals and the exercise of discipline along with the bishops [pastors]."[64]

Calvin taught that in the New Testament deacons were entrusted with the care of the poor. There were also two kinds of deacons: those who distributed alms to the poor, and those who were involved in "hands on" care of the poor. Women often fell into this second category of deacon.[65]

How are pastors to be chosen? Calvin pointed to Acts 14:23, which he translated as "presbyters elected by show of hands in every church," to demonstrate that, though Timothy or Titus may have selected the candidates for office, they were affirmed by a congregational vote.

We therefore hold that this call of a minister is lawful according to the Word of God, when those who seemed fit are created by the consent and approval of the people; moreover, that other pastors ought to preside over the election in order that the multitudes may not go wrong either through fickleness, through evil intentions, or through disorder.[66]

The last aspect of calling a pastor is ordination. While ordination, Calvin confessed, is not a clear New Testament practice, the simple laying on of hands was used continuously by the apostles. And it is worthwhile for the dignity of the office that the ministry be commended to the community by such a sign. Ordination also served to warn the one ordained that he is no longer a law unto himself, but bound in servitude to God and the church.[67]

Calvin had much to say about the historical leadership structure of the church. He pilloried the Church of Rome for overthrowing the original structure of the church in favor of an artificial hierarchy which tyrannized the local congregations and oppressed the freedom of the genuine church. He pointed out how far Rome had strayed from the intentions of the apostles. From the apostles onward, bishops (or pastors) were never free to go beyond God's Word. Nor had any of them ever been infallible. Not even the whole church together possesses such a gift. "For if he [Christ] daily sanctifies all his people, cleanses and polishes them, and wipes away their stains, it is obvious that they are still sprinkled with some defects and spots, and that something is lacking to their sanctification."[68]

On Church Discipline. Calvin felt strongly enough about church discipline to devote a full chapter to the subject in his *Institutes*. He divided discipline into two areas. In addition to a "common discipline, to which all ought to submit," Calvin saw another discipline for "the clergy, who, besides the common discipline, have their own."[69] If the saving doctrine of Christ is the soul of the church, he declared, then discipline should be seen as its sinews, holding the members of the body together, each in its own place.

Discipline in the church, avowed Calvin, should move along the lines of Matthew 18. Private admonition is the first level, whether by pastors or by the individual lay person. If that admonition is rejected, discipline is escalated to the second level—admonition in the presence of witnesses. The third level is appearance before a church tribunal, namely, the assembly of elders. The offender who remained unrepentant even at that level, should be cut off from the church's fellowship. Should the sin be open and flagrant, rather than private or individual, it should be publicly rebuked from the outset.

Church discipline should be seen as a corrective rather than as a punishment. It should seek the repentance and restoration of the offender. "Moreover, anathema is rarely or never used."[70] Disciplinary action should be sufficient, but not excessive.

Calvin cited the writings of the early church in regard to clerical discipline: "No cleric should devote himself to hunting, gambling, or reveling. No cleric should practice usury or commerce; no cleric should be present at wanton dances—and there are others of this sort."[71] The clergy have an obligation to set an example for their people.

On Baptism. Calvin defined a sacrament as "an outward sign by which the Lord seals on our consciences the promises of his good will toward us in order to sustain the weakness of our faith; and we in turn attest our piety toward him."[72] In this view, he confessed to be in complete accord with Augustine's definition of a sacrament as "a visible sign of an invisible grace." It is a token which authenticates God's covenant with His people. In order for a sacrament to be efficacious, however, the Holy Spirit must be actively involved; otherwise it is an empty and invalid thing. Only two Christian sacraments exist: baptism and the Lord's Supper.

Calvin defined baptism as "the sign of initiation by which we are received into the society of the church, in order that, engrafted in Christ, we may be reckoned among God's children."[73] He saw a threefold significance for the believer in this sacrament.

First, it is a token of the recipient's cleansing from sin. While in the past some in the church taught that baptism cleansed only from past sins, and therefore one was in mortal danger if one sinned after that point, they were in error. "But we must realize that at whatever time we are baptized, we are once for all washed and purged for our whole life. . . . For though baptism, administered only once, seemed to have passed, it was still not destroyed by subsequent sins."[74] Let one not think, however, that because he has been baptized, he may sin with impunity. Such action will bring God's judgment and condemnation.

103

Secondly, baptism is a symbol of the believer's mortification and renewal in Christ. Calvin asserted that "those who receive baptism with right faith truly feel the effective working of Christ's death in the mortification of their flesh, together with the working of his resurrection in the vivification of the Spirit."[75] For those who receive baptism in faith, God not only freely pardons their sins and imputes Christ's righteousness to them, He also grants the Holy Spirit's grace to reform the believer to a new life in Christ.

Thirdly, baptism is to be a sign of the recipient's union with Jesus Christ. In baptism the believer is engrafted into Christ and so comes to share in all His blessings. Paul indicates in Galatians 3:26-27 that those who put on Christ in baptism, become children of God and receive all the gifts the Holy Spirit has for them.[76]

Calvin acknowledged that the word "baptize" in the New Testament means to immerse, and that this was the practice of the earliest church.

> But whether the person being baptized should be wholly immersed, and whether thrice or once, whether he should only be sprinkled with poured water—these details are of no importance, but ought to be optional to churches according to the diversity of countries.[77]

Calvin forbade women to perform the sacrament of baptism. This restriction, it should be noted, was not based on any New Testament writer or command, but rather on Tertullian (who later became a member of a sect where women baptized!) and on Epiphanius.

While Calvin upheld the idea of infant baptism, he departed from the Augustinian teaching that an infant unbaptized would not go to heaven upon death. To the contrary, infants are not barred from heaven just because they have not been immersed. Believers may rest assured, stated Calvin, that their children— baptized or not—are children of God under His covenant of grace with their parents. Baptism of a believer's child is not to make that one a child of God, but simply to affirm that the child is a part of Christ's body, the church.[78]

Like many other reformers, Calvin associated infant baptism

with the Old Testament rite of circumcision. The spiritual promises covenanted to the patriarchs have been covenanted to the church (the New Israel). Just as circumcision was God's seal of the Old Covenant, even so baptism is the seal of the New Covenant. Thus, there is a difference only in the mode of confirmation.[79]

Calvin scorned arguments that nowhere in the Scripture is there any evidence of an infant's ever having been baptized. And when one recalls that Christ Himself commanded that infants be presented to Him (Matt. 19:14), how can baptism be forbidden them? Calvin argued, as well, from the infancy of Jesus: "If we have in Christ the most perfect example of all the graces which God bestows upon his children, in this respect also he will be for us a proof that the age of infancy is not utterly averse to sanctification."[80]

Nor would the reformer accept the logical argument that, because infants are incapable of repentance and faith—the biblical bases for baptism—they are not proper subjects for the sacrament. He countered by saying that "infants are baptized into future repentance and faith, and even though these have not yet been formed in them, the seed of both lies hidden within them by the secret working of the Spirit."[81] Children, as they grow, will acquire an understanding and appreciation of their baptism. Moreover, it is a comfort to them to know that they have received God's forgiveness, and they should not be deprived of the sign of such comfort.[82]

On the Lord's Supper. Calvin taught that, as God has accepted us into His family through baptism, so He nourishes us on the life-giving Bread, Jesus Christ Himself, in the sacrament of the Lord's Supper. The signs of the Supper are bread and wine, which represent the invisible food received from Christ's flesh and blood. In partaking of the Supper, believers are made one with Christ, receiving at the same time His immortality and righteousness.[83]

Calvin was not in accord with Zwingli on the significance of the Lord's Supper as purely symbolic. Nor did he see eye to eye with Luther on the literal presence of Christ in the elements. Rather, he sought a mediating position, known as "real presence."

I therefore say (what has always been accepted in the church and is today taught by all of sound opinion) that the sacred mystery of the Supper consists in two things: physical signs, which, thrust before our eyes, represent to us, according to our feeble capacity, things invisible; and spiritual truth, which is at the same time represented and displayed through the symbols themselves.[84]

Through the symbols Christians enjoy the very fullness of Christ Himself, and just as they become one with the bread and wine, so they become one with Him.

Calvin had no use for the Roman Catholic concept of transubstantiation. He recoiled from the idea that the bread became Christ's literal body, "to be touched by the hands, to be chewed by the teeth, and to be swallowed by the mouth."[85] Such doctrine, he purported, was unknown in the purer age of the church fathers.

When the believer eats the bread and drinks the wine of the Lord's Supper, he is receiving Christ spiritually by faith, averred Calvin. All the blessings that Christ offers in His body belong to those who partake in faith. Unlike Luther, Calvin rejected the idea that the spiritually worthy and unworthy alike receive the flesh and blood of Christ in the sacrament. Christ does not descend to earth — being in heaven — but believers are in the sacrament drawn up to Him by the power of the Holy Spirit.[86]

Conclusions. Calvin's ecclesiology was probably the most thoroughly developed of all the reformers. The signs of participation in the church (and the marks of the true church), he argued, are right faith, participation in the sacraments, and an upstanding Christian life. He saw the church and state as mutual servants of God, and he worked in Geneva to ensure that those who were members of the civil community were also saints of the church.

Discipline was an important part of his ecclesiology. It is a vital part of the church's life and work. Its purpose is to restrain those who are Christ's enemies, and to guide those who are His disciples.

Like Luther, Calvin saw faith as integral to the efficacy of the sacraments. He rejected the *ex opere operato* view of Rome.

106

Despite his insistence on the necessity of faith, he advocated infant baptism, although he could find no direct biblical basis for it. Instead, he relied on analogies to circumcision and on references to Patristic theology. He held to a real presence view of the Lord's Supper, but rejected Luther's emphasis on the literal presence of Christ's body and blood. Christ's presence is experienced by the believer's being lifted up to heaven in faith.

A Summary of Reformed Views

The Reformed theologians were essentially in agreement on their definition of the church as the sum total of God's people in Christ from all ages and all nations. The church has its visible expression in the local congregation.

They were also in accord on the relationship between the church and state. Both serve God and should be seen as complementary, each acting to keep the other true to God's purposes for it. Church and state share responsibility for the restraint and guidance of the members of the community.

In regard to the sacraments, Zwingli and Calvin differed to some degree in their views. The majority of Reformed leaders adopted the teachings of the latter more so than the former. Calvin's definition of a sacrament was stronger than Zwingli's. While Zwingli saw a sacrament as a symbol of reality (as a wedding ring symbolizes the act of marriage), Calvin saw it as a means of grace for the faithful.

Calvin's understanding of sacraments was reflected in his views on baptism. While baptism for the Reformed Church was the rite of initiation into the church, Calvin also held (contra Zwingli) that God regenerated the individual in baptism. All of the Reformed leaders advocated infant baptism (although Zwingli wavered on the issue, not really finding it a necessity), but none were able to undergird their doctrine with a solid biblical foundation.

Calvin, in his doctrine of the Lord's Supper, advocated a mediating position between Zwingli's symbolic position and Luther's position of the literal physical presence of Christ. He agreed with the former that Christ is in heaven and so cannot literally be present in the elements, but he also concurred with Luther that the Supper is not mere symbol but a genuine participation in Christ Jesus.

That Calvin was the greater influence on Reformed ecclesiology is demonstrated in the latter documents of Reformed theology. The most authoritative of these—the Heidelberg Catechism (1563), the Later (Second) Helvetic Confession (1566), and the Westminster Confession (1646)—all bear the distinctive stamp of Calvin's theology, especially in regard to the church, its polity, and the sacraments.

THE RADICAL/ANABAPTIST ECCLESIOLOGY

The leaders of the German and Swiss Reformations were more deeply troubled by opposition from radical reformers than from Roman Catholicism. The radicals believed that Luther and Zwingli had stopped short of true biblical Christianity in their reforms and had retained much of the trappings of Roman Catholicism. In short, the Reformers had admitted doctrinal authorities other than the Scriptures, and so they had been lured away from a pure understanding of the church.

The radicals, however, were not united in their theological views. Some, like Jan Matthys and John of Leyden, were fanatical revolutionaries who were further from a biblical faith than were Luther and Zwingli. Others, however, like Conrad Grebel, Felix Mantz, and Menno Simons, were devout and godly people. These folk, who came to be called by their enemies "Anabaptists" (rebaptizers), added a new dimension to Protestant ecclesiology.

The Swiss Brethren

If one were to look to one particular group as the "original" Anabaptists, it would have to be the Swiss Brethren. Their leaders came from a larger Reformation group in Zurich known as the Zwingli Circle. Between October 1523 and September 1524, a number of them engaged in a disputation with Zwingli over his failure to institute major reforms which would bring the church in line with the biblical teaching. A number of this Circle, led by Conrad Grebel and Felix Mantz, broke with Zwingli and began to meet together as "Brethren."[87] Because of their concern for a return to New Testament faith and practice, they had much to say about the church and its ways.

The Church. While the Anabaptists believed, along with the leaders of the German and Swiss Reformations, that the invisible church comprises the saved of all peoples and centuries, they vehemently rejected the notion that its visible expression may include those openly leading sinful lives. "For the Anabaptists, the true church must externally manifest its inner character. As they emphasized repeatedly, it must constantly strive to be, corporately, the bride 'without spot or wrinkle.' "[88] Although perfection eluded even those in the visible church, the sins of believers were sufficiently secret that they were known only to God.

For the Anabaptists, then, the visible church is a community, or brotherhood, of repentant, spiritually regenerate, and voluntarily baptized believers who have covenanted together to engage in holy and disciplined living. Members of the church community practiced the gifts of the Holy Spirit for the common good. And all members are involved in a mutual, spiritual relationship for the purpose of edification and discipline.[89]

The teaching of the Swiss Brethren on the church cannot be understood apart from their teaching on separation from the world. The Seven Articles of the "Brotherly Union of a Number of Children of God" (popularly known as "The Schleitheim Confession") notes that

> everything which has not been united with our God in Christ is nothing but an abomination which we should shun. By this are meant all popish and repopish works and idolatry, gatherings, church attendance, winehouses, guarantees and commitments of unbelief, and other things of the kind, which the world regards highly, and yet which are carnal or flatly counter to the command of God.[90]

Anabaptist historian George H. Williams comments that the phrase "guarantees and commitments" could mean vows the Anabaptists had made while still Catholics or Zwinglians, probably refers to all associations with the unsaved, even to unbelieving spouses.[91] In regard to the separation of believers from both the state and the world, the Anabaptists were going back to Jesus' teachings on the kingdom of God. As Williams aptly observes: "Since true Christians belong to the Kingdom and the

109

community of mutual aid, they have no need of the organs of the state, which are ordained of God for the punishment of the wicked (and the testing of the faith of the righteous)."[92] Furthermore, state institutions are operated by unbelievers, not by kingdom citizens, and so believing brethren will have no truck with them of any kind.

Baptism. The Swiss Brethren affirmed that the only fit subjects for baptism are "those who have been taught repentance and the amendment of life and [who] believe truly that their sins are taken away through Christ, and to all who desire to walk in the resurrection of Jesus Christ and be buried with Him in death, so that they might rise with Him."[93] Belief must always precede baptism if it is to be biblical. Anyone who has been otherwise baptized has not received true baptism and so union with God in Christ.[94]

Baptism in water is an external rite. It is a sign of inner, spiritual baptism having occurred in one's life; namely, that "by faith and the blood of Christ, sins have been washed away for him who is baptized."[95]

Because baptism requires the faith of its recipient, the Swiss Brethren could not accept infant baptism. Conrad Grebel put their case well in a letter to Thomas Müntzer:

> But as to the objection that faith is demanded of all who are to be saved, we exclude children from this and hold that they are saved without faith . . . and we conclude from the description of baptism and from the accounts of it (according to which no child was baptized) . . . that infant baptism is a senseless, blasphemous abomination, contrary to all Scripture.[96]

Melchior Hofmann, a former Lutheran itinerant preacher won to the Anabaptist faith, concurred, teaching that pedobaptism is unequivocally not from God but is observed willfully by those subservient to Satan, contrary to God's commandment, purpose, and desire.[97]

The Lord's Supper. The Swiss Brethren practiced "closed Communion." This practice was reflected in Article III of the Schleitheim Confession:

110

All who desire to break the one bread in remembrance of the broken body of Christ and all who wish to drink of one drink in remembrance of the shed blood of Christ, they must beforehand be united to the one body of Christ, that is the congregation of God, whose head is Christ, and that by baptism.[98]

Anyone who was not a part of the brotherhood could not participate in the Supper. To do so would be to break the unity depicted by the single loaf.

In their interpretation of the meaning of the Lord's Supper, the Brethren followed Zwingli's view. The bread is only bread, and the wine is nothing more than wine. The Lord's Supper is a simple memorial meal, to be eaten in fellowship with one's brothers and sisters. It is neither a Mass nor a sacrament, and it should not be partaken of by oneself alone; for it is an expression of fellowship.[99]

The Pastoral Office. Pastors should be chosen according to the rule of Paul (1 Tim. 3:1-13). "The office of such a person shall be to read and exhort and teach, warn, admonish, or ban in the congregation, and properly to preside among the sisters and brothers in prayer, and in the breaking of bread, and in all things to take care of the body of Christ."[100]

The pastor should be able to expect economic support from the congregation, according to the teaching of 1 Corinthians 9:14. If he should do something deserving of reprimand, such an error must be supported by two or three witnesses. In the event of his banishment or martyrdom, "at the same hour another shall be ordained to his place, so that the little folk and the little flock of God may not be destroyed, but be preserved by warning and be consoled."[101]

Church Discipline. An important aspect of community life among the Brethren was the "rule of Christ," described in Matthew 18, the ultimate enforcement of which was found in the ban. The Schleitheim Confession described it as follows:

The ban shall be employed with all those who have given themselves over to the Lord, to walk after [Him] in His commandments; those who have been baptized into the one body of

111

Christ, and let themselves be called brothers or sisters, and still somehow slip and fall into error and sin, being inadvertently overtaken.[102]

Failure to repent after being publicly admonished led to expulsion from the brotherhood and treatment as a pagan, namely, being let alone.

Conclusions. The Swiss Brethren carried Zwingli's reforms to their logical conclusion. They returned the church to its New Testament roots, engaging in very simple and straightforward fellowship. Like the first church, they were content to pay the price of suffering and martyrdom in order to worship in the fashion they felt the Spirit of Christ dictated. And like the New Testament church, they grew rapidly by multiplication until their influence pervaded all of Europe.

Pilgram Marpeck

Pilgram Marpeck was born into an upper middle class family at Rattenberg, in the Tyrol, toward the end of the fifteenth century. In 1520, he became a member of the guild of mine workers in his hometown and was active in the government of his city. His work brought him into touch with the Anabaptists, and it has been suggested that he was baptized into that faith as early as 1527. In 1546 he died of natural causes. Marpeck was a prolific writer and a capable theologian, laboriously defending Anabaptist doctrines. He left a rich legacy for Anabaptism and for the whole free church movement.[103]

The Church. Marpeck's view of the church was evangelical and not marked by aberrations held by some of the Anabaptist leaders. He saw the existence of two churches in the world, the true and the false. He compared them to Sarah and Hagar. Both had children who sprang from the seed of Abraham (God), but the true church is born of water and blood (of Christ) and are legitimate children; the false church is composed of others, who boast of being God's children, but are without a legitimate mother, for they are born of the flesh since "theirs is only the first birth."[104]

112

Marpeck demonstrated his conviction through his belief that the visible expression of the church quickly went astray. The Asian church defected from Paul; false teachers crept in and replaced grace with law. Division and wrong doctrine abounded. Did such terrible things mean that there was therefore no legitimate church in existence? Of course not! One must realize that "the church of Christ does not come . . . with regard to numbers or persons . . . nor with regard to any place or any time." But where two or three are gathered together in His name, He is there with them.[105] Yet because the sharpness of God's Word had been blunted by carnal teachers, "the church and almost all people's hearts, which should be God's temple, have thereby become a dark cave and a den of thieves over which the powers of the world rule freely." But the true church may be found wherever people come to the wonderful light of God's grace and obediently "serve the Word as the sword of the Spirit."[106]

Baptism. Marpeck's work known as "The Admonition of 1542" *(Vermahnung oder Taubüchlein)* is the most detailed Anabaptist statement in regard to the ordinances. He began it with a definition of sacrament as "anything done in connection with an oath or a similar obligation, and [which] refers to an event that is special and holy or a work that has that kind of connotation."[107] Should an act be carried out with an oath or similar commitment, then it might rightly be termed a sacrament. If one accepts such a definition, then baptism and the Lord's Supper may be called sacraments. To do so, however, places no special or extraordinary holiness upon them.[108]

Marpeck understood the word baptize to mean immersion or dipping under the water (although in his teaching, he included effusion in his views).

> If, however, this takes place in a different manner and with a different understanding than that which Christ commanded and the apostles practiced, then we can say that, in a grammatical and natural *sense*, it can still be called baptism, but not according to the . . . Christian way of understanding baptism. For all immersion into water . . . is the true and correct Christian baptism only if it happens according to the command of Christ.[109]

Baptism should always be properly preceded by instruction so that one may know and understand God's will and may believe in Christ. Following baptism, one should be instructed to be obedient to Christ's teaching.

Baptism, per se, does not save a person. It does save when, "through it, the believer unites himself with God and henceforth denies the desires of the flesh and the lust thereof, and desires with his whole heart to carry out the will of God."[110] Apart from such an act on the part of the believer, baptism is a vain act which mocks God.

It may rightly be said, averred Marpeck, that baptism is a door into the church. Believers are baptized into the one body as they are united with other believers in one confession of God. But such unity does not occur because of immersion or effusion of water, but because the Spirit of Christ unites the body in faith. In addition to baptism, those who would be admitted to the (visible) church, must testify to faith in Christ externally by good works.[111]

Marpeck called for an end to infant baptism, citing it as a prelude "to the destruction and the total apostasy of the holy church."[112] There is no biblical basis for such a rite. Only those who believe the Gospel may be proper candidates for baptism. To suggest that infant baptism does away with original sin is a mockery of the blood of Christ. Original sin is acquired only when there is awareness of good and evil. Children are unaware of such things. Nor can they repent (a necessity preceding baptism).[113]

Marpeck also rejected the analogy of baptism to circumcision. Baptism is based on faith in Jesus Christ, "and not upon external circumcision performed on unknowing flesh."[114] If any analogy exists, it is that baptism is analogous to the spiritual circumcision of the heart, and not to the physical rite. Nor may one baptize infants because Jesus called little children to Himself (Luke 18:16). "To bring something to Christ is not synonymous with bringing it to baptism."[115]

Marpeck was adamant that, since God had ordained children to be born in created innocence, He would not accuse them of any sin. But when children come to an age of understanding, then they may seek instruction and baptism into Christ's perfect way.

The Lord's Supper. Marpeck believed that theologians had put so much effort into disputing the interpretation of the words "This is my body; this is my blood" that they had neglected adequate consideration of what the Supper is and why it was instituted.[116] And while Marpeck allowed that one might properly call the Lord's Supper a "sacrament," given his definition of the word, the word as popularly used obscured the meaning of "the Lord's communion" (as Paul called it).[117]

Marpeck defined the Lord's Supper as "a bodily gathering or *assembly* of Christian believers who *partake* of communal food and drink, as Christ instructed them to do, in remembrance of Him."[118] This eating and drinking signifies the believers' participation in Christ's body and blood and, as such, symbolizes a durable bond of loving fellowship. Thus, believers become united in one body through one spirit of love.[119]

Marpeck concluded that the importance of the Supper does not lie in the meaning of what the bread and cup may be or contain in them, but rather in the reasons for a Christian's participation. When participation flows out of faith in Christ and a desire to obey His commands, the Supper symbolizes the believer's incorporation "into the fellowship of the only true, united church of Christ."[120] As a symbol, then, the Lord's Supper declares its meaning and importance from faith and obedience and not from the nature of the bread and wine. Any notion of transubstantiation, consubstantiation, or real presence places the efficacy of the elements in tension with the efficacy of faith. Moreover only the metaphorical sense of the words has any biblical foundation. "The bread and wine are nothing more than an external signal. However, the power and the might of that which counts rests alone in the heart of the individual who, girded with genuine faith and love, and thus in the church of Christ, can partake of the bread and wine."[121]

The Ban. Unlike the Swiss Brethren, Marpeck believed that the ban tended toward legalism, and wanted no part of it. Indeed, he refused to have fellowship with them until such time as they saw that their behavior was contrary to the Spirit of Christ and ceased its use. He did not believe that a Christian could do as he pleased (a charge leveled against him by the Brethren), but he did hold to freedom in Christ from the law. Indeed, "who-

ever presumes to preserve, rule, and lead the kingdom of Christ
through law . . . yes, through the law of God . . . no matter how
pious it appears, it, too, thrusts the voluntary Spirit of the Lord
Jesus Christ . . . out of His place. . . ." Just as bad, "they thrust the
Lord out, and make sin where there is no sin."[122]

Marpeck avowed that nowhere in the New Testament could
one find Jesus or Paul excluding anyone from fellowship because of minor issues such as self-seeking. The Brethren cut
people off too quickly. Even their pastors "have been excluded
from you and your gatherings at least once, if not twice."[123] To
punish the shepherd is contrary to Christ's Spirit.

In a second letter to the Swiss Brethren, Marpeck suggested
that they were not a true church, because of the division they
were causing through casual use of the ban. He called upon them
to return to the true nature of the Spirit of Christ. "For, there can
be no rift in the body of Christ since there is only one faith, one
Lord, one Spirit, one God and Father of us all. And this fellowship
is without exception, baptized with one Spirit, with water, into
one unsundered, undivided body with united members."[124]

Conclusions. Marpeck held views very similar to those of the
Swiss Brethren in regard to the church and the ordinances.
There were two churches, a genuine one and a counterfeit.
Entry into the true church occurred through believers' baptism
and an observance of the law of love for Christ (and, therefore,
obedience to His commands), which included a separation
from the world (including the state). The Lord's Supper is
purely representative of the body and blood of Christ, but it
does signify participation and membership in the body of
Christ, the true church.

When it came to the ban, Marpeck was his own person. His
position on its use was diametrically opposed to that of the
Swiss Brethren. He considered the ban to be legalistic and so,
subchristian. An extensive use of the ban, he submitted, led to
division in the body of Christ, a sin in itself.

Menno Simons

Although Menno Simons may not be regarded as either a
founder or charter member of the Anabaptist movement, it

would be reasonable to accord him a place as its preserver and promoter. Born in Witmarsum, the Netherlands, in 1496, Menno trained for the priesthood and was ordained in March of 1524. He began his service as a country priest, but confessed to spending much of his time carousing.[125]

As early as 1525, Menno began to entertain doubts about the validity of the Roman Catholic doctrine of transubstantiation. A few years later, he had reason to wonder about infant baptism and concluded that there was no biblical basis for that practice. But it was not until the slaughter of the Münsterites (a revolutionary Anabaptist group) — among whom was his brother — that he sought and obtained God's forgiveness and a new life in Christ.[126]

In 1537, having been rebaptized some time earlier, Menno was reordained as an Anabaptist pastor by Obbe Philips (who left the movement he had spearheaded a few years later). During the remainder of his ministry (he died in 1561), Menno exerted a strong influence on Anabaptist life in the Netherlands and northern Germany. His life was a hectic one; for he was hunted by his enemies and large rewards were posted for his apprehension. Still, he traveled about the countryside preaching, baptizing, ordaining, and planting churches. Timothy George remarks, "When we consider the dangers Menno faced, we are amazed that he was able to die a natural death at the age of sixty-six."[127] His influence on Anabaptist life was sufficient to cause his descendants in the faith to adopt his name as a badge of honor, calling themselves Mennonites.

On the Church. Menno defined the church as

> . . . the community of God . . . an assembly of the pious, and a community of the saints . . . which from the beginning firmly trusted and believed in the promised Seed of the woman . . . Christ . . . [who] believe to the end His Word in sincerity of heart, follow His example, [are] led by His Spirit, and trust in His promise, as the Scriptures teach.[128]

Menno held that the true church was opposed by a counterfeit one. The latter he characterized as "the church of the Antichrist" and "a community of the impenitent, who reject the

117

afore-mentioned Seed, Christ, and His Word; and oppose His will."[129]

Yet the true church, Menno contended, has existed from the beginning, although it sometimes had a different name and ordinance. In fact, all who in unfeigned fear of God live and continue to live according to God's Word and will are a single community, church, or body.[130] All in this community are saved by Christ and enriched by His Spirit.

Menno, like many other reformers, set out certain marks, or signs, that characterize the true church, setting it apart from the counterfeit church, and these were:

1. The salutary and unadulterated doctrine of God's holy Word.
2. The right and biblical use of the sacraments of Christ, namely, baptism and the Lord's Supper.
3. Obedience to the Word, that is, a pious, godly life.
4. Sincere and unfeigned love for one's neighbor.
5. Confession of Christ in the face of the tyranny and violence of the world.
6. Bearing the cross of Christ for the sake of His testimony and Word (i.e., persecution).[131]

Menno agreed with the majority of Christendom that the true church is invisible and is contained in the visible church. Contra Luther and Calvin, however, he contended that the visible church must be intact in doctrines and ordinances, and impeccable in its actions before the world; for human beings are able to judge only that which is visible.[132]

Baptism. Menno held that the ordinance of baptism had been perverted for centuries, and he called for a return to baptism as taught by the New Testament.[133] He condemned the sacramental practice of baptism and the baptism of infants as "accursed idolatry and abomination . . . a rending of the saving ordinances of Christ."[134] Baptism does not save; it is but a symbol of the new birth through faith in Jesus Christ.

> Those who believe receive remission of sins, not through baptism but in baptism . . . through the crimson blood and through the merits of our beloved Lord Jesus Christ. They therefore

receive the holy baptism as a token of obedience which proceeds from faith, as proof . . . that they firmly believe in the remission of their sins through Jesus Christ.[135]

Nor does baptism cleanse one of one's inherited sinful nature; for it persists in the believer following observance of the ordinance. It is, rather, a declaration that the believer desires to conquer and destroy the sin nature within. Any cleansing comes not by baptism but by God's Word.[136]

Although in one section of his "Foundation of Christian Doctrine," Menno referred to baptism as "immersion in water,"[137] he personally practiced affusion. In fact, in the same tract, he later referred to baptism with "a handful of water."[138]

Menno had no use for any doctrine of baptismal regeneration and particularly eschewed infant baptism as "an abominable idolatry."[139] While Menno held that children are accepted into the covenant of God, such acceptance is based on God's grace and not on baptism. Indeed, pedobaptism is nowhere proclaimed in Scripture, and because it is practiced, "the true baptism of Jesus Christ, that is, believer's baptism, is so . . . and trampled upon by all men as an heretical baptism."[140] True baptism represents the believer's death to sin and resurrection to life through faith in Christ, a faith infants cannot invoke and parents or sponsors cannot rightfully promise on their behalf.

What would happen, then, should a child die unbaptized? Menno's response was unequivocal; referring to Christ's statement in Matthew 19:14 (cf. Mark 10:14; Luke 18:16): "Let the little children come to me, and do not hinder them, for the kingdom of heaven belongs to such as these," Menno stated that parents might be certain that their young children are saved and pleasing unto God, whether alive or dead.[141]

The Lord's Supper. Menno had no more use for a sacramental view of the Lord's Supper than he did for a sacramental view of baptism. The Lord's Supper does not bring forgiveness of sins. He criticized those churches that admit all to the rite, regardless of their belief or character, and called upon them to heed the Scriptures. "For your table may more properly be called the table of the devil than the table of the Lord."[142]

He condemned any attempt to suggest that the elements of

the Supper are Christ's literal flesh and blood. To believe such a thing is not only "contrary to nature, reason, and Scripture," but "an open blasphemy of the Son of God; abomination, and idolatry."[143] The Bible teaches that the Supper "is an admonishing sign and memorial to the fact that Christ Jesus the Son of God has delivered us from the power of the devil . . . by the sinless sacrifice of His innocent flesh and blood, and has led us triumphantly into the kingdom of His grace."[144]

Furthermore, the Lord's Supper is a sign of Christian unity, love, and peace. Just as one loaf of bread is composed of many grains, so the true church is composed of many believers baptized into the one body of Christ by the Holy Spirit. "Just as there is harmony and peace in the body and all its members . . . it also becomes the true and living members of the body of Christ to be one: one heart, one mind, and one soul."[145]

The Supper, observed Menno, is also the communion of the body and blood of Christ. It calls upon believers to examine their hearts, asking themselves whether they really partake of Christ. No one should participate in the rite who has not become a new creation in Christ, who is not being led by the Holy Spirit to live the Christlike life.[146]

The Ban. Menno, like the Swiss Brethren, was in favor of excommunication, or the ban. But he went far beyond them, to advocate shunning, including the practice of marital avoidance.

Because the world is so alluring and Satan so deceptive, and because the unity and purity of the body of Christ is so important, God's Word commands that all schismatic, offensive, and greedy people should be excluded from His church. The purpose of the ban is that fallen believers "may be frightened by this ban and so brought to repentance, to seek union and peace and so to be set free before the Lord and His church from the satanic snares of their strife, or from their wicked life."[147]

Not only should offenders be excluded should they fail to repent, but they should be shunned as well. To do so in the hope of their restoration is particularly important in regard to those closest to us; for "they are our dearest friends, yes, our own flesh and blood, and we cannot by any other holy means lead them from evil and turn them to the way of the saints."[148]

Menno was adamant that, when required, a husband should shun his wife, and vice versa. Indeed, true shunning does not refer merely to spiritual fellowship as exemplified in the Lord's Supper, but also to physical fellowship, such as eating with an unrepentant fallen believer, having business dealings with such a one, or even receiving such a person into one's house.[149] Menno based his view on Deuteronomy 13:6-10, where God commanded that a person who tried to subvert a spouse, parent, or other family member from His worship should be executed. In the New Testament dispensation, such a command is obeyed by the ban and shunning.[150]

Preachers and Preaching. Menno called upon the churches to make sure that their preachers are servants of Christ and not hirelings. Preachers must be called into service because of genuine love for God and their neighbor, and through the power of the Holy Spirit.[151]

The duties of the Christian pastor are

rightly to teach in the house of God, that is, to teach in the church of Jesus Christ, with sound doctrine and by a pious and unblamable conduct, to admonish, rebuke, or reprove, and comfort, and assist in paternal love, to administer the Lord's holy baptism and Supper rightly, to ward off diligently with God's Word all seducing and false teachers, and to exclude all incurable members from the communion of the godly, etc.[152]

A carnal pastor is a sign of a carnal congregation. It is obvious that such a one is not called by God and will be punished.

Menno referred to 1 Timothy 3:1-11 and Titus 1:8f in regard to ministerial conduct. "For if disciples have to lead an unblamable life, how much more the teachers, because they govern and supervise the hearers."[153] A shepherd must be a model of the behavior expected in his sheep.

Menno reminded his readers that the true bishop fills an office of humble Christian service and is subject to poverty, pain, and reproach. He castigated the preachers of other (non-Anabaptist) churches who "parade in splendid robes dressed in shining sham . . ." and reminded his readers that "there is not a word to be found in Scripture concerning their anointing,

121

crosses, caps, togas . . . masses, offerings . . . etc."[154] Such preachers are "antichrists, locusts that rise from the bottomless pit. . . ."[155] The wise person, in keeping with the instruction of God's Word, avoids their doctrines, sacraments, and practices.[156]

Conclusions. Menno's ecclesiology was typically Anabaptist. It was consistent with the theology of the founding fathers of the movement, such as Conrad Grebel and Michael Sattler.

In his use of the ban, he differed from many other Anabaptist leaders by going to an extreme. Shunning—especially by one spouse of the other—was a radical action not employed by most other Anabaptist leaders (outside of the Netherlands) at the time. It is significant that most Mennonite groups dropped marital avoidance soon after Menno died.

Summary of Anabaptist Ecclesiology

Anabaptists were not at all interested in reforming the church; they wanted to see it *restored* to its original New Testament luster. The Bible depicted not a powerful political and economic religious institution, but a simple brotherhood of love and faith based on and animated by the movement of the Holy Spirit within its members.

For the most part, the Anabaptist majority view was summed up in the "Brotherly Union" of Schleitheim, concluded in 1527. While there were some variations, Anabaptist groups across Europe generally held doctrines in accord with that statement of faith.

The founders of the modern Anabaptist movement may be said to be the Swiss Brethren, initially a breakaway group from the Zwingli Circle, who felt that the Swiss reformer had failed to return to a biblical base in his efforts. They rejected the commonly held Protestant concept that the invisible church was contained in a visible church containing the saved and the lost, as well as the good and the bad. They insisted that the true church would show itself in its character. They included in the visible church only those people who had repented of their sins, confessed Christ publicly and voluntarily in believers' baptism, and had covenanted together to live a holy, Christlike life. In seeking to live holy lives, Anabaptists separated from the world and championed a total separation of church and state.

Anabaptists also initiated the "ban," a disciplinary tool by which erring believers were motivated to repent and return to fellowship. But not all Anabaptists accepted the ban. Pilgram Marpeck, a leader of Austrian and German Anabaptists rejected it as a violation of freedom in Christ. Others, such as Menno Simons, the Dutch Anabaptist leader, went beyond the ban by adding "shunning," a practice in which believers isolated and avoided the fallen sinner.

There seems to have been unanimity on the ordinances. Anabaptists demanded believers' baptism (a voluntary action), and saw the baptism of infants as an idolatrous practice which harmed the true church. Baptism initiates the believer into the church, but has no efficacy itself. It is completely dependent on the faith in Christ that undergirds it, and it is symbolic of the believer's baptism into the body of Christ by the Holy Spirit. Nor did they see the Lord's Supper as efficacious. They adopted the Zwinglian symbolic view of the rite, eschewing any notion of transubstantiation. The Supper is a simple memorial to the crucified Christ and is symbolic of the unity of the church as the body of Christ. As there is one loaf and one cup, so there is only one church and one faith.

Because of the Anabaptist insistence on separation, they were frequently seen as enemies of the state. This led to severe persecution in much of Europe, particularly in those areas with a strong emphasis on the establishment of religion. But these persecuted evangelicals were also the forerunners of other groups, such as the Baptists, who fostered the freedom of conscience enjoyed in democratic countries today.

ENGLISH REFORMATION ECCLESIOLOGY

The English Reformation began slowly in the fourteenth century with the preliminary work of John Wycliffe (ca. 1329–1384) and his Lollards. But it gathered impetus when Henry VIII quarreled with the pope over his desire to divorce Katherine of Aragon; as a result, the pope's authority was terminated in England and Henry proclaimed himself head of the English church. While he remained a Roman Catholic (albeit excommunicated) until his death, Henry's son Edward VI encouraged reform of the church in England through his advisers, who included Thomas Cranmer, Archbishop of Canterbury. Even though attempts were made by Mary Tudor to return England to Roman Catholicism, the Reformation could not be quenched. It was permanently established by Elizabeth I, who proclaimed herself "supreme governor" (rather than "head") of the Church of England.

Two main groups emerged from the English Reformation: Anglicans (the established church) and Separatists (those who stood against establishment). Out of the latter came two prominent groups, the Congregationalists and the Baptists.

Thomas Cranmer

Thomas Cranmer (1489–1556), more than any other person, was responsible for shaping the Protestant church of England. Born in Aslacton, Nottinghamshire, and educated at Cambridge, he led a quiet, scholarly existence until suddenly propelled into the archbishopric of Canterbury in 1532. Essentially Lutheran in his theology, Cranmer believed in the role of the "godly prince" to uphold society and the freedom of the Gospel, and he devotedly supported Henry VIII in his break with Rome, and guided Edward VI to further reformation of the church. Shortly after the accession of Mary Tudor, a Roman Catholic, to the English throne, Cranmer was deposed and in 1556 was burned at the stake as a heretic.[157]

On the Church. Because he was engaged in a running battle with Rome, Cranmer found it expedient to attack the historical foundations of the Roman Church. Going back to the Patristic era, he accused Rome of having destroyed ancient documents which militated against its authority, and of having hidden others. "And many more things said by the ancients, of the see of Rome, and against their authority, were lost, as appears by the fragments yet remaining."[158]

He pointed out, further, that while Peter and James directed the apostolic council, Christ had named no head. The church had appointed archbishops out of convenience. Nor is there any proof that Peter was ever in Rome. Even if some type of headship were given to Peter in Rome, nothing demonstrates that such power is forever. And, "if a pope with the cardinals be corrupted, they should be tried by a general council, and submit to it"; for "St. Peter gave an account of his baptizing Cornelius, when he was questioned about it."[159] Indeed, history clearly shows that councils have authority over popes, and a pope has no right to attempt to overrule a council.

Cranmer told King Edward VI that the king was "God's vice-regent and Christ's vicar within your own dominions." His duty was to act as a second Josiah, to see "God truly worshipped, and idolatry destroyed, the tyranny of the Bishops of Rome banished from your subjects, and images removed."[160] Like many of the reformers of Europe, the Archbishop believed in a joint service of church and state, the latter ensuring a proper climate of peace and justice in which society could worship Christ.

On the Ministry. Because Cranmer understood the relation of church and state as one of cooperation, he saw no difference between civil ministers and ministers of the Word. All these officials, said Cranmer, should be appointed, assigned, and elected in every place, by the laws and orders of kings and princes.[161]

Because there were no Christian princes in the apostles' time, noted Cranmer, ministers were appointed by uniform consent of the body of believers when these ministers were found to be "replete with the Spirit of God" and full of wisdom and wise counsel. Others were appointed by the apostles and the people accepted those appointments, "not for the supremity, impery, or dominion, that the apostles had over them to command, as their princes and masters, but as good people, ready to obey the advice of good counsellors."[162]

Even though Cranmer admitted that originally the office of bishop and priest were one and the same, he seemed to have no difficulty with a differentiation of the two and the elevation of the former above the latter. Now

> a bishop may make a priest by the Scripture, and so may princes and governors also, and that by the authority of God committed to them, and the people also by their election; for as we read that bishops have done it, so Christian emperors and princes usually have done it, and the people, before Christian princes were, commonly did elect their bishops and priests.[163]

125

While he obviously disregarded his own teaching, Cranmer allowed that neither priests nor bishops needed consecrating after their selection. The Bible did not require it. Election or appointment is sufficient.[164]

Nor does the Bible require a bishop or priest either to excommunicate or to refrain from excommunicating. Where the law of the land gives him the power to excommunicate, he should do so within its parameters. If the law forbids excommunication, he must refrain from so doing.[165]

On the Sacraments. While the Scriptures do not speak of the sacraments as such, the New Testament does use the Greek word *mystērion*, which is translated by the Latin *sacramentum*. Cranmer adopted the ancient definition that a sacrament is the sign of a sacred thing.[166] As to how many sacraments there might be, Cranmer does not say. Scripture is silent on the number, and ancient authorities placed them at more than seven, the number set by Rome.[167]

Scripture, Cranmer avowed, mentioned certain sacraments. Baptism is that rite in which "we be regenerated and pardoned of our sin by the blood of Christ." In the Eucharist, "we be concorporated unto Christ, and made lively members of his body, nourished and fed to the everlasting life, if we receive it as we ought to do, and else it is to us rather death than life." Penance is found in Scripture, but not as Rome sets it out formulating it in three parts, namely, contrition, confession, and satisfaction. Matrimony is also cited by the Bible for "sanctifying the act of carnal commixtion between the man and the wife" for the glory of God in procreation. On confirmation, orders, and extreme unction the Bible is silent.[168]

Cranmer held that Rome had greatly abused the doctrine of the Lord's Supper, especially in the four or five centuries leading up to his own time. He had nothing but scorn for the doctrine of transubstantiation. While it is true that one who eats and drinks at the Lord's Table has everlasting life, let no one suppose that the bread and wine are the literal body and blood of Christ.[169]

The effect of the sacrament, asserted Cranmer, depends upon its recipient. The believer eats and drinks salvation; the unbeliever eats and drinks damnation to himself.[170] Those who

126

3.1   Reformation Ecclesiology

Group	Governance	Baptism	Eucharist	Nature of the Church
Lutheranism	Bishops to administer churches; churches have autonomy and do not have to obey unbiblical dictums.	Baptism is the means of becoming part of Christ. It cleanses one from sin and guilt. But it is empty apart from faith. Endorsed infant baptism.	Consubstantiation — the literal flesh and blood of Christ are "in, with, and under" the bread and wine.	There is only one church, but it stretches across all ages and encompasses all persons of faith. The "visible" church contains all who profess faith.
Calvinism	Presbyterial — teaching and ruling elders represent the local church to the presbytery.	Baptism is a sign of initiation into the church. Infant baptism — like O.T. circumcision — is a sign of being under the covenant.	Real presence — when the believer eats and drinks the elements, he/she receives Christ spiritually by faith.	There is one, invisible church, composed of the elect. It is revealed in the visible church, comprised of all who profess Christ.
Anabaptism	Congregational autonomy. Each church is responsible only to the authority of Jesus Christ as revealed in the Bible.	Baptism of (adult) believers only upon repentance of sins and profession of faith in Christ. It is an external rite symbolic of inner spiritual baptism.	Symbolic — the bread is still bread, the wine is still wine. The Lord's Supper is a simple memorial and not a sacrament.	The invisible church is all who have been saved; it is manifested in a visible community of spiritually regenerated, voluntarily baptized believers.
Anglicanism	Episcopal system. The monarch (government) is responsible for appointment of bishops.	Baptism is sacramental — it regenerates one and cleanses one from sin, even an infant.	The believer spiritually ingests Christ; the unbeliever ingests damnation.	One invisible, apostolic church, actualized and continued in the holy, catholic church (i.e., the Church of England).

come to the Supper with a living faith do spiritually ingest the body and blood of Christ, and in such a way He is present in the elements. As the communicants participate together in the sacred feast they witness to "a brotherly and unfeigned love between all of them that be members of Christ."[171]

What effect does the observance of the Supper have on the participant? Cranmer was unyielding that the sacrament does not constitute a propitiatory sacrifice. Reception of the Supper does not effect forgiveness of sins. While in the Old Testament certain sacrifices were seen as propitiatory in nature, "yet in very deed there is but one such sacrifice whereby our sins be pardoned and God's mercy and favor obtained, which is the death of the Son of God our Lord Jesus Christ."[172] The Lord's Supper is "a sacrifice of lauds and thanksgiving, and . . . a remembrance of the very true sacrifice propitiatory of Christ . . ."; here is found its true significance.[173]

Conclusions. Cranmer readily followed his monarch out of the Roman fold and into a church governed by the king as God's vice-regent. He attempted to return to a biblical basis for church practice, but on occasion accepted the witness of the church fathers in its place. Like Luther, Zwingli, and Calvin, he saw the church and state as equal coworkers in God's kingdom. He went beyond those reformers in the power he accorded the monarch to appoint church leaders.

Cranmer's view of the sacraments was patristic. He disagreed with Luther, holding the Calvinistic idea of the spiritual presence of Christ, along with the need for an underlying faith to validate the sacrament. His concept of the Supper as symbolic was also typically Reformed.

The Congregationalists

Even with the separation of the church in England from the see of Rome, many English Christians remained dissatisfied. A growing group within Anglicanism asserted that their church still retained too many papist trappings and wished to purify it further. This wish led to their being nicknamed "Puritans" after 1560. Puritanism flourished in England. In fact, it had grown to such an extent by 1593 that Elizabeth I passed an act against it.[174]

One part of the Puritan wing, which came to be known as the Independents, wanted Anglicanism exchanged for an established Presbyterian or Congregational Church. Another group, the Separatists, favored complete separation of church and state (i.e., church disestablishment). Both of these groups grew quickly in spite of opposition from both the Crown and the Church of England.[175]

In about 1567 a group of Separatists, led by Richard Fitz, separated from the Church of England to begin an autonomous church whose basis of membership was a covenant of loyalty to Jesus Christ. Another, similar group was organized by Robert Browne in Norwich in 1580 or 1581. Browne and his congregation were forced by persecution to flee to Holland. There, he wrote three tracts outlining the bases of Separatist Congregationalism. The chief of these was *Reformation Without Tarying for Anie*. Browne contended that believers should be united to Christ and to each other by a voluntary covenant. Church officers should be appointed by members of the congregation. Decisions affecting the church as a whole should be made by the congregation as a whole. And each congregation should be completely autonomous. Although Browne apostatized from his faith and became a member of the Anglican clergy soon after this, his views left an imprint on many others.[176]

Another Congregationalist group was organized by John Robinson (ca. 1575–1625) at Scrooby. They, too, were forced into exile in Holland in 1608. From among their numbers came a group who immigrated to Plymouth in America in 1620. By 1631 Congregationalism (in spite of its Separatist beginnings) had become the established church in the New England colonies. Church polity was Congregational and its theology was Calvinistic.[177]

The principles of Congregationalism were set forth in the Savoy Declaration of Faith and Order, adopted by English Congregationalists in 1658 at the Savoy Palace, London. It differs very little from the (Presbyterian) Westminster Confession, except in church polity (congregational rather than presbyterial) and in its denial of the authority of magistrates in church affairs.[178]

The Baptists

A group of Separatists organized in Gainsborough and led by John Smyth and Thomas Helwys were forced to leave England for Amsterdam in about 1607. There, they were strongly influenced by the Mennonites and concluded that believer's baptism was the proper biblical rite of initiation into the church. In 1608 Smyth baptized himself and then the other members of the group.[179] Thus was constituted the first Baptist congregation.

When Smyth and some of the congregation decided to make application to become a part of the Mennonite Church, Helwys and the remaining members excommunicated them. The Mennonites, for their part, were wary of accepting the English into their fellowship and Smyth died in 1611, belonging nowhere.

In 1611, Helwys along with his congregation returned to England where they established at Spitalfields in London a General Baptist congregation. A direct appeal for toleration was rejected by King James I, who clapped Helwys in Newgate Prison where he died about 1616.[180] His church, however, lived on and multiplied.

No more than twenty years after Helwys' death, several Particular (i.e., Calvinistic in doctrine) Baptist congregations had been formed. While their doctrine of the Christian life differed somewhat from the General Baptists', their ecclesiology did not.

The Church. In what is surely the first Baptist confession of faith, penned by Thomas Helwys in 1610, the church is defined as "a company of faithful people separated from the world by the word and Spirit of God, being knit unto the Lord and unto one another by baptism, upon their own confession of the faith and sins."[181]

Even though there is only one church, asserted Helwys, it is represented by many congregations throughout the whole world. Indeed, every congregation, no matter how small, which possesses Christ and salvation, is the body of Christ and a complete church. Thus, when its members come together, whether they have officers present or not, they should "pray, prophesy, break bread, and administer in all the holy ordinances."[182]

The London Confession (1644) of the Particular Baptists

acknowledged the autonomy of the local church, but went beyond it to recognize the interdependence of congregations.

> And although the particular congregations be distinct and several bodies, every one a compact and knit city in itself; yet are they all to walk by one and the same rule, and by all means convenient to have the counsel and help one of another in all needful affairs of the Church, as members of one body in the common faith under Christ their only head.[183]

The Ministry. The General Baptists were far in advance of their time in regard to the gender of church leadership. Helwys contended that the officers of a church, according to Scripture, are elders and deacons, either men or women. These should be chosen from within the congregation of which they are members, and in concord with 1 Timothy 3:2ff and Titus 1:6ff. They should be elected by the congregation with prayer, fasting, and the laying on of hands.[184]

The London Confession did not comment on the gender of church officers. It did add to their number the categories of pastors and teachers. It also maintained that every church should support its officers, but such maintenance should be a free and voluntary act and not legally compelled (as in the established church).[185]

Baptism. The General Baptists saw baptism accompanied by a profession of faith as the necessary rite for membership in the church. Helwys declared "that baptism or washing with water is the outward manifestation of dying unto sin, and walking in newness of life (Rom. 6:2,3,4), and therefore in no wise appertaineth to infants."[186]

The Particular Baptists concurred, but went further to discuss the proper mode which, according to Scripture, is "dipping or plunging the whole body under water." Baptism is symbolic of washing with Christ's blood, of identifying with Christ's death and resurrection, and of assurance of resurrection at the last day to reign with Him.[187]

The Lord's Supper. Early Baptists were Zwinglian (or Anabaptist) in their view of the meaning of the Lord's Supper. It is a symbolic memorial of Jesus' death. Helwys wrote that "the Lord's Supper is an outward manifestation of the spiritual communion between Christ and the faithful mutually (1 Cor. 10:16,17) to declare his death until he come (1 Cor. 11:26)."[188]

Conclusions. Baptists, coming out of the Separatist camp and being strongly influenced by the Anabaptists, insisted on an autonomous covenanting church, but recognized that every congregation should be interdependent because of the unity of Christ. Because of local autonomy, church officers should be drawn by congregational election from among those in the congregation biblically qualified for the task.

The Baptists imitated the Anabaptists in baptism, but moved fairly speedily from affusion to (what they saw as) the biblical mode of immersion. Like the Anabaptists (and unlike the Separatists), they denied baptism to infants, insisting on the voluntary baptism of believers alone.

In regard to the Lord's Supper, they followed Zwingli's view of the elements as symbolic of Christ's body and blood. The Supper was a memorial to His death and signified the unity of believers.

A Summary of English Reformation Ecclesiology

A study of ecclesiological views in England during the sixteenth and early seventeenth centuries reveals a great variety of stances. Although not commented upon in this section, traditional Roman Catholicism was far from dead. A great many people clung to Roman doctrine and practice. The established Church of England was strongly influenced by Thomas Cranmer's teachings, which were largely Lutheran with a substantial flavoring of Calvinism. One wing of Anglicanism, the Puritans, was attempting to cleanse their church of papal trappings in favor of a simpler, biblical Christianity. A more radical group, the Separatists, were antiestablishment, and broke with Anglicanism in order to found their own churches, organized around a covenant of loyalty to Christ Jesus as their Head. Each Separatist congregation was autonomous and Calvinistic in its theology; some were congregational in polity, while others were presbyterian.

Some Separatist groups became independent. Others joined together as Congregationalists. Still others, influenced by the Anabaptists, rejected infant baptism in favor of voluntary believer's baptism. These became Baptists.

With the exception of the Roman Catholics, all churches rejected transubstantiation. Anglicans, Presbyterians, and some Separatist groups accepted the Reformed concept of spiritual presence. Some Congregationalists and all Baptists followed the symbolic notion of Zwingli and the Anabaptists.

Viewpoints contrary to those of the established church were heartily persecuted, but they could not be eradicated. It was not, however, until 1689 that a measure of toleration was finally granted.

CONCLUSIONS

As one surveys the broad diversity of Reformation ecclesiologies, one must wonder whether there is more of a common thread than reaction against Roman Catholicism. Certainly the names "Protestant" and "Reformation" would suggest a response to perceived abuses in the established church of the Western world. While the reformers did attempt to undo the excesses of Roman Catholicism, it is also clear that the ecclesiologies of the Lutheran, Reformed, and Anglican theologians were influenced more by political than by biblical considerations. Even the Congregationalists, although they began with the proper motivation (that is, a desire to return to biblical Christianity), soon succumbed to the theology of politics. Only the Anabaptists and their first cousins, the Baptists, can be said to be free of political taint, for only they stressed the absolute separation of church and state. Only they insisted on absolute freedom of conscience.

Penrose St. Amant notes that magisterial Protestantism (such as the Anglicans, Lutherans, and Reformed) held to the Roman Catholic concept of church and state combined together in a single Christian body, the *Corpus Christianum*, and tried to perpetuate the idea within their own spheres of influence. The Anabaptists and the Baptists, on the other hand, attempted to replace the *Corpus Christianum* with the *Corpus Christi*, the "body of Christ," a voluntary nonpolitical discipling community.[189]

133

The wide variety of views on the church, the ministry, and the sacraments, which were held by the different Protestant groups led to even more divergent views as reactions set in. Second and third generation Protestants and beyond attempted either to change the views of their ancestors or to reinforce them. This tendency is clearly displayed in the scientific and modern ages.

CHAPTER FOUR

The Church in the Scientific Age

Sixteenth-century Europe gave birth not only to new forms of the Christian faith, but also to new forms of technology, philosophy, and political systems. Leonardo da Vinci was an engineer and physicist, as well as a painter and a mathematician. Galileo Galilei was an inventor and a scientist. Francis Bacon was a scientist and a philosopher. These brilliant minds led toward new methods of inquiry—methods which would question the validity and legitimacy of just about every traditional system and process held important. Neither the Christian faith nor the church would be safe from their questioning, as revolutionary paradigm shifts emerged.

The Christian world was in a state of flux between the sixteenth and twentieth centuries. This ebb and flow would be seen in the ecclesiologies of Eastern Orthodoxy, Roman Catholicism, and Protestantism.

EASTERN ORTHODOXY

With the capitulation of Constantinople in 1453 to Islam, the Eastern Orthodox Church found itself largely cut off from normal intercourse with the West. Eastern theology continued its decline begun during the Middle Ages. Because of the sad state of theological education in Greece and Asia Minor, Eastern theologians took their training in Europe. Thus, the conflicts and questions raised in Western theology were introduced into the Eastern church.[1]

Seventeenth-Century Orthodoxy

The Eastern Orthodox Church of the seventeenth century faced assaults not only from the Muslims but also from the Roman Catholics and, to a lesser degree, from the Protestants.

Roman Catholic Persecution. In Poland, where there were large numbers of Eastern communicants, the Patriarch of Constantinople – under whose jurisdiction they came – could exert no real control, and so Orthodox bishops were appointed by the Roman Catholic king. On numerous occasions the Roman Catholic authorities of Poland attempted to force the Orthodox Church to submit to the pope. The Jesuits were in the forefront of this effort.[2]

A substantial group within Polish Orthodoxy recognized the supremacy of the Roman pontiff; they formed a "Uniate" Church, whose members were known as "Catholics of the Eastern Rite." The Eastern church in Poland legally ceased to exist, for authorities recognized only the Uniates.[3]

In the Ukraine, the Orthodox Church organized powerful lay institutes known as *Bratsva*, or Brotherhoods. They, in turn, produced apologetic works against the Jesuit onslaught and organized Orthodox schools.[4] These Brotherhoods reenergized Eastern Orthodoxy and reemphasized the traditional Orthodox Church teachings on doctrinal matters.

Protestant Evangelization. In 1573 an exchange of views began between Protestants and Orthodox when a group of Lutheran scholars from Tübingen visited Constantinople. They hoped to win the Eastern church to the principles of the Reformation. They presented copies of the Augsburg Confession and translations of Lutheran sermons to the Patriarch, Jeremias II. Jeremias' *Answers* (in 1576, 1579, and 1581) reiterated the traditional Eastern positions on Tradition, the sacraments, prayers for the dead, and prayers to the saints. Of all the articles in the Augsburg Confession, he affirmed only its endorsement of the Ecumenical Councils and married priesthood.[5] Ultimately, relations between the two groups were terminated by the Patriarch, but they were always courteous, and no attempt at coercion was made by the Lutherans.

Cyril Lukaris. Cyril (1572–1638) was a Greek priest whose experiences with Roman Catholic oppression in the Ukraine left him with a deep hatred for Rome. When he became Patriarch of Constantinople he devoted all of his efforts to counteracting all Roman Catholic influence within the Turkish Empire. He sought the political help of the Protestant embassies in Constantinople and the theological help of Calvinism to overcome the Romish inroads.[6]

In 1629, Cyril published his *Confession*, a doctrinal statement. It was distinctly Reformed in tone. It emphasized the superiority of Scripture over the church, denied the church's infallibility, accepted only two sacraments, and rejected the notions of transubstantiation and purgatory.[7]

Cyril's reign as Patriarch was troubled and stormy. He was deposed and reinstated five times. Finally, he was strangled by the Turks. His Calvinistic *Confession* was condemned by six ecumenical councils between 1638 and 1691.[8]

The *Confession* of Dositheus (1641–1707) sought to repudiate Cyril's work. He differed from Cyril in his doctrine of the church, the number and nature of the sacraments, and the veneration of icons. In writing on the Lord's Supper, Dositheus adopted both the Latin term *transubstantiation* and the Scholastic differentiation between *substance* and *accidents*.[9] While his work was an effort to present a clear account of Orthodox theology, it was firmly founded on Roman Catholic doctrine. Dositheus did, however, reject the pope as head of the church.[10]

Eighteenth-Century Orthodoxy

Anti-Roman Catholic feelings increased during the eighteenth century. In 1724, a large portion of the Patriarchate of Antioch came under the authority of Rome, and the Orthodox leaders, afraid of other defections, became extremely wary in their relations with the see of Peter. In 1755, the Patriarchs of Constantinople, Alexandria, and Jerusalem decreed that Latin baptism was invalid and that all converts to Orthodoxy must be rebaptized. This provision extended to the end of the nineteenth century, but it was never observed in the Russian Orthodox Church.

4.1   The Disunity of the Church 1500–1700

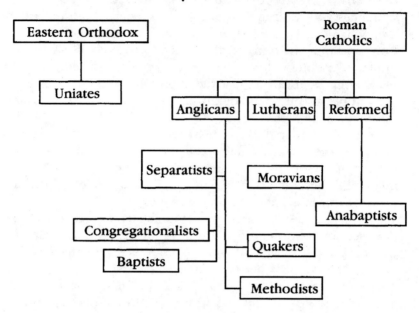

Nineteenth-Century Orthodoxy

Eastern Orthodoxy experienced something of a spiritual revival during the nineteenth century, especially in Russia where there was a flurry of missionary activity, a revived assurance of the distinctive mission of the church, and of Orthodoxy as the channel of its true traditions. In regard to ecclesiology, two names are outstanding: Alexei Khomiakov (1804–1880) and Philaret Drozdov (1782–1867).[11]

Alexei Khomiakov. Khomiakov, a retired Russian cavalry captain and landowner, was a lay theologian (a common Orthodox order). He contended that Eastern theology was something totally distinct from that of the West, either Roman Catholic or Protestant. Consequently, Orthodoxy should not borrow its theology from the West, as it had done for the last two hundred years. Khomiakov returned to early Orthodox theology in order to combat Roman Catholicism and Reformed theology. He was especially concerned with the doctrine of the church, its unity and authority.[12]

Khomiakov stressed the church as community. "We know

that when any of us falls, he falls alone; but no one is saved alone. He is saved in the church, as a member of it and in unison with all its other members."[13]

The Orthodox doctrine of the church is quite different from that of the West. While the latter sees the church christologically as the body of Christ, the former views it in Trinitarian terms: it is (1) the image of the Trinity, (2) the body of Christ, and (3) a continued Pentecost. As such, it is both visible and invisible, divine and human. Because it is composed of people worshiping here on earth, it is visible; but because it also consists of the saints in heaven, it is invisible. Because it is composed of sinful people, the church is human; but it is also divine, for it is the body of Christ. There is no separation between the two; for they entail a single and continuing reality. "The Church, even on earth, is a thing of heaven."[14]

Khomiakov stressed the unity of the church. "The Church is one. Its unity follows of necessity from the unity of God."[15] Because Christ is one, so His body is one. The church therefore remains visibly one on earth, and while there may be schisms from the church, there are no schisms in the church. What holds the church together is not a pope or other hierarchical figure, but the communion of the sacraments.[16]

Herbert Cunliffe-Jones concludes about Khomiakov:

> Khomiakov's conception was more sacramental than mystical. The Church is an actual communion not only in truth but also in grace. He sought to give the Orthodox Churches a new confidence in themselves and to bring back their teaching to the standard of the Fathers and to the experience of actual Church life.[17]

Philaret Drozdov. Drozdov, Metropolitan of Moscow from 1821 to 1867, was likely the most capable theologian of Russian Orthodoxy. While he was in essential agreement with Khomiakov on doctrinal issues, he was more generous with non-Orthodox Christians. In his *Conversation of a Seeker and a Believer Concerning the Truth of the Eastern Greco-Russian Church*, he asserted that the visible church is just the external form of the invisible church which can be grasped only by faith. The Eastern Orthodox Church may be said to be the only true church because it has been true to the original deposit of faith. But even "impure" churches are a part of the mystical unity of Christ. In his *Longer Catechism of the Orthodox Catholic Eastern Church*, Drozdov argued that Tradition is vital as a guide to a proper understanding of the sacraments and their preservation.[18]

Conclusions. The Orthodox Church entered the scientific era in a pitiful state of stagnation and demoralization. It was suffering political oppression at the hands of the Muslims in the Turkish Empire and from the Roman Catholics in Poland and the Ukraine. Nor was it entirely safe from the Protestants, who attempted to evangelize the Orthodox on a number of occasions. Orthodox theologians trained in the West at Roman Catholic or Protestant schools muddied the theological waters of Eastern Christendom. It was not until the nineteenth century that these waters were cleared and the theology of Orthodoxy was somewhat reinvigorated largely through the efforts of unfettered Russian Orthodox thinkers.

ROMAN CATHOLICISM

Roman Catholicism entered the scientific age very much on the defensive as a result of the Protestant Reformation. Its efforts during this period were directed toward the consolidation of its territory and the reclamation of ground lost to Protestantism.

Seventeenth-Century Roman Catholicism

The touchstone of Roman Catholic theology during the scientific age was the Council of Trent (1545–1563). Although a sixteenth-century endeavor, the council saw its outworking in successive centuries.

The Roman Church emerged from the sixteenth century as a highly centralized body which had taken the lead in the Counter Reformation. But these events occurred just as the fledgling nations of Europe were asserting their own independence, often under very authoritarian rulers who did not care for a church within their realm which was loyal to a foreign ruler. As a result, they encouraged those within Roman Catholicism who wished to see the pope's power restricted. Consequently, one of the major issues during the seventeenth to nineteenth centuries was the exact nature and extent of papal authority. Gallicanism, Febronianism, Josephism, and Ultramontanism were all responses to that problem, the final outcome of which was Vatican I.[19]

Gallicanism

In the seventeenth century, nationalist sentiments pervaded Spain, Portugal, and France. Their Roman Catholic rulers opposed and attacked papal power. Because this opposition was strongest in France, it came to be known as Gallicanism.

The French had good reason for opposing papal authority. During the "Babylonian captivity," the kings of France had forced the popes to live at Avignon and had extracted numerous concessions from them. In 1516, Pope Leo X had signed a concordat with Francis I of France which gave the king and his successors considerable authority over the church in that realm. When the French spoke of "Gallican liberties," therefore, they were speaking of traditional practices which were now under attack. As a result, they opposed the Council of Trent and the promulgation of its edicts; for they believed that to affirm them would be to assent to the authority of the papacy over the crown, at least in church affairs.[20]

In 1615, most of the French clergy, tired of waiting for government action on the edicts of Trent, went ahead on their own and declared the council's decrees binding on all Christians. Many French people were strongly opposed to the move.

Edmond Richer. One of those opposed to papal power in France was Edmond Richer (1559–1631), a doctor of theology at the Sorbonne. In his book, *On Ecclesiastical and Political Power*, he claimed that Christ is the only Head of the church, and He has delegated His authority to believers as a whole. They, in turn, have delegated their authority to the clergy. The priests possess sacerdotal power, each in his own parish. Bishops possess juridical authority, each in his own diocese. In council together the bishops are the supreme authority of the church. The pope is the council's servant, executing its policies and reporting back to it regularly.[21]

The Six Articles. In 1663, the Sorbonne published its *Six Articles*. They affirmed that, in temporal affairs, the king was sovereign. Nor did the pope have authority to depose French bishops. They also declared that the pope was not superior over a council, nor was papal infallibility a dogma which had universal acceptance.[22]

Febronianism. A movement strongly supportive of Gallicanism derived its name from its main proponent, Justin Febronius, whose real name was Johann Nickolaus von Hontheim (1701–1790). He claimed that kings are not under the pope's authority, whose power is derived from the church as a whole. Thus, the pope is subject to the church which, in council, may judge and depose him. Nor is he superior to other bishops, and he has no power in dioceses not his own.[23]

Febronianism was merely a German form of Gallicanism. German rulers were no more anxious than the French to permit papal interference in their national affairs.

Josephism. Febronianism turned into Josephism when the Holy Roman Emperor Joseph II applied its principles within his domains. He coupled its theories with measures against religious orders, which he saw as papal infiltration of his empire. His brother Leopold applied its tenets in Tuscany. Josephism was short-lived, dying with Joseph in 1790. It was condemned by Pope Pius VI in 1794.[24]

Conclusions. The French Revolution brought an end to Gallicanism. The murder of the royal family and the overthrow of the nobility led to a separation of church and state. Throughout the nineteenth century the forces of papal authority would be ascendant in Roman Catholicism.

Ultramontanism

Ultramontanism, which means quite literally "beyond the mountains," refers to the pope as supreme head of the church worldwide. It was originally used of those French who looked beyond the Alps to Rome for direction.

With the collapse of Gallicanism under the onslaught of the

French Revolution, Ultramontanism gained momentum, reaching its zenith in the latter part of the nineteenth century.

The Concordat of 1801. When Napoleon Bonaparte quashed the French Revolution and made himself master of France, he discerned that recognition of the Roman Catholic Church was important to the realization of his ambitions. Thus, he came to an understanding with Pope Pius VII in 1801. Roman Catholicism was no longer established, but it was allowed to function openly. Bishops would be nominated by Napoleon, but they would be invested only by the pope, who could also refuse to invest them (and even depose them). Thus, a strong measure of control of the bishops was granted to the papacy. Rome became the authority in religious affairs, and the pope was declared (at least in France) to be superior to the bishops.[25]

Félicité de Lammenais. Abbé de Lammenais (1782–1854) was initially antagonistic toward the French Revolution, but soon came to realize the degenerate state of the monarchy. He contended that the church should be free and separate from any state association. His knowledge of the struggles of oppressed peoples in Europe led him to appropriate liberal and democratic ideas. In 1819 he asserted that the church should ally itself with all those who were seeking independence. Nor should the pope accept concordats with monarchs, but rather he should champion the people directly.[26]

De Lammenais sought the support of Pope Gregory XVI for his ideas. Instead, the pope condemned his views in 1832 and again in 1834. De Lammenais, disillusioned, left both the priesthood and the church. He died in 1854, bitter and unreconciled, so poor that he was consigned to a pauper's grave.[27]

Pius IX. The major figure of nineteenth century Roman Catholicism was Pope Pius IX (1792–1878). He began his reign as a supporter of liberal ideas and actions, only to be besieged by Italian revolutionaries and forced to flee Rome. William Brausch observes that

the net effect was to make Pius forever suspicious of liberalism. He did not condemn it as such but he had become scared of what he saw. Under the influence of his ultra conservative secretaries of state . . . Pius came to see nothing good in any liberal Catholic movement.[28]

Before long Pius arrived at the conclusion that his work was to preserve the character of the church against the liberalism and secularism of the time. In 1854 he issued the bull *Ineffabilis Deus*, a significant milestone in the advancement of papal authority. In it he declared the dogma of the immaculate conception of Mary, proclaiming that Mary had been born without the stain of original sin. The importance of this action was that, for the first time in church history, a pope had specified doctrine by his own authority. Because there was little resistance to this manifesto, Ultramontanes were convinced that it was a fortuitous time for a formal assertion of papal infallibility.[29]

Papal infallibility was the central item for consideration at the First Vatican Council, called by Pius IX in 1868 and begun the following year. *The Dogmatic Constitution on the Church* dealt with the nature and scope of apostolic primacy. The council decided, by a vote of 522 for, 2 against, and more than 100 abstentions, that "the Roman Pontiff, when he speaks *ex cathedra* . . . is possessed of that infallibility with which the divine Redeemer willed that his Church should be endowed for defining doctrine regarding faith or morals. . . ."[30] Another part of the decree declared the pope's authority over the entire church in discipline and morals, as well.

Conclusions. During the nineteenth century Ultramontanism gained the upper hand over Gallicanism. But the triumph was a hollow one; for it has been noted that "the main reason that the doctrine of papal infallibility met such scarce resistance was that the church had lost a great deal of influence in the world."[31]

Cardinal Newman

John Henry Newman (1801–1890), an Anglican cleric and member of the Oxford movement, became a convert to Roman Catholicism in 1845, and ultimately one of the outstanding Roman Catholic leaders in England.

Newman was particularly concerned about the matter of religious authority. He had become enamored of the fourth-century church, and his theology was based upon that era. He criticized Protestantism for accepting the Bible by itself without the interpretation of the church as the definitive authority.[32]

While Newman was not in favor of the dogma of papal infallibility, he did subscribe to the infallibility of the church, of which the pope is head. Thus, he declared that, "We must either give up the belief in the church as a divine institution altogether, or we must recognize it at this day in that communion of which the Pope is the head."[33] At the same time, he counted obedience to conscience above all else.

Cunliffe-Jones summarizes Newman's importance:

> The question that Newman has bequeathed here to the twentieth century is this: is the combination of the supremacy of conscience and an infallible teaching authority a possible one, or if the supremacy of conscience is maintained must not the nature of the Church and its application be understood differently from what it has been?[34]

Conclusions. The Roman Catholic Church began the seventeenth century in a battle over authority. The Gallicans were loyal to their national leaders; the Ultramontanes supported papal authority. During the seventeenth century, Gallicanism held the upper hand, reaching its apex in the eighteenth century. With the French Revolution, however, Gallicanism came to an end and Ultramontanism became supreme. During the nineteenth century the papacy took steps to consolidate its gains by such stratagems as the promulgation of the dogma of papal infallibility at Vatican I. While not all Roman Catholics favored these steps, opponents were in a minority position.

PROTESTANTISM

The scientific era saw a further fracturing of Protestantism as other sects and denominations were established. While Western Christianity once had been unified in its structure—if not its outlook—it now existed in many forms with vast differences in outlook and doctrine. This trend toward increasing pluralization would continue to snowball.

The Quakers

Quakerism has been described as "to a significant degree a fruit of the Radical Reformation as it expressed itself in Puritan dress in seventeenth-century England."[35] While they shared the Calvinistic ideas of God's sovereignty and human depravity, the Quakers also adopted many of the ideals of Anabaptism such as voluntary church membership, separation from the world, freedom of conscience, and nonresistance.

George Fox. George Fox (1624–1691) may be seen as the father of the Quaker movement. The son of a Puritan weaver, and self-taught in theology, he spent a number of years searching for spiritual meaning until, in 1646, he was overwhelmed by Christ's "ocean of light and love." Like many other mystics, such as Teresa of Avila or John of the Cross, he experienced trances and visions, but his main experience gave him victory over sin.[36]

Fox began to move throughout England holding mass meetings and attracting huge crowds. He was particularly welcomed by Separatist groups, many of which supplied him with co-workers who had adopted his vision. Those who believed as he did began meeting regularly as they sojourned together toward the Light.

When Charles II was restored to the British throne in 1659, religious toleration was squelched. All but ministers pledged to use full Anglican liturgy were forbidden to preach. Any who did preach were imprisoned. The Quakers' refusal to swear the Oath of Allegiance made outlaws of all of them. A special "Quaker Act" singled them out for even greater persecution. Hundreds of Quakers died in prison. Eventually after England revolted against the Stuarts, and William and Mary ascended the throne, the Act of Toleration was proclaimed in 1689, granting Quakers some measure of religious freedom.[37] Only a few of the original Quaker leaders were left. But the Quakers began to grow and spread throughout Britain and its colonies, proclaiming their religion of spiritual light.

Quaker Ecclesiology. One of the early Quakers, Robert Barclay, studied under the Roman Catholics at the Scots College in

France and under the Presbyterians at Aberdeen. He was probably the most acute theologian of the group. His *Catechism and Confession of Faith*, published in 1673, set forth the normal Quaker standards of church doctrine.

The church, asserted Barclay, is composed of "them that are sanctified in Christ Jesus (1 Cor. 1:2)."[38] Christ has appointed officers in the church for the work of the ministry, namely, apostles, prophets, evangelists, and pastors and teachers. Their task is to oversee and feed the church to the glory of Jesus Christ. Their demonstration of the power of the Spirit in their own life is much more important than any erudition. Women, as well as men, may preach or prophesy.[39]

The Sacraments. The Quakers were antipedobaptist. They rejected any idea of infant baptism; for there was no biblical basis for such a doctrine. However, their view of believers' baptism was much different from that of the Baptists. They would not accept a material baptism (that is, in water). Rather, "the true baptism is that of the spirit, 'with the Holy Ghost and with fire.' "[40]

In the same way, they rejected a physical celebration of the Lord's Supper. "The true supper of the Lord is the spiritual eating and drinking of the flesh and blood of Christ spiritually."[41] It is through this spiritual eating and drinking that one is nourished to everlasting life. The world, on the other hand, "who takes only the outward figures," eats and drinks damnation rather than a communion.[42]

Conclusions. Fox was of the opinion that the churches had long been in an apostate state. But Christ had now returned in Spirit to review His church and return it to its original pristine condition. He was calling His restored church to a cosmic battle against evil at all levels. The weapon given was the sword of the Spirit. Those who sought to use material things instead, dispensed with the spiritual.[43]

Pietism

Pietism was a reaction against moral decadence in Germany resulting from the terrible devastation of the Thirty Years' War (which ended in 1648). It arose in a context of sorcery, alchemy, exorcism, and the creedal rigidity of a "dead" orthodoxy.[44]

The founder of Pietism was Philipp Jakob Spener (1635–1705). Raised in a devout Lutheran family, Spener could find little connection between the faith on which he had been raised and the theology dispensed by the universities. On a trip to Switzerland he came in contact with Jean de Labadie, a former Jesuit who held that the immediate inspiration of the Holy Spirit was required for a proper understanding of the Bible. While he did not accept all of Labadie's teachings, Spener admired the vitality of his group's faith and decided to foster a similar fervor in German Lutheranism.[45]

In 1666 Spener was made senior minister of Frankfurt. It was here he began small group devotions and published *Pia Desideria*, the handbook of Pietism. In 1686 he became chaplain to the court at Dresden, where he made a disciple of August Hermann Francke. The two men promoted the ideals of the movement throughout Germany: a stress on personal piety, the formation of small groups to promote piety, an emphasis on personal reading of the Bible, and a stress on ministry of the laity. "All of this was placed within an epistemological context in which personal experience was more important than communal faith, and sometimes even more important than historical revelation."[46]

Because of opposition from traditional Lutheranism, the Pietists founded the University of Halle. Francke turned it into an institution for the formation of Pietist leaders. Soon they were to be found throughout Germany and even overseas, as the movement gained strength and expanded (for both Spener and Francke believed that the Great Commission was incumbent upon all Christians).

Pietist Ecclesiology. The Pietists rejected the traditional Lutheran ecclesiology of their day, which claimed that because the church possessed pure doctrine it was therefore infallible. Spener saw such a view as "Romanism," and proclaimed that God's judgment falls even upon the church.[47]

In regard to the visible and invisible church, Spener and Francke considered themselves to be of the same mind as Luther. They believed that the invisible church is composed of all true children of God. The visible (Lutheran) church is a portion of the invisible church which teaches true theology and properly administers the sacraments. But as they began to use certain marks to identify true Christians, the Pietists began to see the invisible church as the true church within Lutheranism, and then as something which went beyond a particular denomination. Not surprisingly (although they denied the charge), the Pietists were accused of the Anabaptist practice of identifying the true invisible church with a separate visible community.[48]

The Sacraments. When it came to the sacraments, Spener tried to walk a middle road: "As in all things, two extremes are possible. It is a deviation to place your trust outwardly in the mere custom of the sacrament and be concerned little with the inward. It is also a deviation when one chooses to despise and set aside the outward because of the inward."[49]

In their teaching on baptism, Spener and Francke were orthodox. They held to pedobaptism and defended it with all the traditional arguments, seeing it as the true path of regeneration and the renewal of the Holy Spirit. And yet there were deviations from tradition. The Pietists rejected any aspect of infant baptism which suggested *opus operatum*. Nor would Spener accept the damnation of unbaptized infants. He also betrayed an Arminian bent in regard to salvation: unless one were obedient to Christ following one's baptism, one stood in danger of losing the new birth.[50]

In regard to the Lord's Supper, the Pietists again purported to be traditionally Lutheran. Spener emphasized that in the Supper we partake of the true natural body of Christ. At the same time, he made no attempt to define the nature of His real bodily presence. He asserted that, while the mature believer certainly remembers and proclaims the death of Christ, the sacrament is more than merely a memorial; for Christ instituted it to participate in it by His presence in the elements. The Supper was instituted for all people, regardless of their worthiness; for Christ gave His life and shed His blood for all.[51]

View of the Clergy. The Pietists contended that no reformation of the church could be successful apart from a reformation of the clergy. Spener believed the greatest danger to the church

149

did not come from the advocates of false religions but from corrupt leadership within its own membership. He declared, "There is no doubt in my mind that we would soon have a completely transformed church if we teachers, or at least a majority of us, were able without embarrassment to call on our congregations as Paul did in 1 Cor. 11:1: 'Be imitators of me as I am of Christ.' "[52]

With a view to transforming the clergy, the Pietists suggested a program which included personal relationships with parishioners, pastoral visitation, Bible classes, and prayer meetings. The pastor must be a shepherd, not just a functionary. His leadership should arise, not out of coercion, but by an exemplary life of purity and holiness. He should preach simply and straightforwardly.[53] This program was the path to the renewal of the clergy and, in turn, of the church.

Pietistic Polity. Lutheranism in Spener's time was set in three inflexible classes — the princely, the priestly, and the lay. Each had its own clearly defined sphere of practice. Spener had no use for social distinctions. In his meetings, servants sat with nobles.[54]

While he was essentially egalitarian in his religious program, Spener nonetheless believed that a leadership structure was vital. His was a presbyterial view. The members of a church should be responsible for its affairs. They should select their own pastor. Both laity and pastors should participate in synods. Elders and pastors together should be involved in church discipline.[55]

One might suppose that such directions might encourage some toward a greater emphasis on the individual. And in some Pietist circles such an emphasis took place. But Spener and Francke deplored such an attitude, stressing the nature of the church as community.[56]

Conclusions. Pietism exerted a substantial influence not only on German Lutheranism, but on world Protestantism. Its effects are still evident.

Pietism fostered many other movements. One of these was Moravianism. Its father was Count Nikolaus von Zinzendorf (1700–1760), a godson of Spener and a student of Francke. In

1727 he created a Christian community, Herrnhut, which sent missionaries worldwide. Another was Methodism. John Wesley received much of his instruction and example from Moravian missionaries. One may say that the Great Awakening was a wave of Pietism. In our own time, such things as sanctification, house churches, and Christian communes are all a legacy of Pietism.

Methodism

Just as many in Germany had reacted against the coldness and corruption of traditional Lutheranism, so many in England found traditional religion in that country equally lacking. Skevington Wood aptly sums up the situation.

> Permissiveness was the order of the day. The orthodox theologians scored an intellectual victory in the fight against Deism. It was sadly ironical that, although the central doctrine of Christianity had been defended, the new life in Christ they were intended to encourage was no longer in evidence. A new dynamic was needed.[57]

Many English Christians attempted to foster renewal by imitating Pietist stratagems. One of the most popular of these was the small group, or religious society, which was intended to complement church worship services. When John Wesley (1703–1791) and his brother Charles (1707–1788) were students at Oxford University, they belonged to such a group, which was first known as "the holy club" and later as "Methodists."[58]

John Wesley, who shortly assumed the leadership of the group, became an Anglican deacon in 1725, and a priest in 1728. He served as a missionary to the colony of Georgia in North America, but soon realized his unsuitability for the task. Returning to Britain, he came under the influence of the Moravians, who guided him on his spiritual formation. On May 24, 1738, his Aldersgate experience took place.

While Wesley appreciated Moravian piety, he objected to their mystical bent. He was especially set against their disdain for the established church. Wesley was a keen Anglican and did not intend for his Methodist societies to be in opposition to the

151

established church. But although he affirmed the *Book of Common Prayer*, his understanding of ecclesiology differed from that of his church.

In opposition to Anglican polity, Wesley ordained leaders for his movement, particularly ministers for his societies in the American colonies. His rationale for so doing was that in the New Testament church presbyters and bishops were one and the same. He had been ordained a presbyter, and therefore he could ordain others to that same function.[59] Indeed, in ordaining Dr. Coke to the position of "Superintendent of the Societies in America," he effectively created a new denomination.[60]

Schleiermacher

Friedrich Daniel Ernst Schleiermacher (1768–1834) may be regarded as the father of modern theology. The son of a Reformed army chaplain who had joined the Moravians, he was influenced by both rationalism and romanticism in his theological formation. In 1794, he was ordained a Reformed pastor.

In 1799, Schleiermacher published *On Religion: Speeches to Its Cultured Despisers*. It was designed to reassert the position religion had lost in the world, and to demonstrate that it was still the province of cultured, well-rounded human beings.[61] In 1821 and 1822, he published *The Christian Faith*, undoubtedly the most influential theological work of the nineteenth century. It was a systematic theology of Schleiermacher's own time. Both books have much to say about the church, but the latter particularly emphasizes ecclesiology.

On the Church. Schleiermacher described the church as "a society which originates only through free human action and which can only through such action continue to exist,"[62] and a "communion or association relating to religion or piety."[63] Its members are those who have perceived that they need redemption and that Christ is the only One who can achieve their redemption. "No one can wish to belong to the Christian Church on any other ground."[64]

In response to the question as to whether Christ ever intended to found a church, Schleiermacher responded that "He could not have exercised any activity whatever of an attractive and therefore redemptive kind, without such a fellowship arising."[65] Thus, when and how Christ actually did found the church is irrelevant. But Schleiermacher was quite willing to concede that, "as long as Christ's personal activity lasted, the Church remained unconstituted [and] merely latent. . . ."[66]

Schleiermacher rejected the commonly held distinction between the visible and invisible church. No grounds existed to distinguish a community of the regenerate who have a genuine standing within the realm of sanctification, and those who profess outwardly to be members of the church, but who are, in fact, unregenerate.[67] But he believed that such a dichotomy should not exist. Indeed, "even if it were possible to keep all the non-regenerate outside the Church, the whole body of the regenerate would only constitute the visible Church in our sense of the term."[68]

Schleiermacher recognized that because even believers possess a worldly element, the visible church always contains some germs of division. But even in spite of division, each portion of the visible church is nonetheless a part of the invisible; for in it Christ is confessed and the Spirit is at work.[69] He also recognized that, because of sin, in every expression of truth there is a measure of error, and so no presentation of Christianity issuing from the visible church is the pure, unvarnished truth. But, he countered, the influence of error within the church "must diminish in proportion as the Holy Spirit takes possession of the organism of thought."[70] Schleiermacher believed that the Holy Spirit can counter all ills and evils, so that the visible and invisible church may become one.

On Baptism. Schleiermacher was emphatic that the admission of a person into the Christian fellowship and that person's regeneration must be one and the same event. It was Christ Himself who declared baptism to be the act of reception into the church. Thus, every such reception is an act by Christ Himself when it is performed in the manner He commanded. The church can neither abandon this model of reception through baptism nor can it doubt that when it carries out Christ's command, He will extend His promised salvation to the one who is received into the church.[71] Consequently, it behooves the church to retain baptism in the form received from Christ.

Such baptism must also occur as it did at Pentecost. Baptism is intended to be evoked by the Holy Spirit. "Without the action of the Spirit, baptism with water is certainly no more than an external rite which Christ Himself declares to be insufficient."[72] Thus, the baptismal candidate's faith in Christ must be a precondition, so that the action is truly what it is supposed to be.

Although Schleiermacher confessed that there was no biblical support for infant baptism (a reasonable conclusion when personal faith is required as a precondition), he nonetheless supported it. He did so in the belief that, in the case of children of believing parents, one may count upon their confessing their faith at a future point. It is therefore the responsibility of the church to bring them into an explicit affinity to the Word of God, and to keep them there until faith is kindled.[73]

Again, he acknowledged that one should not make the mistake of equating such a baptism with that originally instituted by Christ, in which one makes a personal profession of faith in Christ. "Yet this defect does not render the act invalid, as though it were positively wrong; and the Anabaptist assertion that, in the case of persons baptized so, baptism must be repeated, has rightly been felt to give offence." The baptism is valid, but its fitting power is deferred until the one baptized has actually become a believer.[74]

Nor did Schleiermacher hold that infant baptism conferred any magical protection upon its recipients. There is no difference between those children who, although baptized, have not renewed their baptismal covenant, and those who die without any baptism at all. He was quite prepared to fellowship with the Baptists, "if only they will not pronounce our infant baptism absolutely invalid, even when supplemented by confirmation."[75]

The Lord's Supper. While baptism admits one into the living fellowship of Christ, the Lord's Supper nourishes and strengthens this fellowship. It is a twofold affair: the strengthening of the relationship with Christ and with one another.[76]

Schleiermacher's view of the Lord's Supper was not as focused as that of theologians in preceding generations. When Christ spoke of the need for eating His flesh and drinking His blood, he declared, He had in mind no specific act. "He wished rather to indicate in how profound a sense He Himself must become our being and well-being.'"[77] It was another way of saying that we must be related to Him as the branch is to the vine.

Schleiermacher confessed, however, that while spiritual participation in the flesh of Christ can occur more generally in an assortment of fashions, the Lord's Supper is unique. The same result, namely, union with Christ, is tied to this definite action, which has been blessed and consecrated by Christ's own words.[78]

What is the true meaning of the words of the institution of the Supper? The interpretation of Christ's words is essential to the spiritual results, observed Schleiermacher. He saw little difference between transubstantiation and consubstantiation, except that Rome insists on the body and blood of Christ being present after the consecration regardless of context or the spiritual state of the recipients, while Luther would never have affirmed the physical presence of Christ apart from the eucharistic rite. The Zwinglians, on the other hand, declare that Christ commanded merely spiritual participation through the bread and the cup, and the Calvinists assert that Christ enjoined not only spiritual participation, but a real presence of His flesh and blood unavailable in any other context.

> Beyond all question this [last] view is the clearest and the easiest to grasp, for it sets up an exact analogy between the Lord's Supper and baptism, and leaves the real presence of body and blood (which it is scarcely possible to describe) altogether out of account, so that by sacramental participation it can only mean the conjunction of spiritual participation with bodily participation as defined above.[79]

The Calvinistic view, Schleiermacher felt, was an ideal mediating view between the concept of mere symbolism and those of physical presence.

What benefit may be derived from the Lord's Supper? For Schleiermacher, it was the substantiation of our friendship with Christ, as well as the confirming of believers in their union with one other.[80] In the Supper the believer experiences anew the forgiveness of sins, along with a heightening of the powers effecting sanctification. The Supper calls one afresh to the service of Jesus Christ and is accompanied by a renewed impulse to develop one's gifts.[81]

Conclusions. Schleiermacher was much broader and more flexible in his ecclesiological outlook than most of his contemporary coreligionists. While his views were not unlike those of the Lutherans and the Reformed, he went beyond them in conceding that their doctrine was not always based on Scripture or fully faithful to Christ's design. He also saw a picture of Christianity which transcended narrow denominationalism, and seemed to seek a mediating position which could be accepted by many viewpoints. It was this openness which invited the trek toward increasing liberalism.

SUMMARY

The church entered the scientific era sadly divided, with its component parts in friction with each other. The Greek Church, under the heel of Islam in many sectors, fell prey to the depredations of Rome, which attempted to force or coerce Orthodox bishops to acknowledge the supremacy of the pope and which was successful in leading some into the Roman fold. Protestants made efforts to evangelize the Orthodox clergy, but were pacific and largely unsuccessful in their approach. Moreover, some Orthodox theologians trained in the West in Roman Catholic and Reformed seminaries, and were leading the Eastern church away from its traditional theological position. It was not until the nineteenth century that—thanks to a revitalized Russian Orthodoxy—the Greek church returned to its traditional moorings.

The Roman Catholic Church, weakened by the Protestant Reformation, regrouped somewhat under the Council of Trent (the Catholic Reformation), only to find itself once more under attack from European nationalists. The Gallicans, as they were known, wanted the church to be subject to the control of the local (national) bishops or monarch. They were opposed by clergy who held the pope to be supreme over all the church. The latter group (Ultramontanes) won out in the nineteenth century, but it was largely because the Roman Church had lost much of its relevance to society.

Protestantism entered the scientific era in a divided state. Attacks from changing philosophies had led to a widespread dilution of faith (and hence, in many cases, corruption) among the clergy, particularly in the established churches. Several new religious groups sought to counter this slide by evoking a more emotional or mystical context for faith. The Quakers emphasized an experience of inner spiritual light (namely, the Holy Spirit) upon which one could rely for guidance in one's life. The Pietists, disillusioned with traditional Lutheranism in Germany, sought a return to the intimacy of small groups with a stress on Bible study, prayer, and holy living. The Wesleyans, in an effort to counteract a spiritual decline in England, took a similar direction. Schleiermacher sought a "religion of the heart" which was nonetheless very rational in its philosophy. The result was that, by the end of the nineteenth century, Protestantism was more divided than it had ever been, with rational and mystical elements, emotional and cognitive styles, traditional and radical groups, all still mostly at odds with each other.

CHAPTER FIVE

The Church in the Twentieth Century

As the nineteenth century melded with the twentieth, liberal theology was in ascendancy. Liberal theologians were absolutely convinced that, with the aid of education and technology, they would be able to usher in the millennial age. But they were not without their detractors, many of whom were the disillusioned of their own movement. And within two decades of the opening of the new century, a world war had occurred which sent liberalism reeling; within another two decades the movement was spent as a theological force.

NEO-ORTHODOXY

The neo-orthodox movement was born during the latter years of World War I when Karl Barth, then a young pastor in Switzerland, discovered that his liberal theological education had ill-equipped him for ministry in such troubled times and turned to the Bible for direction. Neo-orthodoxy was a road back toward orthodox theology (although it arrived at a somewhat different conclusion).[1] Early heroes of the movement included Barth, Emil Brunner, and Reinhold Niebuhr. Of these three, Brunner had most to say about the church.

Emil Brunner

Emil Brunner (1889–1966) may be viewed as a cofounder of neo-orthodox theology. Born in Switzerland, he studied at

Zurich, Berlin, and Union Seminary in New York. In 1924 he
became a professor of theology at Zurich. Brunner wrote numerous articles and books, and was well-accepted in English-
speaking theological circles, who saw neo-orthodoxy primarily
through his eyes.

The Importance of the Ecclesia. Brunner castigated Calvin's
conception of the church. The latter regarded the church simply as the *ecclesia invisibilis,* and saw the visible church merely
as an external means of salvation. Brunner observed that "the
idea of the invisible church is foreign to the New Testament,
while the interpretation of the real visible church as a merely
external means of salvation is not only foreign to it but completely impossible."[2]

The New Testament *ecclesia* is not a mere means to an end
but rather the body of Jesus Christ, an end in itself. Indeed,
declared Brunner, it is the final saving miracle in the process of
revelation; for the pouring out of the Holy Spirit and the existence of the *ecclesia* are so keenly coupled that they may well
be uniquely associated. He went even further to insist that the
Holy Spirit is in the world as the Spirit given to the community.
"Therefore the community as bearer of the Word and Spirit of
Christ precedes the individual believer. One does not first believe and then join the fellowship: but one becomes a believer
just because one shares in the gift vouchsafed to the fellowship."[3]

Unlike Schleiermacher, who saw the church as a voluntary
human society, Brunner perceived it as flowing from communion with Christ. It is the completion of the revelation of the
triune God, a "quite unique meeting of the horizontal and the
vertical."[4] To be in Christ through faith and to be a part of the
ecclesia are one and the same thing. As a consequence,
Brunner defines the *ecclesia* as

> the community of those who have been reconciled and draw
> their life from the reconciliation. It is nothing other than [per-
> sons] in fellowship, in fellowship with God and in fellowship
> with each other. . . . The New Testament Ekklesia is the true,
> visible brotherhood of the reconciled, even if there may have
> been in it some who only seemed to belong to it.[5]

Brunner took great care to differentiate between the *ecclesia* and the church as two totally separate entities. The former is a pure communion of persons, while the latter is an institution. The *ecclesia* is not institutional in any respect. Thus, it is deceptive to identify any particular one of the historically developed churches, all of which are conspicuously institutional, with the authentic Christian fellowship.[6]

The *ecclesia* transcends the church. It is God's elect people of all time. It is "at the same time spiritual and invisible (intelligible to faith alone) and corporeal (recognizable and visible to all)."[7] It is the *ecclesia*—not the church—which is one and which will endure forever. It has become distressingly obvious that the multiplicity of the churches calls into question the essential unity of the *ecclesia*. But whether this basic oneness of the Christ-community demands expression in a single church is exceedingly dubious. One thing, however, which may be counted on is that God will—with or without the churches—create a genuine *ecclesia* or communion of true brothers and sisters.[8]

On the Sacraments. Brunner did not follow the traditional view of the sacraments as means of grace. Indeed, he referred to them as "so-called sacraments," and explained, "I say 'so-called' because this concept is really not a biblical but a heathen one."[9]

In referring to baptism, he acknowledged the great confusion in Christendom because of the variety of teachings and methods, and asserted that one must return to the Pauline doctrine of baptism if one would know the truth: "it is above all a doctrine about the repentance which is necessarily bound up with faith, about dying with Christ. . . . This dying was also sensibly and symbolically represented by the visible act of submersion."[10] But baptism is more than just dying with Christ; it is also a rising to newness of life.

In baptism one is incorporated into the body of Christ and included in the believers' fellowship. The rite is indicative of one's having become a participant in Christ's sacrifice by surrendering oneself as a sacrifice to Christ. Brunner argued:

The once-for-allness of baptism was in a special manner the sign of the once-for-allness of the sacrifice of Christ, and the irrevocability of the decision for Christ. The [person] who was baptized had thereby surrendered his right to himself, and was henceforth one who belonged to Christ, a member of His Body, and thereby a fellow member with all other members.[11]

Given such sentiments, it is peculiar that Brunner later attempted to make a case for infant baptism by defining baptism as "the event which points to the grace and prevenience of Him Who is the foundation of the Church." Consequently, "Infant Baptism could be acknowledged and rightly administered, as the sign that points to Him, His grace which precedes all preaching and all faith."[12] Brunner argued that because no one knows when the Holy Spirit begins His work in an individual, believers might not be aware of His work in the lives of those who cannot actively participate in the community of faith.[13]

Nor did Brunner see the Lord's Supper as a sacrament. "It is the great miracle of the grace of God, but not the prodigy of the transubstantiation of the elements."[14] Rather, it is an act of fellowship repeated on a regular basis because of Christ's command to do so. Its purpose is to build up His people as a fellowship with Him and with one another. On the night of the original Supper, not only was the ordinance instituted but also the New Covenant itself. That first Lord's Supper became the founding of the "Ekklēsia" as the community of those who were joined to God and to one another by the death and resurrection of the Lord.[15]

The celebration of the body of Christ is dual in purpose. It commemorates the literal body of Christ broken on Calvary. But it also is the feast of the institution of the *ecclesia*, the single fellowship of those who belong to Christ. It binds in a visible manner all believers into a genuine unity.[16]

Because of his elevation of the unity of the body of Christ, Brunner decried an overemphasis on individualism, arguing that the self-avowal of the individual as individual, shatters community. At the same time, the opposite extreme of collectivism oppresses the individual and subjects one to a tragic and hurtful stereotyped routine.[17]

Ministry in the Church. Every member of the *ecclesia* has a responsibility to minister. Scripture knows nothing of a distinction between those members who are active and those who are passive, between those who minister and those who do not. But there is a pneumatic order of ministry functions. "The *diakoniai* . . . should be conceived on the analogy of the organs with their specific functions which inhere in a living body."[18] It is the Spirit who decides the distinction of the functions.

The present-day church possesses a juridical organization rather than a pneumatic ordering. Brunner ascribed such a legal administration as "a compensatory measure which it becomes necessary to adopt in times and places where the plenitude of the Spirit is lacking. Canon law is a substitute for the Spirit."[19]

Conclusions. Brunner was not a typical traditional Reformed theologian. He did not want to identify the church with what Christ had in mind. The church is more legalistic, institutional, and complex than what Christ intended. Rather, Christ had desired a simple fellowship of brothers and sisters flowing out of the abundance of His Spirit.

Sacraments are a part of the church, not the *ecclesia*. Scripture knows nothing of baptism and the Lord's Supper as conduits of salvation. Rather, they are rites which represent one's inclusion in the body of believers and one's continuing solidarity in loving fellowship with other believers and with Christ.

Brunner insisted that Scripture is emphatic on the role of all believers in ministry. All are players; none are spectators. There are, however, different ministry functions. These distinctions are determined by the Holy Spirit.

PENTECOSTALISM

Pentecostalism may be said to have originated with the Azusa Street revival of 1906 in Los Angeles. But should the term be limited only to traditional Pentecostal denominations such as the Assemblies of God, the Foursquare Gospel Church, or the Pentecostal Assemblies of Canada? Or should charismatic and Vineyard churches bear the same label? There is considerable controversy over these questions. Perhaps it is best to follow a conservative line and refer to Pentecostalism (in the traditional sense) and Neo-Pentecostalism (the later, charismatic, sector).

The Pentecostals

The Azusa Street revival gave the impetus for the formation of most of the major Pentecostal denominations. Clergy who were "baptized in the Spirit" returned home to bring their experience to their churches. Churches which were "Spirit-filled" banded together to form Pentecostal denominations.[20] These denominations followed an ecclesiology which in many ways resembled that of their former denominations, but with important differences.

The Church. Traditional Pentecostalism implies a particular, twofold model of the church: "The church is the community of those who are saved; it is a group of people who are individually empowered by the Holy Spirit for service within the community and in external witness; and it is a commissioned community."[21] The first and last emphases are not unlike a number of other denominations, but the second is unique. And yet, it qualifies the other two in a way which—like the Radical Reformation—demonstrates the desire of Pentecostals to regain the nature and work of the church displayed by the New Testament community of believers and its doctrine.[22]

In their early days, most Pentecostals held other denominations (i.e., non-Pentecostals) to be false churches. Other groups were "Babylon"; Pentecostals called upon genuine believers to "leave the whore church of Babylon. The knell of the previous system of Christianity has been sounded and thousands are following the Lamb out of the camp, bearing his shame."[23] As time has gone along, however, the attitudes of Pentecostals toward other churches—especially evangelical churches—has softened and has been replaced by a cooperative spirit. David J. DuPlessis, a white South African Pentecostal leader, was an observer at Vatican II who did much to reconcile Protestants and Roman Catholics.[24]

The Ministry. Even though Pentecostalism sees itself as a movement of the Holy Spirit, it realizes nonetheless that some persons have received gifts that set them apart from the bulk of believers. Their ministry may be for a particular time in a particular context (such as a person who prophesies in a worship service) or it may be a long-term, full-time vocation (such as pastor, evangelist or missionary). But all ministries must flow out of the work of the Holy Spirit.

> What is peculiar to the Pentecostal notion of the church, and what relativizes the contributions so that in the end there is a priesthood of all believers, is a two-fold emphasis: (i) *every* Spirit-filled believer has a contribution to make; and (ii) every contribution is only valid insofar as it can be traced back to the dynamic activity of God.[25]

Pentecostals make no attempt to deny the existence of ministry "offices," when they are descriptive of the individual's ministry. However, any office is valid only insofar as the Holy Spirit has chosen to work that way. It is "in the Spirit" which validates one's office rather than education or credentials. Nor does the office matter; for example, a church treasurer is expected to be filled with the Spirit as much as a pastor. In both cases the source, aptitude, and framework of the ministry must be demonstrably God-conferred.[26]

Baptism and the Lord's Supper. The majority of Pentecostals hold a Baptist view of baptism. They see it as

> an outward sign, seal or expression of an inward death, burial and resurrection, signifying the believer's identification with Christ, in that he has been planted in the likeness of His death, raised by the might of His power to walk in newness of life, yielding his members as instruments of righteousness unto God as those that are alive from the dead.[27]

While some Pentecostals baptize by sprinkling, most Pentecostals see sprinkling as unbiblical and practice immersion instead. Likewise, Pentecostal churches generally reject infant baptism as unbiblical, insisting that "baptism is for believers only."[28] There are even a few monists who baptize in the name of "Jesus only," but Trinitarian Pentecostals generally do not fellowship with them.

The Lord's Supper, which is seen in Zwinglian terms as a simple memorial of Christ's death, is the centerpiece of Pentecostal worship. It represents participation in the divine nature of Christ (2 Peter 1:4), a commemoration of His Passion (1 Cor. 11:26); and a revelation of His Parousia.[29]

Neo-Pentecostalism

The charismatic, or neo-pentecostal movement, is considered to have begun on Passion Sunday in 1960, when Dennis Bennett, an Episcopalian rector in Van Nuys, California, told his congregation how he had been "baptized in the Spirit."[30] From that point, neo-pentecostalism cut across all the mainline denominations. Even Roman Catholicism was susceptible to the "charismatic renewal." Some of those involved broke away from their churches to found separate, independent charismatic churches. Others stayed within their denominational context. Both groups, however, hold views of the church which differ from the traditional.

The strong emphasis of the charismatic renewal is on the church as the body of Christ. James Jones points out that "the reason God wants people filled with His Spirit, the reason He wants His church built up as the full body of Christ, is because He wants us to share in His great purpose" that all creation should be filled with His presence, and that He might be all in all to everyone. The purpose of the Holy Spirit is to unite believers into "the full body of Christ." The Holy Spirit belongs essentially to the fellowship and not to the individual; He is the individual's solely to the degree that the individual in turn belongs to the faith-community. Both the spiritual gifts and the fruit of the Spirit are intended to contribute to the unity of the body. The spiritual gifts contribute to the common good by building up the church; and the fruit of the Spirit transforms believers into the people who can live in fellowship with their brothers and sisters.[31]

Denominational Neo-pentecostalism. Those charismatics who stuck with their original denominations declared the outbreak of the Holy Spirit's power in their midst to be for the renewal of their church. Michael Harper stated the case well in his 1964 book *Prophecy*: "It is the renewal of the Church that God is principly [sic] concerned about—not that of the gifts. The gifts are for the building up of the Church — in order that it may become once more a powerful and influential force in the world. It is recovery of New Testament Church life that is our greatest need today." Neo-pentecostals who stay in mainline denominations attempt to renew the New Testament foundations of the established churches.[32]

Restorationist Neo-pentecostalism. Many of those charismatics who left their original denominations embraced a Brethren view of the church. They rejected all ideas of "special ministry offices" (e.g., professional clergy) and "special membership" (i.e., in a particular denomination), in favor of a local independent church, which is self-sufficient, self-supporting, and self-edifying. Communion between these churches is not a matter of external authority but of voluntary cooperation.[33]

Other charismatics have embraced the house church movement. Some have followed the Brethren model of independence, with each small group claiming autonomy. Others have utilized the fivefold ministries of Ephesians 4:11-12; in this model, they find an apostle (or apostles) overseeing a group of fellowships, and so they have connected with other house church communities.[34]

The Lord's Supper. The Lord's Supper is a vital part of the unity of the body of Christ. The term "body of Christ" in the Eucharist describes both the broken body of the Lord symbolized by the broken loaf, and the community of individuals united in common purpose, as symbolized by the pieces of bread which are a part of the single loaf. "The charismatic *koinonia* provides a communal context in which the sacramental *koinonia* can be lived to the fullest."[35]

Many charismatics who remain in mainline denominations have found that their renewal experience has led them to a much deeper appreciation of the Eucharist. By the ministry of the Holy Spirit within, they become poignantly aware of Christ's sacrifice as they share in the Lord's Supper.

Conclusions. Pentecostals and charismatics are one in their desire to regain the state of the New Testament church. They long for a return to Christian communities energized and empowered by the Holy Spirit. Both groups regard the Lord's Supper as the keystone of worship, symbolizing, as it does, both Christ's sacrifice and the oneness of the body.

From the oneness of the community flows the doctrine of the priesthood of all believers. Every believer is called to ministry by the gifting of the Holy Spirit. As believers are obedient to the call, they build up the body of Christ and accomplish God's purposes for the world.

EVANGELICALISM

Evangelicalism became a force in North America with the founding of the National Association of Evangelicals in 1943. Its founders were well-educated fundamentalists who had tired of fundamentalist isolationism and infighting. They believed that more could be accomplished by dialogue with liberals and non-believers than by shunning them. Their doctrinal views had not changed; they had simply adopted a more flexible attitude toward others.[36]

Since that time, evangelicals have grown and expanded until they have become the main group of conservative Christians in North America. At the same time, they have endeavored to remain on the cutting edge of theological thinking. We may see some of that thinking reflected in the ecclesiology of some of the major evangelical minds of the last quarter century or so.

Millard Erickson

Millard J. Erickson, formerly dean and professor of theology at Bethel Theological Seminary in Minneapolis-Saint Paul, and then professor of theology at Southwestern Baptist Seminary in Fort Worth, is a noted theologian who has written many books and articles and is reckoned to be a foremost spokesman for evangelical theology. His *Christian Theology* is a classic text in evangelical seminaries.

The Nature of the Church. Unlike other foundational doctrines, asserts Erickson, little attention has been focused on the theology of the church, perhaps because most believers simply take the church for granted. Thus, a theology of the church has been

167

neglected, while much work has been done on the relation of the church to rapid social change, to secular society, and so on. Unfortunately, Erickson notes,

> at the present time the focus of most of this literature is not the church itself, but the other entities. It is time to reverse this trend, for if we do not have a clear understanding of the nature of the church, we cannot have a clear understanding of its relationship to these other areas.[37]

Erickson perceives the church to be a divinely established institution, whose essence must be determined by Scripture. Its purpose is to carry out God's will through the power of His Holy Spirit. It is a fellowship of regenerate persons who model themselves on Jesus Christ. These persons, though regenerate, are nonetheless imperfect. Thus, while the church is divinely created, it will not attain a state of perfect sanctification until Christ returns.[38]

The Role of the Church. The church was not created to be an end to itself, but to perpetuate Christ's ministry to the world. Erickson sees the function of the church as fourfold. The first function is evangelism, an imperative of the Great Commission: the church exists to make disciples of all peoples. Its second function is to edify believers through fellowship, teaching, and the many gifts of the Holy Spirit. The third function is worship, the praise and exaltation of God. Worship should always precede evangelism and edification. The last function of the church is to demonstrate a social concern for believers and nonbelievers alike. It must fight oppression and injustice, regardless of the personal cost or inconvenience.[39]

Foundational to the church's activities, Erickson avers, is the Gospel. Nothing is more important than the proclamation of the "good news." Erickson argues that

> we must not think of the gospel as merely a recital of theological truths and historical events. Rather, it relates these truths and events to the situation of every individual believer. . . . We will all be evaluated on the basis of our personal attitude toward and response to the gospel.[40]

In carrying out the ministry of its Lord, the church must manifest His character and spirit. Two of these attributes are crucial to ministry in our ever-changing society, namely, a servant attitude and adaptability. Willingness to serve signifies that the church will not try to control society for its own ends, although it must also be adaptable in accommodating its procedures and strategies to its varying context. If the church holds a sense of mission like that of its Lord, it will discover ways to reach out to people in all places and all situations.[41]

The Ordinances. Erickson's view of the ordinances betrays his Baptist roots. He rejects a sacramental notion of baptism, noting that "unlike repentance and conversion, baptism is not indispensable to salvation. It seems, rather, that baptism may be an expression or a consequence of conversion."[42] Baptism graphically symbolizes one's commitment to Christ, representing the believer's death and resurrection with Christ.

The case for infant baptism, according to Erickson, is based on the notion of it as analogous to the Old Testament rite of circumcision as an entry into the covenant. Because it rests on the premise of baptism as a means of saving grace, he rejects it. "The meaning of baptism requires us to hold to the position of believer's baptism, as does the fact that the New Testament nowhere offers a clear case of an individual's being baptized before exercising faith."[43]

The Lord's Supper, states Erickson, may be seen "as a rite which Christ himself established for the church to practice as a commemoration of his death."[44] He would argue that participation in the Lord's Supper confers a spiritual benefit on the believer. But there are different views of what that benefit might be. Erickson believes that the benefit of the Supper is that one is brought close to Christ, and so comes to know and love Him more intimately.[45]

Conclusions. Erickson holds that the church is a divinely ordained institution, created to achieve God's will through the power of the Holy Spirit. It does this in a fourfold manner: through evangelism, fellowship, worship, and social concern. It effects these with a servant attitude and in a spirit of adaptability to an ever-changing world.

Erickson denies that baptism is a means of grace, necessary to salvation. Nor is infant baptism legitimate. Baptism's significance as commitment to Christ requires believer's baptism.

The Lord's Supper may be seen as a sacrament to the extent that it confers a benefit upon the believing participant. Erickson sees that benefit as a deeper, more loving relationship with the risen Lord.

Donald Bloesch

Donald Bloesch, professor emeritus of systematic theology at Dubuque Theological Seminary in Iowa, has been a leading evangelical thinker for some years. His magnum opus is *Essentials of Evangelical Theology*, a two-volume systematic theology designed "to reconceive evangelicalism so that it can become an effective force for renewal in the church."[46]

The Church. Bloesch is concerned that the secular humanism of contemporary society has pervaded the church. He asserts that

> the enemy is not simply collectivism or nationalism or a new Baalism but a secular or worldly Christianity which has accepted at least in part the values and goals of the surrounding society. When secular values however praiseworthy are uncritically adopted by the church as authentically or even potentially Christian, the tension between the transcendent Word of God and human culture is lost sight of, and the result is a compromised version of the faith.[47]

Consequently, he proposes that the great need of the time is a confessing church which will go into the world bearing witness to its faith in Christ Jesus. Such a church must invade the secular realm with the good news of redemption.[48]

Bloesch calls upon the church to change the world. Not only are its members called to bring light (i.e., God's Word) to a dark world, but also to be light. They are not called to be honey, but salt. Their commission is not to sugarcoat the distress of life, but to bare this woundedness to the light of Calvary; for there can be no genuine recuperation without suffering. The church's task is to preserve society from decay and death, functioning like "white corpuscles that take out the infection in society."[49]

We must realize that Christians, as the elect of God, are in this world as sheep among wolves. As sheep, believers should not resist in the face of evil. Bloesch reminds us that the precept of non-retaliation is not legislation for secular society—it is the decree of the kingdom of God.[50]

A Christian style of life is as important to one's witness as the proclamation of the Gospel. Both words and deeds are vital. The church's commission is not to withdraw from the world but to try to change it.[51] Bloesch bluntly states his view of the church's mission in our day: "It is indeed imperative that we recover the evangelistic zeal and urgency of the first century church and carry the flag of the Gospel into the pagan world of our time, seeking to bring all peoples into submission to the one Lord and Savior, Jesus Christ."[52]

The Unity of the Church. Bloesch finds the lack of unity in the church a scandal of major proportions. But even more outrageous is the disunity that infests evangelicalism, the very group within the broader church that emphasizes faithfulness to the Gospel and to the Scriptures. It is obvious that the evangelical church has lost much credibility on the mission field because of infighting between mission boards and churches. Intra-Christian warfare has prevented the church from proclaiming the Gospel of Christ with a united voice.[53]

What kind of unity should be sought? Unity, contends Bloesch, will never be attained "until there is an awakening to the reality of the oneness and catholicity of the church."[54] Such an awakening can come only in God's good time through an outpouring of His Holy Spirit. Believers can nevertheless pray and seek for this. They can ready the way, but unity must ultimately come as a gift from the Spirit of God.[55]

The Sacrament of Preaching. Bloesch regards the preaching of the Gospel as the third sacrament of the church; for it is the means of salvation to the lost (John 5:24). Not only our Savior, but the apostles as well, taught that "the preaching of the Gospel is the divinely-appointed means by which people come to salvation."[56]

171

Bloesch contends that in its preaching the church must proclaim all of God's Word (John 20:27): not only the Gospel but also God's Law, not only salvation but also sin, not only heaven but also hell. He scorns those neo-Protestants and neo-Catholics who claim that the purpose of preaching is not to convict of sin but to inform people of God's forgiveness and acceptance. Such a view is an insidious universalism. Although God gives grace of His own accord independently of one's own merit, once His grace takes hold of people they will begin to change. God accepts people as they are, but those who remain as they are God has not accepted. As God's Word declares, "if we do not earnestly pursue his righteousness, he will spew us out of his mouth (Rev. 3:16)."[57]

True biblical preaching, rather than modern cultural preaching, is badly needed, argues Bloesch. Genuine biblical preaching will convict people of sin and lead them toward repentance. A fellowship of love *(koinonia)* and the willingness to enter into costly discipleship will be created. Still another aspect will be the desire to evangelize others and bring them to Christ. But sound biblical preaching will also arouse opposition; for it not only upsets sinners who would rather be complacent in their sin, but it also offends the spiritual powers of darkness which it exposes and deposes.[58]

The Priesthood of Believers. Because of faith in Christ as both Mediator and Elder Brother, believers share in His priestly role of offering spiritual sacrifices to God. They also share His kingly rule. And so the church is set as a kingdom of priests who receive power to preach, sacrifice, and intercede for the world. "All its members have been anointed by the Spirit to be witnesses and ambassadors of Christ."[59]

Necessary to a proper understanding of the doctrine of the priesthood of believers, Bloesch avers, is an awareness of the spiritual gifts.

All Christians are called to exercise their priesthood but in different ways, depending on the gifts that have been allotted to them. Calling, indeed, is correlative with charisma. The way we serve in the body of Christ is conditional on how we use the charisms that are bestowed on us in faith and baptism.[60]

172

Bloesch warns that, even though the gifts are important in fulfilling the mission of the church (to build up and extend the body of Christ), they must not be seen as the hallmark of being a Christian. Others, who are not believers, may also demonstrate peculiar gifts. The hallmark of being a Christian is one's confession of Jesus Christ as Lord. Jesus observed that the reason for one's rejoicing should not be the possession of sensational gifts, but in one's election by God to eternal life.[61]

While all true members of the church have a special call and a personal ministry, not all have a part in pastoral ministry. Every believer, nonetheless, has some particular calling and service within the ministry of Christ. The form of the ministry depends on the gifting by the Holy Spirit, who moves and acts as He wills. Bloesch declares that a church in which the charismatic gifts are not in evidence in their many facets is not the church established at Pentecost. A church in which the priestly role is confined to the pastoral office is one where the Spirit has been quenched and/or grieved.[62]

Conclusions. Bloesch is concerned about the threat to the church from a secular Christianity which has capitulated to present-day cultural values. The church must return to a biblical foundation. He longs to see it practicing a New Testament Christianity which will invade the secular realm with the good news of Christ's salvation.

Bloesch is devastated by the disunity of the church, especially of evangelical churches who claim fidelity to the Bible. He rightly observes that the incessant warfare between denominations and mission boards has blunted the effectiveness of evangelism both at home and abroad. And he urges believers to pray for a fresh visitation of the Holy Spirit bringing a new vision of the oneness of the church.

In regard to evangelism, the priesthood of all believers must be emphasized afresh, as must the gifts of the Spirit. Even though not all believers are called to pastoral ministry, all are called to some form of service on behalf of the body of Christ.

Bloesch's ecclesiology issues a "wake-up call" to the church. It is, especially, a call to action for the evangelical wing. His appeal for a fresh outpouring of the Holy Spirit upon today's church is a prayer which should be on the lips of every believer.

Charles Colson

Charles Colson is a former adviser to the late President Richard Nixon and a former Watergate conspirator. As a result of his experiences he became a Christian. In 1976 he founded Prison Fellowship Ministries. While not a theologian in the technical sense like Erickson and Bloesch, Colson has become a popular apologist of note for evangelical Christianity and a prolific author whose works include a best-selling practical theology of the church.[63]

In seeking to define the church, Colson strongly disparages the consumer mentality of the many churches which abandon biblical foundations to pander to the tastes of modern society. He cites the problem succinctly.

> What many are looking for is a spiritual social club, an institution that offers convivial relationships but certainly does not influence how people live or what they believe. Whenever the church does assert a historically orthodox position, one that might in some way restrict an individual's doing whatever he or she chooses, the church is accused of being "out of touch"—as if its beliefs are to be determined by majority vote or market surveys.[64]

Given its attitude toward the church, Colson refers to contemporary society (including many evangelicals) as the "McChurch generation."

While surrendering to consumerism may seem to bring material success to the church, Colson warns that it is a course of action fraught with danger: it dilutes the Christian message by watering down biblical teaching in favor of the idea that Jesus is a friend who brings us happiness and self-fulfillment. To do this changes the very character of the church. The body is changed from a worshiping fellowship into a consoling refuge from life's stresses. Indeed, the gospel of God's grace through His Son is reduced to a message of self-realization. Finally, the church is stripped of its authority. It no longer has the ability to make its members accountable; it loses the facility for discipling and discipline.[65]

Colson decries the idea of Christianity as primarily an individual affair. Christianity is corporate, a community of the re-

174

deemed. It is a re-created society, established for the deliverance of a lost world; it is the kingdom of God that Christ inaugurated continuing on until its full realization.[66]

The essence of the church, Colson holds, is its unity; for it is by definition one. He makes it clear that when the world is unable to see the unity of Jesus' people — the church — it is unable to see the authentication that He is in fact the Son of the living God.[67]

In searching for unity within the church, it is not necessary to pretend that there are no differences between believers. There are, and they must be recognized and respected. But there are basic, fundamental, orthodox doctrines — such as those communicated through the ancient creeds — on which members of the true church can agree. Some of these would include the Virginal Conception, Christ's deity, His atonement, His resurrection, the authority of the Bible, and the Parousia.

Colson finds diversity in the nonessentials to be a valuable corrective. He observes:

> The fact is, we can learn from one another. Personally, while I've formed strong doctrinal convictions, I've been enriched deeply by my fellowship with those who hold different, but equally strong doctrinal convictions — particularly my Catholic, Anglican, Orthodox, and Lutheran brothers and sisters. Doing so has also helped me not to trivialize the ordinances or sacraments and other acts of worship.[68]

Baptism, Colson finds, is the crucial dividing line between the world and the church. Even though Christians may argue over mode or even its significance, all agree upon the need for baptism. It testifies outwardly of the invisible reality. It is a command Christ gives in the Great Commission, and it is the first vow and mark of entry into the church.[69]

The Lord's Supper, he observes, is a physical gesture by which we demonstrate our oneness with Christ. Consequently, believers must be at peace with each other when partaking. The act of participation is, furthermore, the sovereign sign of the internal work of grace in one's life. God holds this act to be of the highest importance. Consequently, for a nonbeliever to participate is to indicate scorn for God.[70]

Some Observations

Bloesch and Colson are concerned that the world appears to be exerting a greater influence on the church than vice versa. Both call upon the church to return to its biblical roots. All three theologians declare the role of the church to be the continuation of Christ's ministry on earth. Erickson delineates that task in a fourfold ministry: discipling, edification, worship, and social concern. Bloesch sees the church's ministry as bearing witness to Christ before the world with a view to its transformation. Colson wants the Christian community to point a lost world to the kingdom to come.

Erickson and Colson hold a typically Baptist view of the ordinances. They are believer's baptism and the Lord's Supper. Bloesch would add a "third sacrament," namely, preaching. It is a means of salvation for the lost.

Both Bloesch and Colson contend for the unity of the church. They agree that disunity blinds the world to the reality of Jesus as the Christ, the Son of God who is the Savior of the world. The unity of the church is paramount in spite of its diversity.

Nor are evangelicals the only ones concerned about the unity of the church. As we shall see in the following sections, unity is of great concern to other sectors of the Christian faith as well.

CONTEMPORARY EASTERN ORTHODOXY

Eastern Orthodoxy, although it has expanded throughout the world, has changed very little over the centuries. Its theology of the church and the sacraments is much the same as it was during the Middle Ages.

The Church

The Orthodox Church claims to teach precisely the identical message which was proclaimed by the undivided church for a millennium. "The Orthodox Christians today . . . proclaim Christ as He was revealed, understood, and taught in the undivided Church."[71] Orthodoxy goes even farther, asserting that every Orthodox believer is in organic unity with the original church.[72]

Man becomes a new creature within the Church, because she is the depository of grace and the means of salvation. The Orthodox Church is not a worldly organization or a social system, but a living organism. . . . Her members are animated by the common means of sanctification: the sacraments, the reading of the Word of God, and the life of prayer. . . . Their faith in Christ is sustained and guarded by the Church as a whole, the conscience of the Church, which is the totality of the faithful, laymen and clergymen alike.[73]

Orthodoxy teaches that when one is regenerated by the Spirit of God, that person becomes a child of God. But this is not the ultimate goal; for there is a further destiny—union with God. This further process is known as deification. All the necessary conditions for union with God are available through the church.[74] While the deification process will be completed only on the other side of this life, it must be increasingly accomplished here and now. Christians attain unity with God by means of prayers, vigils, fasts, alms, and other good works done in Christ's name. "The virtues are not the end but the means, or, rather, the symptoms, the outward manifestation of the Christian life, the sole end of which is the acquisition of grace."[75]

This deification or union with God is not an individual affair. It takes place only within the context of the individual as a part of the body of Christ. Vladimir Lossky states that everything that can be said of Christ may be equally well applied to the church, since "it is a theandric organism, or, more exactly, a created nature inseparably united to God in the hypostasis of the Son, a being which has—as He has—two natures, two wills and two operations which are at once inseparable and yet distinct."[76]

The Sacraments

While the Roman Catholic church has determined the number of sacraments to be seven, the Eastern church has no set number. It really prefers the term "mystery" (the Greek rendering) over "sacrament" (the Latin rendering). In fact, all rites of the church are considered to be "outflowings of the original mystery of Christ" and to "perpetuate the incarnation of Christ and its redemptory effect through the ages."[77]

177

Baptism. Baptism is the initiatory rite of the church. The candidate renounces Satan three times as he faces the west (the direction of the Antichrist), spits three times at Satan, and then turns to the east and surrenders to Christ by being immersed three times.[78] As the Spirit fell upon the disciples in tongues of fire, so He comes invisibly upon the newly baptized person in the sacrament of the holy chrism. In this sacrament He transforms the nature by cleansing it and coupling it to the body of Christ. In this fashion He also confers deity upon the believer.[79]

Closely related to baptism and sometimes called a "Second Baptism," is the sacrament of reconciliation, which both heals and leads to a change of heart. The Western church refers to this rite as penance. Believers confess their sins to the priest, who gives them advice, direction, and absolution, and then suggests an appropriate penance.[80]

The Eucharist. The Eucharist is the primary rite of the Eastern church. In it Christ is revealed and is present among humanity. While the Orthodox Church does not like to use the term "transubstantiation," it does believe that Christ is in the elements "through and through."[81]

In the Eucharist, the baptized believer has access to the tree of life, namely, Jesus Christ, who brings immortality and divine sonship. For the unbaptized, the Eucharist is an invitation to those who would come to God with a sincere heart.[82]

Other Sacraments. Other recognized sacraments in the Eastern Orthodox Church include ordination, marriage, and holy unction. Ordination preserves the apostolic succession of the church. Offices to which one may be ordained are deacon, presbyter, and bishop. While the first two orders may be married, bishops are always chosen from the unmarried so that they may be totally devoted to the care of the church. The totality of the bishops, known as the Synod, constitutes the supreme governing body of the church under the headship of Jesus Christ.[83]

In the mystery of marriage a man and a woman are joined into one body. "By this sacrament the union of two human bodies and spirits is blessed for the procreation of mankind and the integration of their personalities."[84] Orthodoxy opposes

178

divorce, except on the ground of fornication. Upon the granting of a sanctioned divorce, remarriage is permitted.

Unction (not extreme unction as in the Roman Church) is
practiced by the Eastern church. It is a rite for the healing of
the sick. "Healing in the Church stands or falls with our concept of Christ. If Christ were both the physician of the human
soul and the healer of man's body, as the Gospels present Him,
then His Church cannot be anything less."[85] Power over illness,

5.1 Jürgen Moltmann

Jürgen Moltmann

Jürgen Moltmann, longtime professor of theology at Tübing-
en University, may be called the father of the theology of
hope. Out of a context of World War II, the Holocaust, and a
postwar Germany dominated by confrontation between Marx-
ist and Christian thought, Moltmann formulated his theology
of hope, which postulated that the God of the Bible has
"future as His essential nature." He also had much to say
about the church in his book *The Church in the Power of the
Spirit* (1977).

What is the place of the church in Moltmann's eschatological theology? "The church is the people of God and will give
an account of itself at all times to the God who has called it
into being, liberated it and gathered it."[1] It takes part in the
Savior's messianic mission and in the creative mission of
God's Spirit. While it is concerned with proclamation and
administering the sacraments, its work extends beyond these
to being a vehicle for liberation and reconciliation: "The
church participates in the uniting of men with one another, in
the uniting of society with nature and in the uniting of creation with God."[2] The church is the channel of the Christian
faith which brings hope in the midst of seemingly hopeless
circumstances that cloud our human existence. The church's
part may be summarized by saying that it is "participation in
the history of God's dealings with the world."[3]

1. Jürgen Moltmann, *The Church in the Power of the Spirit*, trans.
Margaret Kohl (London: SCM, 1977), 1.
2. Ibid., 65.
3. Ibid.

infirmity, and the demonic has been given to the church. A secondary effect of this sacrament is the forgiveness of sins.[86]

Conclusions. There are many similarities between Eastern Orthodoxy and Roman Catholicism. Both communions stress apostolic succession back to the Lord and His apostles, but the former surely has a better claim. While both observe many of the same feasts, fasts, and sacraments, there are significant differences.

The concept of corporate and personal deification is an Orthodox distinctive. The latter must be accomplished within the context of the former; for the church is the repository of both grace and salvation.

Though both Roman Catholics and Eastern Orthodox accept seven sacraments, the latter prefer the use of the broader term (originating from Greek), "mysteries," and acknowledge that there are more than seven mysteries — indeed, an indefinite number. Of these, baptism and the Eucharist are held most highly.

POST-VATICAN II ROMAN CATHOLICISM

For many centuries Roman Catholicism followed the teachings of Augustine of Hippo and Thomas Aquinas, holding that opposition to scholastic theology was virtually synonymous with opposing God Himself. In the mid-twentieth century, however, a new breed of Roman theologian came to the fore. These scholars were trained in radical higher criticism and increasingly challenged and reinterpreted much of the traditional dogmatic interpretation of the Roman Catholic Church. These challenges were particularly in evidence at the Second Vatican Council (1962–1965).[87]

Vatican II

Initiated at the behest of Pope John XXIII, Vatican II was an intentional effort to renew the Roman Catholic Church and redefine Roman Catholic dogma. Some 2,300 delegates were in attendance for the major votes of four annual sessions, and approved sixteen major texts. The pope, asserting that the world needed healing rather than condemnation, held out an olive branch to other Christian groups, and so exhibited a true ecumenical spirit. Many delegates took him at his word, and a conflict developed between radicals and traditionalists as to the future direction of Roman Catholicism. The documents of the Council reveal an effort to establish some harmony between these two factions.[88]

The Second Vatican Council continued work on the nature and structure of the church begun by the First Vatican Council in 1869–1870. A preparatory commission for the latter had drawn up a substantial declaration on the church, but the outbreak of the Franco-Prussian War as well as the invasion of the Papal States by the armies of Piedmont cut short the Council's deliberations. Instead of promulgating fifteen planned chapters on the Constitution of the church, only the four chapters dealing with the papacy were enacted.[89]

The Second Vatican Council's major document on the church, *Lumen Gentium* ("Light of All Nations"), underwent substantial discussion and revision prior to its final form, accepted by the overwhelming majority of delegates in November 1964 and promulgated immediately by Pope Paul VI. Referred to as a "dogmatic constitution on the Church," *Lumen Gentium* defined no new doctrines, but rather asserted the Roman Church's present understanding of its own nature.[90]

The Mystery of the Church. According to this document, the church is all those who have been called into union with Christ. To these people He has communicated His Spirit and has made them mystically into His own body. Through the sacraments, Christ's life is poured into His people, by which they are united to Him and formed into His likeness.[91]

Christ has established and maintains His church as a visible structure, through which He universally communicates grace and truth.

> But the society furnished with hierarchical agencies and the Mystical Body of Christ are not to be considered as two realities, nor are the visible assembly and the spiritual community, nor the earthly Church and the Church enriched with heavenly things. Rather they form one interlocked reality which is comprised of a divine and a human element.[92]

181

This unique church founded by Christ, which is one, holy, catholic, and apostolic, is in its visible form synonymous with the Roman Catholic Church, governed by the Bishop of Rome and the bishops in union with him. The document admits that many elements of truth and of sanctification are to be found outside of the Roman Church, but because they are gifts appropriately belonging to the church of Christ, they manifest an inward dynamism toward Catholic unity.[93]

The People of God. The church is the new elect, replacing Israel as God's covenantal people. But the church's task is similar: it is intended to be "an instrument for the redemption of all, and is sent forth into the whole world as the light of the world and the salt of the earth."[94]

Vatican II contended that the church is necessary to salvation. In affirming the necessity of faith and baptism (cf. Mark 16:16; John 3:5), Christ also affirmed the necessity of the church. As a result, anyone who would refuse to be a part of the church cannot be saved.[95]

What of non-Roman communions? They do not profess the Latin faith in its entirety, noted the Council. Nor are they in communion with the chair of Saint Peter. At the same time, they honor Scripture as the basis of their belief and practice. They trust in the Triune God, have been united with Christ in baptism, and partake of the sacraments. Thus Vatican II could say

> that in some real way they are joined with us in the Holy Spirit, for to them also He gives His gifts and graces, and is therefore operative among them with His sanctifying power. . . . In all of Christ's disciples the Spirit arouses the desire to be peacefully united, in the manner determined by Christ, as one flock under one shepherd, and He prompts them to pursue this goal.[96]

The church has the task of evangelizing the world in response to the Great Commission. All believers have the right to baptize, but only a priest may offer the Eucharistic sacrifice which completes the building up of the body of Christ. "In this way the Church simultaneously prays and labors in order that the entire world may become the People of God, the Body of the Lord."[97]

182

The Episcopate. Vatican II, in accordance with traditional Roman Catholic policy, grounded the episcopacy in the gifting of the church by the Holy Spirit, especially in the apostolic gifts. Over the other apostles Christ placed Peter. The bishops are successors to the apostles; the pope is Peter's successor and so holds supreme infallible authority in the church.[98] With their assistants, the priests and deacons, bishops have to undertake the service of the community, managing in the place of God over the congregation, as teachers of dogma and priests of sacred worship. The person who attends them, attends Christ, and the one who spurns them, spurns Christ.[99]

The bishops are linked together with one another and with the Bishop of Rome in conciliar assemblies. But the college of bishops has no authority apart from their head, the supreme Pontiff. He has absolute and unlimited power over the church. And he is able always to use this power freely.[100]

While the bishops individually are not infallible, they can nonetheless proclaim Christ's doctrine infallibly. Their authority is heightened in council, where they are teachers and judges of faith and morals for the church, and their teachings must be submitted to. The pope, on the other hand, enjoys infallibility by virtue of his office, when, as supreme shepherd of the faithful, he sets forth a particular doctrine of faith or morals.[101]

The Laity. The clergy alone were not intended to shoulder the entire burden of the saving mission of the church. It is their duty, rather, so to shepherd the laity that all cooperate in advancing the Gospel.

> The laity are gathered together in the People of God and make up the Body of Christ under one Head. Whoever they are, they are called upon, as living members, to expend all their energy for the growth of the Church and its continuous sanctification. For this very energy is a gift of the Creator and a blessing of the Redeemer.[102]

Consequently, the laity must learn to relate life to the praise of God. They must help one another to live holier lives, even in their secular callings. They must also learn how to distinguish between their duties as church members and their duties as

183

members of human society. In the latter they must be guided by Christian conscience; for there is no human activity beyond Divine sovereignty. "Each individual layman must stand before the world as a witness to the resurrection and life of the Lord Jesus and as a sign that God lives."[103]

Conclusions. While retaining much of the traditional Roman Catholic ecclesiology, Vatican II exhibited a renewed and more loving interest in both its own members and non-Roman Catholic believers. A new openness toward including other communions as brothers and sisters in Christ has done much to foster Christian unity.

Karl Rahner

Karl Rahner was born in Germany in 1904 and was ordained a Jesuit priest in 1932. He studied under Martin Heidegger and received his doctorate in 1936. His teaching career was spent in dogmatic theology at Innsbruck, Munich, and Münster. A prolific writer, his magnum opus is the sixteen-volume *Theological Investigations*, published between 1954 and 1984.

The Nature of the Church. Rahner saw the church as "the people of God," an idea he explained by saying that, "by the gracious coming of the Logos in the flesh, in the unity of the race, in the one history of humanity, mankind as a whole has become a consecrated humanity, in fact the people of God."[104] Such a definition dovetails well with Rahner's concept of the "anonymous Christian." He declared that even when one does not know Christ explicitly, one may still be a justified person who abides in the grace of Christ.[105] Consequently—and in accord with the findings of Vatican II—a person might be a dedicated Moslem, Hindu, Confucian, and so forth, and nonetheless be an unknowing Christian.

Not only is the church the people of God, but it is the body of Christ, as well. Rahner sees the church as "the continuation, the perpetual presence of the task and function of Christ in the economy of redemption, his contemporaneous presence in history, his life."[106] As the union of humanity with Divinity, the church is a sign of God's abiding grace-giving presence in the world. The church is faithful to its nature when it teaches, testifies to Christ's truth, carries His cross through the ages, loves God through its members, and delineates in the sacrifice of the mass the saving grace that it possesses.[107]

Rahner argued that the Holy Spirit is in the church to such a degree that its ecclesiastical ministry cannot abuse its authority. The supreme example of this is the pope, who has the competence to determine his own competence. "When he invokes his ultimate authority in making a decision, this action is itself the only guarantee that he has remained within the limits of his competence"; for he is assisted by the Spirit of God Himself.[108]

The Local Church. Rahner held that the Christian church has always been a "local church." It is in the local church that the Gospel is proclaimed and the Eucharist is celebrated. The "parochial principle," as he termed it—the parish church as the locus of Christian life—is a valid and valuable one. The living center of its multifaceted activity must be the altar where believers, as members of God's holy people, encounter the self-sacrificing, servant-nature of the Lord.

> If every pastoral work finds its central point in the Altar of Christ, then the life of the parish, issuing from the altar of the parish church, is and remains the basic form of the care of souls. In this way we also have a guarantee that individual pastoral endeavors preserve their mutual relations and proper proportion, by the very fact that in the parish they reach man under the very respect which even by nature is one of the most many-sided and yet most uniform, viz. man as member of a natural, spiritual community.[109]

The Sacraments. Since the church is the sign of God's grace in the world, it must seek to make that grace efficacious for the sanctification of each individual. This is accomplished through the sacraments.[110]

The Eucharist is the central event of the church. It is incorporation into the mystical body of Christ. Taking part in the physical body of Christ by receiving this sacrament bestows the grace of Christ to the participant as long as that person demonstrates an effectual evidence of a renewed and personally ratified in-

185

corporation in that body of Christ. In such a fashion one can share in His Holy Spirit, namely, the church.[111]

Baptism is a twofold act; it is both an act of incorporation into the church, as well as a proclamation of acceptance of the church's belief that the person baptized receives full membership in the body of Christ and is vivified by the Spirit. In fact, even those baptized people who become heretics or schismatics, retain a connection to the church by virtue of the enduring fact of their baptism. Such a connection does not belong to a person who is unbaptized, even if he or she is justified.[112]

Confirmation is the conferral of the Holy Spirit (who was not received at baptism). Through this sacrament the charismata of the Holy Spirit are bestowed upon believers through the laying on of hands. These gifts are many and varied, and are given for the edification of the church and the carrying out of its mission in the world.[113]

The sacrament of penance is the rite by which the community deals with a sinful member. According to Rahner,

> this cannot be a matter of indifference to Christ's Church. . . .
> She must react against such a sin, through which the member of
> the community not only puts himself in contradiction to God
> but also to the Church of Christ, for the Church is in her mem-
> bers and by their holiness must be the primal sacramental sign
> of the victorious grace of God.[114]

Consequently, the offender must be excluded from the fellowship of believers. But efforts at reconciliation should be made. Contrite sinners are not condemned; for the church receives their confession and imposes a penance, granting God's mercy and forgiveness to the penitent.[115]

Conclusions. The church is the definitive people of God, established at the incarnation of Christ and manifested on Pentecost. The church is the Roman Catholic Church in all of its hierarchical organization with the bishops and pope at its head. But this larger church meets the individual Christian through the local, or parish, church. Through the exercise of the various sacraments the church holds out to human beings God's offer of grace and love, and it carries out its task of mission to the world. It is absolutely necessary to the salvation of human beings, although they may relate to it in different ways according to the light they possess.

Hans Küng

Born in Switzerland in 1928, Küng studied at the Sorbonne, and in 1960 assumed the chair of theology at the Roman Catholic Theological Faculty of Tübingen University, later serving as professor of dogmatic and ecumenical theology as well as director of the Institute for Ecumenical Studies at the same school. Because of his radical stand theologically, and because of his unceasing opposition to papal infallibility, he was banned in 1978 by Pope John Paul II as an accredited teacher of Roman Catholic theology.

One of Küng's important works is *The Church*,[116] in which he critiques the contemporary church in the light of both history and the Gospel.

The People of God. Küng sees the church as the new eschatological people of God, successors to ancient Israel, in whom all the divine promises to Israel have been fulfilled. All believers belong to the church and all are equal. There can therefore be no differentiating between "clerics" and "laity." Such a distinction is not to be found in the New Testament.[117]

Because those who belong to the people of God do so by virtue of His call, Küng insists that the church cannot be private or exclusive. It is always completely dependent upon God's election, without which there would be no church. Since God's call is a prelude to any action and any faith on the individual's part, and since this call confronts all God's people, the individual never stands alone, but always within the fellowship, just as the individual fellowships are part of the one fellowship, the church. The church originates, not with one pious person, but with God.[118] While the church is composed of individuals, it can be seen only in terms of the individual who has been called by God and who has responded by becoming and remaining a member of the church.

Although membership in the church is dependent on God's

call, it is also dependent on human decision. Free human assent is necessary to its existence. Voluntary obedience and faith are integral to the people of God. "The people of God is anything but a flock of sheep with no will of their own."[119]

The Church and the Holy Spirit. Küng criticizes Roman Catholic theology and the church for having neglected the charismatic nature of the church. He places the cause with a legalistic clericalism which mistrusts any movement of the free Spirit of God. A second cause he cites is the Roman Catholic ecclesiology which is based on that of the pastoral epistles and Acts rather than on the Pauline epistles (which are much more pneumatic in scope).[120]

It would be a misconception, avers Küng, to consider charisms (gifts of the Spirit) as exceptional or sensational phenomena. Paul was not at all adverse, he declares, to any spiritual gifts, although he reduced tongues in importance, and limited this gift. And because of the commonness of signs and wonders among non-believing Hellenists, he set forth two criteria for ascertaining whether a spirit is from God: first, the Spirit which comes from God enables one to affirm the lordship of Christ, and second, the true spiritual gift brings a sense of responsibility toward the community and the desire to assist and edify it. Nor should Christians desire the more sensational gifts, but instead should seek the best one of all—love.[121]

Charisms are various rather than exceptional phenomena, and they are spread throughout the church rather than restricted to an elite group. Nor are they peripheral phenomena, maintains Küng, but essential and foundational to the church. The significance of charisms, he says, is that they denote "the call of God, addressed to an individual, to a particular ministry in the community, which brings with it the ability to fulfill that ministry."[122] Because all charisms are expressions of God's grace and power through His Spirit, they all direct us toward the one great charism of God, namely, eternal life.[123]

Baptism. Baptism goes back to the very beginning of the church, Küng determines. The community baptizes in memory of Jesus; it is a dying to sin and a resurrection to new life in Him. Baptism is administered "in the name of Jesus." "By being baptized in the name of Jesus," Küng argues, "a person becomes a subject of Jesus, and is committed to the rule and to the care of the risen Lord. He becomes the property of the risen Lord and has a share in him, in his life, his Spirit, his Sonship of God."[124]

Baptism by itself, declares Küng, is valueless. Baptism must be coupled with repentance and faith. Both baptism and faith are based in the saving act of God in Christ. "Baptism comes from faith, and faith leads to baptism."[125]

Baptism is never an individual affair, involving only the believer and Christ. It is bound up with the community of faith in a deep and meaningful way; for by sharing in Christ's death and resurrection, one becomes a part of the Christian community. "The believer does not . . . make himself a member of the community, but he is made a member."[126]

Like Rahner, Küng sees baptism as a vehicle for a radical new character. It can never be repealed. One can only accept it or deny it. Even those who abandon the church hold an abiding connection, even though a wrong one, with the church.[127]

The Lord's Supper. The words of institution Küng takes as indicating that Jesus was giving His disciples a share in His sacrificed body and outpoured blood, that is, a part in the saving work of His death. He was also allowing them a share in the coming kingdom of God (as represented by the common eschatological meal).[128]

Küng rejects a purely symbolic interpretation of the Lord's Supper. While bread and wine are indeed symbols, they are symbols filled with reality. "They are *signs*, but *effective signs*, containing what they represent."[129]

Lest one misunderstand, Küng observes that Christ's presence comes not from the power of the elements, but through the power of His Word. While He is absolutely present in the preaching of the Word, He is present in a special way in the Eucharist. By so saying, Küng is not affirming transubstantiation, but real presence. According to Küng, the Lord is not in the Lord's Supper in the way He was present as a historical person on this earth, nor as He will be when He returns as the glorified Lord. But He is there in the Spirit.[130]

The Supper is more than an individual matter; it is a fellow-

ship in Christ. Those who participate in the communion become partners with Christ. Because believers share the body of
Christ in the rite, they are a part of each other. "By their
communio the sharers in the meal are made into one *body*,
because the bread is the body of Christ."[131]

Unity and Plurality within the Church. Küng is concerned
about polarizations (which he calls "parties") and tensions
within the church. While the church has included certain socio-
political, cultural, and sexual contradictions within its membership, can it in the interests of unity admit ecclesial parties?

He admits that pluralism may be a foundation of liberty and
ingenuity in the church. Christian truth has many aspects, and
difference is not bad unless it hardens into elitism. Associations
and movements of all sorts, if they are not in conflict with one
another, may have fruitful interaction.[132]

At the same time, it is widely recognized that plurality without limits can pose extreme danger to the unity of the church.
Indifferent pluralism blights the character of the church as the
community of believers. "Pluralism may be accepted, but pro-
miscuity is rejected."[133] And while certain types of plurality may
be allowable, sectarianism which brings dissension into the
church—tearing apart the fabric of unity—is not.

As he studies the New Testament, Küng concludes that parties in the church may be accepted, not for division, but for the
sake of its unity. Indeed, he concludes, "the formation of
groups is permitted and desired as an aid to unity and communication, for the building up of the community and for mission,
and especially for the service of men."[134] At the same time, he
feels that, when possible, organized groups in the church
should be avoided. It is much better to have a community of
faith and love declare its spiritual oneness as mutual openness
free of polarizations.[135]

While sometimes splits and factions are unavoidable—such as
at the time of the Reformation—Küng wants to avoid at all costs
a return to "the old days." Instead, he would like to see
churches of all stripes and hues work together to become parties within the church which are in full communion with each
other in spite of their differences. But how can such a thing
happen? According to Küng:

190

We must expose ourselves fully to Christ and his gospel and together look at God and our fellow men and accept all the consequences of this attitude. We must be open to the Spirit and in sympathy with each other whenever we differ. We must learn to speak more freely to each other and to listen to each other in vital questions of faith. We must keep a sense of proportion . . . and take seriously the plurality of culture and the resulting pluriformity in the expression of the Christian faith. We must try to understand more deeply the conciliar process through which the Church lived in the past and in which it will find new life.[136]

Women and the Church. Küng reveals himself as an egalitarian in male-female roles within the church. He argues that the animosity toward women of the church fathers and subsequent theologians originated not with Jesus but with contemporaries of Jesus. Jesus had a remarkable openness to women.[137]

In looking at Mary, the Mother of Christ, Küng accuses the church of having taken away her sexuality. "Only a Mariology which does not avoid a historical analysis of her virginity and accepts Mary as a complete woman, instead of simply as an exemplary humble handmaid, can help people of today to a better understanding of the Christian message."[138]

If the Roman Catholic Church is to become representative of all human beings and not just men, declares Küng, then it must admit women to all levels of decision-making within its ministry. Women should be encouraged to study theology and should be admitted to all degree programs within Roman Catholic seminaries. The admission of women to the diaconate should be reintroduced (it was abolished in the early ages of the church), and they should be permitted to go on to ordination as priests. "For a long time both in theory and practice, the Catholic Church has discredited and defamed women and at the same time exploited them. Along with the dignity due them, it is time to guarantee women an appropriate juridical and social status."[139]

Conclusions. Küng is an outstanding thinker who might seem better to belong to Protestantism than to Roman Catholicism when one considers his position on certain issues. He does not

191

seem to mind rejecting traditional Roman views in favor of those he considers more biblical and more in line with the mind of Christ. While one may not agree with everything he holds to, nonetheless he is to be admired for his fearlessness in proclaiming what he deems to be right.

5.2   A Summary of Contemporary Ecclesiology

Group	Nature of Church	The Ministry	Sacraments
Neo-orthodox	Final saving miracle in the process of salvation. Bearer of the Word and Spirit of Christ. The *ecclēsia* transcends the church—it is not institutional.	Every believer has an obligation to minister. The Holy Spirit decides ministry functions. A judicial rather than pneumatic organization indicates a lack of the fullness of the Spirit.	Baptism is incorporation into Christ by dying and rising with Him. The Lord's Supper commemorates the body and blood of Christ and the institution of the *ecclēsia*. It binds all Christians in a unity.
Pentecostals	Community of the saved; a group of people individually empowered by the Spirit; a commissioned community.	All believers are spiritually gifted, but some have gifts which set them apart to be a pastor, evangelist, or other special servant.	Baptism is the outward sign of an inward death, burial, and resurrection in which the believer identifies with Christ. The Lord's Supper is a simple memorial of the Lord's death.
Evangelicals	Fellowship of regenerate persons who model themselves on Christ; the company of the elect.	Need for a servant mentality. All believers are appointed to be witnesses and ambassadors for Christ; they minister according to their spiritual gifts. All have personal ministry but not necessarily pastoral ministry.	Baptism is the outward testimony of an inward reality; it is necessary for the Christian life. It is the entry to the Christian fellowship. The Lord's Supper is the sign of oneness in Christ. It commemorates His death.

192

Eastern orthodox	Every Orthodox believer is in organic union with the original Christ. The Orthodox Church is not an earthly organization, but a living organism, a theandric entity united with Christ.	The goal for the believer is deification—unification with God. Clergy help to facilitate this process as shepherds and priests.	There are numerous sacraments. Baptism is the initiatory rite in which the believer is cleansed of sin and coupled to the body of Christ. There is a literal view of the elements in the Eucharist. In it the believer has access to the tree of life. Unction is the rite of healing for the sick.
Roman Catholicism	All those called into communion with Christ. The visible structure is the Roman Church. The church is the new elect, which replaces Israel.	The pope is the successor to Peter. The bishops are the successors of the apostles. With the priests and deacons they oversee the community as God's chosen representatives.	Baptism is incorporation into the church. Confirmation confers the Holy Spirit. The Eucharist bestows Christ on the believer.

A Summary

Through Vatican II, many new ideas found a home in the theology of Roman Catholicism and some old ideas received new interpretation and a fresh emphasis. Especially inviting was the stress on the unity of the church and the recognition of Protestants as fellow believers (along with sincere adherents to other religions).

Roman Catholic theologians (represented by Rahner and Küng) built on the findings of the Second Vatican Council. Some, such as Küng, went beyond the conciliar parameters, trying to return to a more biblical Roman Catholicism. It is not surprising that the magisterium of Rome punished them for exceeding the limits.

CONCLUDING OBSERVATIONS

While there are a number of differences among the groups and individual representatives cited—which should be no surprise considering their greatly varied denominational and theological contexts—one should note the many similarities in emphasis that they possess. That they share many similar concerns will be more amazing than their differences.

There is both agreement and disagreement on the sacraments or ordinances. Baptist evangelicals such as Erickson and Colson would deny the sacramental nature of baptism and the Lord's Supper; in this they are joined by Brunner and by the Pentecostals. The Eastern Orthodox Church and Roman Catholicism would affirm sacramentalism of a transubstantial nature in the Lord's Supper, although Küng would dissent, but hold to a real presence sacramentalism in this rite. In the same way, the former grouping would deny the efficacy of infant baptism, while the latter would affirm it. All would see baptism as the rite of initiation into the church and the Lord's Supper as the rite of continuing fellowship.

Particularly strong is the emphasis on the need for the unity of the church. Brunner argued against the overemphasis on individualism in the church, seeing it as destructive of fellowship. While there is little overtly to suggest a desire for unity in the church, Pentecostals and Neo-Pentecostals keenly desire a return to the state of the New Testament church; that surely suggests a desire for unity. Donald Bloesch finds disunity in the church a scandal of horrific proportion, and calls for a seeking of the Holy Spirit to bring the need for reconciliation and harmony to fruition. Charles Colson insists that the essence of the church is its unity. Although Eastern Orthodoxy proclaims itself to be the only true church (and therefore others are schismatics), its practical warmth and openness to other communions would suggest its desire for the unity of the faith. Vatican II proclaimed the desire of Roman Catholicism for unity among all Christian brothers and sisters; these sentiments have been strongly echoed by Hans Küng.

The increasing emphasis on the desirability of church unity is a good omen for its future. Yet unity must be grounded in truth—the truth found in God's authoritative biblical revelation.

194

Evangelicals correctly argue that the church is in danger of bowing to pressure to accommodate the world's standards in many areas. Only as it unites in Christ will the church find strength to persevere as the people of God, truly the body of Christ.

PART 2

A Biblical Theology
of the Church

CHAPTER SIX

The People of God in the Old Testament

When discussing the church, questions are frequently asked as to its place in regard to the Old Testament. People sometimes call the church a "spiritual Israel." Does that mean that Israel in the Old Testament is synonymous with the church in the New Testament? Does Old Testament Israel occupy any place in God's plans for His church?

THE DEBATE OVER ISRAEL

When one asks such questions, the responses are myriad. Theologians are not at all in agreement. Dispensationalists rigorously differentiate between Israel and the church, insisting that "the Church stands distinct from Israel and did not begin until the Day of Pentecost, and thus did not exist in the Old Testament period."[1] God has two very distinct objectives in mind for Israel and for the church, and the two must not be muddled. Promises made to Israel are not intended for the church and may not rightly be assumed to apply to it.

At the opposite end of the spectrum are covenant theologians who maintain that "the Church is not simply a New Testament phenomenon . . . [but] the historical continuation of Old Testament Israel."[2] Because Israel disobeyed God, and because it rejected Christ as its Messiah, Israel has been replaced by the church, which has become heir to all the (spiritual) promises made to her in the Old Testament. The church, to put it simply, is the "new Israel" in God's economy.

Who is right? George Ladd has aptly suggested that, "as is often the case, the Biblical solution to the problem lies between the two extremes."[3] Thus, while it is inappropriate to speak of Old Testament Israel as the church, it is accurate to call the Hebrews "the people of God." In the Old Testament, the people of God were the Hebrews; in the New Testament, they are the church. In this light, Ladd observes that

> there is . . . but one people of God. This is not to say that the Old Testament saints belonged to the Church and that we must speak of the Church in the Old Testament. . . . The Church properly speaking had its birthday on the day of Pentecost, for the Church is composed of all those who by one spirit have been baptized into one body (I Cor. 12:13), and this baptizing work of the Spirit began on the day of Pentecost.[4]

6.1 Jewish and Gentile Salvation History

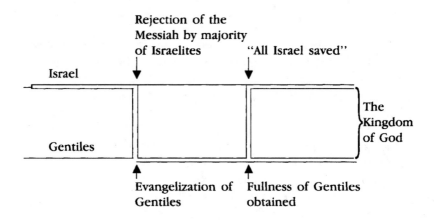

The People of God

A favorite term applied by Israel to itself was "the people of God." It is a reiteration of the covenant God made with Abraham, Isaac, and Jacob. When Israel was in Egyptian bondage,

200

the Lord appeared to Moses and commanded him to tell them that "I will take you as my own people, and I will be your God. Then you will know that I am the Lord your God, who brought you out from under the yoke of the Egyptians" (Ex. 6:7). As the Hebrews prepared to enter the Promised Land, Moses reminded them that "you are a people holy to the Lord your God. The Lord your God has chosen you out of all the peoples on the face of the earth to be His people, His treasured possession" (Deut. 7:6). God told David when he was anointed as king, "You will shepherd my people Israel, and you will become their ruler" (2 Sam. 5:2b). He also promised the Hebrews that when they sinned, "if my people, who are called by my name, will humble themselves and pray and seek my face and turn from their wicked ways, then I will hear from heaven and will forgive their sin and will heal their land" (2 Chron. 7:14). When Nehemiah was mourning in prayer the state of destroyed Jerusalem, he reminded the Lord that the exiles who had returned to live in its ruins "are your servants and your people, whom you redeemed by your great strength and your mighty hand" (Neh. 1:10). These concepts are repeated over and over again throughout the Old Testament.

When one looks at the New Testament, however, one finds the language applied to the church. Paul, in writing to warn believers in Corinth against partnership with unbelievers, quotes the Old Testament to remind them of their place in the divine economy: "As God has said, 'I will live with them and walk among them, and I will be their God, and they will be my people' " (2 Cor. 6:16). And he emphasizes in his letter to Titus that Christ "gave himself for us to redeem us from all wickedness and to purify for himself a people that are his very own, eager to do what is good" (Titus 2:14). Peter calls upon his Christian readers to remember that "you are a chosen race, a royal priesthood, a holy nation, God's own people" (1 Peter 2:9, NRSVB). All of these references draw from the notion of Old Testament Israel as the people of God.

One might suppose, considering the above, that the Reformed covenantal view is correct, and that the church has indeed supplanted Israel as the people of God. But examination of Romans 9–11 indicates that such conclusions are premature.

Israel as God's People

As one begins to read Romans 9, the idea of Israel's being rejected in favor of the church seems to be born out. Paul observes that "not all who are descended from Israel are Israel. Nor because they are his descendants are they all Abraham's children" (9:6-13). Then he proceeds to quote Hosea 2:23 to the effect that God "will call them 'my people' who are not my people" (9:25) to demonstrate that God will go outside of Israel to elect a people.[5]

In chapter 10, Paul chronicles the path to eternal life that is set out by faith.

> If you confess with your mouth, "Jesus is Lord," and believe in your heart that God raised him from the dead, you will be saved. For it is with your heart that you believe and are justified, and it is with your mouth that you confess and are saved (10:9-10).

Tragically, Israel rejected the path of faith in favor of the legalistic dead end. As a nation they rejected the good news of the Gospel of Christ. In his commentary, F.F. Bruce aptly notes, "They understood well enough, but they refuse to obey. They have shown their envy and indignation when the Gentiles accepted the message, but they would not believe it themselves."[6]

Paul's opening remarks in chapter 11, then, come as somewhat of a shock; for the natural response to his question, "Did God reject His people?" (11:1a) would be resoundingly affirmative. But the apostle's reply is, "By no means!" (11:1b) Indeed, Paul constructs the question so as to require a negative response: it might be rephrased, "God did not reject His people, did He? By no means!" And this emphatic statement is the theme of the whole section.[7]

Paul reiterates his assertion in 11:2: "God did not reject his people, whom he foreknew." God's foreknowledge of Israel is ample proof that He would not exclude them; for it denotes His deliberate attachment of them to Himself in faithful, sacrificial love.[8]

Nor did all of Israel reject the path of faithful obedience. The Lord always set aside a faithful remnant unto Himself. Likewise, after citing Elijah's diatribe against Israel and the Lord's response that 7,000 had not bowed the knee to Baal, Paul affirms that, "So, too, at the present time there is a remnant chosen by grace" (11:5). Thus, the spiritual seed of Abraham has always existed in Israel, even up to and including the Church Age.[9] But because Israel had disobeyed God, He hardened their hearts to the truth, and it became a stumbling block for them (11:7-10).

As if to reinforce his point against those who might still insist that the church is a sign of God's rejection of Israel, Paul once more poses and answers a question: "Again I ask: Did they stumble so as to fall beyond recovery? Not at all!" (11:11) Indeed, God allowed Israel to fall from grace so that the gospel of salvation might be proclaimed to the Gentiles. As Walter Kaiser remarks:

> This, in turn, would once again provoke the Jew to jealousy (Rom. 11-14; cf. Deut. 32:21). So Israel did not fall into an irreversible tumble. In fact, marveled Paul, if the casting away of Israel for a time has meant the reconciliation of the Gentile world to Christ, how much more spectacular will be the result when Israel returns to the Lord?[10]

Paul emphasizes that here (11:13) he is addressing the Gentile believers in Rome, those who might claim that they replaced Israel as God's chosen people. The nation of Israel, he declares, remains the Lord's chosen people. In spite of all that has happened, Israel will be His medium of redemption. The Apostle Paul points out to his readers that because the "firstfruits" of Israel (namely, the patriarchs) were holy, therefore the whole batch (that is, the nation) is holy: "if the root is holy, so are the branches" (11:16b). The people of Israel continue to be a holy people whom God has chosen for His salvific purpose in the world.[11]

The Parable of the Olive Tree

While there has been much ado about whether Paul was acquainted with the agricultural methods of his day, such considerations are not really germane.[12] When he compares the people of God to an olive tree, he is simply using an analogy to make his point about Israel and the church.

6.2 The Olive Tree Analogy

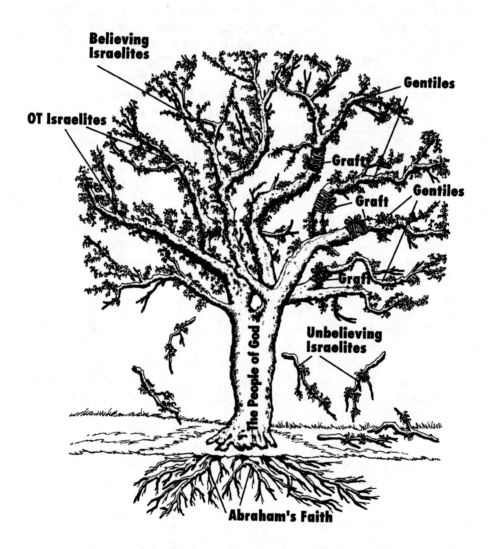

There is a single tree, a single people of God. At its base stand the patriarchs, while the original branches are the nation of Israel of Old Testament times. In the New Testament era, however, most of these natural branches have been broken off (because of Israel's unbelief) and branches from a wild olive tree (that is, the Gentiles) have been grafted on in their place (because of the faith of these Gentiles in Christ Jesus).

The Gentiles in the church must beware of boasting or of deriding the natural branches. The former were not grafted in on account of any merit of their own, but because of God's grace. They must remember that the natural branches were broken off because of Israel's unbelief: "Do not be arrogant, but be afraid. For if God did not spare the natural branches, he will not spare you either" (11:20b, 21).

The Gentile faction of the church must also realize that, should the unbelieving Hebrews repent of their unbelief, they will be restored, grafted back into the trunk of faith from which they have been severed. God can and will perform such a miracle.[13]

To sum up the matter: Israel has undergone a partial blindness where only a small remnant has heeded the Gospel message. But Israel's temporary blindness has occurred so that God may bless the Gentiles. When He has brought into the gospel fold all those Gentiles who are to be saved, then He will turn back to Israel, "and so all Israel will be saved" (11:26a). Of course this does not mean that every single Jew will be saved, but rather that the nation as a whole, or in general, will be saved.[14] But, the point remains, God has not permanently laid Israel aside; He will again work in Israel as a people—the people of God. By God's grace, Israel and the church will be grafted into the same tree.

Conclusions

It is a serious error to believe that God has rejected Israel in favor of the church. Yet it is equally problematic to believe that God has two peoples—Israel and the church—and has different purposes for each.

God has only one people. The people of God are seen as a massive tree rooted in the faith of Abraham, Isaac, and Jacob.

Out of that single trunk grow many branches. Some may be labeled "Israel" and some "the church" (some may be doubly labeled; for there are Jews who are also a part of the body of Christ). God has cut off the apostates of Israel, those who refused to acknowledge Jesus as Messiah, and He has grafted in their place those Gentiles who by faith became a part of the Christian community. When the time of Gentile salvation has been achieved, the nation of Israel will be grafted back into place. Israel will be saved by a miracle of God's grace.

The lesson to be learned here is that God has called a people to Himself. He has not made distinctions; for "all have sinned" (Rom. 3:23). But even as God's wrath falls upon all people, so His grace has abounded to all. God is loving and merciful to Jew and Gentile alike. As many as turn to Him in faith are a part of His people: in the Old Testament, the nation of Israel; in the Christian era, the church; when the time of the Gentiles is completed, Israel once more; and in eternity all who have trusted Him will be His people.

ISRAEL: THE COVENANT PEOPLE OF GOD

Because God has but one people, the church should not spurn Israel; for, in so doing, it spurns itself—past, present, and future. Along with Markus Barth Christians must affirm that

> [the church] is built upon the Old Testament witness and the New Testament witness to God. She does not stand only upon that of the disciples of Christ, but on the search, foretelling, and witness of the old prophets as well (cf. 1 Peter 1:10-11). This is said in Eph. 2:20. The Church, built upon the apostles and prophets, can neither stand "in love" on its root and ground (3:17), nor grow internally or externally (2:21f.; 4:13-16) unless it listens and learns continuously from the Old Testament people of God, and from the testimony given to and by them.[15]

Such artificial divisions between branches of the people of God were never constructed by the New Testament church. A study of the epistles will strongly suggest that Gentile believers were made familiar with the Old Testament immediately upon their conversion to Christianity; they often quote the Old Testament as a recognized authority and assume a familiarity with Old Testament teachings. It was, after all, the Scripture of the church at that time. Thus, the history and teaching of Israel as God's covenant people were vital to the church. And this holds true today; for the church is also God's covenant people.

The Nature of the Covenant Relationship

The idea which gave Israel definition and impetus as a nation was that of the covenant.[16] The Hebrew word signifying covenant is *berith*. Its etymology is in scholarly dispute. Some hold it to be a derivative of *brh*, "to eat, dine," reflective of the libation accompanying the covenanting ceremony. More convincingly, others associate it with the Akkadian *biritu*, "clasp, fetter," carrying the concept of a binding agreement.[17]

The original significance of the Hebrew covenant was not simply a contractual agreement between two parties,[18] but rather an imposed obligation. Again, there is a similarity to Akkadian tradition where a king would impose a set of regulations on his officials, citizens, or vassals. In return for their loyalty and obedience, he promised to protect and look after them.[19] In the case of the Hebrews, God was the King, promising Israel security, prosperity, and a multitude of physical and spiritual blessings in return for loyalty and obedience.

Thomas McComiskey tells us that there were two basic types of Old Testament covenant between God and Israel: the promissory and the administrative. They are, however, so closely tied together that to separate them would be to damage irreparably the biblical concept of covenant: "The promissory covenant states and guarantees the elements of the promise; the administrative covenants set forth stipulations of obedience and, except for the covenant of circumcision, explicate the elements of the promise."[20]

The Covenant with Abraham. The earliest covenant pertaining directly to Israel is found in Genesis 15:18-21. It is a promissory covenant established unilaterally by God without any attached conditions. At the same time, the context makes it clear that this covenant is based on Abram's devout trust in God's promises (15:1-6).

On that day the Lord made a covenant with Abram and said, "To your descendants I give this land, from the river of Egypt to the great river, the Euphrates — the land of the Kenites, Kenizzites, Kadmonites, Hittites, Perizzites, Raphaites, Amorites, Canaanites, Girgashites and Jebusites" (15:18-21).

While this covenant contained only the promises of descendants and land, a reiteration of it in Genesis 17 went considerably further. Abram's name was changed to Abraham (meaning "father of many") because he would father many nations (17:4-6). Kings would be his descendants (17:6b). The covenant would be an everlasting one between God and Abraham's descendants (17:7). The land of Canaan would be their everlasting possession (17:8). And God would be the God of Abraham and his descendants after him (17:7b, 8b). Again, in Genesis 22, because of Abraham's willingness to obey God to the point of sacrificing his only son, Isaac, the Lord added to His covenant the promise that "through your offspring all nations on earth will be blessed" (22:18).

The Covenant of Circumcision. The rite of circumcision is introduced in Genesis 17:10 as a covenant which Abraham and his descendants were to observe "for the generations to come" (17:12). Circumcision signified participation in the promissory covenant God had established with Abraham (17:11, 13), and those who refused the rite indicated their refusal to stand under the covenant: "Any uncircumcised male, who has not been circumcised in the flesh, will be cut off from his people; he has broken my covenant" (17:14).

The covenantal significance of circumcision may be seen in the years of Israel's wanderings in the wilderness en route to the Promised Land. During this period of punishment and God's disfavor, children born were not circumcised (Josh. 5:5). Barton Payne suggests:

> The reason is not stated in so many words, but Numbers 14:33 had revealed that the children were "to bear the whoredoms" of their fathers over the entire forty-year period. Israel's refraining from circumcision may then have been done intentionally, so as to provide the people with a concrete symbol of God's disfavor, or perhaps of their own physical sufferings.[21]

At any rate, immediately upon crossing the Jordan into Canaan, the rite was reinstituted by God's command at Gilgal, along with the proclamation by the Lord that "today I have rolled away the reproach of Egypt from you" (Josh. 5:9). And while exactly what this reproach was has become shrouded in the mists of time,[22] it does seem to signify the renewal of God's approval of Israel and the divine removal of the guilt of its fathers.

McComiskey points out that circumcision was related both to the promissory and the administrative covenant, although not completely identifiable with either. He notes that "circumcision was inextricably bound to the promise covenant in that it was a sign of that covenant";[23] at the same time, "the immediate context in which circumcision was introduced (Gen. 17:9-14) contains no formal statement of the elements of the promise."[24] On the other hand, "it is considered an administrative covenant in this work only because it shares one function with them, that is, the governing of an aspect of obedience."[25] It might be best to see the rite as a *tertium quid*, separate from two basic types of covenant.

The Mosaic Covenant. The covenant established at Sinai with Israel contains both promises and legislation, binding the two together in one irrevocable covenant.

In this new covenant, the patriarchal covenant was reaffirmed (or, regarded as still in force). In the Deuteronomic historian's account of the matter, Moses is recorded as telling the Hebrews:

> You are standing here in order to enter into a covenant with the Lord your God, a covenant the Lord is making with you this day and sealing with an oath, to confirm you this day as his people, that he may be your God as he promised you and as he swore to your fathers, Abraham, Isaac and Jacob (Deut. 29:12-13).

Not only were the promises to Abraham validated afresh in this manner, but they were expanded substantially. These heightened promises, however, were not unconditional.

Not only would Israel be a great nation with the Lord as their God (promised to Abraham), but "if you obey me fully and keep my covenant, then out of all nations you will be my treasured possession. Although the whole earth is mine, you will be for me a kingdom of priests and a holy nation" (Ex. 19:5-6). Brevard Childs comments that Israel would be "God's own people, set apart from the rest of the nations . . . dedicated to God's service among the nations as priests function in society."[26] In other words, this special relationship to God as priests implied a pastoral and missionary function on the part of Israel, witnessing on God's behalf to the other nations and mediating on their behalf before the Lord. They would become co-laborers with Him in effecting the world's redemption.

While previous covenants had established the Lord as God of Israel and Israel as His chosen people, this new covenant emphatically restated the nature of the covenant relationship. And during Moses' leadership, the Lord would continually call Israel to remember the covenant relationship and to be faithful to it (e.g., Ex. 6:6-8; 29:45-56; Deut. 4:20; 7:6; 14:2; 27:9).

Nor was the promise of the land forgotten. It was heightened by the very fact of Israel's physical progress toward Canaan. The promise was tied to obedience to God's covenant commands in Deuteronomy 4:1, "Follow [these laws] so that you may live and may go in and take possession of the land that the Lord, the God of your fathers, is giving you."

> This new covenant was ratified (or, sealed) through sacrifice. Moses . . . took the Book of the Covenant and read it to the people. They responded, "We will do everything the Lord has said; we will obey." Moses then took the blood, sprinkled it on the people and said, "This is the blood of the covenant that the Lord has made with you in accordance with all these words" (Ex. 24:7-8).

It should be noted that this sacrifice establishing the covenant was once for all. While sacrifices for sins committed would have to be made on a regular basis, the covenant sacrifice could not be repeated, but created the covenant relationship for all time.[27]

The Davidic Covenant. The covenant God concluded with David (2 Sam. 7; cf. 2 Chron. 7:18; 13:5) has similarities to the Abrahamic covenant. The context of its establishment was the desire of David (expressed to Nathan the prophet) to build a temple to the Lord. While David was forbidden by God to build Him a temple, it was promised that his son would construct it (2 Sam. 7:12-13).

The Lord promised David, like Abraham, "that I will make your name great, like the names of the greatest men of the earth" (7:9b). Israel would be so situated that the people would not be disturbed in their own land (7:10), and David would enjoy a reign of peace (7:11). Like Abraham, David was promised progeny (7:11-16); in fact, God would establish through him a dynasty of monarchs. Through David's son who would build the temple, God would establish his throne forever (7:13, 16, 24-26, 29).

As with the Abrahamic covenant, God's establishment of the Davidic covenant was completely unilateral and unconditional. In fact, God promised David concerning his descendants that

> when he does wrong, I will punish him with the rod of men, with floggings inflicted by men. But my love will never be taken away from him, as I took it away from Saul, whom I removed from before you. Your house and kingdom will endure forever before me; your throne will be established forever (7:14-16).

The latter prophets envisioned the eternal establishment of David's throne as a promise of the Messiah. Micah promised that from Bethlehem, the city of David, would come "One who will be ruler over Israel, whose origins are from of old, from ancient times" (5:2). Isaiah spoke of One who would reign on David's throne forever; His name would be "Wonderful Counselor, Mighty God, Everlasting Father, Prince of Peace" (9:6). Ezekiel noted that the Messiah would be a member of the Davidic dynasty who would reign forever (37:24-28).

The New Covenant. As God punished the Hebrews' covenant unfaithfulness by allowing Babylon to sweep over Judah, the Prophet Jeremiah envisioned the establishment of a new covenant between God and His people.

> "The time is coming," declares the Lord, "when I will make a new covenant with the house of Israel and with the house of

Judah. It will not be like the covenant I made with their forefathers when I took them by the hand to lead them out of Egypt, because they broke my covenant, though I was a husband to them," declares the Lord (31:31-32).

A new covenant was in view, not because there was any defect in the old one, but because the Israelites had rendered it null and void by breaking it, in spite of God's mighty acts demonstrating His lordship over them.[28] Jeremiah had no quarrel with the older covenant; to the contrary, he affirmed the perpetuity of the law set out in it.[29] But the new covenant would overcome the weakness of the people in regard to their reception of, and obedience to, the law. "I will put my law in their minds and write it on their hearts" (31:33b). Indeed, "there could be no obedience and no recognition of Yahweh's sovereignty as long as the covenant was externalized. It needed to touch the life deeply and inwardly in mind and will."[30] Only then would the promise be completely fulfilled that the Lord would be Israel's God and they would be His people. It was precisely because of guaranteed obedience that this new covenant would last forever: "I will make an everlasting covenant with them, and I will inspire them to fear me, so that they will never turn away from me" (32:40).

The new covenant promised, as well, a new relationship between humans and the Lord. No longer would the people have to seek God through a human mediator, but "they will all know me from the least of them to the greatest" (31:34). Each person would enjoy an inward, personal experience of God's presence and grace; even the least of believers would enjoy the same privileges of approach to God as did the prophets of the old covenant.[31]

Furthermore, God would forget the sins of the people (31:34). Because God's recognition of one's sin was what separated Him from a person, His forgetting of sin was tantamount to announcing His reconciliation of human beings to Himself. "The new covenant affirms God's faithfulness to his promise and provides the theological ground for the blessings of justification by faith. It envisions that great day when in the dusk of an upper room the words were spoken, 'This cup is the new covenant in my blood.' "[32]

Ezekiel, too, proclaimed God's new covenant (16:60-63; 34:25-31; 37:26-28). Many of the aspects of the Abrahamic and Davidic covenants were evident: its eternal duration (16:60; 37:26), a promise of security in the land (3:27), references to progeny including inferences to the Messiah (34:23; 37:25), and a special relationship between God and His people (37:27).

As in the new covenant of Jeremiah, the new covenant of Ezekiel carried the promise of sins forgiven (16:63). Moreover, "I will give you a new heart and put a new spirit in you; I will remove from you your heart of stone and give you a heart of flesh" (36:26). The indwelling of the Holy Spirit would bring these things about, and would move the people to obedience (36:27).

Isaiah was a third prophet to speak of the new covenant. While many of the same aspects mentioned by Jeremiah and Ezekiel were present here, Isaiah took a somewhat unique tack. It was the servant of God who was actually to be the covenant: "I will keep you and will make you to be a covenant for the people, and a light to the Gentiles, to open eyes that are blind, to free captives from prison and to release from the dungeon those who sit in darkness" (42:6-7; cf. 49:8). In explaining how a person could be a covenant, R.H. Whybray tells us this covenant is not to be seen as a mutual relationship, but as an obligation: "The person addressed here, then, is to 'become an obligation' to the nations of the world: that is, he is to be the agent who imposes Yahweh's obligations on them."[33]

Conclusions. A covenant is a binding legal obligation effected between two parties. When one party is superior to the other, the covenant is a statute or regulation imposed by the more powerful on the weaker. Payne declares that

> when the parties concerned are God in His grace and man in his sin, on whose behalf God acts, the [covenant] becomes God's self-imposed obligation for the deliverance of sinners. It becomes an instrument for effectuating God's elective love (Deut. 7:6-8; Ps. 89:3,4). Through it, He accomplishes the gracious promise that is found from Genesis to Revelation, "I will be their God; they shall be My people."[34]

213

The covenants applied to God's people. But to be included in the people of God—that is, to be included in the benefits of the covenant—one had to bear the covenantal sign (i.e., circumcision).

A covenant contained stipulations binding on the two parties. In return for God's promises, Israel was obliged to render obedience to Him and His commandments. If only Israel would obey His commandments they would enjoy the benefits of living in covenant relationship with God. But failure to keep God's commandments was a sinful fracturing of the covenant relationship—a willful sin to be punished by God.

History demonstrated that Israel was unable to keep the provisions of the covenant. God therefore proposed a new covenant which, instead of being imposed upon the people externally, would be inscribed on their hearts and spirits. The indwelling Spirit of God would ensure obedience to these covenantal obligations. The inference of Isaiah was that God's special servant (the Messiah) would be the enabler of this new covenant.

The Purpose of the Covenant Relationship

The covenant gave definition and identity to the Israelites from the Exodus on. It served as the basis of relationship between God and His people. The entire course of Hebrew history from Sinai to the postexilic era manifested the influence of the covenant relationship. As a consequence, the task of setting forth the theological significance of the covenant is vital.

The Self-Disclosure of God to a Particular People. Walther Eichrodt insists that "God's disclosure of himself is not grasped speculatively, not expounded in the form of a lesson; it is as he breaks in on the life of his people in his dealings with them and moulds them according to his will that he grants them knowledge of his being."[35] God in His sovereignty elected a particular people and shaped them into a spiritual community: "I will take you as my own people, and I will be your God" (Ex. 6:7). The terminology whereby the significance of this election was made clear arose in a covenantal context, a well-known device of the ancient world.[36]

214

6.3 Israel and Its Covenants

Name	God's Promises	Human Conditions
Abrahamic (with Abraham)	Land. Many descendants.	None—but it was based on Abraham's faith.
Circumcision (with Israel)	Inclusion in covenant with Abraham.	To be circumcised.
Mosaic (Sinai) (with Israel)	Great nation. God's own people. Treasured possession. Security in the land.	Honor God as Lord. Obey God's laws.
Davidic (with David)	Great name. Reign of peace. Descendants. Eternal throne.	None—but it was based on David's faith.
New Covenant (with God's people)	God's own people. Security. Progeny. Eternal in duration. Written on heart.	Obedience with help of God's Spirit. Obedience imposed through Messiah.

Through the covenant God set Israel apart from the other nations. The covenant became Israel's "very raison d'être. She had been created for a very special purpose."[37] The Hebrews had been prepared for this purpose by the covenant terms which dictated how they should live. Following the covenant commands would make Israel a model of the right human relationship with God. While this model was certainly incumbent upon the individual Hebrew, the real stress was on the shaping of a spiritual community.

The terms of the covenant—both the promises and the conditions—revealed to Israel much of who God was and what He was like. For example, in Exodus 3:14-16, the covenant name for God was revealed as *Yahweh*, "I am who I am" or "I will be who I will be." The stress here was upon a God who actively existed, a God who acted in the world.[38]

> The character of the name ought to be clear when the patriarchal promises are borne in mind. Israel must now recognize in Yahweh the only real existent Deity, who directs her future. The very nature of the disclosure is at once an assertion by Yahweh of his uniqueness, his exclusive right over, and his relationship with, Israel.[39]

Consequent to an understanding of God's name was the realization that He was a personal God. In so many ways He acted like a human being. Indeed, Eichrodt maintains that the foundation of Old Testament faith "is his personhood—a personhood which is fully alive, and a life which is fully personal, and which is involuntarily thought of in terms of the human personality."[40] At the same time, God was also perceived as the fullness of perfection, His powers heightened beyond all human capabilities.

While one might mention other characteristics of God revealed through the covenant relationship—such as holiness, wrath, and love—one trait which is starkly set forth is His sovereignty. In His love for, protection of, and discipline of Israel, the God of Israel is exalted in hymns as a mighty warrior-hero, awful and glorious in His holiness, a doer of miracles. Not only was He Creator and Ruler of nature, but He was also absolutely sovereign in human history, moving humanity toward His own goal, allowing nothing to interfere with His purposes.[41]

The Self-Disclosure of God to All Humanity. In His covenant relationship with Israel God intended to grow a relationship of wider scope which would extend to all the nations. The Lord had promised Abraham that through him "all nations on earth will be blessed, because you have obeyed me" (Gen. 22:18; cf. 12:3; 18:18). If nothing else, the idea given was that those of other nations would consider Abraham to be an ideal, one who should be emulated if they wished to be blessed.[42]

Similar sentiments were echoed by the prophets, especially Isaiah. One of the tasks given by the Lord to His Servant was the renewal of Israel. But now the scope of His mission was

216

being extended to becoming "a light for the Gentiles, that you may bring my salvation to the ends of the earth" (Isa. 49:6). God's intention for Israel went far beyond her own salvation; through her He would reveal Himself to all humanity.[43] Even though the Hebrews rarely took it up, an evangelistic burden had been laid upon them to witness to their neighbors.

A Clear Explication of God's Will. Because the Fall had clouded the original relationship between God and humanity, sinful people lived in a climate of doubt as to God's will for them and as to how the damaged relationship might be repaired and renewed. This common human ignorance appeared clearly in the religious rituals practiced by most peoples in an effort to placate heaven and learn the divine mind in regard to themselves.

The remedy for human ignorance of God and His will would be found only within a divinely initiated covenant. The covenant set forth in no uncertain terms the relationship between God and His people. "I will be your God and you shall be my people." The covenant

> provides life with a goal and history with a meaning. Because of this the fear that constantly haunts the pagan world, the fear of arbitrariness and caprice in the Godhead, is excluded. With this God men know exactly where they stand; an atmosphere of trust and security is created, in which they find both the strength for a willing surrender to the will of God and joyful courage to grapple with the problems of life.[44]

The Creation of Community. The covenant was an instrument for welding the loosely tied Hebrew tribes into a closely knit community with a common purpose, law, worship, and sense of destiny.[45] Israel was the people of God both by covenant and by redemption. While these people might have been united by other things they held in common, it was in the covenant that they were declared a people, namely, God's people. In this common allegiance to the one God whose supply and instruction they had experienced, the Hebrews were unified into one people. Israel's unity was not merely cultural—it was a spiritual unity.[46]

The covenant community was at the same time both exclusive and inclusive. Any who rejected the covenant sign of circumcision were excluded, as were those who gave their devotion to gods other than the Lord. But membership in the community was not limited to Hebrews; for "the decisive requirement for admission [was] not natural kinship but readiness to submit oneself to the will of the divine Lord of the Covenant and to vow oneself to this particular God."[47] Wherever non-Hebrews were ready to obey the Lord and accept the covenant sign on their bodies, they were welcomed into the community as an integral part.

A Testing of Authenticity. It has been said that the covenant was a device whereby Israel was to test her authenticity as the people of God.[48] It stood as a test of her faithful obedience—of her commitment—to God alone. Joshua saw this clearly in his call to covenant renewal (Josh. 24), reminding the Hebrews that their legitimacy as a people lay in their relationship to God, in heeding His Word. Consequently, he informed them as they took the covenant oath afresh that "you are witnesses against yourselves that you have chosen to serve the Lord" (Josh. 24:22). The covenant would serve as a standard by which they would measure their corporate behavior and test their corporate fidelity (or lack thereof) to their commitment.[49]

The covenant gave shape to Israel as a holy community. A fracture of that covenant could be punished by the dissolution of the covenant community. H. Strathmann notes how Israel was God's own people.

> He has rescued it from Egypt and revealed Himself to it. Hence, He and He alone is Israel's God. . . . Yahweh has separated Israel to Himself (Lev. 20:26). He now expects that Israel will separate itself for Him. Yahweh has shown Israel His love. He now expects that Israel will love Him and keep His commandments (Deut. 7:9). Israel is holy: it has been taken from the sphere of the secular world of nations for Yahweh. But this indicative carries with it the imperative: Ye shall be holy! . . . Israel is Yahweh's people only if it conducts itself accordingly.[50]

What is in view here is responsibility. Upon entering into the covenant relationship, Israel enjoyed a special responsibility to

God and to the surrounding nations. If the Hebrews failed in their responsibility, they could lose their election as God's people. Indeed, "the Deuteronomist, and even more so the Chronicler, went so far as to evaluate the history of the monarchical period in these same terms."[51] And, in due course, Israel did fail the test: the Northern Kingdom was destroyed as a people and the Southern Kingdom had to endure conquest and exile for a period of some seven decades.

Leadership Under the Covenant

In the Old Testament, leadership properly began as Israel started to emerge as a national unit, that is, with the Exodus from bondage in Egypt. As the corporate structure of the Hebrews developed, so did various forms of leadership. Eichrodt's classification of Israelite leaders into two broad categories—charismatic and official[52]—provides a distinction helpful for understanding Israel's leadership.

Charismatic Leaders. When it comes to leadership, there can be no question that Moses was the pioneer in Israel. The renewal of monotheism (some might argue, the rise of popular monotheism[53]) and the transformation of religious thinking in Israel was the spiritual lifework of this great man.

While there is no doubt that Moses was a charismatic leader, he was unique in the annals of Hebrew history and defies specific categorization. If anything, he must be seen as a composite of the various leadership models.

> The prophetic type of Moses belongs to the earliest stage of Israelite prophecy. Moses is an antique model of an apostolic prophet; he is a leader and judge having political authority. Like Deborah, Gideon, Samson, and Samuel, he makes his appearance in time of trouble. Like them, he "judges" Israel all his life. Like Gideon, Elijah, and Elisha he fights idolatry and personally works judgments on idols and their worshipers.[54]

To the above may be added aspects of the functions of priest, seer, and lawgiver. It is evident, then, that Moses cannot be placed on the same stratum as "those more ordinary servants of

God or consecrated men whose operations were confined to a restricted sphere."[55]

One category of charismatic leaders may be called the "seers." The Hebrew *rā'a* means "see, perceive." Its participial form *rā'eh* has generally been rendered as "seer." The *rā'eh* seems to have been a person who revealed secrets by seeking a direct answer from the Lord (1 Sam. 9:9). While some suggest on etymological grounds that the seer's revelation always was a visual one, there are no biblical indications that seers were visionaries or dreamers of dreams.[56]

Hāzeh, another Hebrew word rendered "seer," is used in connection with three musicians appointed by David to oversee various aspects of corporate worship (see 1 Chron. 25:5; 2 Chron. 29:30; 35:15). It is also applied to certain court holy men in Judah, such as Gad (2 Sam. 24:11; 1 Chron. 21:9; 2 Chron. 29:25), Iddo (2 Chron. 9:29; 12:15), and Hanani (2 Chron. 19:2). These seers proclaimed God's Word to the king, generally in connection with the king's actions or intended actions, and chronicled them in writing. In such a setting it may be said that the seer was a royal adviser to the king, informing him of God's will.[57]

The Nazirites were a second class of charismatics among the Old Testament Hebrews. These people took a vow to be separate from worldly concerns so that they could be completely devoted to God (Num. 6:1-8). Their vows might require a lifetime commitment—as with Samson, Samuel, and John the Baptist—but Hebrew tradition also prescribed periods of thirty to one hundred days.

Nazirites adhered to certain restrictions. These included abstinence from intoxicants and the refusal to approach or touch a dead body (even a close relative). While obeying the vow, they were to refrain from cutting their hair or beard; long hair evidently was a sign of a Nazirite's commitment to the Lord (Num. 6:7). Eichrodt aptly summarizes their relevance to the Hebrew life and culture:

> The direct significance of the Nazirites was their contribution to the strengthening of the sense of nationhood and of the religious basis on which that was built. They certainly did not a little to awaken Israel's sense of its distinctive character, and to lay

forceful emphasis on the truth that the election of the nation by the jealous God entailed its separation from all things Canaanite. The Nazirites thus became a major factor in keeping the religion of Israel from drifting into a compromise with that of Canaan, and in urging it to assert itself and to develop to the full its unique character.[58]

The "judges" were charismatic leaders during the pre-monarchy period who came to the fore to save Israel from her enemies. They were a vastly differing group of individuals: "Some (e.g., Gideon) rose to their task at the behest of a profound experience of divine vocation; one (Jephthah) was no better than a bandit who knew how to strike a canny bargain; one (Samson) was an engaging rogue whose fabulous strength and bawdy pranks became legendary."[59]

The Hebrew title *shofet* went beyond our English rendition of "judge" in the sense of a legal referee. While it included the former, it also signified one who secured the right of the people by military means. The term might better be interpreted "ruler," for the *shofet* was not only a legal arbiter but a military deliverer of the people.[60]

This office was not hereditary. Judges arose by virtue of their empowerment by the Spirit of the Lord. Because of this divine possession their authority was accepted beyond their own clan or tribe (see Jud. 4:5; 6:34-35; 14:6).[61]

The prophet was unquestionably the most prominent charismatic leader in Israel. The Hebrew *nabi'* (from the Akkadian *nabu*, "to call, announce") refers to a spokesman for the divine will. James Ward tells us that

the message of the prophets, first and last, was a message for Israel. It originated in and for the people of YHWH. Everything they did presupposed their participation in this community. They were formed by it, and they were representative of it. Thus the prophets were the voice of Israel, in dialogue with God.[62]

The prophet's authority was not self-derived but resulted from his utter conviction of divine commissioning. As a consequence, the prophet's voice could shake kings and kingdoms: "Thus says the Lord."[63]

During the early period of Israelite history (from Moses through the united monarchy), most prophets seem to have been ecstatics. Numbers 11:24-29 describes how the spirit of Moses was transferred to the elders of Israel and caused them to prophesy ecstatically. Samuel, in anointing Saul as first king of Israel, promised him that "the Spirit of the Lord will come upon you in power, and you will prophesy with [other prophets]; and you will be changed into a different person" (1 Sam. 10:6). Under the power of the Spirit amazing things happened, as in the case of Elijah, who outran King Ahab's chariot with superhuman strength (1 Kings 8:46).

Many of these ecstatic prophets belonged to guilds or schools, and were known as "the sons of the prophets." They appear to have been under the authority of a senior prophet, referred to as their "father." We see Elijah and Elisha as leaders of prophetic schools at Bethel and Gilgal (see 2 Kings 2:3; 4:38). These prophetic schools were itinerant, traveling about the country giving divine counsel as needed.[64]

Other prophets were tied to the major worship centers of Israel (e.g., Jerusalem and Bethel). These "cultic prophets" seem to have been in a collegial relationship with the priests, and played a special role in worship, especially in intercessory prayers. They also brought answers from the Lord to the petitioners.[65]

The prophets were frequently in conflict with the official leadership of Israel, especially when they perceived the latter to be departing from the Lord's expectations. Ward observes:

> The basis of the prophets' criticism of the kings and the other leaders of Israel was a set of convictions concerning the nature of true community and the proper service of God. In other words, their presuppositions were ethical and theological . . . the prophets' social criticism . . . was based on ethical principles . . . rooted in faith in God's righteousness and motivated by commitment to the service of God.[66]

Official Leaders. Israel's earliest official leaders were priests—a leadership role which Israel recognized early in its history and persisted through the New Testament era. While the official priesthood dates back to the time immediately following the

222

Exodus, the Book of Exodus 24:5 indicates that there were priests in Hebrew society prior to that time.

While the priesthood was limited to the tribe of Levi (beginning with Aaron and his sons and their descendants), not all Levites—or even males of Aaron's line—could become priests. Certain physical and ceremonial restrictions existed (see Lev. 21). There were three essential levels to the priesthood: the high priest, the priests, and the Levites. Although the Levites began as servants to the Aaronic priesthood, in Deuteronomy they appear to have been equated with the priests (see Deut. 17:9, 18; 18:1, etc.).[67]

The priest was set apart from the people by an elaborate installation ritual. He was seen as one chosen by God and dedicated to Him, one who represented God to the people and the people to God. His main function was the ministering of the Torah to the people (Deut. 33:10). He also possessed certain secondary responsibilities, such as judging certain types of leprosy and their cleansing (Lev. 13–14), discerning cases of ritual impurity (Lev. 15), and the judging of certain legal infractions (Num. 5:11-21; Deut. 21:5; 2 Chron. 19:8-11).[68] "All the dealings of the people of Jahweh with its God were imposed upon the priestly office: the priest was thus pre-eminently the person competent to mediate any kind of divine decision."[69]

The highest level of official leadership in Hebrew society was the king. Eichrodt maintains that the monarchy shared its origins with the priestly and prophetic offices, "namely *the office of the primitive chieftain endowed with divine powers,* and exercising both priestly, prophetic and royal functions."[70]

With the advent of the monarchy in Israel there was a shift from charismatic to official, established national leadership. While Saul was a charismatic type differing little from the judges who preceded him, David combined the charismatic and official aspects in establishing a dynastic monarchy. His successors were increasingly non-charismatic and official as kings. And as the charismatic flavor of the monarchy decreased, the king increasingly gave way to the prophet as God's spokesperson, although the former continued to represent (or symbolize) the people before the Lord. Thus, as the monarch went, so went the people. If he became apostate, Israel was punished; if he was faithful, Israel received divine blessing.

Breaking the Covenant

Implicit in the nature of a covenant as an agreement binding on two or more parties is the possibility that one of the parties may not honor it. The idea of a possible annulment of the contract is further implied by the addition to the covenant of a series of curses as the consequence of unfaithfulness to its stipulations.[71] For example, in Deuteronomy 28:15ff, Joshua warns the Hebrews that if they fail to obey the Lord's commands a multitude of curses will overtake them (and there follows a fearsome catalog!). J.A. Thompson comments on this aspect of the covenant:

> Israel was God's covenant people. God, in sheer grace, displayed many mighty acts of deliverance on her behalf and took her into covenant. In gratitude Israel accepted His invitation. It was her covenant with Yahweh which created, sustained and gave meaning to her nationhood. To disobey Yahweh was to betray and to reject the very source of her life. . . . Out of fellowship with Yahweh she was cut off from life.[72]

Our chief concern is the covenant between God and Israel mediated by Moses at Sinai. This "covenant of obligation"[73] was based on the patriarchal covenant, but stressed human obligation along with the consequences of human behavior in regard to the continuance of the divine-human relationship as spelled out in the covenant. Here, the stipulations were geared to individual Israelites and required their compliance, but the community was corporately responsible to God for the behavior of its members. Each citizen, then, had a twofold obligation under the regulations of the covenant: to conform to the demands as an individual, and to take part in the systematic execution of justice and fairness, so participating in the community's obligation before God. How the Hebrews both individually and corporately fulfilled their dual duty would determine the destiny of their nation.[74]

Grave problems, therefore, would occur when numerous individuals broke covenant fidelity and the nation as a corporate entity failed to mete out appropriate justice. Such an incident is recorded in Jeremiah 34:8-22 where Zedekiah, king of Judah, made a covenant with the people of Jerusalem to liberate all the slaves. This covenant was in accord with the Mosaic covenant of Sinai which stipulated that after a Hebrew slave had served six years he was to be freed. The people "agreed, and set them free. But afterward they changed their minds and took back the slaves they had freed and enslaved them again" (34:10b, 11). Because of this covenant violation, "I now proclaim 'freedom' for you, declares the Lord—'freedom' to fall by the sword, plague and famine" (34:17b). The kingdom would be utterly destroyed by the Babylonians. David Noel Freedman explains:

> Merited judgment cannot be put off forever. . . . Once the agreement was broken, it was up to the divine Suzerain to decide whether to renew it or not. And the time came when, after many periods of grace and renewals of the relationship, the patience of the long-suffering Deity was exhausted, the curses of the Covenant were enforced against the condemned nation, and it fell."[5]

The Hebrew people made a serious mistake in assuming that because God had chosen Israel as His people He was therefore obliged to keep them safe and secure regardless of their behavior. And so they not only believed that they could sin with impunity, but that God would punish their enemies and bless them forever. They eagerly looked forward to that "Day of the Lord."

The prophets, however, knew differently. They attempted to confront the people by proclaiming an approaching cataclysm because of national sin. They warned that the Day of the Lord would be one of tragedy and not triumph (Amos 5:18), that God was poised to strike down apostate Jerusalem (Isa. 9:8-21), and that it was too late to avoid His visitation of doom (Hosea 4-5; Micah 1:3-7).

Such terrible utterances of divine judgment were necessary if the prophets of God were ever to make Israel recognize the gravity of her sinful behavior. Covenant-breaking led to alienation from a holy God. Such deliberate wrongdoing further resulted in an inner perversion totally destructive of personal relationships, not only human-divine but also human-human encounters.

The more the hideous power and extent of this inner perversion, swelling into a demonic compulsion, a cancer corrupting the whole history of the nation, is disclosed, the more shatteringly can the irremedial character of its breach of faith be brought home to the people, and the more unbreakable the inner coherence between guilt and punishment shown to be. Israel is placed on a par with the nations; and in the day when Yahweh establishes his universal sovereignty she can look forward not simply to the punishment of the heathen, but primarily to her own condemnation.[76]

So the Hebrews succumbed to God's judgment.

With the destruction of Judah and the exile to Babylon of its leading citizens, it was presumed by many that God's curse on the nation because of its covenant failure had occurred. Accordingly, when the opportunity to return from exile to Palestine occurred, and Jerusalem and its temple were being rebuilt, it was also presumed that the covenant was being re-established.

The prophets were persuaded that God's grace in bringing His people back to their promised home would result in a transformed Israel. He was still committed to this people in spite of their regrettable history. And yet, a renewal of the old covenant would not suffice. A new and more effective covenant was needed. To reinstitute things as they had been prior to the destruction of the nation would be effectively to promise a fresh national catastrophe. Consequently, the Lord promised a new agreement. Its basis would be God's unconditional guarantee. The new covenant would quite literally set apart a new people unto the Lord.[77]

Nor would the element of human obligation be lacking. But since Israel had demonstrated an inability to keep the covenant stipulations, a special divine grace would be given, namely, God's own Spirit indwelling the human heart: "I will put my Spirit in you and move you to follow my decrees and be careful to keep my laws" (Ezek. 36:27). Freedman summarizes the idea nicely: "Yahweh's irreversible commitment to Israel flows into the blessings which he bestows on an obedient people who, through the power of his Spirit, fulfil all the requirements of the Covenant."[78]

226

The Eschatological Fulfillment of the Covenant

While the restoration of Israel to her homeland brought about expectations of a new covenant in which God would restore the greatness and fortunes of the Hebrew people, these expectations did not last long. Many Jews stayed in Babylon and Persia, preferring the security of their existing conditions; those who did return faced famine and physical dangers, as well as opposition from other peoples who had settled in the region. Under such threatening conditions, the temple took some twenty years to construct, and it was such a poor edifice that those older people who recalled Solomon's temple wept in humiliation and frustration. John Bright observes that "morale in the community was dangerously low. How little these were the purged and purified people of God . . . we may see from a reading of Haggai, Malachi, and Nehemiah."[79]

The Rise of Apocalyptic. During the postexilic period prophecy as it had been known gradually died out. But hope did not die with it. In its place arose a futuristic theology known as Apocalyptic. Its name is taken from the word Apocalypse (unveiling, revelation), referring specifically to a revelation enshrouded in highly symbolic terms concerning the end time or Day of the Lord and thought to be imminent in its occurrence. Apocalyptic writings were not systematized; for their authors were absolutely certain that the end was at hand. They were convinced that a tremendous conflict between God and Satan was already in process, and undoubtedly moving toward a final resolution.

> Since the age of prophecy had ended, apocalypticists were obliged, their works being of a predictive nature, to place their words in the mouths of prophets and worthies long dead. They were fond of describing bizarre visions in which nations and historical individuals appear as mysterious beasts. They sought by manipulating numbers to calculate the exact time of the end—which would be soon. They reinterpreted the words of earlier prophets to show how they were being fulfilled, or were about to be.[80]

Apocalyptic enjoyed popular attention between 200 B.C. and A.D. 100. While only two books of this genre were included in the canon of Scripture (Daniel in the Old Testament and Revelation in the New), multitudes of others were produced. All of them stressed that, even though evil might seem to have gained the upper hand in this world, God was nonetheless sovereign. He would judge the world, redeeming His own people and casting Satan and those who followed him into eternal punishment. Instead of the turning point in history envisioned by pre-exilic Hebrew society, the Apocalypse held out the picture of a new and recreated world outside of history.[81] As Bright summarizes the significance of this age:

> The Apocalypse was thus a legitimate outgrowth, albeit to us a strange one, of Israel's faith in God who is Lord of history. In times of darkest despair, when the kingdoms of this earth exercised their tyrannical and unbroken rule, it affirmed and kept alive Israel's historic confidence in the triumphant Kingdom of God. It asked for a solution of man's dilemma in terms of divine intervention. Like all the hope of Israel, it pointed to a solution beyond itself.[82]

Other Eschatological Strains. One must not make the mistake of thinking that Apocalyptic was the only genre of eschatological thinking in Israel. The hope of salvation may be traced back to before the monarchy.

In the period of the Judges and in the early monarchy, two types of salvation-hope may be distinguished, one militaristic and one pacific.[83] The former strain is represented by the Balaam oracles in Numbers 23 and 24. The first oracle (23:7-12) indicated Israel's uniqueness among the nations because of her divine election and called to mind the Lord's fulfillment of the covenant promise to make of Abraham's progeny a great nation. The second saying (23:18-24) asserted God's utter reliability and the surety of His covenant promises. What He had promised (namely, to bless Israel), He could not fail to do.[84] The remaining oracles (24:3-18) identified the Lord God as the Source of life and were highly eschatological in language. In an ecstatic state Balaam saw a figure removed in time, a figure somewhat obscured but who was called "a star out of Jacob" and "a scepter from Israel" (24:17). He would conquer and destroy Israel's enemies. Timothy Ashley notes that the passage "surely does give some of the first glints of messianic hope, even if only in a highly indirect form."[85]

The latter strain occurs in the oracle pertaining to Judah in Jacob's Blessing in Genesis 49:8-12. Judah would be the focus of his brothers' praise and obeisance; for he would rise to prominence among them and to a position of rulership. Indeed, the essence of the Blessing was that "the scepter will not depart from Judah, nor the ruler's staff from between his feet until he comes to whom it belongs and the obedience of the nations is his" (49:10). In other words, Judah would have dominion over Israel until a future ruler arrived (from Judah) whose dominion would be expanded to include all peoples.[86] The remaining verses describe the peace and prosperity which would attend this latter ruler's arrival. Old Testament theologian, Gerhard Von Rad says of the One to come, "He is almost a Dionysiac figure."[87] Certainly, a strong argument may be made for an eschatological interpretation of this passage.

The two excerpts, above, fit in well with the Hebrew concept of history as moving under God's sovereignty to a final consummation. The future is not something new and radical, but is rather an integral part of God's eternal plan unfolding as the ages progress.[88]

This attachment of eschatological hope to current reality became even more evident during the monarchy period. Because of the covenant God had concluded with David establishing his throne forever, their kings were regarded by the Hebrews as the Lord's direct representatives and imbued with almost superhuman qualities. The royal psalms refer to the king as God's son by adoption (Ps. 2:7) who will administer with equity the terms of the Mosaic Covenant (Ps. 72:1-19), and on whose behalf the Lord will crush all enemies.[89] While acknowledging that these psalms were aptly descriptive of David, Derek Kidner hastens to assert that "the painful inadequacies of the actual kings [after David] helped to raise men's eyes towards the One to come."[90] It is not for nothing that Psalm 2:2 refers to the figure of the king as God's "Anointed One" (literally, "Messiah"), and as time progressed, the idea of "messiah" was transferred from the current monarch to the anticipation of a future Davidic ruler who would fulfill God's covenant and usher in eternal paradise.[91]

229

A more traditional eschatological concept was evidently co-existing alongside of the salvation-hope. It was the idea of the Day of the Lord.[92] The Hebrews looked forward to that day when God would intervene in history to elevate Israel and destroy or subjugate her enemies forever. Beginning in the eighth century before Christ, the prophets were more universalistic and less optimistic in their approach. The Prophet Amos was representative:

> Woe to you who long for the day of the Lord! Why do you long for the day of the Lord? That day will be darkness, not light. It will be as though a man fled from a lion only to meet a bear, as though he entered his house and rested his hand on the wall only to have a snake bite him (5:18-19).

Thus, contrary to popular belief, the Day of the Lord would not be Israel's advancement and glory. "This does not in itself constitute a decisive change in the concept . . . for the coming of the Lord on his day includes both, from the start: disaster and judgment for the enemies of the Lord, but salvation and deliverance for the remnant faithful to the Lord."[93] A remnant would be set aside. And out of the remnant would be fashioned a new Israel for a new era of paradise (see Amos 9:11-15; Hosea 2:21-23; etc.).

In Isaiah, eschatological consummation was focused on the Servant of God. While some have suggested that the Servant should be interpreted as the nation of Israel (and certain passages, such as 45:4 and 49:3, might lead in that direction), He is spoken of as "an individual charged with the responsibility of restoring Israel to favor with God (cf. 49:5). Furthermore, He is said to be righteous and innocent of all wrongdoing (cf. 53:9,11), something that certainly could not be said of the nation as a whole (cf. 42:19-25)."[94] Eichrodt understands the Servant to be the figure of a Savior-King, arising out of the Davidic Messiah of other prophecies (see above) and perhaps proclaimed in a liturgy of an annual royal festival.[95]

In Isaiah's portrait the coming Savior-King was not a figure of militaristic power or cataclysmic judgment. His depiction is both positive and universal, ushering in paradise for all peoples.[96]

Conclusions. The Hebrews had always believed that God would never allow them to be overcome by enemies. He was almost obligated to protect them no matter what, and so the majority of their society looked forward with eagerness to that day when God would break through and make them supreme in the world. When Israel fell to the Babylonian hoards, however, that confidence was shaken and the people realized that they had broken God's covenant and were being punished. With the subjugation of Babylon to the Persians and the subsequent restoration of the Jews to their homeland, there was a fervent hope that a restored Israel would receive all that had been foretold by the prophets. But with the decline of prophecy and the advent of further persecution by heathen peoples, hopes were transferred to the apocalyptic anticipation of God's creation of a new order beyond history, to that time when He would bring history to a close, destroy His enemies (who were Israel's foes, as well), and exalt His people, the Jews.

But there were always eschatological strains in Israelite history. From its early history as a national entity, Israel held a belief that God would at some point bring history to a consummation and redeem His people. There seem to have been two concurrent strands of thought: one which envisioned a catastrophic, earth-shaking time of war and judgment; and one which was much more gentle in its scope, focusing on a kingly figure who would dispense paradise on a universal scale. In both of these scenarios Israel played a prominent role and was a focal point of God's plan of action.

CHAPTER SEVEN

The People of God
in the Gospels

From Genesis to Revelation the Bible deals with God's election of a people to be His own. The Old Testament is the account of God's calling of Israel as His people. Frank Stagg rightly observes that, "when national Israel proved to be 'flesh,' . . . God turned to the creation of a remnant. The remnant itself proved elusive, and it finally came to realization in one person . . . even Jesus Christ."[1] When Israel as a nation rejected Jesus, God called into being as His people a new entity, the church.

Hans Küng makes a very clear distinction, on biblical grounds, between Israel and the church, declaring that

> the name Israel still applies to the ancient people of God, even after Christ, and cannot be taken away from it and simply transferred to the New Testament ekklesia. On the other hand the New Testament ekklesia clearly remains, outwardly and historically as well as inwardly and actually, linked to Israel, the ancient people of God.[2]

There can be no question that the New Testament church believed in this continuity and applied to itself, as the people of God, the promises of God to His Old Testament people.

JESUS' INTENTION

There has been considerable scholarly controversy over whether Jesus ever intended to create the church. In his work,

232

L'Evangile et l'Eglise, Alfred Loisy wrote, "Jesus announced the kingdom, and what came was the Church."[3] While Küng has maintained this statement to be a positive one, identifying the church with the kingdom of God, other scholars have decried this identification. Friedrich Nietzsche, for example, contended that "the Church is precisely that against which Jesus inveighed—and against which He taught His disciples to fight."[4]

H.E.W. Turner has responded to and summarized the controversy appropriately.

> The question, "Did Jesus found the Church?" is capable of a wider and a narrower range. If we mean, "Did Jesus intend that His mission and message should be enshrined and mediated in a community living under His allegiance?" we can with great probability give the answer "Yes." If, however, we identify the Church as He envisaged it with any particular body of Christians living now, and take it to include the sum-total of their beliefs and practices, we are compelled to answer "No."[5]

The majority of those who confess the name of Jesus are compelled along with Turner to assert that He came to this earth to proclaim God's kingdom and to effect a community of persons under God's gracious rule. That the word "church" (*ekklēsia*) occurs only twice (Matt. 16:18; 18:17) in all of the Gospels should not be interpreted as evidence against Jesus' intention for the church; for the evangelists use many other terms to denote the people of God. Some of the more common ones deserve careful attention.

The Disciples

In contemplating Jesus' ministry, it is important to note the great gap between His movement and the other comparable movements in Israel of that time. The Pharisees, Essenes, and Zealots constituted sects or parties which attempted to influence the direction of Israel as a believing community. Jesus, however, made no such effort. Instead, He called everyone to repent and accept God's salvation. Those who responded to His invitation followed Him as disciples. In fact, the only sociologically identifiable group that materialized was a tiny band of disciples.[6]

It was these disciples who linked the pre-Pentecost people of God with the post-Pentecost people of God. E.P. Sanders argues cogently that, while a few of His disciples may have believed that Jesus was promising political liberation from Roman oppression (e.g., Judas Iscariot), most of them understood that His kingdom involved some form of "otherworldliness." He writes:

> I think, then, that we must grant an element of continuity between what Jesus expected and what the disciples expected after the crucifixion and resurrection. . . . The resurrection did not change political, military and nationalistic hopes (based on misunderstanding) into spiritual, heavenly ones, but otherworldly-earthly hopes into otherworldly-heavenly. What the disciples originally expected, I propose, was a kingdom which did not involve a military revolt, but which was a good deal more concrete than either a collection of nice thoughts about grace and forgiveness, or a *message* about God's love for sinners and his being near.[7]

The Call to Discipleship. Jesus established His band of disciples by challenging individuals to join Him: "Follow me!" (Matt. 4:19; Mark 1:17-20; 2:14) In this respect He differed markedly from the rabbis, whose students solicited them. Jesus' manner of approach in bringing people into fellowship with Him and with one another was more after the fashion of the call by God to the Old Testament prophets.[8]

It was made very clear to these followers that their call took precedence over all else in life. Nothing was to come before it, not even one's own life: "If anyone comes to me and does not hate his father and mother, his wife and children, his brothers and sisters—yes, even to his own life—he cannot be my disciple" (Luke 14:26).

The call was not simply to an emulation of Jesus' teachings, but to an adherence to His person. Dietrich Bonhoeffer has made the application accurately and, although he intended it for contemporary application, it applies equally well to the "called" of Jesus' day:

> When we are called to follow Christ, we are summoned to an exclusive attachment to his person. The grace of his call bursts

all the bonds of legalism. It is a gracious call, a gracious commandment. It transcends the difference between the law and the gospel. Christ calls, the disciple follows; that is grace and commandment in one. "I will walk at liberty, for I seek thy commandments" (Ps. 119:45).[9]

Some have suggested that one might be a follower of Christ without being a disciple.[10] But such a conception is entirely foreign to the Gospels. The redemption of Christ and the Lordship of Christ go hand in hand.[11] The kingdom of heaven was always communicated through some connection to Jesus' person in trusting obedience.

Discipleship and the Church. Upon realizing that Jesus called people to a personal relationship as disciples, it becomes possible to understand why He did not establish a party or sect. Only a very few were able to share Jesus' person and presence in His earthly ministry, and then only for a limited time. Leonhard Goppelt remarks, "As long as Jesus was bound to time and space, the goal of his ministry could not be achieved within the givens of a historical setting, because its character was in the final analysis, eschatological."[12]

At the same time, while restricted by time-space limitations, Jesus was gathering together the people of God who would form the nucleus of the post-resurrection church.[13] Indeed, this band of disciples was the church in embryo (born on the Day of Pentecost).

The Flock

The picture of the shepherd and his flock was not an unfamiliar one to the people of biblical times. The Old Testament abounds in pastoral imagery. Psalm 100:3 reminded the Hebrews, "Know that the Lord is God. It is he who made us, and we are his; we are his people, the sheep of his pasture." And Isaiah 40:11 noted that "he tends his flock like a shepherd; he gathers the lambs in his arms and carries them close to his heart; he gently leads those that have young." The Gospels display a similar literary concern. In Luke 12:32, Jesus encourages His disciples, "Do not be afraid, little flock, for your Father has been pleased to give you the kingdom." And John 10:1-18 likewise employs the pastoral metaphor. Here, Jesus assures His disciples that "I am the good shepherd; I know my sheep and my sheep know me—just as the Father knows me and I know the Father—and I lay down my life for the sheep" (10:14-15).

In describing the chaos of the coming night of His betrayal, Jesus compared the disciples to a flock of sheep. "This very night you will all fall away on account of me, for it is written, 'I will strike the shepherd, and the sheep of the flock will be scattered' " (Matt. 26:31). And when the post-resurrection Jesus restored Peter, who had denied Him three times on the night of His betrayal, He did so through a pastoral analogy: "Feed my lambs" (John 21:15c); "Take care of my sheep" (John 21:16c); "Feed my sheep" (John 21:17d).

Jesus certainly saw His "flock" as the people of God. The New Testament church carried over the identification of "flock" with the church (Acts 20:28; 1 Peter 5:2). As Frank Stagg correctly observes, "The presence of the 'flock' analogy in the Gospels does supply a part of the answer to the problem of the few occurrences of *'ekklēsia'* in the Gospels."[14]

The True Vine. While the word "church" (*ekklēsia*) does not occur in John's Gospel, the idea is nonetheless present in Jesus' analogy of the vine and its branches (John 15:1-8).[15] This teaching is closely connected to the concept of God's chosen people; for the Jews saw themselves as God's vineyard (see Isa. 5:1-7; 27:2-6; Jer. 2:21; Ps. 80:8-16), planted by God Himself.

In John 15:1, Jesus declared, "I am the true vine." By so doing, He was claiming to supersede Israel as the genuine locus of God's people. The true vine was Jesus and all those in union with Him: His disciples were the branches, deriving their sustenance from Him and, in turn, producing His fruit.[16]

Rudolf Schnackenburg believes this vine metaphor parallels the Pauline concept of the body of Christ. He says that

> what Jesus says here to his band of disciples in view of his departure is after all only realized in the church. Only in the Church is the abiding in Christ and the promise of Christ's abiding in them possible; the disciples and the later believers could

236

not have understood this in any other way (even as regards the supplementary exhortation "to remain in his love" and as regards brotherly love).[17]

It is in the context of the church as His body that one is joined to Christ.

The Apostolate

That Jesus deliberately poured His mission into twelve disciples (Matt. 10:2-4; Mark 3:13-19; Luke 6:13-16) is beyond question. The number twelve was symbolic, signifying the twelve tribes of Israel, the fullness of God's people. Since the conquest and deportation of the Northern Kingdom in 722 B.C. had left only two tribes, twelve was an eschatological sign of restored Israel.[18] Joachim Jeremias maintains that Jesus' use of the number twelve was intended to demonstrate that salvation was not to be limited to the empirical Jewish people, but rather announced an eschatological people of God to which even the Gentiles would be attached.[19]

This special group was commissioned by Jesus not only to accompany Him about the land, imbibing His person and proclamation, but also to represent Him throughout Israel. They were to imitate both Jesus' words and actions, announcing the day of salvation and the imminence of the kingdom, and demonstrating its power by casting out demons. In these aspects, too, they were a vanguard of the church triumphant. That they were Christ's representatives is established by Matthew 10:40, "He who receives you receives me, and he who receives me receives the one who sent me" (cf. Luke 10:16). Goppelt notes:

> Their model of commissioning was not the ordination of the rabbi's pupil, but the model of a non-religious institution, i.e., the personal representation of—to choose a modern image—a power of attorney in legal transactions. This person was called the *shaliah*, the one deputized and sent in place of the other.[20]

It would appear, then, that Jesus had a dual intention in regard to the Twelve. First, they should be representative in the future sense of the people of God's rule. Secondly, they should

237

continue His ministry in the sense of being His personal agents or representatives.

The Prayer for Unity

John 17 takes place in the context of the Last Supper, and is actually the last of five chapters containing Jesus' final discourses to His disciples. It has been suggested that these discourses are somewhat analogous to the "Testaments" of famous individuals which were well-known to both Jewish and Hellenistic writers, the most notable Testament being Deuteronomy, which contains Moses' parting instructions to Israel. George Beasley-Murray, in commenting on the similarity of these two discourses, observes:

> The parallel may have been present in John's mind, for the concept of Jesus as the new (or rather greater than) Moses, bringing about a second Exodus for life in the kingdom of God, is an important theme in this Gospel. In Deuteronomy Israel is on the point of entering the promised land as God's chosen people; the disciples are about to be launched as leaders of renewed Israel to summon the nations into the kingdom of God. The readers of the Gospel know that he who speaks in these discourses is now the crucified and risen Lord . . . Chapters 13-17 thus convey to the church the message of the Lord from the table of the Lord "until he come."[21]

Chapter 17 signals the conclusion of the discourses with a farewell prayer. This prayer, termed "the high-priestly prayer" by sixteenth-century Lutheran theologian David Chytraeus, may be divided into four sections: (1) Jesus' prayer for Himself in relation to His followers (17:1-5); (2) His prayer for His disciples (17:6-19); (3) His prayer for the unity of His people (17:20-23); and (4) His prayer that believers might be perfected in His glory (17:24-26).[22]

Jesus' Prayer for Himself (17:1-5). The purpose of this prayer is twofold: that God the Father may be glorified by Jesus' utter faithfulness right to the end (i.e., that Jesus would serve God as devotedly in dying as He had in living), and that He would

238

through the completion of His earthly ministry impart eternal life to those given Him by the Father. Ray Summers declares that "all that God has done in providing redemption for sinful man redounds to his glory and his praise. It was that for which the Son prayed as he prayed for himself that even in the agony and shame of a Roman crucifixion, he would bring glory to the Father."[23]

One item of supreme importance in this prayer for formulating a theology of the church is the emphasis on those who compose the people of God. They are those whom God has given to Christ (i.e., the elect) and to whom He has granted eternal life (17:2). An understanding of Jesus' definition of eternal life in 17:3 is crucial: "Now this is eternal life: that they may know you, the only true God, and Jesus Christ, whom you have sent." The word "know" in the original (Greek) language, ginosko, suggests experiential rather than informational knowledge; the encountering of God's eternal being will be life eternal.[24]

With the accomplishment of His earthly ministry, Jesus looked forward to reacquiring the glory He had enjoyed with the Father prior to His incarnation (17:5). His reglorification would be different, however; for it would be in His glorified humanity, an eternal testimony to His redemptive work on earth.[25]

Jesus' Prayer for His Disciples (17:6-19). Jesus expressed two principal desires for His disciples: that the Father "protect them" (17:11) and "sanctify them" (17:17). He would soon be reunited with the Father, but they would have to remain in the world; therefore, He asked God to protect them "by the power of your name" (17:11). Some would interpret this through the connection of God's name with His character as revealed by Christ to the disciples; that is, that the disciples should be kept in fidelity to that revelation.[26] A better idea, however, seems to be that of instrumental power (in keeping with the NIV's translation of the Gk.); precedence for such a rendering is found in Old Testament passages such as Psalm 54:1: "Save me, O God, by your name; vindicate me by your might." The context would favor the latter interpretation, particularly in view of the following clause, "the name you gave me," which would then be interpreted as "the power that you gave me." Thus, Jesus was asking the Father to protect the disciples with the same power He had given His Son.[27] In any event, Jesus' prayer was that the Father would keep His disciples in firm adherence to the revelation that Jesus Himself had brought to them from God "so that they may be one as we are one."

This prayer for their preservation is amplified in 17:15. During His earthly ministry, Jesus protected His disciples from harm. With His departure close at hand, He was concerned for their safety, not so much from the hatred of the world, but rather from the one who was behind its malevolence, namely, Satan. As a consequence, He prayed, "My prayer is not that you will take them out of the world but that you will protect them from the evil one."

In the context of 17:17, "sanctification means to be made holy by being set apart for a special purpose. Negatively, the word implies separation from all evil, and so is used in contrast to being involved in the world. Positively, it means dedication."[28] Jesus had dedicated Himself to His mission of world redemption. As He commissioned His disciples to go into the hostile world to continue His work, He prayed that they would be sanctified "by the truth." Like their Master, the disciples must be dedicated to making God's truth—His Word—known throughout the world.[29] Just as He had consecrated Himself to His task, even to the point of death, so He expected His disciples to be completely consecrated to the redemptive mission (17:19).

Jesus' Prayer for Unity (17:20-23). As Jesus prayed for His disciples, His mind envisioned all those who would receive the message of truth and believe on Him (17:20). Summers notes:

> In the sense that the faith of all future believers could be traced in chainlink fashion back to the witness of the apostles after Pentecost, Jesus prayed for the believers through the ages. It is in that sense that believers since Pentecost, even in our own day, have been able to say, "Jesus prayed for me."[30]

Jesus' prayer was "that all of them may be one, Father, just as you are in me and I am in you. May they also be in us so that

240

the world may believe that you have sent me" (17:21). It expresses a unity based in a common nature originating both in the Father and the Son. Merrill C. Tenney has pointed out that Jesus did not pray for complete harmony of mind, nor for consistency of expression, nor for union of visible structure, but for the basic homogeneity of spiritual nature and of affection which would permit His people to bear a convincing witness to the world.[31]

Jesus' Prayer for the Perfection of Believers (17:24-26). This last prayer is somewhat of a reprise of the first in that both have to do with His glory. In the first prayer (17:5), Jesus had prayed that God would glorify Him with the glory they had shared prior to His incarnation. Now He prays, "Father, I want those you have given me to be with me where I am, and to see my glory, the glory you have given me because you loved me before the creation of the world" (17:24). The form of Jesus' prayer here is not a request but a statement of His will in regard to the Father-Son relationship within the Trinity. It is an expression of the ultimate heavenly union of Christ and those who belong to Him. He looked forward to that moment when all of His people would witness His eternal glory with the Father.[32]

The prayer of 17:24 is built squarely on 17:25-26. Jesus Christ was envisioning His parousia, the consummation of history and of the divine redemptive mission. The objective for which He came to earth and gave His life is clearly elucidated in 17:26, "that the love you have for me may be in them and that I myself may be in them." G.R. Beasley-Murray sums up the passage well:

> It has a variety of implications: an ever-increasing understanding of the love of the Father for the Son, an ever fuller grasp of the wonder that that love is extended to believers, an ever-growing love on their part to the Father, an ever deeper fellowship with him in the experience of abiding in the Son and he in them. In this way the love command of 13:34 attains its ultimate fulfillment and the prayer of verse 24 its final exposition: the glory of Christ is the glory of God's love; seen by his people it transforms them into bearers of Christly love.[33]

241

THE CHURCH IN MATTHEW'S GOSPEL

As demonstrated above, the occurrence of the Greek *ekklēsia* (church) only twice in the Synoptic Gospels does not negate Jesus' intention to establish a community of those committed to His lordship. Many other synonyms occur in a multitude of Synoptic settings. These two mentions of *ekklēsia*—both of which appear in Matthew (16:18-19 and 18:17)—nonetheless are important contributions to the biblical theology of the church. Both are solidly embedded in the text of the First Gospel and neither can be excluded on textual critical grounds. Each of these occurrences should be carefully considered.

Matthew 16:18-19

This passage occurs in the context of the question to Simon Peter at Caesarea Philippi as to just who Jesus was. When asked his opinion, Simon replied, "You are the Christ, the Son of the living God" (16:16). It was in response that Jesus asserted:

> Blessed are you, Simon son of Jonah, for this was not revealed to you by man, but by my Father in heaven. And I tell you that you are Peter, and on this rock I will build my church, and the gates of Hades will not overcome it. I will give you the keys of the kingdom of heaven; whatever you bind on earth will be bound in heaven; whatever you loose on earth will be loosed in heaven (16:17-19).

The Church on the Rock. When Jesus said that He was going to build His church, the Greek word He would have used was *ekklēsia* and the Hebrew word was *qāhāl*. The former refers to the assembly of the called out; the latter, to the people of God assembled together. What is in view here is the Lord's people in a general, or universal, sense. There is no thought of a specific denomination or local body, but rather the church in its totality.[34]

In 16:18 Jesus has made a play on words: Peter is the Greek *petros*, and the word "rock" is similar, *petra*. The question has arisen as to what Jesus meant by this statement. The Roman Catholic Church has taken the statement literally, making Peter the rock on which the church is founded. Protestantism has taken the statement less literally, making the rock on which the church is built Peter's confession of faith (16:16). It might be better to admit that it is not a matter of "either-or," but of "both-and." George Eldon Ladd contends that when Peter made his confession of Christ's messiahship, he became the rock; but since he had made that confession as the representative of the Twelve, the rock is the apostolate as a whole.[35] Küng proceeds along much the same line.

> Without the witness and ministry of these first public witnesses authorized by Christ, without the witness and ministry of Peter and the twelve . . . the Church could not exist. The Church is founded on the apostolic witness and ministry, which is older than the Church itself. The apostles are the beginners, the continuing foundation-stones of the Church, the cornerstone and keystone of which is Christ himself.[36]

The Gates of Hades. Jesus was confident that the gates of hades would not overcome the church (16:18). The *King James Version* has done its readers a disservice by rendering *pulai hadou* "the gates of hell," thus giving the impression that Jesus had in mind the powers of evil. In actual fact, Hades is the place of the dead; the *Revised Standard Version* is more accurate in rendering the phrase "the powers of death." What our Lord had in mind was the indestructibility of the church. Such an assurance was essential in light of Jesus' imminent death (16:21). His followers would also be expected to accept the way of the cross (16:24-28). "Death would come to him and to them, but death could not destroy his *ekklēsia.*"[37]

The Keys of the Kingdom of Heaven. While the metaphorical use of "keys" was widely accepted by the ancient Near-Eastern world, including Judea, the term "keys of the kingdom of heaven" is unique to Christian literature. What exactly does the expression mean?

Some biblical comparisons may help. In Luke 11:52 Jesus condemned the Jewish religious leaders for taking away the key of knowledge, unwilling to enter the kingdom of God themselves, and unwilling to permit others to enter. Matthew 23:13

says much the same thing: "Woe to you, teachers of the law and Pharisees, you hypocrites! You shut the kingdom of heaven in men's faces. You yourselves do not enter, nor will you let those enter who are trying to." The biblical concept of knowledge goes beyond the simple accumulation of content awareness; it is a spiritual progression grounded in revelation. Ladd tells us that "the authority entrusted to Peter is grounded upon revelation, that is, spiritual knowledge, which he shared with the twelve," and so the keys of the kingdom are divine insights given to Peter which would allow him to lead others on the same revelatory path he himself had trod.[38]

Succeeding clauses in 16:19 comment on the nature of the authority involved in possessing the keys of the kingdom. The verbs "bind" and "loose" are found in Rabbinic literature in connection with actions that are forbidden or permitted by scribal determination based on an authoritative rendering of the Torah. It was also used in connection with placing under or removing from the "ban" from the synagogue (i.e., a declaration of guilt or innocence in some offense). Hence, it refers to "Peter's authority to declare people forgiven or condemned according to their response to the proclamation of the message of the kingdom, and thus his authority to announce their eligibility to enter the kingdom."[39]

Matthew 18:17

The second mention of *ekklēsia* in Matthew occurs in the context of church discipline. When a brother in Christ continues recalcitrant in an offense, "tell it to the church; and if he refuses to listen even to the church, treat him as you would a pagan or tax collector." This admonition is followed in 18:18 by a declaration on binding and loosing which is similar to that in 16:19.

The Church. While in 16:18 the church mentioned is the "church universal," in this instance *ekklēsia* has to do with a local body; for an offender could not be brought before the universal church. At the same time, the New Testament never sees the local body as only a part of the church, but always as possessing the character of wholeness.[40]

In addition, Jesus here indicates that the church is the final arbiter in relational difficulties between believers. The church represents Jesus Christ in such matters. If repeated attempts fail to reconcile believers, "tell it to the church."

Treated as a Pagan or Tax Collector. Offending believers who have been given every opportunity to repent, and have spurned all of them, are to be excluded from the Christian community: "treat him as you would a pagan or tax collector." While some Bible teachers are presently teaching that this injunction means that the church should treat the unrepentant offenders with compassion, making every attempt to lure them back, the context militates against such an intention. The Jews of Jesus' day shunned pagans and tax collectors. They were pariahs, outcasts from the religious community. The synagogues banned such transgressors; the church was to do the same with unrepentant Christian offenders.

Binding and Loosing. As mentioned earlier, the passage on binding and loosing is essentially the same as that in 16:19. But it goes beyond the latter; for it is extended beyond Peter to the church as a whole. When the church's message of redemption and reconciliation is accepted, the doors to the kingdom are opened wide (loosed), but when that message is spurned, the doors are tightly shut (bound).

Conclusions

Jesus used the word *ekklēsia* to denote all those people — past, present, and future — given to Him by the Father, and forming one community participating under His lordship in the kingdom of God. That single fellowship is the church universal. But Jesus used that same word (*ekklēsia*) to denote a local expression of the body of saints: "There is the reality of wholeness in the local church precisely because Christ is embodied in it, and he is never a fragment."[41]

Our Lord has built His church on Peter and his fellow apostles, all weak and flawed human beings. The church is founded on their commitment to the lordship of Jesus as Messiah. Against such a firmly founded structure the powers of death

245

cannot succeed and are only doomed to failure.

To the apostles initially, and then to the church as a whole, have been given the keys of the kingdom of heaven. This revelatory trust includes the power to bind and loose, that is, to proclaim the condemnation or forgiveness of individuals, according to their acceptance or rejection of the revelation of Christ.

THE CHURCH AND THE KINGDOM

The synoptists make it clear that the central theme of Jesus' public ministry was the approach of the kingdom of God. One of Jesus' favorite phrases was *hē basileia tou theou*, the kingdom of God, which He used interchangeably with *hē basileia tōn ouranōn*, the kingdom of heaven. The latter has the same meaning as the former; for *hoi ouranoi*, literally "the heavens," is simply a synonym for God.[42] From the beginning, Jesus proclaimed the coming kingdom: "The time has come. . . . The kingdom of God is near. Repent and believe the good news!" (Mark 1:15; cf. Matt. 4:23; 9:35; Luke 4:43; 8:1; 9:2, 60)

Jesus clearly intended to establish the church, the community of those who accepted His Messiahship. And given the importance of the kingdom in His preaching, it is likely that He connected the church and the kingdom.

In his monumental *A Theology of the New Testament*, George Eldon Ladd warns against seeking to identify the kingdom with the church. The two are *not* one and the same. The former is the rule of God; the latter, a society of human beings. And yet, there is a connection, which Ladd sets out in five basic statements,[43] each of which will now be examined.

The Church Is Not the Kingdom

Nowhere in the New Testament writings are believers equated with the kingdom. When Jesus Christ commissioned His followers to go out and preach, the good news they proclaimed was that of the coming kingdom of God (Luke 9:2), not the coming church. Nor were His disciples seen as representatives of the kingdom; Jesus Himself was God's personal emissary in that regard, as verified (in Luke 11:20) by His casting out of demons. And the New Testament church understood and accepted the difference; for the first missionaries emphasized the kingdom in their teachings (Acts 8:12; 19:8; 20:25; 28:23, 31), and one could not with any measure of credibility substitute "church" where the term "kingdom" appears. George Ladd emphasizes that "the church is the people of the Kingdom, never the Kingdom itself. Therefore it is not helpful even to try to say that the church is a 'part of the Kingdom,' or that in the eschatological consummation the church and Kingdom become synonymous."[44]

The Kingdom Creates the Church

Because of God's dynamic rule in the world as manifested in the life of Jesus Christ, men and women have been confronted and transformed in such a manner that they have come together in a community fellowship. And from the time of the New Testament, that community has been the church.

Several of Jesus' parables set forth a community concept. The Parable of the Mustard Seed illustrated the amazing results attained from small beginnings (Mark 4:30-32). The Parable of the Great Net (Matt. 13:47-52) portrays the kingdom as inclusive in its scope, but necessitating a process of choosing the righteous and rejecting the unholy at the end of the age. "The present state of the kingdom cannot, therefore, be identified with the pure church, but the latter clearly rises out of the former."[45]

The Church Witnesses to the Kingdom

The church is not the kingdom, nor can it become the kingdom. Its task is to faithfully testify to the kingdom. Originally, this ministry belonged to Israel as the people of God. They were to be "a light to the Gentiles," confronting them with the claims of the sovereign God. But when Israel proved unfaithful, God in Christ constituted a new people, the church, to witness to His rule. They were to model kingdom life (Matt. 5–7). In fact, this demonstration of kingdom life would be an integral component in the testimony of the church to the kingdom of God.[46]

247

The Church Is the Instrument of the Kingdom

In their life of submission to Christ, the disciples became instruments of God's kingdom. Their authority as instruments of the kingdom was demonstrated as they forgave sins (John 20:23), healed the sick (Matt. 10:1), and cast out evil spirits (Mark 6:7). This authority is expressly what Christ seeks to wield through the church by sending His followers to all peoples to summon them all to discipleship, to bring them under His rule visibly and productively, and to uphold them as His followers through the teaching and order of His spokespeople (cf. Matt. 28:19-20).[47]

The Church Is Custodian of the Kingdom

The Jewish religious leaders of Jesus' day taught that Israel was the custodian of the kingdom of God. God's rule had been entrusted to Israel through the Law. Since Israel was custodian of the Law, by extension she was also custodian of God's kingdom on earth. Gentiles might enter the kingdom, but only through becoming proselytes to Judaism and submitting to the Law. Israel was held to mediate the kingdom of God to the non-Hebrew world.[48]

Because the nation rejected the Messiah God had sent them, Israel was removed from its role. Those individuals who did receive Jesus as their Messiah were formed into a community under the rule of God. This community, the *ekklēsia*, not only witnesses to the kingdom, but serves as its custodians, as well. The church's custodianship of the kingdom is manifested in Jesus' statement to His disciples, "He who receives you receives me, and he who receives me receives the One who sent me" (Matt. 10:40).[49]

Conclusions

While the kingdom of God and the church are two completely distinct and separate entities, they are nonetheless inextricably intertwined. The church arises out of the kingdom of God; apart from the latter, the former would not exist. God has ordained the church to witness to His rule. It is the instrument of His kingdom. But it is more. In a very real way the church is the custodian of the kingdom; and through its witness it mediates the kingdom to the world. In the present age, membership in the kingdom of God cannot be had apart from membership in the church.

IN SUMMARY

The very heart of our Lord's preaching was the message "The kingdom of God is at hand." While different interpreters have placed a variety of meanings on the significance of the kingdom,[50] none would disagree that its approach occupied a major part of Jesus' energies and ministry.

While some would deny that Jesus ever intended to establish the church, the testimony of the Gospel writers demonstrates His determination to form a community under the rule of God as represented by God's Son the Messiah. Thus the church arises out of the kingdom of God. The Matthean references to "the keys of the kingdom" and to "binding" and "loosing" demonstrate the close connection between the church and the kingdom. The church is the instrument of the kingdom, testifying to it and challenging people to submit to the rule of God as set out in Jesus' teachings. Those who do so are promised eternal life; for "the gates of hades" cannot prevail against the church. Indeed, those who constitute "the called out" are to persist in proclaiming the kingdom until that day when it is realized in its fullness.

CHAPTER EIGHT

The Apostolic Concept of the People of God

If the Gospels record the gestation of the church in the mind of Jesus, the Acts of the Apostles sets forth its birth through the power of the Holy Spirit, the Epistles describe its structure and organization, and Revelation portrays its consummation. Each of the apostolic writers will be examined in turn in order to distill his particular theology of the church.

THE PEOPLE OF GOD IN THE BOOK OF ACTS

The Book of Acts serves as a bridge between the Gospels and Epistles. It shows how the church as the people of God detached itself from Israel and became a separate community which moved to embrace first the "God-fearers" and then all the Gentiles. The writer, Luke, reveals trends in the development of the church which become full-blown in the Epistles.[1]

The Birth of the Church

Even though Jesus had spoken of the church during His public ministry, He had never made any calculated effort to found a separate community. And yet, within a few weeks of the crucifixion, His disciples were among the people, proclaiming the good news of the glorified Messiah, and assembling a messianic community.[2] What happened to cause such a change?

The Resurrection of Jesus. No event was more crucial to the

250

transformation of the disciples than was Jesus' resurrection. The Gospels portray the disciples as having expected Jesus to establish an earthly kingdom which would liberate the Jews from foreign occupation and make them the premier power in the world. The Crucifixion had devastated their hopes. Upon Jesus' arrest His disciples had run away, abandoning Him. Following His death they had gone into hiding, meeting together behind barred doors.

In spite of such craven behavior, within a matter of weeks these same disciples were sallying forth with a new message which they boldly proclaimed with no regard for threats from the authorities. Such a sudden transformation hinged on the resurrection of Jesus; and this same event formed the content of the message they now boldly proclaimed: "After His suffering [i.e., His crucifixion], He showed Himself to these men and gave many convincing proofs that He was alive" (Acts 1:3). Thus, Hans Küng declares:

> The oldest circle of Jesus' disciples based its account, with considerable emphasis, on meetings which they really and unquestionably had with Jesus, whom God had raised from the dead. The Church sprang not from imaginings, not out of a baseless credulity, but from real experiences of encounters with one who was truly alive; from the standpoint of unbelief these encounters may be challenged, but no interpretation of the disciples' witness can explain them away.[5]

Through His resurrection, Jesus proved the truth of His statement in Matthew 16:18-20 that the powers of hades did not have the final say. He was the guarantee of the promise that those who committed to His lordship would live for eternity.

The proclamation of the resurrection of Jesus became a rallying point for His disciples. Whenever believers met they greeted one another with "The Lord is risen!" and "He is risen indeed!" As they preached the good news of His resurrection, the primitive community demonstrated that through His resurrection, the Jesus of history had become the Lord of glory, the Christ of faith: "Therefore let all Israel be assured of this: God has made this Jesus, whom you crucified, both Lord and Christ" (Acts 2:36).

251

The Charter Membership. The Book of Acts sets the size of the original post-resurrection Christian community at about 120. These included the Twelve (excepting Judas Iscariot, who had committed suicide [Acts 1:15-19]) and the women who had supported Jesus' ministry, along with Jesus' mother Mary and His half brothers (1:11-14). That there was some significance to the band of the Twelve is indicated by the decision to select Matthias as a successor to Judas. At the same time, the community as a whole seems to have been involved in the selection (1:22-26).

The Pentecost Experience. The event which traditionally has been termed the birth of the church is the descent of the Holy Spirit on the Day of Pentecost. The word "birth" should be used loosely; for the community was already in existence. It was, however, the moment of animation of the church.

In relating the Pentecost event, Luke was seeking to portray the church as a community of the Holy Spirit, under His control and direction.[4] And because the Holy Spirit founded the church in Jerusalem, Luke naturally identified the church with Israel. Indeed, Luke adopted a very positive attitude toward the original people of God (e.g., Acts 4:10; 13:17), and did not include the prophecy against them on hardening (Isa. 6:9-10) until the very end of his book (Acts 28:26-27).[5] Even after persecution broke out and the bulk of the church fled Jerusalem, the apostles remained (8:1). And when the faith spread to the Gentiles throughout Asia Minor and Greece, Jerusalem retained its premier position as the center of Christianity.

That the Holy Spirit descended on the Day of Pentecost was also significant. According to Rabbinic tradition, it was on Pentecost that Moses received God's Law on Mount Sinai; it was believed, moreover, that Moses had understood the law in 70 languages. It has been suggested that a possible Lucan motif was connected to this idea: "Just as the law which united Israel to the old covenant was available to people in 70 languages, so the Spirit of God united the new community of God in a new covenant with the capability of communicating the good news in all languages."[6]

The events of Pentecost were simply described by Luke. The community was assembled together on the morning of Pentecost:

Suddenly a sound like the blowing of a violent wind came from heaven and filled the whole house where they were sitting. They saw what seemed to be tongues of fire that separated and came to rest on each of them. All of them were filled with the Holy Spirit and began to speak in other tongues as the Spirit enabled them (2:2-4).

Because of the Feast, members of Diaspora Judaism were in Jerusalem. The sound brought them to the disciples, and they were astounded to hear these Galileans praising God in their own native dialects. Peter took advantage of their bewilderment to preach the good news of Christ's earthly ministry, passion, and glorification. "Those who accepted his message were baptized, and about three thousand were added to their number that day" (2:41).

The Direct Results of Pentecost. Acts 2:42-47 summarizes the immediate results of the descent of the Spirit. Not only were 3,000 added to the church in one day, but they were quickly assimilated into the *koinōnia*, or fellowship. The believers paid close attention to the teaching of the apostles. And the strong spirit of community pervading their fellowship could be seen not only in their attitude toward material possessions, but also in the way that they ate together and worshiped together. In this context, "the Lord added to their number daily those who were being saved" (2:47b). Bruce has suggested that "those who were being saved" could virtually be translated as "the remnant," because "the 'remnant' of the old Israel also formed the nucleus of the new Israel."[7]

Further Visitations of the Spirit. With the descent of the Spirit on the church at Jerusalem, the community of faith began to grow like wildfire (cf. Acts 4:4; 5:14; 6:1, 7). Opposition by the Jewish religious leadership and a persecution (which included the martyrdom of Stephen) served merely to spread the Christian witness throughout Judea and Samaria.

The story of Philip's evangelistic activity is the account of the Holy Spirit's advancement of the church into Samaria (Acts 8:4-25) and, quite literally, "to the ends of the earth" (8:26-40). The mission to Samaria signified the first intrusion of the post-resurrection church into a non-Jewish community. David Dockery declares that

> God in his providence withheld the gift of the Holy Spirit until Peter and John laid their hands on the Samaritans. Peter and John, two leading apostles who were highly thought of in the mother church at Jerusalem, were accepted at that time as brothers in Christ by the new converts in Samaria. Luke's story communicates that in this initial advance of the gospel outside Jerusalem, God was not only working to advance the gospel in Samaria, but was working to bring about the acceptance of these new converts by the church in Jerusalem.[8]

The ancient world regarded Ethiopia as being on the southernmost edge of the world. Thus, Luke may well have felt that Philip's conversion of this Gentile government official was a fulfillment of Acts 1:8.[9]

The conversion of Cornelius was a further advance of the Spirit in the world. A Roman centurion, he was a "God-fearer," a believing Gentile who had not undergone proselyte baptism or circumcision. He was well-known in the area as a man of deep spiritual devotion and social concern. The whole episode leading to his conversion was divinely orchestrated. An angel commanded Cornelius to send to Joppa for Peter (Acts 10:1-8). While Cornelius' emissaries were en route, Peter received a divinely sent vision directing him not to "call anything impure that God has made clean" (10:9-16). Then the Spirit told him to go to Joppa and speak to Cornelius (10:19-23). As Peter preached to the Roman household, the Holy Spirit fell on those listening. It was the Pentecostal experience all over again. "The circumcised believers who had come with Peter were astonished that the gift of the Holy Spirit had been poured out even on the Gentiles. For they heard them speaking in tongues and praising God" (10:45-46). The result was the Gentiles' conversion and inclusion in the Christian community.

Other Christians from Jerusalem had sought refuge from persecution in Antioch of Syria. Initially, they proclaimed the Gospel only to the Jews, but Christian Jews from Crete and Cyrene began to witness to Greek Gentiles. Barnabas was sent out by the Jerusalem church to investigate. "When he arrived and saw the evidence of the grace of God, he was glad and encouraged them all to remain true to the Lord with all their hearts" (Acts 11:23). Antioch was the center from which the Spirit commissioned Barnabas and Paul to undertake mission journeys to Asia Minor and Europe.

The Mission of the Church

Matthew concludes his Gospel with a record of Jesus' commissioning of the disciples.

> Then Jesus came to them and said, "All authority in heaven and on earth has been given to me. Therefore go and make disciples of all nations, baptizing them in the name of the Father and of the Son and of the Holy Spirit, and teaching them to obey everything I have commanded you. And surely I will be with you always, to the very end of the age" (28:18-20).

Luke has his own version of this commission in Acts 1:8: "But you will receive power when the Holy Spirit comes on you; and you will be my witnesses in Jerusalem, and in all Judea and Samaria, and to the ends of the earth."

The Kerygma. For Luke the mission of the church was to witness to Jesus Christ. This witness was accomplished through preaching, an extensive record of which is found in Acts. The contemporary term used in connection with proclamation — and which is used to define its content — is *kerygma.*

Foundational to the kerygmatic concept was the work of British scholar C.H. Dodd. In his work *The Apostolic Preaching and Its Developments* (a collection of lectures given in 1935), he declared that the unity of the message of the New Testament is to be had in the kerygma, the center of which is the arrival of a new era in the person and ministry of Jesus.[10] From his study of Peter's sermons as recorded by Luke in Acts, Dodd made several observations on the kerygma with regard to the mission of the church.

1. The age of the fulfillment of prophecy had occurred. When Peter stood at Pentecost and proclaimed the Gospel of Jesus Christ, he stated flatly "this is what was spoken by the

prophet Joel" (2:16). The New Testament church now saw that "this is how God fulfilled what he had foretold through all the prophets" (3:18). "Indeed, all the prophets from Samuel on, as many as have spoken, have foretold these days" (3:24). The New Testament church was absolutely convinced that the Messianic age had dawned.[11]

2. This new age had occurred through the ministry, death, and resurrection of Jesus. The Petrine sermons stressed Jesus' Davidic lineage (2:30-31); His ministry, approved by God with signs and wonders (2:22); His death, which occurred through the foreknowledge of God (2:23); and His resurrection from the grave (2:24-31).[12]

3. Because of Jesus' obedience to death, God not only raised Him up from the dead, but exalted Him in glory as the Messiah.[13] "The God of Abraham, Isaac and Jacob, the God of our fathers, has glorified his servant Jesus. . . . He must remain in heaven until the time comes for God to restore everything, as he promised long ago through his holy prophets" (3:13a, 21).

4. The Holy Spirit in the church was an indicator of Christ's present power and glory. "We are witnesses of these things, and so is the Holy Spirit, whom God has given to those who obey him" (5:32).[14]

5. The Messianic Age would shortly be consummated by Christ's return (3:21).[15]

6. The kerygma always concluded with a plan for repentance: "Repent and be baptized every one of you, in the name of Jesus Christ for the forgiveness of your sins. And you will receive the gift of the Holy Spirit" (2:38). "Salvation is found in no one else, for there is no other name under heaven given to men by which we must be saved" (4:12).[16]

Baptism. Those who accepted the message of the Gospel repentantly were baptized (Acts 2:38, 41; 8:12, 36; 9:18; 10:47-48; 16:15, 33; 19:5; 22:15). Küng discusses the meaning of baptism in the post-resurrection community.

Eschatological salvation has become reality through the death and resurrection of Jesus, and although baptism still remains indeed a "baptism of repentance for the forgiveness of sins" it takes on a new meaning because "God has made him (Jesus)

256

both Lord and Christ" (Acts 2:36). Repentance must now mean a turning to *Christ*, and the forgiveness of sins reveals that *Christ* now has the authority to do this; for God *through Christ* has given man the promised salvation, has created the new eschatological community of salvation and bestowed on it his Holy Spirit.[17]

Thus, the New Testament church baptized "in the name" of Jesus (Acts 2:38; 8:12; 10:48; 19:5). The one baptized became subject to Jesus, under His authority. By the very nature of the event, the one baptized was deemed to be surrendered to the work of the Holy Spirit. Thus, the promise of the Spirit belonged with baptism from the outset. Baptism, together with the filling of the Spirit, indicated a wholehearted acceptance of the kerygma and a union with the people of God in the community called the church.[18]

The Ministry of the Church

The Book of Acts demonstrates quite clearly that the Jews saw the post-resurrection church as a religious party within the nation, not unlike the Pharisees or Essenes. While Jesus had questioned the validity of the Law, His disciples were faithful in their observance of Jewish customs, and their special teachings and observances seemed to offer little occasion for them not to be considered Jews.[19] One might suppose, as a result, that the organization of the earliest church would be heavily influenced by Jewish administrative concepts.

The Apostolate. The office of apostle was one of major significance in the primitive Christian community. The apostles were the spontaneous leaders in the Jerusalem church. After Judas' suicide, the fledgling church almost automatically replaced him so that the apostolic band could remain at twelve (Acts 1:12-26). Peter, the natural head of the group, led the church in its selection of a replacement. Certain requirements were set out: "Therefore it is necessary to choose one of the men who have been with us the whole time the Lord Jesus went in and out among us, beginning from John's baptism to the time when Jesus was taken up from us. For one of these must become a witness with us of his resurrection" (Acts 1:21-22).

While it might be argued that the apostolic office was modeled on Jewish structures, it is more probable that its significance came from Jesus' personal appointment of the Twelve. In spite of Matthias' having been appointed to take Judas' place, oddly there is no further mention of him. In fact, only Peter, James, and John are mentioned in any meaningful way. While Barnabas and Paul are called apostles (14:4, 14), Luke seems to have made some distinction between them and the Twelve (Acts 15:2).[20]

The Diaconate. Whether Acts 6:1-7 is the account of the appointment of the first deacons is open to debate (at least, in the sense of deacons in 1 Timothy 3:8-13. Some would prefer to call these appointees "the Seven."[21] But tradition has regarded the passage as the introduction of deacons.

The appointment of this category of leadership arose because of the development of a problem within the church at Jerusalem when the Hellenistic Jews began to complain that the widows of the native Hebrew-speaking Jews were being favored in the regular distribution of food (6:1). Evidently, charitable assistance was part of the apostles' responsibility, and it had gotten beyond them.

> And so the Twelve gathered all the disciples together and said, "It would not be right for us to neglect the ministry of the word of God in order to wait on tables. Brothers, choose seven men from among you who are known to be full of the Spirit and wisdom. We will turn this responsibility over to them and will give our attention to prayer and the ministry of the word" (6:2-4).

One of those appointed, Stephen, was a gifted preacher and apologist. A second, Philip, was a capable evangelist. Essentially, however, the ministry of teaching and preaching remained the responsibility of the Twelve.[22]

The Eldership. The position of elder dated back to early Old Testament times in Israel. There are no descriptions outstanding of the institution of elders; for their existence was a given.

In the Jewish colonies of the Diaspora, the synagogues were under the supervision of elders. Thus, the idea of elders was one with which the primitive Christian community was familiar.[23]

The Book of Acts suggests that all the Christian communities had elders, but nothing is mentioned as to how they were appointed, or by whom. They just turn up in Acts 11:30 in connection with the gathering of a collection for the Jerusalem church, again in 15:2-29 in connection with the Jerusalem Council, and finally in 21:18 where Paul reported on his ministry to James and the elders. Küng suggests that the elders of the Jerusalem church, along with James and the Twelve, constituted the highest court of authority for all the church. "It is possible that the local elders at Jerusalem had already extended their authority, in the Judeo-Christian tradition familiar to Luke, into a teaching and juridical authority binding on the whole Church."[24]

Other Ministries. There were other ministries occurring within the Jerusalem church, but which did not involve administrative functions. One of these was the prophets. Agabus appears to have predicted a coming severe famine (Acts 11:27-28), and later, Paul's imprisonment should he visit Jerusalem (21:10-11). Another ministry was that of the evangelist. Although mention is made of evangelists elsewhere in the New Testament, only Philip is called an evangelist in Acts (21:8). Interestingly, his four daughters had the gift of prophecy (21:9).

Some Observations. The organization of primitive churches was very flexible. Acts does not present a consolidated church, but numerous house churches scattered in a multitude of cities throughout Palestine, Asia Minor, and Europe. The word used of these house churches by Luke is *ekklēsia*. Earl Radmacher insists that Luke's "usage of the word *ekklēsia* involves both the universal and local aspects of the church. In his mind they are closely related." Furthermore, "the particular local *ekklēsia* represents the universal *ekklēsia* and, through participation in the redemption of Christ mystically comprehends the whole of which it is the local manifestation."[25]

Governance of the local church was charismatic; that is, the church was led by the Holy Spirit. One reads such statements as, "the Holy Spirit said" (Acts 13:2) and "it seemed good to the Holy Spirit and to us" (15:28). The direction of the Spirit was determined not just by the leadership, but by the whole assembly of believers.

The Pauline Concept of the Church

The Apostle Paul was not only a pioneer church planter but also a theologian. He both founded numerous churches and provided direction for their organization and operation. Paul's understanding of the church in all its aspects warrants careful attention.

Images of the Church

One of the most extensive theological treatments of the church found in the Pauline epistles has to do with its nature. A series of images, or metaphors—some extensive and some minor—sheds considerable light on the apostle's understanding of the church.

Before surveying these images and their significance, Paul's use of the word *ekklēsia* needs to be understood. Generally, his references are to local expressions of the church found in each community. For example, he addresses his Corinthian correspondence to "the church of God in Corinth" (1 Cor. 1:2; 2 Cor. 1:1); he addresses his Thessalonian epistles "to the church of the Thessalonians in God the Father and the Lord Jesus Christ" (1 Thes. 1:1; 2 Thes. 1:1); his epistle to Philemon is sent "to the church that meets in your home" (Phile. 1:2). From these salutations it is obvious that *ekklēsia* is used to denote a corporate group in a local community.

But Paul does on occasion use the term to denote the church universal. This sense occurs only in Ephesians and Colossians, where Paul is discoursing on the theology of the church in a very broad sense. He discusses the relationship of Christ to His church: "And God placed all things under his feet and appointed him to be head over everything for the church, which is his body, the fullness of him who fills everything in every way" (Eph. 1:22-23; cf. Col. 1:18-19). There is no question that Paul has in mind the unified church of all the ages. Guthrie observes that "it is a natural progression from local groups to think of the sum total of these groups as a unified concept. Yet it would not be correct to say that the universal church was simply a conglomerate of many local communities for each local community was in essence the church of God."[26] The relationship of the local churches to the universal church may be seen in the images or analogies that Paul has composed.

The People of God. The first analogy Paul used to explain the mystery of the church was drawn from the vital Old Testament idea of the people of God. In Hebrew thought, the people constituted a whole, a corporate entity to the extent that the individual was perceived to be involved in the future of the entire group, even in a supra-temporal way.[27]

With Israel's rejection of Jesus as the Messiah, it should not be surprising to find Paul, who had been an Israelite of Israelites, describing the church as the true people of God. As with their Hebrew predecessors, a corporate personality characterized the new people of God, the community of those who trusted in the risen Christ. The new people of God comprised the faithful remnant of Israel (that is, those Jews who had accepted the lordship of Christ), and so had a legitimate and continuing link with the original people of God, but they had expanded to include believing Gentiles.

Behind the establishment of this new and true people of God was the reality of the risen Christ, "who gave himself for us to redeem us from all wickedness and to purify for himself a people that are his very own, eager to do what is good" (Titus 2:14). Paul's statement was an allusion to Ezekiel 37:23, which reiterates an ancient formula in regard to the eschatological people of God: "They will be my people and I will be their God." All those who have been redeemed by trusting Christ have been made God's people. They are the fulfillment of another Old Testament prophecy: "I will give them an undivided heart and put a new spirit in them; I will remove from them their heart of stone and give them a heart of flesh. Then they will follow my decrees and be careful to keep my laws. They will be my people and I will be their God" (Ezek. 11:19-20; cf. Jer. 31:33).

261

Just as Old Testament Israel was called, or elected, by God to be His particular people and His servants, so the church was chosen by Him. Paul wrote to believers: "For he chose us in him before the creation of the world to be holy and blameless in his sight. In love he predestined us to be adopted as his sons through Jesus Christ, in accordance with his pleasure and will" (Eph. 1:4-5).

The Body. The most singular image Paul constructed was that of the *sōma Christou*, or body of Christ. The apostle saw the physical body in a different light from the traditional Greek view of that day. The Greeks saw the body as formed matter; Paul considered it an organism of acting members. This is why he could say to the Corinthians, "Now you are the body of Christ, and each one of you is a part of it" (1 Cor. 12:27). Believers were "members of Christ himself" (1 Cor. 6:15); they were His mouth, His hands, His feet, and consequently in their totality His body; for He was at work historically through each of them. "Because he was present as the One at work in this way through all of them, and not through a community-for-action with whose cause they should join forces, they were bound to each other."[28]

The analogy of the body gives expression to Paul's desire to establish the proper relationship between believers. There is a single body, but it consists of many members, whose functions vary substantially. Because in Corinth the church tended to laud the more spectacular gifts such as tongues and to depre-cate the less prominent gifts, there were rifts in the ranks. Paul sought to show Christians that every member was integral to the operation of the body of Christ. Indeed, "God has com-bined the members of the body and has given greater honor to the parts that lacked it, so that there should be no division in the body, but that its parts should have equal concern for each other" (1 Cor. 12:24-25).

In the Prison Epistles the analogy was advanced somewhat when Paul stipulated that Christ is head of the body: "And he is the head of the body, the church; he is the beginning and the firstborn from among the dead, so that in everything he might have the supremacy" (Col. 1:18; cf. Eph. 4:15). These epistles make a very clear dichotomy between the Person of Christ and

His body the church; for Christ is declared to be the Savior of the body (Eph. 5:23). Paul depicted the body as receiving its nurture and unity from the head (Col. 2:19); the body is to grow and mature in every respect in Him who is its head (Eph. 4:15). Even more than earlier epistles, Colossians and Ephesians stress the absolute dependence of the church upon Christ for everything. This also signifies that the church is Christ's instrument in this world, "the fullness of him who fills everything in every way" (Eph. 1:23).[29]

To summarize, in this body metaphor the teaching of the headship relation is emphatic. The source of everything—including unity and nourishment—is Christ. The different members, as they relate to each other and to Christ, are the instruments of the head's work and communication.[30]

The Bride. Although wedding imagery was used both by Jesus (Matt. 25:1-13) and John the Baptist (John 3:29), it was not until Paul theologized on the church that the wedding metaphor was applied to the Christian community. The outstanding passage in this regard is Ephesians 5:25-30.

> Husbands, love your wives, just as Christ loved the church and gave himself up for her to make her holy, cleansing her by the washing with water through the word, and to present her to himself as a radiant church, without stain or wrinkle or any other blemish, but holy and blameless. In the same way, husbands ought to love their wives as their own bodies. He who loves his wife loves himself. After all, no one ever hated his own body, but he feeds and cares for it, just as Christ does the church—for we are members of his body.

Another significant use of this metaphor is found in the second letter to the Corinthians: "I am jealous for you with a godly jealousy. I promised you to one husband, to Christ, so that I might present you as a pure virgin to him" (2 Cor. 11:2).

In both of the above passages Paul depicted the church as a bride betrothed to Christ. From the very moment of betrothal, a woman was regarded in the same light as one married. Only divorce could sever an espousal, and any breach of fidelity was counted as adultery. The bride's property became the property of her intended, and he became her heir. The universal church, comprising the saved from Pentecost to the Parousia, is the bride of Christ whose marriage to Him will be consummated at His return.

Several lessons may be learned from this analogy. One is the indissoluble union between the Lord and His church, a union of loyalty and love. Human marriage is analogous to this bond. The self-sacrificing love the husband is to have for his wife is exemplary of the way Christ loves the church and gave Himself for her.

The love mentioned here is, of course, *agapē*, which is not a sentimental emotion, but a willful spiritual affection, reasoned out and thought through. Radmacher observes that "this love is even more amazing in the light of the infinite distance of nature between the lover and the beloved. . . . Never has there ever been an instance of such love to those so far from being capable of benefiting the lover."[31]

Another lesson drawn from this metaphor is the exalted position of the bride, or church. The *mōhar*, or bride-price, was Christ's own blood on Calvary. That transaction having taken place, the bride now awaits the coming of the Groom for her. Paul describes that day.

> For the Lord himself will come down from heaven with a loud command, with the voice of the archangel and with the trumpet call of God, and the dead in Christ will rise first. After that, we who are still alive and are left will be caught up with them in the clouds to meet the Lord in the air. And so we will be with the Lord forever (1 Thes. 4:16-17).

When the marriage is consummated, the bride will share the glory of the Groom.

The Building. Jesus spoke of building His church on the rock which was the apostolic confession of His messiahship (Matt. 16:18). Paul expanded that theme in his development in 1 Corinthians and Ephesians of the building metaphor.

His use of the building analogy with the Corinthian Christians came in connection with pastoral instruction on dissension in their ranks. Some were claiming to follow him; some,

Apollos; and so forth. Factionalism was rife. In response, Paul taught that God is sovereign, not some human leader: "For we are God's fellow workers; you are God's field, God's building" (1 Cor. 3:9). The apostle, who had planted the church at Corinth, reminded his readers that he had laid the foundation like a careful master-builder, that foundation for the church being Christ only. Now that he was no longer with them, others were building on his foundation, "but each one should be careful how he builds" (3:10); for a day would come when the superstructure erected would be tested. Everything built on the one foundation would be tested by the sovereign God.

In a related metaphor, the apostle observed that just as the church is a building, so each one of its members is a temple of God, indwelt by the Holy Spirit (1 Cor. 3:16). Just as the Spirit of God inhabited the Holy of Holies in the Jerusalem temple, so now He indwells the church by inhabiting every individual believer. Guthrie notes that

> this not only shows an advance in thought, in replacing an external by an internal reality, but also demonstrates the negation of the idea of a special temple. If the believer himself (and consequently the whole body of believers) is the dwelling place of God, location ceases to have importance. Whatever value attached to the central sanctuary for Israel, the Christian church had no need for one. The notion of a building became wholly metaphorical and therefore spiritual.[32]

In his letter to the Ephesians, Paul described the entire church as God's temple, with each individual believer being a stone. Members of the community are "built on the foundation of the apostles and prophets, with Christ Jesus himself as the chief cornerstone" (2:20). What did Paul mean? Did he change his opinion (as expressed in 1 Cor. 3:11) that Christ is the sole foundation? Gerstner suggests that the passage means that it is a foundation belonging to, or proceeding from, the apostles and prophets.[33] That is, it is a foundation of the apostolic and prophetic proclamation of Jesus Christ as God's Messiah.

Who are the apostles and prophets from whom this foundation issues? The order would suggest that the prophets followed the apostles. The passage in all likelihood, then, refers to

New Testament (rather than Old Testament) prophets. Tying the apostolic and prophetic proclamations together and so creating a single solid foundation is the chief cornerstone, namely, Jesus Christ Himself.

The Church's Worship

Christian worship demonstrates the same kind of relationship to Hebrew worship that Christian Scripture does to Hebrew Scripture. The Hebrew Scripture was the Scripture of the New Testament church, and so the traditions about the amazing things God in Christ had done for humanity were originally formulated and then recorded in the context of familiarity with the Old Testament. In much the same way, much Christian worship arose out of Hebrew traditions, worship practices, and Scripture.[34]

Despite its links to Judaism, Christian worship was distinctive. As the Holy Spirit superintended the primitive community's devotion to Jesus' ministry and its eschatological outworkings, there arose a freedom unknown in Jewish worship. Ferdinand Hahn maintains:

> The irruption of the eschaton, which was already taking place in the old aeon, made it impossible simply to adopt the worship of Judaism. Not only had Jesus himself breached and abrogated the traditional cultic order . . . it was the present reality of God's eschatological activity that demanded new forms of worship. . . . There were circles in the primitive community that adhered much more closely to Jewish tradition than others; but . . . now the saving and fulfilling act of God in Christ was the focus of attention for the community as it offered praise, thanksgiving, and intercession.[35]

We shall examine the various aspects of worship — both those similar to and those divergent from Judaism — to which Paul refers.

The Day of Worship. The Jews of the very early Christian era held to a very rigid observance of the Sabbath as *the* day of worship. The typical belief of the rabbis was not only that the

Jews were constrained by the Sabbath, but that even God Himself had conformed to Sabbath regulations from before creation.[36]

Jesus, however, was not given to such a strict observance. Indeed, He taught that "the Sabbath was made for man, not man for the Sabbath" (Mark 2:27), and He practiced what He preached (Matt. 12:1-13; cf. Mark 2:23–3:6; Luke 6:1-11). As a consequence, the primitive Christian community felt free to select a different day of the week to meet corporately for worship. They decided upon the first day of the week. It was on this day, designated as *the* Lord's Day, that Jesus had risen from the grave to gain the victory over sin, and it was on this day that the Spirit in His fullness had descended upon the church.

It has been suggested that the phrase "the Lord's Day" may have been a truculent Christian response to "the Emperor's Day," which was observed in Egypt and Asia Minor on the first day of each month in honor of the Roman emperor.[37] Whatever reason the church had for holding this day special, it is assumed by Paul in 1 Corinthians 16:2 as the appropriate day for gathering. While this is the very first piece of evidence for the Lord's Day (and the only Pauline mention of it), it would seem clear that it was their habit from the very beginning.[38]

Hymns and Songs. The primitive church was one given to displaying its joy in the Lord (Gal. 5:22; Phil. 4:4; cf. Rom. 14:17) in music. The victory of Christ over sin and the grave, in which believers shared through the action of the Holy Spirit within them, gave them a spiritual zest and energy, which they naturally expressed in songs of praise and thanksgiving.

Hymns and spiritual songs (Col. 3:16) were not unknown to Judaism. Antiphonal singing was used in the preexilic period of Hebrew history (Ex. 15:21; Num. 10:35-36; 21:17; 1 Sam. 18:7). Many of the psalms were composed for singing in corporate temple worship (e.g., Pss. 24; 118; 134; 145). Choirs sang responsively during the postexilic period (e.g., Ezra 3:11 and Neh. 12:43). During the century prior to Christ, hymnody was developed to a high degree by the sect of the Therapeutae. And musical aspects of worship were also used extensively by the Qumran Community.[39]

Numerous hymns and fragments of hymns are to be found throughout the Pauline corpus, as are exhortations for the use of hymns, psalms, and spiritual songs during times of corporate worship. Paul told the Corinthians, "When you come together [to worship], everyone has a hymn, or a word of instruction, a revelation, a tongue or an interpretation. All of these must be done for the strengthening of the church" (1 Cor. 14:26). He encouraged the Ephesians to "speak to one another with psalms, hymns and spiritual songs. Sing and make music in your heart to the Lord" (5:19; cf. Col. 3:16). While attempts have been made since the Patristic period to define just what constituted psalms, hymns, and spiritual songs respectively, most scholars would agree that it is difficult to hold any sharp distinctions. Suffice it to say that they were used by believers in corporate worship to edify, instruct, and exhort one another.[40]

The most compelling example of New Testament hymnody is undoubtedly Ephesians 5:14: "Wake up, O sleeper, rise from the dead, and Christ will shine on you."

It is likely that this is a tiny fragment of a primitive hymn, possibly from a baptismal service; for conversion to Christ and baptism were referred to as an enlightenment (cf. Heb. 6:4; 10:32). Three analogies of regeneration are set forth, one in each line: awakening from sleep, resurrection from the dead, and emergence from darkness into light.[41]

Philippians 2:6-11 is a whole, self-contained hymn to the Christ.

Who, being in very nature God
did not consider equality with God something to be grasped,
but made himself nothing,
taking the very nature of a servant,
being made in human likeness.
And being found in appearance as a man,
he humbled himself
and became obedient to death—
even death on a cross!
Therefore God exalted him to the highest place
and gave him a name that is above every name,
that at the name of Jesus every knee should bow,
in heaven and on earth and under the earth,
and every tongue confess that Jesus Christ is Lord,
to the glory of God the Father.

This hymn is a paean of praise to Christ, who exemplified obedience to, and dependence on, God. Had He so desired He could have used His equality with God to grasp rulership of the universe; that is, He could have—by an act of self-assertive pride—rebelled and sought to be Lord in His own right. Instead, He emptied Himself of all rights and took on human form, humbling Himself and becoming obedient to death on a cross. Consequently, God has raised Him to the highest possible station. At His name, every knee will bow, "even denizens of the underworld as well as inhabitants of heaven are included along with dwellers on earth,"[42] because God has made Him Lord.

In 1913, the German scholar Edward Norden determined that Colossians 1:15-20 was a hymn in two strophes: verses 15-18a, which depicted Christ in relation to creation, and verses 18b-20, dealing with Christ and the church:

A

He is the image of the invisible God, the firstborn over all creation.
For by him all things were created: things in heaven and earth, visible and invisible,
whether thrones or powers
or rulers or authorities;
all things were created by him and for him.
He is before all things,
and in him all things hold together.
And he is the head of the body, the church.

B

He is the beginning and the firstborn from among the dead,
So that in everything he might have the supremacy.
For God was pleased to have all his fullness dwell in him,
and through him to reconcile to himself all things,
whether things on earth
or things in heaven,
by making peace through his blood, shed on the cross.

Paul used this apparently already existing hymn to discredit an incipient gnostic heresy which denied the supremacy of

269

Christ and His unique role as Mediator. This is a use to which hymns have been put ever since—to encourage believers to reject heresy by affirming the true faith.[43]

Confessions and Creeds. While official, fixed creeds were not a part of the church's life until the third and fourth centuries, the content of the Christian faith was expressed from very early in the New Testament era in concise, creed-like formulas which may be regarded as their predecessors.[44] Ralph Martin tells us:

> The Church which greets us in the pages of the New Testament is already a believing, preaching and confessing community of men and women; and this fact implies the existence and influence of a body of authoritative doctrine (although in an embryonic form in certain matters, such as the belief in the Trinity) which was the given and shared possession of those who formed the nascent Christian communities in the world of the Roman Empire.[45]

Paul made good use of these confessional statements in his epistles for worshiping, teaching, and apologetic purposes.

As far as we can tell, the oldest New Testament confessional statement is based on Peter's response to Jesus' question at Caesarea Philippi (Mark 8:29): "Jesus is the Christ." Among the Jews of Palestine and the Diaspora, the matter of Jesus' messiahship was an important issue. But as the church increasingly confronted the Gentile world the debate about messiahship lost its importance, and the term "Christ" was joined to "Jesus" as a personal name. Paul used "Lord" instead, and changed the formula to "Jesus is Lord": "if you confess with your mouth, 'Jesus is Lord,' and believe in your heart that God raised him from the dead, you will be saved" (Rom. 10:9). "For we do not preach ourselves, but Jesus Christ as Lord" (2 Cor. 4:5). Various suggestions have been made about the purpose of this confession; Gerald Borchert infers that it may have been a Christian equivalent (perhaps a refutation?) to pagan confessions about their gods or to the Roman proclamation of Caesar as lord;[46] Martin, however, argues that it was probably a baptismal formula.[47]

One of the more important, older confessions quoted by Paul

to reassure believers and exhort them to remain steadfast in the faith was 1 Corinthians 15:3-5:

> That Christ died for our sins according to the Scriptures,
> that he was buried,
> that he was raised on the third day according to the Scriptures,
> and that he appeared to Peter, and then to the Twelve.

The Greek actually uses Cephas rather than Peter, the former being the Aramaic form, which would suggest that the confession dates to very early in the church.

First Timothy 3:16 concisely sets forth the Gospel message, contained in six lines of truth regarding the person and work of Christ:

> He appeared in a body,
>   was vindicated by the Spirit,
> was seen by angels,
>   was preached among the nations,
> was believed on in the world,
>   was taken up in glory.

This confession features two world orders—the divine and the human—and demonstrates how Christ has joined the two by His incarnation and exaltation. "Thus heaven and earth are joined, and God and man reconciled."[48]

Corporate Prayer. Although the New Testament church confessed Jesus as Lord and sang about His incarnation and the salvation available through His blood, when it prayed, it directed those prayers to God the Father through Jesus (Rom. 1:8). Paul was typical of the Christian community: he was theocentric rather than christocentric in his theology.[49]

In Romans 8:15 and Galatians 4:6, Paul pointed out to his readers that the indwelling Holy Spirit could lead a believer to come to God in prayer in such a way that they would relate to Him as a small child to his father, and they would cry out "Abba, Father." This was, of course, the form by which Jesus addressed God in prayer (Mark 14:36).[50] The pious Jew would never have used such a term, finding it too brazen to use to address the Creator and Lord of the universe. Instead, he used a less intimate word, *Abinu*, "our Father." But Jesus not only used *Abba*, "dear Father," He also taught His followers to do the same.[51]

Paul also terminated his prayers with *Amen*, a term borrowed from the Jewish liturgy of that day. It was a term of response to, and wholehearted endorsement of, the words of another. The apostle used it at the end of doxologies which ascribed praise to God and to His Christ (Rom. 1:25; 9:5; 11:36; 16:27; Gal. 1:5; Eph. 3:21; Phil. 4:20; 1 Tim. 1:17; 6:16; 2 Tim. 4:18).[52]

In 2 Corinthians 1:20-22, Paul took his readers back to an early service of worship: "For no matter how many promises God has made, they are 'Yes' in Christ. And so through him the 'Amen' is spoken by us to the glory of God. Now it is God who makes both us and you stand firm in Christ. He anointed us . . . [and] set his seal of ownership on us." C.K. Barrett observes that "Amen" infers a liturgical context; the Amen of the Christian community to whom Paul is writing is like God's "Yes"; it is not only spoken, but acted upon. "The fulfillment of God's purposes, of which the person and work of Jesus constitute the primary affirmation, is reaffirmed by Christians, but reaffirmed by them through Jesus, in whom they are related to God and his purposes."[53]

Stewardship. An important part of the worship of the church has always been giving for the work of Christ. It is an inheritance from Old Testament Judaism, which had much to say about "tithes and offerings."

In his letters to the churches, Paul sounded a similar theme, often writing about stewardship and charity. One of the most important passages is 1 Corinthians 16:1-4.

> Now about the collection for God's people: Do what I told the Galatian churches to do. On the first day of every week, each one of you should set aside a sum of money in keeping with his income, saving it up, so that when I come no collections will have to be made. Then, when I arrive, I will give letters of introduction to the men you approve and send them with your gift to Jerusalem. If it seems advisable for me to go also, they will accompany me.

While this is the first mention in Paul's surviving writings, it was important to him (see, as well, Rom. 15:26; 2 Cor. 8:1-15; 9:1-15). These moneys were destined for the impoverished saints in Jerusalem. There were many charitable groups in New Testament times. The Greek peoples had associations called *eranoi*. If a member became financially disadvantaged, his club brothers would raise an interest-free loan to help him out. The synagogues had officers who collected from those who were well off and gave to those who were in dire straits. Nor was it unusual for wealthy Jews in the Diaspora to send messengers to Jerusalem with large contributions for the poor. Paul undoubtedly wanted the churches to be even more generous in giving than the Jews and the pagans.[54]

There was a more spiritual reason. This collection was a way of showing the unity of the church. It was one method of demonstrating to the scattered believers that they were not just members of a local congregation but a part of the universal church, and that each part was responsible for the whole. It was also a means of helping these believers actualize the teaching of Jesus on love.[55]

It is noteworthy that this collection was to take place on Sunday. This is the first clear data to show that the church routinely celebrated that day, although there is no justification to suppose that it was not their practice from the very beginning.[56]

Baptism

When Jesus had finished His earthly mission and was preparing to return to the Father, He gathered His followers together and commissioned them to "go and make disciples of all nations, baptizing them" (Matt. 28:19). And from the outset of the church, baptism was the rite by which one signified one's intent to follow Jesus in discipleship. Paul's epistles contain much to affirm and promote the concept of baptism as initiation into the body of Christ.

Romans 6:1-14. This passage is undoubtedly the most profound teaching on baptism in the New Testament. The question has been asked, however, as to what degree these verses reflect Paul's teaching and to what degree they are taken from tradition. His declaration in verse 3 — "Or don't you know that all of us who were baptized into Jesus Christ were baptized into his death?" — suggests that Paul expected the Roman Christians to know that baptism into Christ meant participation in His death. Some scholars believe that Paul was making use of an existing baptismal liturgy or hymn,[57] although George Beasley-Murray observes that it is "plausible that in Rom. 6, as in his oral instruction, Paul used both traditional and liturgical phrases, without however citing an already formulated liturgy."[58]

What does Paul mean when he states that we "were baptized into his death"? According to Beasley-Murray:

> If we take into account Paul's theology generally — indeed the text and context provide enough evidence — it can be shown that his interpretation of baptism in relation to the redemptive event of Christ has a three-fold reference: first, it relates the baptized to the death and resurrection of Christ, involving him in the actual dying and rising of Christ Himself; secondly, it involves a corresponding event in the life of the baptized believer, whereby an end is put to his old God-estranged life and a new one begins in Christ and His Kingdom and His Spirit; thirdly, it demands a corresponding 'crucifixion' of the flesh and a new life in the power of the Spirit that accords with the grace received, which 'dying' and 'rising' begins in the baptismal event.[59]

While Paul is obviously referring to the external rite of baptism (as the believer is immersed in water, he is "buried" with the Lord, and when he comes up out of the water, he "rises" with the Lord), it would be a serious error to think of baptism, therefore, as "merely symbolic." For Paul, what baptism symbolizes really occurs, and it occurs through the ordinance of baptism. In order to illustrate this potent reality, Paul uses the very strong language of verse 5, "If we have been united with Him like this in His death, we will certainly also be united with Him in His resurrection." Anders Nygren tells us that "the verb is chosen with the thought that we were not formerly members in Christ's body; but we became such through baptism and henceforth belong inseparably with the Head."[60]

That Paul saw baptism as burial is reasonable considering its nature as immersion. The Greek words for baptize are *baptō* and *baptizō*. The former means "dip" or "dip into a dye"; the latter is an intensive form of the former and means "dip" or "cause to perish."[61] In the dyeing of material, the cloth must be fully submerged in the liquid in order to be completely transformed in color. In the same way, when one is buried, that person is fully covered by soil. Furthermore, the nature of baptism as immersion fulfills what Paul says in Romans 5:17: "For if, by the trespass of the one man [i.e., Adam], death reigned through that one man, how much more will those who receive God's abundant provision of grace and of the gift of righteousness reign in life through the one man, Jesus Christ." It was Christ's obedience unto death that counted with God; through baptism the believer shares in that death. Baptism/immersion's significance may be seen even more clearly in 2 Corinthians 5:14-15: "For Christ's love compels us, because we are convinced that one died for all, and therefore all died. And he died for all, that those who live should no longer live for themselves but for him who died for them and was raised again." In baptism the "old man" is buried with Christ and a new creation arises with Him.

Galatians 3:27-28. This passage has been said to be part of an early baptismal liturgy:[62] "for all of you who were baptized into Christ have been clothed with Christ. There is neither Jew nor Greek, slave nor free, male nor female, for you are all one in Christ." To be "clothed with Christ" assumes that one has already discarded the clothing of the old, sinful self. Paul, then, is viewing baptism in much the same light as in Romans 6. There he had stressed the negative consequences—the death of self; here in Galatians, he emphasizes the positive results—union with Christ through sharing His sonship and also oneness with His church.[63]

Paul's intent in this passage is to show that baptism with faith makes the believer a son of God. The term "son" here should not be rendered "child" (as the NRSVB has done) in an effort to avoid gender chauvinism; for male and female believers alike attain the status of sons. In that day and age sons had privileges and inheritance rights that daughters did not share. All who are baptized in faith are sons of God and, therefore, are all equals, regardless of their national origins, social standing, or gender. All those baptized in faith have become one in Christ.

Colossians 2:11-12. In this passage Paul presents baptism in the context of a polemic against ineffective means of righteous living, such as following Jewish observances, especially circumcision; for "in him you were also circumcised, in the putting off of the sinful nature, not with a circumcision done by the hands of men but with the circumcision done by Christ, having been buried with him in baptism and raised with him through your faith in the power of God, who raised him from the dead."

The circumcision done by Christ should not be seen as synonymous with baptism, but rather with His crucifixion, His finished work on Calvary. Murray Harris exegetes the verse appropriately, noting that verse 11 "presents spiritual circumcision, not baptism, as the Christian counterpart to physical circumcision."[64] We should not think of baptism being compared to circumcision. Rather, it is contrasted with it, for not until verse 12 does the language of baptism begin. Beasley-Murray asserts that "when we consider the 'existential' nature of baptism as described by Paul and the importance of faith for its efficacy, it becomes difficult to believe that Paul placed circumcision on a comparable level with baptism, or interpreted the latter in the light of the former."[65]

Other Mentions. While the previous passages are foundational to Paul's theology of baptism, there are other, less important references which should be mentioned.

The first of these is 1 Corinthians 6:11: "And that is what some of you were. But you were washed, you were sanctified, you were justified in the name of the Lord Jesus Christ and by the Spirit of our God." Although the word "baptism" is not used, the sense of what is happening here is best explained in the context of the washing of baptism. The word for washing, *apelousasthē*, refers to a decisive action on the part of the person which achieves a complete washing away of sin. The action results in sanctification (a setting apart to God's service) and in justification (legal acquittal). These results are accomplished in Christ by the power of the Holy Spirit.[66]

In 1 Corinthians 12:13 Paul appeals to the Christians at Corinth to seek unity because of their baptism: "For we were all baptized by one spirit into one body—whether Jews or Greeks, slaves or free—and we were all given the one Spirit to drink."

There is a similarity here to Galatians 3:27-28. The unity achieved in baptism transcends any existing distinctions. By being baptized, they were brought into the sphere of the Holy Spirit who now indwelled them abundantly.[67]

It has been argued that Ephesians 4:5-6 is taken from a liturgical formula,[68] and that may be so: "one Lord, one faith, one baptism; one God and Father of all, who is over all and through all and in all." Markus Barth insists that this is a reference to the ordinance of baptism, namely, "to that baptism into the name of Jesus Christ which derives its oneness and weight directly from the 'One Spirit . . . One Lord . . . One Father,' and which is received by the One Body (the Church) in One Faith and One Hope (4:4-6)."[69]

As in 1 Corinthians 6:11, the word "baptism" is not mentioned in Ephesians 5:25-27.

> Husbands, love your wives, just as Christ loved the church and gave himself up for her to make her holy, cleansing her by the washing with water through the word, and to present her to himself as a radiant church, without stain or wrinkle or any other blemish, but holy and blameless.

Paul takes the individual baptisms of believers as a collective whole, inferring that the object of baptism is the calling out of a holy community. Exactly what is the meaning of "the word" is uncertain. It may apply to the kerygma, or to a confession of Christ's name by the person baptized, but it is nonetheless a statement of faith in Christ as mandated by the Gospel, and so marks the beginning of the believer's sanctification.[70]

Conclusions. Baptism is initiation into fellowship with Christ and inclusion in His body, the church. It must be preceded by faith in Jesus Christ. Baptism involves participating in the death of Christ by being buried with Him in the hope of being raised with Him. By baptism one receives in faith the status of "son of God." Because all believers are sons of God there is equality throughout the church; the walls dividing one from another begin to be broken down, as believers become one body, the church. In baptism, the Holy Spirit not only fuses believers into the church, but He also indwells each individual Christian.

The Lord's Supper: The Continuing Fellowship

Sharing a common meal was a frequent practice of the New Testament church. Acts 2:42 tells us that these early believers "devoted themselves to the apostles' teaching and to the fellowship, to the breaking of bread and to prayer," and 2:46 says that "they broke bread in their homes and ate together with glad and sincere hearts."

Was there something distinctive about these meals? The eminent New Testament scholar, C.F.D. Moule, declares that their significance was "that those who had now been baptized into the ownership of Jesus Christ and into His allegiance would find in each meal together at least a very vivid reminder of the One who had so often broken bread with His disciples during His ministry, and who after His resurrection was made known to the two at Emmaus as He broke the bread."[71] In all probability they also recalled not only the many meals they shared with their Lord, but also the New Covenant in His blood symbolized in the supper of the Upper Room at Passover time.[72]

In the primitive Christian community the Lord's Supper seems to have been observed in conjunction with the *agapē* or love feast (the common fellowship meal). The word for supper in Greek is *deipnon*, the evening meal, which was the only real meal of the day.[73] The two acts which constituted the ordinance—breaking of bread and drinking from the common cup—were now observed at the conclusion of the meal (originally, they were separated by the *agapē*) and thus had become the focal point of the meal.

Problems in Corinth. Paul wrote about the Lord's Supper in the context of a Corinthian church in a terrible state of chaos. In one situation he confronted brazen immorality on the part of a member—a man having sexual intercourse with his father's wife (1 Cor. 5:1-13). In another instance, some converts continued to attend pagan worship services. Others frequented feasts where meat was served which had been consecrated to a pagan deity; these feasts were sacramental; for those consuming the meat believed that it brought them into an intimate relationship with the god. While Paul knew that these idols were nothing, underlying them were demons, and so these people were

278

consorting with the demonic (1 Cor. 10:20).[74] In still another case, the church was plagued with cliques. Wealthy people were attending the love feasts and eating together without waiting for the poorer people (such as slaves and laborers) who could not be present at the designated time. "The supper had thus degenerated into a shocking exhibition of the cleavages within the church, with the result that Paul was obliged to complain bitterly that 'it is no longer possible to eat the Lord's Supper' (1 Cor. 11:20)."[75]

1 Corinthians 5:6-8. In regard to the man who was engaging in out-and-out immorality without the discipline of the church, Paul wrote:

> Don't you know that a little yeast works through the whole batch of dough? Get rid of the old yeast that you may be a new batch without yeast — as you really are. For Christ, our Passover lamb, has been sacrificed. Therefore let us keep the Festival, not with the old yeast, the yeast of malice and wickedness, but with bread without yeast, the bread of sincerity and truth.

If the church did not take action to excise the perpetrator from their midst, this small amount of "yeast" (sin) would pollute the whole assembly. They too had a Passover lamb — Christ — who had been sacrificed on their behalf.

> It is probable that the idea of Christ as a paschal lamb was quite familiar to the Christians of Corinth, because it was common property in the early Church, as we know from the New Testament. Since it probably goes back to the Lord's comparison of himself with the paschal lamb at the Last Supper, the phrase "Christ our Passover has been sacrificed" is an allusion to the Eucharist.[76]

1 Corinthians 10:14-17. Here Paul was speaking to the idolatrous tendencies of some Corinthian converts. In so doing, he reminded them of the significance of the ordinance: "Is not the cup of thanksgiving for which we give thanks a participation in the blood of Christ? And is not the bread that we break a participation in the body of Christ?" (10:16) Through the receiving of the bread and the cup in faith, the believer participates in Christ's sacrifice. And just as believers are united with Christ at His table, even so they are united with one another: "Because there is one loaf, we, who are many, are one body, for we all partake of the one loaf" (10:17). This idea was similar to Jewish temple observance, where eating part of the sacrifice created a partnership with all who ate (10:18).[77] Those who are one with Christ must not become one with a demon: "You cannot drink the cup of the Lord and the cup of demons too; you cannot have a part in the Lord's table and the table of demons" (10:21).

1 Corinthians 11:17-34. In this passage Paul dealt with the divisions rending the Corinthian congregation. As part of his call for unity, he recounted Jesus' institution of the Lord's Supper: "For I received from the Lord what I also passed on to you" (11:23a). How Paul received this revelation is not clear. It may be that it came directly while he was in the Arabian desert (Gal. 1:17). Or it could have been in a tradition passed down from the actual event. Whatever the case, Paul clearly hoped for unity within the church at Corinth—a unity focused on the Lord's Table.

He concluded by giving a strict admonition to his readers.

> Therefore, whoever eats the bread or drinks the cup of the Lord in an unworthy manner will be guilty of sinning against the body and blood of the Lord. A man ought to examine himself before he eats of the bread and drinks of the cup. For anyone who eats and drinks without recognizing the body of the Lord eats and drinks judgment on himself. That is why many among you are weak and sick, and a number of you have fallen asleep. But if we judged ourselves, we would not come under judgment. When we are judged by the Lord, we are being disciplined so that we will not be condemned with the world (11:27-32).

There are two basic views of this passage. The first stipulates that eating and drinking unworthily involves regarding the elements as ordinary food and missing their significance as the body and blood of Christ. Failing to discern the body is essentially the same thing. The illnesses and deaths which occurred in the Corinthian church because of poor behavior at the Supper were a reaction to the elements wrongly perceived, which had therefore become poisonous.[78]

The other interpretation has even more going for it. Eating and drinking without properly discerning the body means failure to recognize the church for what it is, the body of Christ, indwelt by the living Lord. Because the members of the church had shown contempt for the body of Christ, the Lord was punishing them by illnesses and deaths in the congregation. Though these were afflictions from Christ, they were punishments designed to change the sinners' behavior so that they might escape being condemned along with the world.[79]

Some modern scholars combine elements of the two interpretations. Geoffrey Wainwright states that Paul intended a dual understanding of "body" in 1 Corinthians 11:29, namely, both the eucharistic and ecclesial.[80] Gunther Bornkamm notes that, in verse 29, Paul was appealing to his readers to respect the elements as "the body of Christ who joins us to his body."[81] Charles Talbert stresses that failure to discern the body implies the failure to "perceive the Christian unity rooted in the sacrifice of Christ and actualized in the sacred meal."[82]

Conclusions. When Paul told the story of how Jesus instituted the Lord's Supper, he not only reminded his readers that it is a memorial to the Savior's death on the behalf of sinners, but also exhorted them to be unified by their participation in His body. Indeed this is Paul's primary purpose here, to see believers knit together in unity with Christ. Anyone who would partake of Christ, the One who died and rose again, must be completely loyal to Him; there is no room for unity with other gods (or the demons they represent). If one is united with one's fellow believers through participation in the Supper, then there is no room for cliques or for ignoring those who are dissimilar in social or economic standing. For the body of Christ will not be divided.

Leadership in the Church

For Paul, church leadership was all under the authority of its Head, Jesus Christ. Christ is the supreme authority without

281

whom no leadership structure is possible. But even His leadership must be recognized as organic and not organizational. As Guthrie points out: "The head essentially belongs to the body as the body belongs to the head. It is the most intimate kind of authority, since the body functions efficiently only when it responds at once to the dictates of the head. Any officials who are mentioned must be regarded as exercising their various functions under the direction of the head."[83]

Paul does not mention clergy in his writings (except for the appearance of "priest" in a metaphorical sense in a wide range of activities). The New Testament church stressed function much more so than position.[84] The only detailed information on church leadership positions is in the Pastoral Epistles, but Paul also mentions them in his other letters. The Epistle to the Philippians was written to the church at Philippi, "together with the overseers and deacons" (1:1b). The First Epistle to the Corinthians speaks of charismatic gifts which include leadership roles: apostles, prophets, teachers, and those with gifts of administration (12:28). To the Ephesians, Paul wrote about gift-offices: apostles, prophets, evangelists, pastors, and teachers (4:11). It is in 1 Timothy and Titus that Paul discussed the qualifications of two orders of officials, the overseer and the deacon.[85]

The Overseer. Exactly what were the duties of an overseer or bishop (*episkopos*)? Did the overseer differ from the elder or presbyter (*presbyteros*)? While the New Testament offers no answers, it does give a few hints. After Paul spoke of elders in Titus 1:5-7, he quickly ties them to overseers in verses 7-9, thus indicating that they were almost identical. And from a list of required virtues, it is clear that the office was given a high profile. Such a person was indeed a worthy representative of the local assembly.[86]

Paul wrote to Timothy, "If anyone sets his heart on being an overseer, he desires a noble task" (1 Tim. 3:1). The qualifications he set forth for this position include the overseer's personal character, family, and relationships with those inside and outside the church.

In his personal character the overseer must be above reproach (1 Tim. 3:2; Titus 1:6). While the Greek words differ in the two epistles, the meaning of both demands unimpeachable character. He must be the husband of one wife (1 Tim. 3:2; Titus 1:6), literally "a one woman man." Remarriage is not considered here and rejected; it is not considered at all.[87] Rather, Paul was making a demand for fidelity in an age when a great many married men used prostitutes and mistresses. Other qualifications required the overseer to be temperate (1 Tim. 3:2), self-controlled (1 Tim. 3:2; Titus 1:8), and respectable (1 Tim. 3:2), that is, conducting himself properly. In Titus, Paul also added not overbearing (1:7) or stubbornly inflexible, nor pursuing dishonest gain (1:7), but upright, holy, and disciplined (1:8).

In his family life the overseer had to be in alignment with God's order as depicted in the Scriptures.[88] In 1 Timothy, Paul declared that the overseer "must manage his own family well and see that his children obey him with proper respect. (If anyone does not know how to manage his own family, how can he take care of God's church?)" (3:4-5). His ability to oversee his family will reflect on his ability to oversee the church.[89] Ronald Ward comments, "The parallel between the home and church should be noticed. The bishop [overseer] should be no stranger in exercising his compassion. *God's church* is a home and *a household*, a family derived from God and ideally a pattern for society (cf. Eph. 3:15)."[90] In Titus, the apostle held out the expectation that he must be "a man whose children believe and are not open to the charge of being wild and disobedient" (1:6).

Interpersonal relationships were also vital. The overseer could not be "given to drunkenness" (1 Tim. 3:3; Titus 1:7). The Greek can mean one who is nasty when drunk.[91] Allied here is the prohibition against being violent or quarrelsome (1 Tim. 3:3). Positively, the overseer must be hospitable (1 Tim. 3:2; Titus 1:8), able to teach (1 Tim. 3:2), and so capable of both propounding and defending the Gospel (Titus 1:9). He must be one who enjoyed a good reputation with those outside the church (1 Tim. 3:7). And in all things he had to be a lover of what is good (Titus 1:8).

Spiritually, "he must not be a recent convert, or he may become conceited and fall under the same judgment as the devil" (1 Tim. 3:6). Satan succumbed to the sin of pride and so was cast out of heaven; his end will be in the lake of fire (Rev. 20:10, NASB). One who is appointed prematurely to the position of overseer may be overtaken by the same sin and suffer a similar condemnation. Rather, "he must hold firmly to the trustworthy message as it has been taught" (Titus 1:9).

To conclude, the qualities set forth for overseers are so foundational that one wonders if it infers a lack of suitable candidates. It is obvious that Paul's main goal was that these officials should model the appropriate Christian lifestyle. They were expected to be capable teachers because their task was to communicate to others what they themselves had been taught (cf. 2 Tim. 2:2).[92]

The Deacon. The term "deacon" translates the Greek *diakonos*, "servant" or "minister." It denoted (originally) a slave who waited on tables. In New Testament writing it was used of varying sorts of service. It described the ministry of Jesus (Mark 10:45), of the apostles (2 Cor. 3:6; 6:4; Eph. 3:7; 1 Tim. 1:12), and of others who served the cause of Christ (1 Cor. 16:15; Col. 4:7).

The origin of the office of deacon is as much shrouded in mystery as that of overseer. Traditionally, the connection has been made to the appointment of the Seven in Acts 6:1-7. There are both pros and cons to the idea,[93] but no one can say with certainty either way.

The qualifications for the office of deacon are essentially parallel to those for the overseer; for the passage concerning the deacon — 1 Timothy 3:8-13 — begins with "Deacons, likewise." Once again the emphasis is on character.

In their personal character, deacons must be "men worthy of respect [and] sincere" (v. 8). The *New English Bible* puts it well, "Deacons, likewise, must be men of high principle, not indulging in doubletalk." Like the overseer, such a person must not be a tippler, "indulging in much wine" (v. 8), nor one who pursues "dishonest gain" (v. 8). "If deacons had the handling of money, it should be known in advance that church finances were perfectly safe with men who were not interested in feathering their own nests."[94] In other words, deacons must be expected to have the highest ethical principles in all areas.

Spiritually, no less than overseers, "they must keep hold of the deep truths of the faith with a clear conscience. They must first be tested; and then if there is nothing against them, let them serve as deacons" (vv. 9-10). In the conduct of their pastoral activity, deacons need a solid theological foundation. Nor can they be novices in the faith, or else, like the immature overseer, they may fall prey to pride and its subsequent condemnation.

The family life of deacons, no less than that of overseers, must be above reproach: "A deacon must be the husband of but one wife and must manage his children and his household well" (v. 12). A man is no saint to his family unless that honor is deserved. The deacon's Christian walk must begin in his home.

There is some question as to whether Paul also gives instruction to a group of female leaders. Substantial debate has surrounded verse 11, which the *New International Version* translates: "In the same way, their wives are to be women worthy of respect, not malicious talkers but temperate and trustworthy in everything." Yet, the *New International Version* margin would replace "wives" by "deaconesses." The Greek word at issue is *gynaikes* and, while in some cases it may be rendered "wives," it is generally translated "women." Arguments are substantial on both sides, but nothing clear-cut may be ascertained.[95] One might even posit a group here known just as "the women," who had a ministry similar to the deacons'. Certainly, "women ministers were by no means unknown in the apostolic Church."[96]

Paul concluded his list of requirements for deacons by observing that "those who have served well gain an excellent standing and great assurance in their faith in Christ Jesus" (v. 13). The "standing" here probably refers to spiritual place in the kingdom of heaven rather than promotion to a higher position in the church.[97] Nothing is more important than assurance of standing with Christ.

Ministry in the Church

While the faith of the members of the New Testament church was based on God's redemption in and through the risen Christ, it was attested to them and to new converts by the gift of the Holy Spirit. The Spirit revealed Himself clearly by the gift of transforming power. G.B. Caird informs us that "in the New Testament the Spirit is always the gift of Christ, whereby men are enabled to participate in his ministry and purpose."[98]

The Spiritual Gifts. The power of the Spirit was manifested in the lives of believers by the *charismata*, or spiritual gifts (also known as spiritual graces). Paul discussed them in three different epistles: Romans (12:6-8), Ephesians (4:11), and 1 Corinthians (12:8-11, 27-30; 14:1-25).

Paul stressed the gifting of every believer by the Holy Spirit: "All these [gifts] are the work of one and the same Spirit, and he gives them to each one just as he determines" (1 Cor. 12:11). Because a variety of needs existed and a variety of services were needed, a wide range of gifts were given: "There are different kinds of gifts, but the same Spirit. There are different kinds of service, but the same Lord. There are different kinds of working, but the same God works all of them in all men" (1 Cor. 12:4-6). Gary Inrig observes that

> a corollary of this diversity of spiritual gifts is the importance of every spiritual gift to the life of the church. Just as our physical body depends upon our various members . . . so it is with the gifted members of Christ's body. When individual believers do not know their spiritual gifts or do not use them, the whole body is curtailed in its effectiveness. This is the apostle's emphasis in 1 Corinthians 12:20-26.[99]

Inrig has classified the gifts into three categories: foundational gifts, ministry gifts, and sign gifts.[100]

The foundational gifts are those on which the church is built: "Consequently, you are no longer foreigners and aliens, but fellow citizens with God's people and members of God's household, built on the foundation of the apostles and prophets, with Christ Jesus Himself as the chief cornerstone" (Eph. 2:19-20). The premier gift was that of apostle (1 Cor. 12:28; Eph. 4:11). There appear to have been two classes of apostles: the Twelve and Paul, and official representatives of local assemblies. The former category is in view here; an apostle was one who had both seen the risen Christ and had been chosen by Him. The second gift was that of prophet (Rom. 12:6; 1 Cor.

286

12:10, 28; Eph. 4:11). In fact, Paul exhorted the Corinthians to "eagerly desire spiritual gifts, especially the gift of prophecy" (1 Cor. 14:1). Again, two classes may be distinguished: there were those whose calling was to prophesy—men like Agabus, who foretold a great famine (Acts 11:27-28); there were also believers in local congregations who prophesied from time to time. The first type of gift is foundational.

Ministry gifts are those which concern the continuing life of the local church. One of the most important of these was teaching (Rom. 12:7; 1 Cor. 12:28; Eph. 4:11). Teaching new converts the precepts of the Lord was vital to the growth of the New Testament church (as it is in the church today). The next gift was that of pastor (Eph. 4:11). Actually, in Ephesians 4:11, "pastor and teacher" go together as a unit. The gift of pastor shepherds God's flock, feeding and caring for them.

Another ministry gift is seen in Paul's instruction to Timothy, when Paul exhorts him to "do the work of an evangelist" (2 Tim. 4:5). Every believer may find it necessary on occasion to perform such a task, but the gift is a special ability regularly to evangelize people (Eph. 4:11). In New Testament times there were numerous itinerant evangelists who shared the Gospel wherever they went.

At other times Paul mentions a variety of spiritual gifts. Among these were the gift of giving a word of wisdom (1 Cor. 12:8) and the word of knowledge (1 Cor. 12:8). The word of wisdom applies the truth of God practically; the word of knowledge brings insight into the teaching of God's truth. The gift of faith (1 Cor. 12:9) brings a special vision for God's work even though it may seem impossible. The gifts of administration (1 Cor. 12:28) and leadership (Rom. 12:8) are probably similar involvements in governance. The gift of service (Rom. 12:7) is a general term, probably much the same as that of helping others (1 Cor. 12:28). Encouraging (Rom. 12:8) is a gift of affirming others and lifting them up as they serve God. While all believers are expected to give to the Lord's work, the gift of giving (Rom. 12:8) brings a special generosity. Showing mercy (Rom. 12:8) is a gift connected to grace; it is the ability to dispense love and help to those undeserving of it. The gift of distinguishing between spirits (1 Cor. 12:10) is the ability to test a prophetic spirit to see whether it is of God or Satan. All these gifts contributed to the daily ministry of the church.

Another class of gifts, the sign gifts, were of a miraculous nature. They pointed to a great spiritual truth that God had for people. In the New Testament church, healing (1 Cor. 12:9, 28, 30), miracles (1 Cor. 12:10), tongues (1 Cor. 12:10, 30; 14:1-13), and the interpretation of tongues (1 Cor. 12:10; 14:13, 27) were such gifts. Healing was a gift that allowed one to bring both spiritual healing and physical recovery to an ill person, while miracles (actually in the Greek, *dynameis*, "mighty works") were akin to those wonders done by Jesus in His messianic power.[101] Tongues (not to be confused with the tongues of Acts 2, etc.) were the capacity for speaking in a "spiritual language" or "ecstatic speech," a message from God interpreted by someone with the gift of interpretation of tongues.

8.1 A Summary of the Spiritual Gifts

Romans 12:6-8	1 Corinthians 12:8-11	1 Corinthians 12:28-31	Ephesians 4:11
Prophecy	Word of wisdom	Apostles	Apostles
Serving	Word of knowledge	Prophets	Prophets
Teaching	Faith	Teachers	Evangelists
Encouragement	Healing	Miracle workers	Pastor-teachers
Giving	Miraculous powers	Healers	
Leadership	Prophecy	Helpers	
Governance	Discernment of spirits	Administrators	
Mercy	Tongues	Tongues	
	Interpretation of tongues	Interpretation of tongues	

Order and Discipline. Although the administration of the church was charismatic in nature, it was not chaotic. Paul made sure of that, issuing the dictum that "everything should be done in a fitting and orderly way" (1 Cor. 14:40). The Greek rendered "orderly way" is from a military term signifying the type of discipline exercised in the army. It described the well-aligned functioning of society.[102] The apostle also wrote to various churches, giving pastoral advice and admonition in regard to specific problems; these admonitions are redirected to us as general principles.

In 1 Corinthians 5, Paul dealt with a problem of incest in the Corinthian church: a man was sleeping with his father's wife (the wording is such that the woman in question was not the man's mother), a situation which even pagans found repugnant. In this case the local assembly was to take action: "Hand this man over to Satan, so that the sinful nature may be destroyed and his spirit saved on the day of the Lord" (5:5). Such an action involved exclusion from the Christian community. The perpetrator would, hopefully, see the error of his ways. Jack MacGorman suggests the significance of the statement more clearly: "Evidently the church was a haven where believers enjoyed the protection and guardianship of Jesus Christ during their sojourn on earth. Outside of the church or in the world was the sphere in which Satan held sway."[103] When repentance took place, the offender was to be restored to fellowship: "you ought to forgive and comfort him, so that he will not be overwhelmed by excessive sorrow" (2 Cor. 2:7). In a similar manner, in his first letter to Timothy, Paul spoke about Hymenaeus and Alexander. They had made shipwreck of their faith, and so he had handed them over to Satan so that they might learn not to blaspheme (1 Tim. 1:19-20).

Much the same sort of advice was given to Titus: "Warn a divisive person once, and then warn him a second time. After that, have nothing to do with him. You may be sure that such a man is warped and sinful; he is self-condemned" (Titus 3:10-11). It is evident that Paul was very protective of the purity and unity of the church.

The apostle was also concerned that the church should be orderly in its worship life. To that end he wrote the Corinthians about their worship services.

What then shall we say, brothers? When you come together, everyone has a hymn, or a word of instruction, a revelation, a tongue or an interpretation. All of these must be done for the strengthening of the church. If anyone speaks in a tongue, two—

or at the most three—should speak, one at a time, and someone must interpret. If there is no interpreter, the speaker should keep quiet in the church and speak to himself and God (1 Cor. 14:26-28).

Worship is not an individual matter, but a corporate concern. Paul's intent in this passage was to remind the Corinthians of that very thing. Worship should be orderly so that the whole congregation would understand and grow in the Lord.

In just the same way, prophecy during public assemblies needed regulation. Order and proper procedure were the primary requirements.

Two or three prophets should speak, and the others should weigh carefully what is said. And if a revelation comes to someone who is sitting down, the first speaker should stop. For you can all prophesy in turn so that everyone may be instructed and encouraged. The spirits of the prophets are subject to the control of the prophets. For God is not a God of disorder but of peace (1 Cor. 14:29-33).

The need for order in all things is dictated by the very nature of God; for He is not a God of confusion and chaos, but a God of peace (the Hebrew word *shalom*, which would naturally be in Paul's mind, means "integrity" and "wholeness"). When every part of the body is functioning in its proper place and order, then the church possesses "peace" (i.e., wholeness, unity).[104]

Women in the Church

The New Testament does not give us much detailed information on the pattern of leadership in the primitive Christian assemblies. Attempts to reconstruct the "typical" New Testament church worship service have failed to determine the "typical" leadership arrangement for each local assembly. Thus it is impossible to arrive at definite conclusions about the role of women in the early church.[105]

The difficulty is accentuated by the context in which the church existed. The world of Paul's day generally considered

women inferior to men. While a few areas in the Greek world —
like Macedonia — allowed women some rights, most kept them
subjected and isolated. Nor did the Jews accord women much
in the way of privilege; for women were the property of their
husbands or fathers in Jewish culture. Neither were they given
any education as a rule. It was in such an ethos that the Christian church developed.[106]

Paul had more to say about women in the church than did
any of the other New Testament writers. How did he view their
role in the church? An examination of those passages which
involve women and the church will give us some idea.

Galatians 3:28.[107] All passages relating to women and the
church must be interpreted in the light of this most revolutionary statement of Paul's: "You are all sons of God through faith
in Christ Jesus, for all of you who were baptized into Christ
have been clothed with Christ. There is neither Jew nor Greek,
slave nor free, male nor female, for you are all one in Christ
Jesus" (3:26-28). This passage has been dubbed "the magna
carta of Christian liberty." It declares every person who has
been baptized by faith into Christ to be a son of God, regardless of race, social standing, or gender. All believers receive the
same standing before God.

1 Corinthians 11:2-16. This passage has given rise to substantial
speculation; for each verse in this passage admits more than
one interpretation. Additionally, the customs of society at the
time in regard to hair and head coverings are not known.[108]

Paul was writing to the whole assembly on a matter which
concerned both men and women alike — appropriate dress at
public services of worship. The very comment that "every woman who prays or prophesies with her head uncovered dishonors
her head" (v. 5) is a clear indication that women were participating in worship leadership in Corinth. That the apostle took
care to address the matter of normal dress for women involved
in leadership demonstrates his approval of their role.[109]

It would appear that Paul had previously written the church
at Corinth that in their assemblies women must have their
heads covered when they prayed. Evidently, however, some
were ignoring that teaching. It may be that, in their zeal for the

Lord's parousia, these women were doffing their headdresses because they believed that they had transcended their sexuality and were to live as the angels.[110]

When Paul heard what was happening (either from a letter or from those visiting him), he admonished them to wear a veil, citing the order of creation (vv. 3-12), a sense of proper conduct (v. 13), the teaching of nature (vv. 14-15), and the general practice of the church (v. 16).[111] That they were to do so did not restrain their role in leading worship; it merely demonstrated that men were still men and women were still women, and they all should be conscious of that fact.

1 Corinthians 14:33b-36. Given what 1 Corinthians 11:2-16 implies about Paul's view of women praying and prophesying in public services of worship, 1 Corinthians 14:33b-36 may come as somewhat of a surprise.

> As in all the congregations of the saints [many believe that v. 33b should complete v. 33a, and not begin v. 34], women should remain silent in the church. They are not allowed to speak, but must be in submission, as the Law says. If they want to inquire about something, they should ask their own husbands at home, for it is disgraceful for a woman to speak in the church. Did the word of God originate with you? Or are you the only people it has reached?

A common interpretation of the passage is a literal one. It was common practice in all the churches for women to be silent. Silence during worship was a sign of submission to one's husband, just as the Law set forth. If a woman wanted to know something about proceedings that she did not understand, she should wait and ask her husband at home.

The objections to such an interpretation, however, are many and compelling. To take the passage as prohibiting female participation in public worship is to negate utterly what Paul had just written in 11:5. Nor can one find any Old Testament passages which teach such an admonition. Besides, Paul was hardly one to appeal to the Law. And how can one relate verse 35 to single women, widows, and women with non-believing husbands? Adhering to such an interpretation also brings into question the severe rebuke in verse 36.[112]

Talbert provides a significant alternative to the literal interpretation. Verses 34-35 are an assertion made by the Corinthians in their correspondence to Paul. They contain two admonitions along with two bases.

> Admonition one: "the women should keep silence in the churches." Basis one: "for they are not permitted to speak, but should be subordinate, as even the law says." Admonition two: "if there is anything they desire to know, let them ask their husbands at home." Basis two: "for it is shameful for a woman to speak in church."[113]

These statements are indicative of the general views in Greco-Roman society. Writers of the day talked sarcastically of women who boldly intruded on councils of men. Philo declared that men should pass on knowledge of the laws to their wives, while Josephus contended that the Law held women to be inferior to men, and therefore women should be submissive.[114]

Paul refuted these statements in verse 36, which begins with the Greek particle—rendered by the *Revised Standard Version* as "What!" which indicates that what has preceded it is refuted by what follows it. In other words, Paul has rejected these assertions by the Corinthians (a stance which would harmonize with what he stated in 11:5).[115]

1 Timothy 2:8-15. The interpretation of this passage will rest, to a large extent, on who was the author of the Pastoral Epistles. Many commentators—probably a majority—attribute authorship to a source later than Paul, possibly one of his disciples.[116] Consequently, it may be argued that this writer was a believer in Jewish tradition (or local Greek culture) rather than Pauline freedom when it came to women's roles in the church. "In line with contemporary practice, he wrote that women must be silent and submissive (v. 11)."[117]

What of those of us who hold to Pauline authorship of this epistle? Certainly, the wording seems at odds with what Paul wrote about women to the Corinthians and Galatians.

> I want men everywhere to lift up holy hands in prayer, without anger or disputing. I also want women to dress modestly, with

decency and propriety, not with braided hair or gold or pearls
or expensive clothes, but with good deeds, appropriate for
women who profess to worship God. A woman should learn in
quietness and full submission. I do not permit a woman to teach
or to have authority over a man; she must be silent. For Adam
was formed first, then Eve. And Adam was not the one deceived;
it was the woman who was deceived and became a sinner. But
women will be kept safe through childbirth, if they continue in
faith, love and holiness with propriety.

Verses 9 and 10 pose no apparent problem. Men are to pray
without anger or quarreling. The word "also" in Greek can be
translated "likewise." In other words, women should—like
men—pray with proper decorum, but they should also dress
appropriately.

Beginning with verse 11, however, problems arise. A very
literal rendition goes counter to the spirit of Galatians 3:28 and
in total opposition to 1 Corinthians 11:5. But taken in broad
context, it may be seen as saying something very different. The
Pastoral Epistles seem to be seeking to refute an incipient
Gnosticism which elevated Eve as the possessor of a secret
knowledge which led to salvation. These women against whom
Paul is writing may have been teaching this view. As a result,
Paul forbade them to teach the men in the church, who had a
deeper knowledge of Scripture. Instead, the women were to
learn submissively and quietly, a standard expectation for students of that day (males included). Roger Omanson argues, "In
light of passages such as 2 Timothy 3:1-9; 1 Timothy 4:1-16;
and Titus 2:4-5, one may conclude that women were being won
over to the heretical views and became teachers of these
views—views such as saying that marriage, sexual intercourse,
and procreation are evil. Surely it must be allowed that
1 Timothy 2:11-12 . . . may have had local or even temporary
significance."[118]

Some consider verses 12-16 to be a total prohibition of any
female at any point in history ever exercising authority over or
teaching a man, much less leading worship. The reasons are
based on the order of creation.[119] But "I do not permit" is just
as well translated "I am not permitting" for the tense is present
indicative active, a continuing present meaning, "I am not at

this time permitting." Such an idea is reasonable, considering the educational state of women at that time.[120]

"To have authority" renders the Greek word *authentein*, a word originally connected with suicide and then assassination, but which had come — at least by the later patristic era — to denote a negative and domineering type of leadership.[121] Catherine Kroeger infers that *authentein* in Paul's time had come to connote the exercise of sexual wiles (such a view is born out by John Chrysostom, one of the great church fathers), and that women in the Ephesian church were teaching sexual license.[122] Such a view would fit in well with the idea of a cult of Eve operating in that community. Verse 13 would then be seen as an appropriate rebuke. Those exalting Eve would do well to keep in mind that Adam — not Eve — was created first, and that Eve was the one who was deceived by Satan, not Adam. But, "while Paul is clearly drawing some comparison between Eve's having been deceived and women at Ephesus, it seems unlikely that he thought of such a tendency as being an integral part of the nature of woman as opposed to man."[123]

Verse 15 is one which defies any sure interpretation.[124] Nor does it really have anything to do with women and the church per se. While there are many possible ways of looking at this verse, one suggested by Guthrie, to my mind, makes the most sense in the context of Pauline theology, namely, that the effects of the Fall on women's childbearing will not impede their salvation.[125]

Conclusions. Paul's view of women in the church is based on Galatians 3:26-28, that "all are one in Christ." Nonetheless, men are men and women are women; oneness in Christ does not do away with sexual differences. When it came to worship, however, Paul did not specify different activities for each sex. Both could pray, prophesy, and sing. "Paul's strong stress on order and the avoidance of causing offence probably meant in practice that the women of the church sometimes would have to subordinate their own rights to the well-being of the whole church, just as all the church members had to do."[126] However nothing in Paul's epistles requires the conclusion that he perceived the role of women in worship to be different from that of men.[127]

THE LATTER APOSTOLIC PERIOD

While the General Epistles do not contain the volume of material pertaining to a theology of the church that is found in other New Testament materials, there is still much of value to be learned. We shall examine each epistle—Hebrews, James, 1 and 2 Peter, 1, 2, and 3 John—in turn, omitting Jude because of a dearth of church doctrinal material in it.

The Epistle to the Hebrews

Hebrews is shrouded in mystery. During the church's early years its inspiration seemed to be in question for, even though Clement and Origen knew and admired it, the book was not included as canon until the time of Athanasius (mid-fourth century).

Many scholars believe that the epistle was written to second generation Christians. Because of its content, they would date it somewhere between the persecutions of Nero and Domitian (about A.D. 64 and 85). There are those who would argue for a date prior to 70, because Hebrews seems to assume that the Temple cult is still in operation.[128] On the other hand, New Testament theologian Leonhard Goppelt is typical of the majority, noting that, while "a time of composition after the year 70 is thinkable," sometime between 85–90 is more in line.[129]

The epistle was written to a long-established church (5:12) which had previously suffered persecution (10:32-34). This church had enjoyed prominence and superb teaching and leadership (13:7); it was a church known for its generosity (6:10). Based on 13:24, it has been suggested that the epistle was written to a church in Italy by an expatriate. Because of its complexity of thought, it was probably written to a scholarly group who may have been preparing to teach. But the author, who may have been their instructor, was afraid that they were drifting away from the truth, and so he wrote to them, exhorting them to remain true in spite of suffering and persecution,[130] reminding them that they were aliens in a foreign land sojourning to a heavenly homeland, and so they must expect to be treated as foreigners. No one knows who wrote Hebrews. Solutions to this problem have ranged from Barnabas to Aquila to Phoebe, but no one is certain.

296

Because the emphasis of Hebrews is on christology and not ecclesiology, there is not much in it concerning the church. What there is, however, is worthy of note.

The House of God. While Paul's emphasis was on the church as the body of Christ (Rom. 12:5; 1 Cor. 12:12; Eph. 1:22-23; 4:12; 5:23; Col. 1:18, 24), the writer to the Hebrews made no use of this analogy but instead employed the image of the church as the house of God.

> For every house is built by someone, but God is the builder of everything. Moses was faithful as a servant in all God's house, testifying to what would be said in the future. But Christ is faithful as a son over God's house. And we are his house, if we hold on to our courage and the hope of which we boast (3:4-6).

Moses was only a servant, "working in the anticipation of something yet to come," but Christ is the Son for whom the house was created. He "has come to inhabit us."[131]

The epistle writer placed a condition on the believer's being God's house, by way of admonition: we must hold on to our courage (in the face of persecution) and our devotion to the hope of glory. Barclay observes

> that building of the Church will only stand indestructible and foursquare when every stone in it is firm; that is to say, when every member of it is strong in the proud and confident hope he has in Jesus Christ. Each one of us is like a stone in the Church. If one stone is weak the whole edifice is endangered. The Church only stands firm when each stone in it is rooted and grounded in faith in Jesus Christ.[132]

The City of God. As the writer of Hebrews exhorted believers to remain steadfast in their faith, the writer reminds them of the glories that await faithful Christians: "But you have come to Mount Zion, to the heavenly Jerusalem, the city of the living God . . . to the church of the firstborn, whose names are written in heaven" (12:22-23). The city of God is a synonym for the kingdom of God,[133] of which the church is a part. Those who compose the church are assured of sharing the life of Christ, their names inscribed in heaven.

297

On Worshiping God. Little is said in Hebrews concerning corporate worship in the first-century Christian community. There is, however, a strong admonition to maintain regularity in meeting together for worship: "Let us not give up meeting together, as some are in the habit of doing, but let us encourage one another—and all the more as you see the Day approaching" (10:25). Some evidently were guilty of deviating from the common practice. And while the passage does not lay out the worship practices of the community, it clearly shows that the author of Hebrews regarded worship as of utmost importance.[134]

An even more important principle emerges from this passage when it is examined in its context. The preceding verse exhorts believers, "And let us consider how we may spur one another on toward love and good deeds." Under the pressure of an intense persecution, no believer should be "going it alone." There was strength in unity, a mutual dependence for mutual encouragement. But the author evidently was concerned that the bonds of unity were weakening. A lack of concern for the health of the body, of which they were all members, would be a sign of the selfishness which breeds isolationism. And so he admonished them to demonstrate genuine Christian love in their personal relationships and mutual concern for the faith community. Failure to heed such a warning would not only demonstrate selfish individualism (specifically illustrated by not meeting together regularly), but would also portend the danger of apostasy (one of the themes of the epistle).[135]

All who refused to apostatize would enjoy the right worship of their Lord and an eternal place in the kingdom: "Therefore, since we are receiving a kingdom that cannot be shaken, let us be thankful, and so worship God acceptably with reverence and awe, for our God is a consuming fire" (12:28-29). In view of what lay in store for faithful believers—a harmonious peaceful kingdom where all is joy and light, in comparison to their present chaotic and oppressive circumstances—the writer exhorted his readers to offer God acceptable worship in reverence and awe, allowing nothing to disturb that relationship with the Father which will effect their salvation when this age passed away. "If a man is true to God, he gains everything," says Barclay, "and if he is untrue to God he loses everything. In time and in eternity nothing matters save only loyalty to God."[136]

The Epistle of James

The Epistle of James takes its name from its author who identifies himself merely as "James, a servant of the Lord Jesus Christ" (1:1a), but which James we do not know. As with the Epistle to the Hebrews, some parts of the early church initially questioned the inspiration and authority of this letter. Yet here too, the authority of the Epistle of James soon was widely recognized.

The epistle makes two contributions to our appreciation of the theology of the church. The first involves the treatment of people who gathered in assembly for worship:

> My brothers, as believers in our glorious Lord Jesus Christ, don't show favoritism. Suppose a man comes into your meeting wearing a gold ring and fine clothes, and a poor man in shabby clothes also comes in. If you show special attention to the man wearing fine clothes and say, "Here's a good seat for you," but say to the poor man, "You stand there," or, "Sit on the floor by my feet," have you not discriminated among yourselves and become judges with evil thoughts? (2:1-4)

Discrimination is not compatible with faith in Jesus Christ. The writer illustrated how such discrimination—in this case between rich and poor—was occurring. A wealthy, well-dressed man enters the meeting place at the same time as a man in shabby clothes. By honoring the wealthy man and disdaining the poor man, the church fell into sin. James' conclusion is clear: God regards what is inside people rather than what appears on the outside. In fact, God has chosen the poor of the world "to be rich in faith and to inherit the kingdom he has promised to those who love him" (2:5). The church should display the priorities of its Lord. Furthermore, James notes that the wealthy are not prone to repay such partiality in kind; rather, in return they exploit and manipulate.[137] Thus James calls the church to spurn worldly priorities in favor of the values of the kingdom.

James also calls the church to respond to the needs of its constituents.

> Is any one of you sick? He should call the elders of the church to pray over him and anoint him with oil in the name of the Lord. And the prayer offered in faith will make the sick person well; the Lord will raise him up. If he has sinned, he will be forgiven. Therefore confess your sins to each other so that you may be healed. The prayer of a righteous man is powerful and effective (5:14-16).

Every member of the church had the right to call for the help of the elders of the community. In this case, the ill in the church were instructed to call for the elders to anoint them with oil (a traditional practice among the Jews). When they (the elders and the ill person) prayed in faith, the Lord would heal the ill person. "What is important for our present purpose is that the community had elders in whom special authority in matters of prayer and faith were vested. This seems to suggest that corporate intercession is more effective than individual.[138] One should not suppose that there is any implication in the words "and the Lord will raise him up" of future salvation. The connotation is simply that God will bring about healing.[139] The author advocated confession within the assembly so that prayer might be forthcoming, because a righteous person's prayers were highly effective.

The Epistles of Peter

The two epistles credited to Peter have been the subject of debate over the years both as to dating and authorship. The writer of the first epistle claims to be "Peter, an apostle of Jesus Christ" (1:1a). If the noted apostle was the author, then it would be dated sometime prior to A.D. 70, probably during the reign of Nero. But many scholars question both the excellent Greek of the text and its failure to mention the words or ministry of the earthly Jesus; they would place its probable date during the reign of Domitian, A.D. 81–96.[140] The second epistle has been more disputed. No canonical book is less supported by the church fathers, although Eusebius claimed that Clement of Alexandria had it in his Bible. And there are traces of it in 1 Clement (A.D. 95). It was not fully recognized as canonical until the Councils of Hippo and Carthage in the fourth century. Looking at the text, if it came from the same hand as 1 Peter, then an amanuensis must have been used for the former.[141]

First Peter is written to suffering Christians, calling on them to stand firm in the faith despite persecution. In that context there are numerous instructions for the discipling of new converts.[142] Second Peter warns against false teaching of a gnostic strain, and holds out to wavering believers the hope and warning of the Parousia.[143] In such a context, there is little by way of instruction on the doctrine of the church.

Living Stones. Like Jesus and Paul, Peter used the analogy of the church to a building.

> As you come to him, the living Stone—rejected by men but chosen by God and precious to him—you also, like living stones, are being built into a spiritual house to be a holy priesthood, offering spiritual sacrifices acceptable to God through Jesus Christ. For in Scripture it says: "See, I lay a stone in Zion, a chosen and precious cornerstone, and the one who trusts in him will never be put to shame." Now to you who believe, this stone is precious. But to those who do not believe, "The stone the builders rejected has become the capstone," and, "A stone that causes men to stumble and a rock that makes them fall." They stumble because they disobey the message—which is what they were destined for (1 Peter 2:4-8).

Peter invited those believers who were possibly wavering in their faith to "keep on coming" to Christ (the Greek verb is a present participle which denotes continuing action). Using Jesus' own metaphor, Peter identified Christ as "the living stone—rejected by men but chosen by God and precious to Him." He is more than just another stone; He is the stone which holds the building together. Even more so, being a "living" stone, He is not a monument, but living, resurrected and life-giving.[144]

From the idea of the cornerstone the writer jumped to his next thought, that his readers are the stones of the spiritual building Christ was holding together. Bo Reicke interprets this verse to mean that "the church is not to be made up of individuals who are cold and dead, but who enrich their environment with life-giving love."[145] Certainly, the emphasis is on the unity of believers; all the stones are necessary to a strong and whole edifice.

Those who have accepted Christ will also become priests to God, mediators with God on behalf of their fellow human beings. Those who have rejected Him will find Him to be a stone of condemnation.

The People of God. In language taken from the Old Testament, Peter described the company of believers that God was forming—the church would be His called out people:

> But you are a chosen people, a royal priesthood, a holy nation, a people belonging to God, that you may declare the praises of Him who called you out of darkness into His wonderful light. Once you were not a people, but now you are the people of God; once you had not received mercy, but now you have received mercy (1 Peter 2:9-10).

All of the titles used in this passage are corporate. "A chosen people" was taken from Isaiah 43:20; "a royal priesthood," from Exodus 19:6. The Greek word rendered "royal" is *basileion*, a noun meaning "palace" or "king's court." Alan Stibbs tells us that the phrase may be understood "as describing the Christian community as a 'king's house' or 'royal residence,' " but even more likely "is that Christians are described as sharing with Christ in kingship or sovereignty as well as in priesthood. They are therefore a true hierarchy, called to reign as well as to serve."[146] "A holy nation" came from Exodus 19:6; the church is set apart to God's purposes. "A people belonging to God" combined terms from Exodus 19:5, Isaiah 43:21, and Malachi 3:17; it denoted corporate believers as the covenant people of God.[147]

In all this Peter stresses the corporate identity of the church: by grace the church has become the people of God. Verse 10 indicates how the people of God should live. In language reminiscent of Hosea 1:6-10 and 2:23, Peter notes that because they have been brought out of darkness into light and have experienced God's mercy, it was incumbent upon these believers to live up to the lifestyle God demanded and, above all, to be unwavering in their loyalty to him.[148]

On Baptism. The one place in which Peter mentions baptism is an exegete's nightmare. It is helpful to examine it in a slightly wider context.

> He [Christ] was put to death in the body but made alive by the Spirit, through whom also he went and preached to the spirits in prison who disobeyed long ago when God waited patiently in the days of Noah while the ark was being built. In it only a few people, eight in all, were saved through water, and this water symbolizes baptism that now saves you also—not the removal of dirt from the body but the pledge of a good conscience toward God. It saves you by the resurrection of Jesus Christ (1 Peter 3:18b-21).

Exactly what is meant by Christ's preaching "to the spirits in prison" is uncertain and will not be examined here because it is not relevant to our search for a biblical theology of the church. But it brought the writer to Noah and the ark. Peter Davids tells us that the epistle's readers could well identify with Noah for, like him, they were a tiny, oppressed minority surrounded by a host of disobedient people; "but Christ's triumphant proclamation and the citation of the narrative of the deluge remind them that they will be the delivered minority just as Noah and his family were, which is surely comforting in a time of suffering."[149] Peter depicted the water of the flood as analogous to the water of baptism, the eight in the ark as related to the recipients of baptism, and the deliverance of the ark's occupants as analogous to the salvation of believers. To ensure that his readers would not misconstrue his meaning, Peter observes that baptism is not simply an external washing, but a commitment of faith and obedience made operative through the resurrection of Jesus Christ.[150]

On Church Leadership. Written in the context of the persecuted people of God, 1 Peter 5:1-4 has instructions for church elders.

To the elders among you, I appeal as a fellow elder, a witness of Christ's sufferings and one who also will share in the glory to be revealed: Be shepherds of God's flock that is under your care, serving as overseers—not because you must, but because you are willing, as God wants you to be, not greedy for money, but eager to serve; not lording it over those entrusted to you, but being examples to the flock. And when the Chief Shepherd appears, you will receive the crown of glory that will never fade away.

Because of the circumstances of the epistle's readers, the church's nurturing was essential. As a result, the writer depicts the church as "God's flock." And he admonishes the elders to be shepherds of the flock God has placed in their care. "The imagery of 'the flock' pictures the church as a nurturing community. This notion also implies the church's dependence upon its leaders as shepherds."[151]

The writer carefully used three antitheses to summarize the task of shepherding or overseeing the church. The first antithesis focused on the right basis for the elder's role. The elder was warned not to accept his position because of pressure but rather out of a willing spirit arising from a recognition of God's direction in his life. The second antithesis stressed the motivation for serving as an elder. One was not to function out of a desire for money. The Greek term means "a fondness for dishonest gain." Instead, he should be moved by a zeal for service. The third antithesis discussed the manner in which the elder was to exercise oversight. He was not to be domineering, abusing his position of authority. Instead, he was to be a model believer for those in his charge, patterning himself after Jesus Christ, the Chief Shepherd.[152] As Gerald Borchert keenly observes:

These powerful exhortations to the elders are not left by Peter as mere commands. On the contrary, they are contextualized within the eschatological perspective of verse 4. Elders whose perspectives are rooted in proper motivations with respect to their roles and functions are reminded that when the chief shepherd is manifested they will be granted "the unfading crown of glory."[153]

The Johannine Epistles

The Johannine Epistles should probably be dated from during the reign of Domitian, apparently addressing issues from several decades into the life of the church. The writer was concerned with a gnostic strain of teaching in the church which was promoting Docetism. In spite of this problem, there is virtually no mention of the nature or government of the church. Rather, its nature as community is assumed.[154]

Many interpreters believe that "the chosen lady and her children" mentioned in 2 John 1 was a local church and its members.[155] If so, then those who taught false doctrine were to be cut out of the church's fellowship (vv. 10-11).

Third John portrays a conflict within a local assembly. One man, Diotrephes, was evidently acting in a dictatorial fashion. John accused him of a lack of hospitality, a major sin in the church of that day. Even worse, he was browbeating those who wanted to be hospitable, ejecting them from the fellowship (vv. 9-10). Verse 11, which warns against evildoing, implies that Diotrephes in particular needed to heed this warning.

Revelation

The Book of Revelation was written as a book of comfort and encouragement. It depicted the ultimate victory of God's people who were being persecuted. John identified with them in their suffering "because of the word of God and the testimony of Jesus" (1:9). There is debate over both the authorship and dating of the book. Majority opinion favors a dating during the reign of Domitian; a minority, the reign of Nero. Some scholars endorse John the Apostle as author; others, a believer named John the Elder. Whether the occasion of writing was the reign of Nero or that of Domitian, "it is clear that by John's last days the church faced a society that was hostile."[156]

Although the emphasis of Revelation is eschatological, one may uncover some helpful insights into church affairs. The book is addressed to the seven churches of Asia Minor, which are addressed respectively in chapters 2 and 3. They are, nonetheless, seen in a corporate light. The "letters to the seven churches" give us some idea of the function of the church in

Asia Minor. What their "works" were is not made clear, but John makes it clear how they rejected heretical teaching (2:2, 13-16, 20; 3:8-9). The writer admonished, exhorted, or encouraged these assemblies to purity and an utter devotion to Jesus Christ.[157]

The Bride. John described the church as the bride of Christ: " 'Let us rejoice and be glad and give Him glory! For the wedding of the Lamb has come, and His bride has made herself ready. Fine linen, bright and clean, was given her to wear.' (Fine linen stands for the righteous acts of the saints)" (19:7-8). George Eldon Ladd observes that, while the church is Christ's bride, "the consummation of this relationship is an eschatological event awaiting the return of Christ."[158]

The analogy is repeated in 21:9, where the bride is associated with the Holy City, Jerusalem: "One of the seven angels who had the seven bowls full of the seven last plagues came and said to me, 'Come, I will show you the bride, the wife of the Lamb.' " In 22:17, the bride is linked with the Spirit in inviting readers to eternal life: "The Spirit and the bride say, 'Come!' Whoever is thirsty, let him come; and whoever wishes, let him take the free gift of the water of life." Until the Day of the Lord, when repentance will be impossible, the Spirit invites men and women to come to Christ; the church re-echoes His invitation to partake freely of what Christ offers, life abundant and eternal.[159]

On Worship. The central contribution of Revelation to an understanding of the church is its emphasis on worship. The book is replete with liturgical passages which recapitulate a form of heavenly worship upon which church worship may well have been modeled (e.g., 4:8, 11; 5:9-10, 12-13; 7:10, 12; 11:15, 17-18; 12:10-12). Certainly, there can be no argument as to the writer's exalted view of worship.

Conclusions

The General Epistles and Revelation highlight two factors involved in shaping the people of God during the latter apostolic period. These were persecution and the increase in doctrinal heresy, and they had a strong influence on the direction of the church. We see constant signs of this influence in the glimpses these books give us of the nature and worship of the church.

After the destruction of Jerusalem in A.D. 70, the church developed into a community separate from Judaism. It was a community which found only hostility in Roman society. As a result, the writer to the Hebrews, the author of 1 Peter, and the Johannine writer emphasized the need for unity and mutuality in the church. James stressed the obligation of the church to nurture its members and meet their needs. A necessary adjunct was the exhortation to believers to dissociate from heretical teachers. In Revelation, through the medium of eschatological worship, John encouraged believers to persevere despite persecution.

SUMMARY

After His resurrection and just prior to His ascension, Jesus gave His disciples what was to be the commission for His church: they were to witness to Him in Jerusalem and Judea, throughout all of neighboring Samaria, and to the farthest reaches of the globe. But before they carried out His command, they were to wait for the power of the Holy Spirit to come upon them (Acts 1:8). On the Day of Pentecost the church was born as the Spirit descended upon 120 believers gathered together in prayer. Some 3,000 were added to the church that day and, in the weeks following, those numbers multiplied.

From its inception, the church was controlled by the Holy Spirit. There was no formal organization. Those who occupied positions of leadership did so because they had been gifted by the Holy Spirit. In obedience to Him, believers were an organic unity analogous to a body. Christ was the Head of His body, the church, and individual believers were members of His body.

Admission into the fellowship of the body occurred through baptism. Immersion in the water symbolized participation in the death and burial of Christ. Emergence from the water symbolized resurrection with Christ to newness of life. At the same time, one was reborn through the Spirit and indwelt by Him.

Continuing fellowship was expressed in the celebration of the Lord's Supper. In partaking of the bread and cup, believers were participating in the body and blood of the Lord. Equally important, because believers were one with the Lord, they were also one with each other. Thus, the Supper also symbolized the church's unity.

Just as the church was one even though its members were many, so it was one even though there were many local expressions of it in many diverse geographical locations. Each local assembly was a microcosm of the universal church.

In Christ, the Holy Spirit had broken down all the barriers that divided human beings. The oneness of the church meant that all of its members were equal. They might differ racially or socially or in gender, but in Christ — in the fellowship of believers — there was no difference among them.

There were many threats to the church both from without (persecution) and from within (heretical teaching and members quarreling). Such dangers made the unity of the fellowship all the more important. One may, in fact, derive from the apostolic writings that one of the most important themes is the unity believers share in and through Christ Jesus. As we look at a systematic theology of the church, we shall see the persistence of that theme and its great relevance to our own age and society.

PART 3

A Systematic Theology
of the Church

CHAPTER NINE

The Origin
of the Church

The origin of the church is a matter of considerable debate, not so much in regard to who founded it as to when it originated. The response to that concern ranges all the way from the time of creation to the ministry of the Apostle Paul.

John Macquarrie comments that the church was implicit in Creation. He defines Creation as the self-outpouring of Being. "The Church is a necessary stage in this great action of Being, so that to believe in creation is already to believe in the Church, and there is a sense in which the Church was there 'in the beginning' and is coeval with the world."[1]

Louis Berkhof asserts that the church is to be found back in history as far as the patriarchs. "At the time of the flood the Church was saved in the family of Noah, and continued particularly in the line of Shem. And when true religion was again on the point of dying out, God made a covenant with Abraham."[2]

Donald Guthrie maintains that the church originated in the earthly ministry of Jesus. "It is impossible to account satisfactorily for the rise of the concept of the church, if Jesus himself did not originate it."[3]

A majority of scholars would place the origin of the church at Pentecost when the Holy Spirit descended. Millard Erickson is representative, contending that "the fact that Luke never uses εκκλησια [ekklēsia] in his Gospel but emphasizes it twenty-four times in Acts is also significant. It would seem that he did not regard the church as present until the period covered by Acts. . . . We conclude that the church originated at Pentecost."[4]

311

Some theologians of an ultra-dispensationalist bent believe that the church of Acts was not a real church. They contend that the genuine church began during the ministry of the Apostle Paul.⁵

When did the church originate? This chapter will seek to answer that and related questions.

AN OLD TESTAMENT CHURCH?

Was there a church in the Old Testament? To answer that question one must examine the meaning of the word "church" in its Old Testament context.

"Church" in the Old Testament

The most common biblical word translated "church" is the Greek *ekklēsia*. Prior to both the Septuagint and the New Testament, *ekklēsia* had to do with a political institution in the Greek city-state. It was the assembly of all full citizens through which democratic decisions were made. It had no religious connections.⁶

Qāhāl. The Hebrew word in the Old Testament most commonly translated *ekklēsia* in the Septuagint is *qāhāl.* The word signifies an assembly or congregation and can be used for just about any type of gathering of people. Its purpose may be for good or ill, political, social, or religious. While *qāhāl* is used for the congregation of Israel (Num. 16:3; Micah 2:5), it is also used for the congregation of angels (Ps. 89:5).⁷

'Edhâh. A more focused Hebrew word which more closely approximates the New Testament meaning of *ekklēsia*—even though it is usually translated by *synagogē* in the Greek—is *'ēdhâh.* The word was coined for the assembly which gathered before the tent of meeting (Ex. 33:7-11), and expresses an idea of corporateness which emphasizes not the sum total of individuals but rather the unity of the fellowship. It is sometimes qualified by the addition of "of Israel" (e.g., Ex. 12:3; Num. 16:9) or "of the sons of Israel" (e.g., Ex. 16:9; Num. 1:2; Lev. 4:13).⁸

Conclusions. Some scholars, in attempting to demonstrate a continuity between Israel and the New Testament church, have argued for the use of *qāhāl* as a technical term for Israel in the Old Testament signifying the people of God.[9] But a compelling case cannot be established. Coenen declares:

> If one compares the use of the two Heb[rew] words, it becomes clear, from the passages in which both occur in the same context (e.g., Ex. 12:1ff.; 16:1ff.; Num. 14:1ff.; 20:1ff.; 1 Ki. 12:1ff.) that *'ēdhâh* is the unambiguous and permanent term for the covenant community as a whole. On the other hand, *qāhāl* is the ceremonial expression for the assembly that results from the covenant . . . and, in the deuteronomistic sense, for community in its present form.[10]

Thus, the meaning of the two words is not greatly different. On the basis of the words for "church" (*ekklēsia* or *qāhāl*), one cannot make a case for an Old Testament church. The assembly could meet for any purpose. "The *ekklēsia* is never contemplated as a spiritual fact, independent of spatial and temporal limitations . . . there is no place for reading the church back into the Old Testament on the basis of the prevalent use of *ekklēsia*."[11]

The People of God

We have argued that Israel was chosen by God to be His special people. God promised the Israelites that "out of all nations you will be my treasured possession" (Ex. 19:5). At the same time, there was a condition to being the people of God — obedience to His covenant with them. Yet the Hebrew people as a whole were not faithful. As a result, God punished them time and again. Their apostasy grew to the point where He permitted the Northern Kingdom to be destroyed, never to be reconstituted. Within a few decades the Southern Kingdom came under attack. Jerusalem was conquered by the Babylonians, the temple was destroyed, and the leading citizens were taken away into exile.

Even though the Jews were restored to their homeland after seventy years, God recognized that the existing covenant simply was not effective. As a consequence, He ordained that a new covenant was to be enacted: " 'The time is coming,' declares the Lord, 'when I will make a new covenant with the house of Israel. . . . I will put my law in their minds and write it on their hearts' " (Jer. 31:31, 33b).

When Jesus brought God's new covenant to earth, He offered God's kingdom to Israel. When the disciples were sent out to preach, He commanded them, "Do not go among the Gentiles or enter any town of the Samaritans. Go rather to the lost sheep of Israel" (Matt. 10:5b-6). George Ladd says of Israel:

> The Kingdom was theirs by right of election, history, and heritage. So it was that our Lord directed his ministry to them and offered to them that which had been promised them. When Israel rejected the Kingdom, the blessings which should have been theirs were given to those who would accept them.[12]

Because of Israel's rejection of their promised Messiah, God fulfilled His prophecy through Hosea: "you are not my people" (Hosea 1:9). He elected a new people, namely, the church, to take Israel's place. Israel has not been totally forsaken, however, but only "until the full number of the Gentiles has come in" (Rom. 11:25). At that time, "all Israel will be saved" (Rom. 11:26).

Conclusions

No case can be made for an Old Testament church either linguistically or theologically. Israel is called "the people of God" as is the church. Both are a part of the kingdom of God. But they are not one and the same. The church has replaced Israel as God's elect until His purposes for the nations (Gentiles) have been fulfilled. At that time Israel will once more take its place as His people.

JESUS AND THE CHURCH

When Christ began His earthly ministry, He began to call God's people together. He selected disciples, bidding them to "follow me." Edmund Clowney observes that

314

this choosing created a division among men. It began a "gather-ing" and "scattering." The disciples themselves were called to share in the gathering process as laborers in the harvest field and as fishers of men. . . . As he was rejected by an unbelieving Israel, he declared the rejection of those who refused to be gathered to him.[13]

As a result, Christ proceeded to constitute a new people of God. It is important to realize how often the concept of the founding of a new fellowship is carried in the Gospel accounts of Jesus' ministry and message, and that this concept is charac-teristic of the Gospel as a whole. It was Jesus' desire and inten-tion to assemble a new people, a family prepared for God's kingdom.[14]

This new people of God was founded upon Simon Peter's confession of Jesus as Messiah (Matt. 16:16). His confession of Jesus as God's Son was, moreover, in sharp contrast to the lack of belief manifested by the crowds. Clowney asserts:

Upon this confessing apostle the church was to be built. The foundation of the church is not Peter's confession in the abstract apart from the confessing Peter . . . but neither is Peter the foun-dation apart from his confession. . . . Nor is Peter to be separat-ed from the eleven. . . . It is only Peter as confessing, in his distinctive apostolic work, who is the rock.[15]

As Peter's confession demonstrates, the concept of the church as a fellowship assembled about the Messiah cannot be divorced from the messianic idea. Proceeding from this aspect one can hardly deny that the church which originated at Pente-cost not only had its foundation in Jesus' teaching and work, but that it was also consonant with His purpose. The connec-tion between Jesus and the apostolic church is intact.[16] But while there is an unquestionable link between Jesus Christ and the church, there was no church as such during His earthly life and ministry. Nor is there anything in the Gospel to suggest its existence. In fact, the saying of Matthew 16:18 clear-ly denotes the fashioning of a church in the future rather than in the present. That future would be the first post-Easter Pentecost.[17]

315

THE FORMATION OF THE CHURCH

The church belongs to God. It has its origin in God's finished work in Jesus Christ. Christ came to this earth to usher in the kingdom of God; to that end He gathered about Him a group of followers who would assist Him by witnessing to what He had done. While this group was of vital significance in the formation of the church, it was not the church (during His ministry).[18] The church was a fellowship of Christ's followers created by the Holy Spirit on the Day of Pentecost.[19]

The Work of the Spirit

The church is the work of the Holy Spirit who transformed the social group of Jesus' followers into a spiritual fellowship set apart unto God. Dale Moody observes:

> The fellowship of the Spirit is a term found only twice in the New Testament (2 Cor. 13:14; Phil. 2:1), but the idea supplements the fellowship with the Father (1 John 1:3) and the fellowship with the Son (1 John 1:3; 1 Cor. 1:9) to give the very essence of the Church. Devotion "to the apostles' teachings and fellowship, to the breaking of bread and the prayers" (Acts 2:42 RSV) is something more than voluntary association with one another or participation in the Spirit. It is nothing less than the access through Christ, in the Spirit, to the Father (Eph. 2:18) by all who have been reconciled to God through the blood of the cross of Christ.[20]

The church was established through the baptism by the Holy Spirit. Paul wrote to the Corinthians, "For we were all baptized by one Spirit into one body . . . and we were all given the one Spirit to drink" (1 Cor. 12:13). In baptism through the Holy Spirit (symbolized by baptism in water), the believer is accepted by God and incorporated into the body of Christ. Through this work of the Spirit "the individual is taken into and made a lovely but still distinct member of the one body."[21]

Paul's analogy of the building demonstrates this same reliance on the Spirit for the maintenance of the church: "in him [Christ] you too are being built together to become a dwelling in which God lives by his Spirit" (Eph. 2:22). It was not until the Spirit came to indwell believers that the church was formed as the temple of the Lord.[22]

The Day of Pentecost

The pouring out of the Holy Spirit which formed the church took place on Pentecost. Prior to His ascension, Jesus had commanded His followers: "Do not leave Jerusalem . . . [for] in a few days you will be baptized with the Holy Spirit" (Acts 1:4-5). While it is true that the word *baptized* does not occur in this account of Pentecost (Acts 2), one can easily demonstrate that this was the realization of Jesus' prophecy. In reporting to the Jerusalem church on the Spirit's coming to Cornelius and his household (Acts 10:45), Peter said, "As I began to speak, the Holy Spirit came on them as he had come on us at the beginning. Then I remembered what the Lord had said: 'John baptized with water, but you will be baptized with the Holy Spirit' " (Acts 11:15-16). Peter is clearly equating "the beginning" to Pentecost, and so marking it as the point of the baptism with the Holy Spirit.[23]

The Universalization of the Church

While Jerusalem was the site of the origin of the church, it was not long before believers were carrying the faith beyond its walls to other parts of the country and to far-off lands in obedience to their Lord's command (Acts 1:8).

Jerusalem had been the center of Jesus' ministry. It was there that He celebrated the Passover shortly after His baptism; there that He cleansed the temple. It was there that He did much of His teaching and many of His miracles; there that He made His entry in triumph and spent the last week of His life. He was tried in Jerusalem, crucified, and buried there. He rose again and made several appearances to His followers there. It was from the Mount of Olives, just outside the city, that Jesus commissioned His followers and ascended to His Father. And in Jerusalem the Holy Spirit descended upon and baptized those initial disciples, thus originating the church. It was only natural, therefore, that the city should be regarded as the "headquarters" for the church, even after it had spread to Asia Minor, Greece, and Italy.

317

On the Day of Pentecost, when the fellowship of the Spirit was formed, devout Jews from every nation of the known world were in Jerusalem and witnessed the amazing events attending the church's birth. Many of these people were converted and baptized, becoming a part of the church themselves. They undoubtedly evangelized the home areas to which they returned; for churches existed in various world centers (such as Rome) with no biblical explanation as to how they came to be.

During the church's early days, people from surrounding villages—drawn into Jerusalem by reports of miracles—were led to Christ and returned home, evangelizing Judea. With the outbreak of a persecution beginning with the martyring of Stephen, believers fled Jerusalem to places throughout Judea and Samaria and points beyond, preaching the Gospel wherever they went. Churches were begun in Samaria and Syria.

With the conversion of Saul of Tarsus to Christian faith, and his acceptance by the Christian community in Jerusalem (thanks to Barnabas), the faith was set for transmission to all parts of the Roman Empire. On an initial mission thrust, Paul and Barnabas traveled throughout Asia Minor planting churches. After that venture, they split up, Barnabas going on a mission to Cyprus, Paul back through Asia Minor and on to Greece. Nor were Paul and Barnabas the only missionaries; for the former wrote of the apostles and brothers of the Lord who took their wives along as they traveled (1 Cor. 9:5).

The expansion of the church throughout the world was so rapid and extensive that, within about 150 years of Christ's ascension, the church father Justin Martyr could write:

> There is no people, Greek or Barbarian, or of any other race, by whatever appellation or manners they may be distinguished, however ignorant of arts or agriculture, whether they dwell in tents or wander about in covered wagons, among whom prayers and thanksgivings are not offered in the name of the crucified Jesus to the Father and Creator of all things.[24]

SUMMARY

The church of Jesus Christ is the elect people of God, but so was Israel. Israel, by statement of inspired prophecy, is the

318

covenant-people of God—which is exactly what the church is. Because both are the people of God—and God has only one people, not two—it is only natural to suppose that Israel was the Old Testament church. But the two are not synonymous; for "the fellowship founded by Jesus realized that it was something wholly new, namely, the fellowship of those who through Jesus Christ share in the New Covenant and the new aeon."[25]

Israel, furthermore, should not be equated with the church; for the former rejected its Messiah. When that occurred, God cut Israel off as a nation and initiated a new people—the church—which allowed the participation of all persons regardless of race, social status, or gender. Israel is not completely out of the picture; a remnant is represented in the church and, in God's timing, Israel will be offered another opportunity to take its rightful place among the people of God.

The church began in the mind of Jesus Christ. He began preparing it in His earthly ministry, choosing a band of disciples to live in intimate, daily community with Him and with each other, modeling for them life as a subject of the kingdom of God. They were not the church, but a foundation for it (Matt. 16:18).

The church was birthed in Jerusalem on the first post-Easter Pentecost. The descent of the Holy Spirit upon Jesus' followers welded them into an eschatological fellowship, into the body of Christ on earth.

While the church began at, and centered in, Jerusalem, it did not stay confined to that city. Aided by the *pax Romana*, believers spread far and wide throughout the Roman Empire. Within a century or so of its inception, the church was to be found in just about every tribe and nation of the known world.

CHAPTER TEN

The Nature
of the Church

In the past few years, books on the church have proliferated. However, most of these books have operated without any coherent theology of the church as they have sought to understand other aspects of the church. Nor is such a situation very new. Almost twenty years ago John Macquarrie complained, "We hear about the Church in relation to rapid social change, the Church in a secular society, the Church and reunion, the Church in mission. But however valuable some of the insights gained in these various fields may be, they need to be guided and correlated by a theological understanding of the Church."[1]

One reason for the dearth of theologies on the church may arise from the difficulties involved in understanding the nature of the church. Dale Moody has observed that "the nature of the church in the New Testament has been obscured through the conflicts of church history."[2] Down through the ages doctrinal and denominational rivalries have perverted the biblical teaching on the nature of the church.

This chapter seeks to clarify the nature of the church by a detailed examination of its leading characteristics.

DEFINING THE CHURCH

Many misunderstandings of the nature of the church result from the many uses in English of the word "church." It is popularly used of a building used by a congregation for worship. It may be used of a local assembly of believers; one refers, for example, to the Bethany Baptist Church. Or, it may be used of a denominational grouping of churches, such as the Roman Catholic Church or the Evangelical Free Church. As a consequence, it is important to construct a pointed and clear definition of the church, firmly founded on biblical teaching.

The New Testament Language

Chapter 9 noted that the chief New Testament word for "church" is *ekklēsia*, a term denoting an assembly of citizens called out to make political decisions. While originally devoid of any religious meaning, the term in New Testament parlance was used to describe an assembly of people called out by God in Christ to worship Him and to minister on His behalf.

Why not "synagogue"? One might have supposed that Jesus' followers would have referred to their worship assembly by the Greek term *synagogē*. It was, after all, the institution of worship and learning with which they were most familiar. The word represented both the meeting place of the congregation and the congregation itself. But the term (with the single exception of James 2:2) is never used in the New Testament writings. L. Coenen explains why:

> The name synagogue which was originally a technical term for the Jewish assembly came to be regarded in time as the "symbol of the Jewish religion of law and tradition" (W. Schrage, *ZThK* 60, 1963, 196ff.). It was no doubt also felt that a word with such connotations could not be used to describe a fellowship and an event, at the centre of which was the proclamation of a gospel of freedom from law and of salvation available only through faith in Jesus Christ.[3]

Ekklēsia in the New Testament. With the exception of Matthew 16:18 and 18:17, the word *ekklēsia* is never used in the four Gospels. It is significant that Luke does not use the word at all in his Gospel, but uses it twenty-four times in Acts. The reason is that all the early Christian writers use only *ekklēsia* as a technical term signifying the Christian people of God; there are times when it is used less technically, along with modifiers

321

(see 1 Thes. 1:1; 2:14; 2 Thes. 1:1). Since these epistles were written fairly early, and modifiers are missing in latter epistles' use of the word, a development of *ekklēsia* from nontechnical to full technical term appears to be indicated. "Through use, it became so completely identified with the specific Christian assembly that the term took on that particular meaning itself and could stand for that assembly without being confused with others."[4] Most New Testament uses of *ekklēsia* fall into this category.

Conclusions. The term *ekklēsia* is used in the New Testament to describe the post-resurrection fellowship of believers. It is never used to indicate the building in which believers assemble for worship. Nor does it ever signify a group of Christian assemblies holding a particular doctrinal or polity position.

The Trinitarian Nature of the Church

Like many other areas of Christian theology, the nature of the church must be seen in a Trinitarian light. Moody asserts that "the church is that fellowship of faith created by the living God as Father, Son, and Holy Spirit to the praise of his glory."[5] The church is unquestionably related to all three members of the Godhead.

The People of God. The Apostle Paul made a distinct connection of the church to God in a number of passages in his epistles. For example, he addressed his first letter to the Corinthians "to the church of God in Corinth" (1 Cor. 1:2). He also referred to "the church of God" in 1 Corinthians 10:32 and 15:9. His second epistle to Corinth was similarly addressed (2 Cor. 1:1). In Galatians 1:13 he wrote of having persecuted "the church of God." And in his first letter to Timothy he mentioned "God's church" (3:5) and "the church of the living God" (3:15). In 1 Corinthians 11:16 and 1 Thessalonians 2:14 he talked of "the churches of God."

The Israel of God. God has always had a community of faith, an elect people. In Old Testament times, His chosen people were the Hebrews. But their failure to accept Jesus as God's Messiah led Him to declare to the Jews that "the kingdom of God will be taken away from you and given to a people who will produce its fruit" (Matt. 21:43). Paul reiterated much the same thing: "And Isaiah boldly says, 'I was found by those who did not seek me; I revealed myself to those who did not ask for me.' But concerning Israel he says, 'All day long I have held out my hands to a disobedient and obstinate people' " (Rom. 10:20-21).

Because of Israel's lack of faithfulness, God elected a new people, the church. Paul and the other members of the primitive Christian community held the church to be the successor of Israel, the "Israel of God" (Gal. 6:16). "The church (εκκλησια) was the assembly that God had summoned, just as Israel was the nation that he had chosen."[6] In fact, Paul used many other descriptive terms in depicting the church as Israel's replacement, such as "the commonwealth of Israel" (Eph. 2:12, 19, RSV) and "the circumcision" (Phil. 3:3).

Peter followed suit in terming believers the people of God. He told Christians that they are "a chosen people, a royal priesthood, a holy nation, a people belonging to God. . . . Once you were not a people, but now you are the people of God" (1 Peter 2:9). Although Peter never used the word *ekklēsia* in his epistles, he definitely propounds the idea that the Christian community of faith is the continuing people of God.[7]

Children of Abraham. It may be difficult for some to understand why the church should see itself as the rightful successor to Israel when Israel was a distinct biological unit descended from Abraham, Isaac, and Jacob, whereas the church was a disparate group from a multitude of ethnic backgrounds.

Paul explained that the basis of fellowship among the people of God is faith, whether in the Old Testament economy or the New. None was ever saved by observance of the Law, not even the patriarchs. He put it bluntly: "A man is not a Jew if he is only one outwardly, nor is circumcision merely outward and physical. No, a man is a Jew if he is one inwardly; and circumcision is circumcision of the heart, by the Spirit, not by the written code" (Rom. 2:29-30). Jesus had confronted the Jews of His day when they claimed privilege with God because of their family connection with Abraham: "If you were Abraham's children . . . then you would do the things Abraham did" (John 8:39). Paul admonished the Galatians, "Understand, then, that those who believe are children of Abraham. . . . If you belong to Christ, then you are Abraham's seed, and heirs according to the promise" (Gal. 3:7, 29).

In regard to the Jews as God's people, Harold Bender right-fully notes:

> Historically, by no means were all Jews after the flesh Jews after the Spirit. . . . The true people of God were always the spiritual people, not the biological people, and they were a remnant, produced by God's judgment and grace. Only a part of the eth-nic group were the people of God, for a major part was always in spiritual apostasy.[8]

The church was the continuation of spiritual Israel, not of ethnic Israel. The latter continued outside of God's purposes.[9]

Conclusions. Certain implications arise from the depiction of the church as the people of God which impact our understand-ing of its nature.

The first implication is that the church is not a counterpart of physical Old Testament Israel, but only of the remnant that remained faithful to God. Nor is the church, like Israel, restrict-ed to a particular geographical location. "The church is a com-pany of concrete living persons in the flesh, living in time and space."[10]

A second implication is that the church has been elected by God Himself. Like Old Testament Israel, the church is God's people by virtue of a covenant He has effected with them. There was nothing in them personally to merit His favor any more than Israel was deserving; it was a matter of His sovereign grace. The covenant offered was the new covenant in Christ's blood. "The church is created by God's mighty acts, and she continues to exist only because God dwells in her midst—she is His temple. The new people are the elect."[11]

Thirdly, the church is a people who respond to God. It is true that God is the initiator; He is the dispenser of grace; He elects a people and calls them out. But they become His people only when they respond to His call. Had Abraham not obeyed

God and left home and kin, God would not have made him a great nation and a blessing to all humankind. Israel became God's covenant people because it accepted the covenant and pledged faithfulness to God.

> As Israel, so is the church. The church came into existence likewise in response to God, by repentance and faith. The church does not exist apart from believing in Christ; it is a believing people. . . . The offer of salvation is indeed made by God, but the acceptance is an act of the responder.[12]

And like Israel, when the church does not respond as it should, or is unfaithful in its response, the result is self-destruction. The church has the freedom to apostatize if it so desires; for the love of God does not force anyone to obedience. The church's response of faith, on the other hand, is to produce spiritual fruit.

The Dominion of Christ

Not only was the church in the mind of God from the beginning, but we have already shown (in chap. 7) that it was Jesus' intention to found a church. To that end He gathered together a band of followers and prepared them to be citizens of the kingdom of God by pouring His life and message into them. Jesus founded the church on Simon Peter's confession of Him as Messiah. Gustaf Aulén avers that the ground of the church is the concluded work of Christ and that the church emerges as a vital reality in and through His exaltation. The Christian church is the church of Easter and of Pentecost. Indeed, should the exaltation be the inauguration of His ensuing work, this ensuing work is solidly linked to the church, for the church is ultimately nothing less than His work continuing down through the centuries.[13]

The Eschatological Fellowship. Christ came to earth as herald of the kingdom of God. His victorious resurrection and subsequent exaltation have ushered in the kingdom. While the kingdom is not synonymous with the church as far as this earthly life is concerned, Aulén declares:

When this reign of Christ is established, it means the beginning of a new age, a new aeon, the new "time of fulfillment." The old age remains, but in the midst of this new aeon the church as *regnum Christi* [dominion of Christ] represents the new age. The church lives in this world, but is not of this world. . . . It is the messianic fellowship, the true Israel, the new covenant, *Kyrios-Christus* united with his own in the world.[14]

Thus, the church is an eschatological community with its gaze fixed on the Parousia which will occur when the old age has come to an end and the glory of God's kingdom is revealed. But the church on earth even now participates in the new aeon which has come as a consequence of Christ's victory over the oppressive and demonic powers which have kept human beings in servitude.[15]

The Body of Christ. The church and Christ are an inescapable unity. One cannot think of the church without Him, nor can one conceive of Christ without His dominion and the connection with the community of saints. "Christ has become embodied in his church."[16]

One can best understand the church as the body of Christ in the light of the Hebrew concept of corporate personality, which may be seen in the passages on the Servant of God (Isa. 53), the Son of Man (Dan. 7:13-14), and Adam (Rom. 5:12-14). Paul, in his teaching on the body, focused on its members, its head, and its unity under the head, Jesus Christ.[17]

The apostle dealt with the members of the body in a number of passages. He scored the Corinthians for their failure to discipline a man guilty of incest because the believer's body is a part of Christ's body: "Do you not know that your bodies are members of Christ himself?" (1 Cor. 6:15a) This same fact was reason for believers to examine themselves before participating in the Lord's Supper; for the partaking of the loaf was a participation in Christ's body (1 Cor. 10:16): "For anyone who eats and drinks without recognizing the body of the Lord eats and drinks judgment on himself" (1 Cor. 11:29). Moody reminds us, "The body of Christ is nothing less than the presence of Christ himself in the life and service of the Christian community. This does not mean that the church is Christ, but it means that there can be no true church apart from vital union of the members with Christ."[18]

Christ is the head of His body the church (Col. 1:18), "for God was pleased to have all His fullness dwell in him, and through him to reconcile to himself all things" (Col. 1:19-20). Through the Apostle Paul, the Holy Spirit promised that "all things in heaven and on earth" would be brought "together under one head, even Christ" (Eph. 1:10). Because He is head of the body, Christ is also ruler of the church: "For in Christ all the fullness of the Deity lives in bodily form, and you have been given fullness in Christ, who is the head over every power and authority" (Col. 2:9-10). Christ is the church's Master, and it is to be advised and regulated by Him.[19]

Paul gives extensive attention to the unity of the body of Christ in his letter to the Ephesians. "In Ephesians the headship of Christ is described in reference to the past, present, and future."[20] Ephesians 1:15-23 is a prayer for spiritual enlightenment (1:15-19a) and spiritual energy (1:19b-23) because of Christ's resurrection and exaltation to God's right hand. That glorification is not just something past or future, but a present reality among His people; for Christ fills the church with His presence, so that it becomes "His body, the fullness of Him who fills everything in every way" (1:23). The past fact of Christ's exaltation is viewed as a present fact in the body's activity.[21]

The Bride of Christ. The analogy of marriage to represent the relationship of God to His people is a common one in both the Old and New Testaments. Looking toward Israel's restoration after the Babylonian exile, Isaiah told the people, "your Maker is your husband — the Lord Almighty is his name — . . . The Lord will call you back as if you were a wife deserted . . . a wife who married young, only to be rejected" (Isa. 54:5-6). Jeremiah, in attempting to forestall Judah's destruction, brought a similar message from God, " 'Return, faithless people,' declares the Lord, 'for I am your husband' " (Jer. 3:14). While not a frequently used image in the New Testament, the analogy of the church as the bride of Christ is nonetheless an important one for understanding how the church relates to its Lord.

The major use of this image is found in Ephesians 5:22-33,

where Paul relates the union of Christ and His church to human marriage: "Now as the church submits to Christ, so also wives should submit to their husbands in everything. Husbands, love your wives, just as Christ loved the church and gave himself up for her" (5:24-25).

Even though it has been set out as the standard for married love, the love of Christ for His bride has gone far beyond any human love of a bridegroom for his intended. For Christ loved not only the lovable, but the unlovely as well (Rom. 5:8-10). And He did not give a traditional "bride price" (the Jewish custom of His day), but His own life. Such a love transcends our understanding and knowledge. It remains, nonetheless, the paramount object of all authentic knowledge and the subject of all authentic experience of the bride.[22]

Even though the bride initially is not just enjoined to love her husband, there is nonetheless a response to his love. The Apostle John defines the church's response to her Lord as "love." John writes, "We love because he first loved us" (1 John 4:19). Paul, by way of contrast, rarely refers to the believer's attitude toward the Lord as one of love, but instead prefers to spell it out because of believers' failure rightly to interpret it.[23]

Just as a wife is to be faithful to her husband, so the church must be faithful to Christ. Paul was concerned about the fidelity of the faith community to its Lord. Consequently, he wrote to the Corinthians, "I am jealous for you with a godly jealousy. I promised you to one husband, to Christ, so that I might present you as a pure virgin to Him" (2 Cor. 11:2). He was afraid that they might be seduced by Satan away from a wholehearted devotion to their Lord (11:3). The Corinthians were threatened by seduction through the guile of false teachers of another gospel. Until the church was ultimately united to her Lord, it needed to be watchful against the enticing and yet false enchantments used by Satan to pull her away from Christ.[24]

The Creation of the Spirit

Even as the institution of the church was God's plan from before the foundation of the world, and crystallized in the mind of Christ, so the church is a creation of the Holy Spirit of God.

It is the Holy Spirit who descended upon the followers of Christ on the Day of Pentecost and welded them into a unity, a single body. According to the Book of Acts, the uniqueness of Christianity lay in the immense transformation created in the individual believer by the Holy Spirit and in the energizing power of the Spirit infusing the church. Thus, the church is a fellowship of the Holy Spirit.[25]

Emil Brunner reflects upon the way the Holy Spirit works in the world in establishing and maintaining the church.

> If we search the New Testament documents themselves in order to discover some characteristic signs of [His] mode of being and operating, we shall have to affirm for example that the "pneuma" is there, manifesting [His] presence and operating in a self-authenticating manner—even so it is said of Jesus that He preached with authority and not as the scribes; [His] effects are incomprehensible, striking the beholders with amazement and awe.... [He] manifests [Himself] in such a way as to leave one wondering why and how, and in such a way as to demolish the walls of partition separating individuals from each other.[26]

Apart from the Spirit's animating energy, there would be neither power nor fellowship nor even a church at all.

The Formation of the Body. The Holy Spirit is the basis for the existence of the church. He fills it, nourishes it, sustains and guides it. The church is controlled by the Spirit of God.[27] He has taken a motley crew of men and women and made them into a fellowship with a ministry of service.[28]

Having formed the church on the Day of Pentecost, He now indwells the church both individually and collectively. Paul not only tells the Corinthians "that you yourselves are God's temple and that God's Spirit lives in you" (1 Cor. 3:16), but he also reminds the Ephesians that "in Him you too are being built together to become a dwelling in which God lives by His Spirit" (Eph. 2:22). The life of the Spirit is the life of the church.

The church, furthermore, is empowered by the indwelling Spirit for God's service. The Holy Spirit indwells each believer, giving each member at least one spiritual gift for the purpose of ministry. No organism can perform satisfactorily unless differ-

329

ent members are fulfilling different functions. The church is designed by God to be such an "organism," and the Head of the church has made a wholly ample arrangement for it: the ministry of the Holy Spirit, to furnish spiritual gifts to every Christian.[29] One may define a spiritual gift as "an enablement which the Lord Jesus gives through His Spirit to every believer to enable him to serve God in some specific way."[30] The purpose for these spiritual gifts is that "we all reach unity in the faith and in the knowledge of the Son of God and become mature, attaining to the whole measure of the fullness of Christ" (Eph. 4:13).

The Filling of the Spirit. Not only does the Holy Spirit fill the church, but He is ready and willing to fill every believer. Paul exhorted the Ephesians, "Do not get drunk on wine, which leads to debauchery. Instead, be filled with the Spirit" (Eph. 5:18). The sense of the latter verb in the Greek is a present imperative — "be being filled." All believers should allow themselves to be fully possessed by the Spirit of God. All Christians should seek to give the Spirit continuing control of their lives. Moody observes, "It was this spiritual fullness that led some observers at Pentecost to conclude that Spirit-filled men were 'filled with new wine' (Acts 2:13), but this filling of the Spirit is the source of power in the worship and work of the church."[31]

The Sword of the Spirit. God has empowered the church with spiritual weapons. Paul urged the Ephesian believers, "Take the helmet of salvation and the sword of the Spirit, which is the word of God. And pray in the Spirit on all occasions . . . be alert and always keep on praying for all the saints" (Eph. 6:17-18). The church is in a spiritual battle against the world. It has a powerful weapon in the living Word of God, wielded by the Holy Spirit like a sword battering into destruction every power of darkness.[32] And in the arsenal, as well, is prayer. Mutual prayer in the Spirit for believers is a mighty force in maintaining the strength and well-being of the church.

Conclusion

The church is Trinitarian in its nature. It is related closely to all three Persons of the Godhead. The church belongs to God; it is

His people, elected by Him by virtue of His grace. It is also the messianic fellowship, founded by Christ to advance the work of the kingdom of heaven. It is a corporate entity relating to Christ as Head of the body. He loves it with an everlasting love; it responds to His love with fidelity and devotion. The church was created by the Holy Spirit, and He fills it and empowers it with special spiritual gifts for the purpose of building it up and edifying it. He has provided believers with the most powerful weapons of all: God's Word and prayer "in the Spirit" are invaluable in the fight against the powers of this world.

THE CHURCH AND THE KINGDOM OF GOD

Jesus' earthly ministry began with a call to His hearers to repent because the kingdom of God was approaching (Matt. 4:17; Mark 1:14-15). The kingdom was basic to Jesus' whole understanding of His purpose in coming to minister to humankind. Because of the importance of the kingdom of God to Jesus, it is vital to understand the meaning of the kingdom in relation to the nature of the church.

The Nature of the Kingdom

What is meant by "the kingdom of God"? There are several definitions which might be considered. Edgar Mullins defines it as "a divine society wherein God and man are associated in loving fellowship; where the will of God is done by men; where love is the expression of their relations with and conduct toward each other; and where God graciously manifests himself in the fullness of his grace to man: this is the New Testament teaching as to the kingdom of God."[33] Rudolf Bultmann describes it as "the regime of God which will destroy the present course of the world, wipe out all the contra-divine, Satanic power under which the present world groans—and thereby, terminating all pain and sorrow, bring in salvation for the People of God which awaits the fulfillment of the prophets' promises."[34] C.H. Dodd determines that the kingdom of God signifies "the manifest and effective assertion of the divine sovereignty against all the evil of the world."[35] And George Eldon Ladd speaks of the kingdom as "God's rule or sovereignty . . . that God's will be done on earth, i.e., that his rule be perfectly realized."[36] While all of these definitions are all right as far as they go, all are inadequate to describe fully the nature of God's kingdom. Further reflection is needed.

A Spiritual Kingdom. While some scholars, like Bernhard Weiss (in his *Leben Jesu*), believed that Jesus had intended to establish a theocratic kingdom under His rule but was diverted by the cross and so turned to a spiritual kingdom, the New Testament indicates differently. Jesus' intention was always to set up a spiritual kingdom. Such an intention was demonstrated by the Beatitudes (Matt. 5:3-12), as was His defense of His disciples for feasting rather than fasting (Matt. 9:14-17).

The Jews, including Jesus' own followers, believed that the Messiah would reestablish the Jewish empire founded by David and enlarged by Solomon, that with a cataclysmic burst of power He would shatter Roman rule and make Jerusalem supreme. Even after the Resurrection, Jesus' disciples were looking for the restoration of a physical kingdom (Acts 1:6). William Stevens avers that

> Jesus endeavorsto make them conceive of a kingdom free from national, racial, and political limitations, one embodied in himself as future Lord and present Son of man. In fact, he very seldom applies the term Christ, or Messiah, to himself, for it brings to the Jewish mind a concept far from what he desires. So he chooses the obscure title Son of man, as found in the famous passage of Daniel 7:13ff., and pours into this unexpected term the concept of himself that he wishes the world to have . . . the Suffering Servant idea of Isaiah 53.[37]

A Universal Kingdom. The kingdom of God extended beyond Israel to the whole world. Jesus never refused anyone; "whosoever is thirsty, let him come; and whoever wishes, let him take the free gift of the water of life" (Rev. 22:17b).

In His earthly ministry, Jesus declared His mission to His hometown by quoting Isaiah 61:1-2: "The Spirit of the Lord is on me, because He has anointed me to preach good news to the poor. He has sent me to proclaim freedom for the prisoners and recovery of sight for the blind, to release the oppressed, to proclaim the year of the Lord's favor" (Luke 4:18-19). He then announced, "Today this scripture is fulfilled in your hearing" (Luke 4:21).

Jesus carried out His mission to all with whom He came in contact. The type of people to whom He preached, the level of society to which He ministered, and the diversity of persons he invited are all expressive of the kingdom's universality. He proclaimed the kingdom to the poor (Matt. 16:5); and He sought the lost (Luke 19:10). Tax collectors, loose women, and sinners comprised the largest cluster of people forging into the kingdom. Jesus' ministry obviously went well beyond the pale established by the religious Israelites of His day, extending to all classes and groups of people.[38] The universality of His kingdom was demonstrated by His Great Commission. His followers were given the mandate to "make disciples of all nations . . . teaching them to obey everything I have commanded you" (Matt. 28:19-20).

The "Already, But Not Yet" Kingdom. A study of the New Testament teaching on the kingdom of God shows us that the kingdom is not only a present reality but a future hope.[39] The tension manifested between these two spheres is found in the nature of faith itself, which is synonymous with hope, and yet not exactly the same as it. "Faith is the future as present, it is the anticipation of the future."[40] John writes, "Dear friends, now we are children of God, and what we will be has not yet been made known" (1 John 3:2). Faith in Jesus Christ saves one here and now, and yet, one's salvation is also in the future when sin is destroyed at the close of the age.

There are a number of New Testament passages which show the kingdom as present now, and there are a number which show it as future reality. Jesus declared to His detractors, "But if I drive out demons by the Spirit of God, then the kingdom of God has come upon you" (Matt. 12:28). He publicly proclaimed, "The time has come, the kingdom of God is near" (Mark 1:15). He also promised, "I say to you that many will come from the east and the west, and will take their places at the feast with Abraham, Isaac and Jacob in the kingdom of heaven" (Matt. 8:11). And, at the Last Supper, He asserted, "I tell you, I will not drink of this fruit of the vine from now on until the day when I drink it anew with you in my Father's kingdom" (Matt. 26:29).

The Church and the Kingdom

Chapter 7 demonstrated that church and kingdom are not synonymous terms; but the two are connected. The church is God's people; the kingdom is God's rule in the lives of His people. The constituents of the church are also constituents of the kingdom, but the church is God's instrument for carrying out the work of the kingdom in the world.

John Bright has aptly observed in his classic work *The Kingdom of God* that the New Testament has no inclination to equate the church with the kingdom of God. Indeed, he warns that

> the church that makes such an identification will soon begin to invite God to endorse its own very human policies and practices, will equate the people of God with those nice people who share its particular beliefs and participate in its services, and will reckon the advance of the Kingdom in terms of its numerical growth. But it will not be the New Testament Church.[41]

In the mind of Jesus, the kingdom of God was all-important. Indeed the kingdom—not the church—continually occupied His mind. Nonetheless, the Lord Jesus was well aware that the spiritual life of the kingdom would be centered in the fellowship of the faith community—the church.[42]

THE CHURCH VISIBLE AND INVISIBLE

Jesus told His followers, "I will build my church" (Matt. 16:18). But is the church He founded the same institution with which believers identify today? Are the true church and the institutional church one and the same? Are there people in the visible church who are not a part of the invisible and greater body of Christ? And, in the same vein, are there some people who belong to the invisible church but have never been a part of a local community of believers? These and related questions are a part of an active debate among Christians over the visible and invisible church.

The Apostolic Succession

Roman Catholicism—and, to some degree, Eastern Orthodoxy and Anglicanism—holds that there is no invisible church; the true church is and always has been visible. Hans Küng is representative of this view.

> A real Church made up of real people cannot possibly be invisible. The believing Christian least of all can harbour any illusions about the fact that the Church he believes in is a real one and therefore visible. There is no place here for fantasies about a Platonic idea. The Christian's starting-point . . . is a real Church.[43]

When Jesus declared His intention to found a church, He initiated a real, tangible institution. When He granted the apostles possession of the keys of the kingdom (Matt. 16:19), He was bestowing on them the ability to define doctrine and convey grace (that is, saving grace). They in turn transmitted to their successors this same ability.[44]

These denominations hold that apostolicity is the criterion of a true church. Only a church which stands in the "apostolic succession" is genuine. People may organize themselves into a religious institution and call themselves a church, but apart from a historical connection to Christ and His apostles, they do not constitute a church, nor are they Christians.[45] The true church is apostolic in both its teaching and ruling authority, in its priestly office and sacramental service, in its obedience to the Lord's command to be baptized, and in its approbation of a common faith and lordship as taught first by the apostles.[46]

Individual Commitment

At the other end of the spectrum is the view that only an individual's personal commitment to God in Christ can make that one a Christian. A church is simply a gathering of such regenerate persons which effect a valid church. Those who hold to this view insist that "those who are savingly related to Christ make up the church, whether or not they are assembled into any visible group. Membership in a visible group is no guaran-

335

tee whatsoever of justification in God's sight, so the visible organization is relatively unimportant."[47] Thus, church membership is of minimal importance. One may be a part of a parachurch group, a nondenominational chapel, or a house church, and be part of the invisible body of Christ.

Some of the proponents of such a view hold to a dispensational theology which sees the church as incidental to God's program for the world. His central plan is based on Israel—not the church—as His special people. When Israel rejected Jesus as its Messiah, God moved His focus to the Gentiles, but only for a time. In due course, His attention will move back from the church to Israel. Israel will not become a part of the church; it will be reconstituted as God's chosen nation. Because the church is only a transient phenomenon, membership in the visible church is not really needed.[48]

10.1 Views on the True Church

	Apostolic	**Individual**	**Dualistic**
Groups holding view	Roman Catholic, Greek Orthodox, Anglican	Brethren Bible Churches	Reformation churches (e.g., Lutheran, Presbyterian, Baptist, etc.)
View of Church	No invisible church; the true church always has been visible, and is the church which has existed historically from the Day of Pentecost; the church is marked by the Apostolic Succession.	Those individuals who have been regenerated in Christ by the Holy Spirit compose the true (invisible) church whether they are members of a local (visible) church or not.	There are two churches—visible and invisible. All who profess faith in Jesus Christ and have followed Him in baptism are members of the visible church; those who are truly saved (and have been baptized) are members of the invisible and universal church.

A Mediating View

The above two perspectives are extremes. There is a mediating view, held largely by Reformation groups. This view holds that membership in the invisible church comes only through faith in the Christ who died as an expiation for the world's sins. It (membership) has nothing to do with joining a local church, nor with observation of the sacraments as a means of grace, nor with any attempt to imitate the Lord's example by seemingly patterning oneself on Him. Only a sincere believer in Jesus may be a member of His church (Acts 16:31).[49] Furthermore, "all unbelievers and hypocrites *(mali et hypocritae)* who outwardly belong to visible churches are really outside the pale of the Christian Church."[50]

By so saying, the proponents of this view are not denying the benefits of the ordinances. Theologian John Mueller, who is representative of this Reformation position, properly asserts that "a sincere believer never despises the ordinances of Christ, Luke 7.29, 30, So that a true member of the Church neglects neither Baptism nor the Lord's Supper."[51] One of the signs of love for (i.e., faith in) Christ is obedience to His commandments.

Conclusions

In spite of talk about a visible and invisible church, there are not two separate churches, but only one. These are simply two aspects of the one church, which is the body of Christ. The church on earth is both visible and invisible. As Louis Berkhof observes, "The Church is said to be invisible, because she is essentially spiritual and in her spiritual essence cannot be discerned by the physical eye; and because it is impossible to determine infallibly who do and do not belong to her."[52] All that the Bible says about the church's glorious attributes pertains to the invisible church, the spiritual body of Christ, not to the church as an external institution.[53] All those who by faith have confessed Christ as personal Savior and Lord are members of His body.

Just as the human spirit is joined to a body through which it manifests itself, so the invisible church is joined to an external structure through which it manifests itself on earth.[54] This is the institutional church. While some people who belong to the invisible church may never belong to the institutional church — such as those who make deathbed conversions — it is unthinkable that mature believers would want to separate themselves from fellowship with the Lord's people in the institutional church.

10.2 A Statement on the Church

1. The catholic or universal Church, which is invisible, consists of the whole number of the elect, that have been, are, or shall be gathered into one, under Christ the head thereof; and is the spouse, the body, the fullness of him that filleth all in all.

2. The visible Church, which is also catholic or universal under the gospel (not confined to one nation as before under the law) consists of all those, throughout the world, that profess the true religion, and of their children; and is the kingdom of the Lord Jesus Christ, the house and family of God, out of which there is no ordinary possibility of salvation.

3. Unto this catholic visible Church Christ hath given the ministry, oracles, and ordinances of God, for the gathering and perfecting of the saints, in this life, to the end of the world: and doth by his own presence and Spirit, according to his promise, make them effectual thereunto.

4. This catholic church hath been sometimes more, sometimes less visible. And particular churches, which are members thereof, are more or less pure, according as the doctrine of the gospel is taught and embraced, ordinances administered, and public worship performed more or less purely in them.

5. The purest churches under heaven are subject both to mixture and error; and some have so degenerated as to become no churches of Christ, but synagogues of Satan. Nevertheless, there shall be always a Church on earth to worship God according to his will.

6. There is no other head of the Church but the Lord Jesus Christ: nor can the Pope of Rome, in any sense be the head thereof; but is that Antichrist, that man of sin and son of perdition, that exalteth himself in the Church against Christ, and all that is called God.

— **Ch. XXV of *The Westminster Confession* (1646)**

SUMMARY

The church is the post-resurrection fellowship of Christian believers. Like Old Testament Israel, God has elected the church to be His covenant people; it is composed of those who have responded to His call.

The church is also inseparably related to Christ. He came to earth to herald God's kingdom, and the church which He has founded is the instrument of God's rule in the world. Indeed, Christ is embodied in His church. The relationship of Christ to the church is illustrated by the analogy of marriage, although His love for His bride goes far beyond the love of a man for his wife. It is this incomprehensible love which motivates human beings to respond in love to Christ.

The Holy Spirit is the Creator of the church. He not only controls the church but empowers it for God's service. He does so by gifting the members of the body with special spiritual abilities designed to build it up and to edify it. The church is also empowered by the "sword of the Spirit, which is the word of God" (Eph. 6:17).

The true church which Christ founded is both visible and invisible. While it is possible for one to be a member of the visible church but not of the invisible, it is unlikely that a member of the invisible church would not want to be a member of the visible church. Such an idea would have been unthinkable to the apostles and the New Testament church.

CHAPTER ELEVEN

The Mission
of the Church

God created human beings with a purpose in mind—fellowship with Him. But human sin disrupted that purpose. God nonetheless had a redemptive plan which attained its apex in the earthly ministry of Jesus Christ, who came to seek and to save the lost (Luke 19:10). Jesus understood His mission to be redemptive, "to preach the good news to the poor . . . to proclaim freedom for the prisoners and recovery of sight for the blind, to release the oppressed, to proclaim the year of the Lord's favor" (Isa. 61:1-2; Luke 4:18-19).

To help Him in His mission and ministry, Jesus Christ called disciples. He modeled for them the life of the citizen of the kingdom of God, and He commissioned them to go out into the community and proclaim that coming kingdom. Following His crucifixion and resurrection, He gave to His disciples—and His church—the mandate which has come to be known as the Great Commission:

> All authority in heaven and on earth has been given to me. Therefore go and make disciples of all nations, baptizing them in the name of the Father and of the Son and of the Holy Spirit, and teaching them to obey everything I have commanded you. And surely I am with you always, to the very end of the age (Matt. 28:19-20).

The mission of the church was and is to be an extension of Jesus' ministry.[1]

340

THE NATURE OF THE CHURCH'S MISSION

In examining the New Testament, four Greek words stand out in connection with the nature of the mission of the church: *martyria*, or witness; *diakonia*, or service; *koinōnia*, or fellowship; and *leitourgia*, or worship.

Martyria: The Mission of Witness

The primary mission of the church at all times and in all contexts is to bear witness to the work of Jesus Christ.[2] The implementation of this mission forms a major theme in the Book of Acts. Indeed, at the beginning of Acts, Luke recounts Jesus' promise to His disciples: "But you will receive power when the Holy Spirit comes on you; and you will be my witnesses in Jerusalem, and in all Judea and Samaria, and to the ends of the earth" (Acts 1:8). Throughout the remainder of Acts, Luke recounts how the Holy Spirit fulfilled Jesus' promise, by empowering the church to witness to what God in Christ has achieved, namely, human redemption. Dale Moody tells us that

> there are six "books" in Acts. Each closes with a summary on the spread of the gospel (6:7; 9:31; 12:24; 16:5; 19:20; 28:30f.). The climax of his [Peter's] crusade was before the household of Cornelius. . . . Peter's preaching was that: "We are witnesses to all that he did both in the country of the Jews and in Jerusalem. They put him to death by hanging him on a tree; but God raised him on the third day and made him manifest, not to all the people but to us who are chosen of God as witnesses . . . (10:39-41). The primacy of the witness of Peter and the twelve was preached by Paul, although he believed he had been chosen as a special witness to the Gentiles (13:31; 22:15; 26:16).[3]

Several important implications arise from this concept of witness.

The Focus of Witness. The church witnesses not to itself, but to its Lord. Like John the Baptist, it is to direct attention to the Lamb of God who takes away the sin of the world.

Its witness is historically grounded. As Harold Bender points out, the center of the Gospel is the chain of events which make up the total Saviorhood of Jesus Christ for humanity and its salvation. But the purpose of this historical witness is not just for remembrance, but to make the incarnation, atonement, and exaltation of Christ a present living reality. Christ must be born not only to the apostles and New Testament witnesses, but to us and *in* us. While He was crucified once for all and can die no more, people today must also die with Him and rise with Him to newness of life. The proclamation of the cross, a historical fact, is designed to make Him who was crucified at Calvary present as Savior and Lord.[4] Thus, the church must witness not only to the historic Christ (although this is a vital part of its mission), but also to Christ as a living and potent reality in our own day.

A Witness by Practice. The church does not perform its mission of witness unless it is practically demonstrating the abundant life which comes from experiencing the presence of Christ. "The real presence of Christ is not in word or in sacrament, which can only be symbols, or at the most signs of His presence, but in His personal effect on men."[5]

The church must model the results of God's redemption of believers through faith in Jesus Christ. Why should sinners accept the church's message of forgiveness and transformation unless they see it animated in the lives of its witnesses? They must also be able to see the message of forgiveness — along with the practice of the transformed life — being carried on between members of the church. "The grace to forgive is a witness to the grace by which we are forgiven, because it is the same grace; for there is only one grace, the grace of our Lord Jesus Christ."[6] Lost humanity cannot come to a saving acceptance of the Gospel unless practice accompanies preaching.

Diakonia: The Mission of Service

While witness is primary in the mission of the church, service does not come far behind.[7] Jesus set the tone with His "new commandment": "A new commandment I give you: Love one another. As I have loved you, so you must love one another. By this all men will know that you are my disciples if you love one another" (John 13:34-35). The New Testament church gave substance to the commandment in many different ways. The best example probably is the great collection taken up by Paul and his friends among the Gentile churches to help a suffering Jerusalem Christian community. This collection is mentioned in 1 and 2 Corinthians, Galatians, and Romans.

In A.D. 46 there had been a severe famine in Judea (Acts 11:27-30). The following year was a sabbatical for the Jews, their fields lying fallow. The church at Antioch had taken a collection to help the Jerusalem Christians in their suffering, displaying true service (*diakonia*).[8]

One of the conditions of the Jerusalem Conference in A.D. 49 (Gal. 2:1-10) was that a second collection would be made in the Gentile churches to help the Jewish believers in their next sabbatical year of A.D. 54–55; thus, the significance of Paul's word to the Galatians: "Anyone who receives instruction in the word must share all good things with his instructor" (6:6).[9]

Paul exemplified the service motif more than any other figure in the New Testament (excepting Christ Himself). In a number of places (Rom. 1:1; 2 Cor. 3:6; Gal. 1:10; Phil. 1:1), he described himself as a servant, or slave (*doulos*), of Jesus Christ. In his letter to the Romans (15:7-12), he described Christ as a servant (*diakonos*) to both the Jews and the Gentiles. Through this service to the Jews, Jesus was fulfilling God's promise to the patriarchs (cf. Gen. 12:3). Part of that promise included being a blessing to all the nations.[10] Paul, for his part, was emulating Christ's example in seeing to the offering for the saints and delivering it from the Gentile churches to Jerusalem. Dale Moody cautions that

> any effort to separate witness and service in the mission of the church contradicts the purpose of Paul. The material blessings from the Gentiles was a thankful response for the spiritual blessings from the Jews. Indeed, there is a beautiful balance between witness, service and fellowship in 15:26f.[11]

The Priesthood of Believers. In his first letter, Peter referred to believers as "a royal priesthood, offering spiritual sacrifices acceptable to God through Jesus Christ" (1 Peter 2:5). John described Christians as having been made "a kingdom and priests" through Christ "to serve His God and Father" (Rev. 1:6). Paul exhorted believers to "offer your bodies as living sacrifices, holy and pleasing to God—this is your spiritual act of worship" (Rom. 12:1), an implication of priesthood.[12]

The Reformers referred to this aspect of doctrine as "the priesthood of all believers." Their idea was that believers needed no human intermediary to approach God. While that is true, the priesthood of believers entails much more. Another term which may be used is "the ministry (*diakonia*) of all believers." Bender observes:

> The church's ministry is best understood as a direct succession to and imitation of Christ's ministry as His service of love and compassion to men, first of all on behalf of their salvation and spiritual health, but also for other needs. . . . [Jesus] said to His disciples who were striving for the greatest posts in His kingdom: "Whoever would be great among you must be your *diakonos*, and whoever would be first among you must be *doulos* of all" (Mark 10:44).[13]

Priesthood beyond the Church. The servant attitude of the church must extend beyond its boundaries to those who are not believers. While Jesus commanded believers to love one another with His love for them, He also told them to love their neighbors as themselves. And to illustrate His point, He told the parable of the Good Samaritan (Luke 10:27-37). In this case, the Samaritan helped one who was hurt, even at high personal cost.

The Epistles contain similar admonitions. James, in particular, stresses practical faith. He declared that "religion that God our Father accepts as pure and faultless is this: to look after orphans and widows in their distress and to keep oneself from being polluted by the world" (1:27). He added, furthermore, that, "as the body without the spirit is dead, so faith without deeds is dead" (2:26). The Apostle John is equally adamant: "Dear children, let us not love with words or tongue but with actions and in truth" (1 John 3:18).

Millard Erickson writes:

> The church is to show concern and take action wherever it sees need, hurt, or wrong. There will be differences of opinion as to

the strategies and tactics that should be employed. In some cases, the church will work simply to alleviate the hurt. . . . In others, it will act to change the circumstances that produced the problem. There will be times when the church acting collectively will be able to accomplish more than will Christians acting individually; in other situations the reverse will be true.[14]

Not only the church corporately, but every individual Christian, must evince a servant demeanor.

Koinōnia: The Mission of Fellowship

The third aspect of the church's mission — along with witness and service — is fellowship. The Greek word is *koinōnia*, which means "what is held in common," or "sharing." In the New Testament about half of the uses of *koinōnia* have to do with a sharing of spiritual resources and about half concern a sharing of material resources.

The first Christian church brought very diverse groups of people together. The gift of tongues on the Day of Pentecost made the Gospel comprehensible to people from nations all over the known world (Acts 2:5-11), thus reversing the divisions caused at the Tower of Babel (Gen. 11:1-9). These people became one in Christ: "All the believers were together and had everything in common" (Acts 2:44). The work of the Spirit in uniting different peoples carried over, pulling in Samaritans (Acts 8:4-25), an Ethiopian (8:26-29), some Italians (10:1ff), and Greeks (11:19-34).[15]

Thomas Finger observes that the fellowship of the primitive Christian communities was not only spiritual, but also effected new and radical social changes. Gender, social, and economic gulfs were bridged. At the same time, "early church fellowship was a quality of spiritual and interpersonal communion which transcended any mere social arrangement, yet which engendered and was further enriched by novel social patterns."[16]

The Basis of Fellowship. This brief study of fellowship has thus far revealed that the essential basis of *koinōnia* rests upon an awareness of a common faith in Jesus Christ, a common experience of transformation, and a common hope of salvation, all of which issue in a common expression of Christian love. This perception must be conveyed interpersonally by the testimony of the members to one another of their shared experience and by mutual counsel to Christian obedience and action; it must be deepened by an ever-growing knowledge of and gratitude for God's grace as it operates in the community.[17]

Danger to Fellowship. There are two dangers in particular which assail the full expression of fellowship by the church. The first of these is individualism, the second, institutionalism. Individualism emphasizes personal privilege and self-importance and culminates in an abandonment of the common life, an insistence on one's own way, and the refusal to share with others or to take counsel or discipline from Christian brothers and sisters. Individualism "turns the rightful and needed sense of individual responsibility before God, and the need for a personal experience of Christ and the Holy Spirit, into the corrupted spirit of self-exaltation."[18]

The second danger, institutionalism, establishes a church polity where only a few privileged persons minister, while excluding others from responsible participation in the common life of the community. As a result, the church stagnates in its endeavors to know the Lord and to take care of the different members of the body. "The result is a breakdown in fellowship and a denial of the very nature of the church."[19]

Leitourgia: The Mission of Worship

It has been said that one of the most important tasks of the church "is to celebrate with joy the salvific action of the Lord in history."[20] The church is to worship its Lord. The New Testament church gathered for worship regularly. Acts 2:46 suggests daily worship. First Corinthians 16:2 infers that the church met on the first day of the week. Hebrews 10:25 exhorts believers not to forsake assembling together for worship, as some are wont to do. And Revelation depicts worship as it will be in heaven.

Praise. The Book of Acts allows us to see a church whose keynote was rejoicing. On the Day of Pentecost, all of the believers were filled with the Holy Spirit and spoke in other languages as the Spirit enabled them, "declaring the wonders of God" (2:11). The primitive Christian community met together daily, "praising God and enjoying the favor of all the people" (2:47). Their elation was similar to that of the lame man who, upon being healed, went into the temple with them, walking and dancing and praising God (3:8; cf. 5:41-42; 8:39). Interestingly, from very early on, the vitality of this joy stimulated friction between the fellowship and others. And so its worship was frequently highlighted by entreaties for direction, and by the Spirit's continuing reply (4:24-31).[21]

Jürgen Moltmann speaks of the joy of worship as a "messianic feast," and asserts that it

> is not an ecstasy that transports us into another world; it is the experience of the qualitative alteration of this world. Joy in the divine liberation is therefore accompanied by the expression of suffering over the godliness that restricts life; rejoicing in the presence of the Spirit is accompanied by the utterance of the sighs of expectant creation. . . . The service of worship reveals the heights of life, but also the poverty of the depths of our own lives. These dissonances are part of its harmony. They make it at once realistic and hopeful.[22]

The joy experienced through worship should not be confused with the pleasure so often manufactured by our contemporary Western society. Joy is not of such a superficial genre. True joy flows from the experience of brokenness by identifying with Jesus' suffering and the hope that the Lord will somehow resurrect His people from the dead (Phil. 3:10-11). Joy and praise come with the realization that the Lamb upon the throne has overcome the accuser of God's people (Rev. 12:10).[23]

Prayer. Prayer is very near to worship, and much that one could say about worship might also be said about prayer. But worship and prayer are not synonymous; prayer is an element in worship. Prayer refers to "ways in which the worshipper expresses himself verbally. It is true that we sometimes talk of 'silent prayer,' but such silence, like silence in music or a significant silence in conversation, has meaning only in a context

347

that can be heard and understood."[24]

Through prayer, Christians express their innermost thoughts, hopes, and fears, and hold them before God. Prayer is that "very special form of discourse, giving shape and definiteness to that mysterious communion between God and man which is founded on the very structure of our existence as beings whom Being not only let-be but has made open in their being so that they can be understanding, answering, and responsible."[25]

The goal of prayer is not to cause God to change His mind, but to affirm that God's will be done. Gustaf Aulén rightly points out that Christian faith holds that God is pure love; His purposes are always the achievement of that love. Thus, no real Christian would want to change God's will. "Prayer, therefore, is principally a petition that we might grasp and understand fully and clearly this divine will and its purposes, and that this will shall entirely subdue us."[26]

In worship, prayer is used to demonstrate our thanksgiving and praise to God for His gift of Himself to humankind. The one who prays is prostrated in adoration before the unfathomable splendor of divine love which deigns to approach those who are frail dust and do not deserve to abide in His presence.[27]

Offering. Those who worship God thankfully offer Him all they are and all they have; Paul expressed this concept succinctly in Romans 12:1, urging believers to offer their bodies to God as living sacrifices, which "is your spiritual act of worship." Worship in the New Testament church was generally connected with sharing material possessions (Acts 2:44-47). The evangelists portray both the offering of praise and of material possessions in sacrificial language.[28] Peter told his readers: "you also, like living stones, are being built into a spiritual house to be a holy priesthood, offering spiritual sacrifices acceptable to God through Jesus Christ" (1 Peter 2:5). And Paul exhorted the Corinthian Christians to give cheerfully and generously: "You will be made rich in every way so that you can be generous on every occasion, and through us your generosity will result in thanksgiving to God" (2 Cor. 9:11).

Offering our possessions and the fruit of our endeavors is a fitting activity of worship. But Finger warns against the offering simply as a means of financing the church; rather, "what is given should be celebrated as a manifestation of the worshipers' self-giving, and of the transformation that the *eschaton* is already producing in the physical world and in human labor."[29]

11.1 The Fourfold Foundation of the Church's Mission

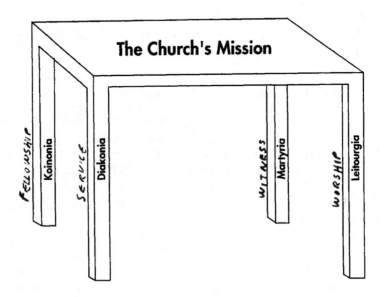

Some Observations

The mission of the church is fourfold. The most important aspect is witness. The church's witness to Christ's saving power, however, must be not only vocal but also lived out in the everyday lives of its members.

Service follows close behind witness. The church must faithfully act on Jesus' command to love. It does so by imitating Christ's servant ministry—to one another and to the world at large.

Fellowship is the third aspect of the church's mission. The Greek word *koinōnia* speaks of community. The Holy Spirit, working in and through believers, tears down the barriers that separate them. Christians are brought together and share

349

together because of their common experience of salvation in Christ.

The fourth aspect is worship. Christians celebrate their redemption and worship the Triune God who wrought their salvation. Praise, prayer, and offering are all components of the joyful acknowledgment of God's supreme expression of love for humankind.

These four aspects of the church's mission must not be isolated from each other. All four are necessary to the church's success in the world.

THE SCOPE OF THE CHURCH'S MISSION

Jesus set the scope for the church's mission in the Great Commission (Matt. 28:19-20; cf. Acts 1:8); its witness is to be to the whole world. Not only is the church to evangelize the whole world, but the completion of this task will be a sign of the close of the age: "And this gospel of the kingdom will be preached in the whole world as a testimony to all nations, and then the end will come" (Matt. 24:14).

Karl Barth noted that all who testify to Christ before the world bear the mark "by which the true community of Jesus Christ may be infallibly known."[30] Christ's commission is bound up with the very nature of the church. It is part and parcel of what the church is called to be—the salt of the earth, the light of the world (Matt. 5:13-16). Without this activity, the church cannot be the church of the Lord Jesus. The Great Commission "is not to be understood as an accidental commission, a command that could not be expected from the reality of the Church."[31]

The Great Commission by and of itself is insufficient to motivate the church to mission. An inward motivation is required, namely, the impelling of the indwelling Spirit of God. Thus the Holy Spirit internally compels Christians to testify to what God has done, even as the Great Commission externally constrains them to bear witness. Without the Holy Spirit, the church would become a static institution floundering in self-sufficiency and failing to advance the kingdom through the riches Christ has given. However, the eminent theologian G.C. Berkouwer cautions:

The riches of the Church cannot be understood unless the Church is in motion in the "going forth" that Jesus commanded as "the most profoundly necessary step." Therein it is clear that God loved the world (John 3:16), that He was in Christ reconciling the world to Himself (2 Cor. 5:19), and that Christ is the Savior of the world (John 4:42). That is a continuing reminder of the *missio Dei*, the "mission of God. . . ."[32]

The history of the church from its beginning is a history of missionary outreach, confronting the world with the Gospel of Christ's redeeming grace. The church today must "extend that confrontation by proclaiming the gospel to all persons everywhere, by watering the seed when planted (1 Cor. 3:5-10), and by praying for the Lord of the harvest to provide laborers (Matt. 9:38)."[33]

11.2 A Covenant Expressing the Church's Mission in the World

As we trust we have been brought by Divine grace to embrace the Lord Jesus Christ, and by the influence of his Spirit to give ourselves up to Him, so we do now solemnly covenant with each other, as God shall enable us, that we will walk together in brotherly love, that we will exercise a Christian care and watchfulness over each other, and faithfully, warn, rebuke, and admonish one another, as the case shall require; that we will not forsake the assembling of ourselves together, nor omit the great duty of prayer, both for ourselves and for others; that we will participate in each other's joys; and endeavor with tenderness and sympathy to bear each other's burdens and sorrows; that we will seek Divine aid to enable us to walk circumspectly and watchfully in the world, denying ungodliness and every worldly lust; that we will strive together for the support of a faithful evangelical ministry among us; and, through life, amidst evil report and good report, seek to live to the glory of Him who hath called us out of darkness into his marvellous light.

—**William Crowell,** ***The Church Member's Manual***
(Boston: Gould, Kendall and Lincoln, 1847), 231-32.

SUMMARY

The church is called to extend the mission of Jesus Christ on this earth. It does this in four basic ways: through witnessing to the saving grace of God in Christ, through modeling Christ's love by serving fellow believers and the lost world, through mutual fellowship with believers, and through regular worship.

The scope of the church's mission is universal. While it must involve itself locally and regionally, the church must go beyond its comfort and cultural zone to the whole world. Carrying out this mission requires more than a legalistic obedience to Christ's command; the church must be motivated by the Holy Spirit working in it and through it. As the church moves out into the world extending Christ's ministry, it anticipates His return: "Amen. Come, Lord Jesus" (Rev. 22:20).

CHAPTER TWELVE

The Ministry
of the Church

The church exists for ministry. Its purpose is the shared life and ministry of its Lord. Even though it cannot be viewed as an extension of the Incarnation (which is the unique, personal role of Jesus Christ), the church nonetheless demonstrates the ongoing love and mission of Christ through its life and ministry. The church, empowered by His Spirit, is Christ's body and the continuation of His ministry.[1]

The starting point and norm for Christian ministry must be the person and ministry of Jesus. At the same time, the form of present ministry does not need to be copied directly from the Gospels. All that occurs in the church's life—doctrine, ritual, organizational patterns, cultural formulations—needs redefining on occasion, in part because sin taints all things human, so that continuing transformation is needed, and in part because the world which needs redeeming is not static but always in flux.[2] The ministry of the church, while it must be a contemporary form of ministry, must nevertheless be grounded in the ministry of Jesus as set forth in the Gospels. Thus, the church must understand clearly who Jesus is and what He did while He was on earth.

The chief trait of Jesus' ministry was service. He declared that servanthood must be the hallmark of those who would be great in God's kingdom: "whoever wants to become great among you must be your servant, and whoever wants to be first must be slave of all. For even the Son of Man did not come to be served, but to serve, and to give his life as a ransom for many"

(Mark 10:43-45). Jesus was the fulfillment of Isaiah's prophecy of the Servant of God (Isa. 42:1-4; 49:1-6; 50:4-7; 52:13–53:12).

MINISTRY: TASK OF THE WHOLE BODY

Because Jesus saw His ministry as one of service, all who are united to Him are also called to serve. This call to be ministers extends to all Christians, and not just a small, elite group. Regardless of their place or position in the church, all are expected to be ministers or servants. Indeed, Paul describes himself and fellow leader Apollos as "servants, through whom you came to believe" (1 Cor. 3:5). Rodman Williams observes, "Christ is the only Lord, so that Christians in high positions are still servants, even slaves, of all others. They, like all believers, are ministers of Christ."[3]

Unfortunately, as early as the end of the first century, ministry was made the private preserve of church leaders. A distinction was created between the common people, the laity, and those in leadership (the clergy). The latter group became professional ministers, and the former group were largely excluded from God's service.

The Reformation stressed the priesthood of all believers, but this denoted only that all believers have direct access to God through Christ. With the exception of the Anabaptists, ministry was still the special work of the clergy. In fact, the Second Helvetic Confession (1566) asserted that "the ministry . . . and the priesthood are things far different one from the other. For the priesthood is common to all Christians; not so is the ministry."[4]

It was not until the second half of the twentieth century that a strong movement toward the ministry of all God's people took place. People like the great Quaker leader Elton Trueblood stressed that the laity are intended by God to be His ministers.[5] It is now generally accepted that all of God's people are to be His ministers.

The Fundamental Ministry of God's People

The fundamental ministry of the church is described by Paul as "the ministry of reconciliation."

All this is from God, who reconciled us to himself through Christ and gave us the ministry of reconciliation: that God was reconciling the world to himself in Christ, not counting men's sins against them. And he has committed to us the message of reconciliation (2 Cor. 5:18-19).

The ministry of reconciliation has been committed by God to all who have been reconciled to him through Christ Jesus. Clearly, the ministry of reconciliation is the responsibility of *all* the church. All believers are ministers; all believers share in Christ's own ministry of reconciliation. It is this ministry of reconciliation which Peter had in focus when he referred to Christians as "a holy priesthood, offering spiritual sacrifices acceptable to God through Jesus Christ" (1 Peter 2:5).[6]

This ministry of reconciliation is grounded in the finished work of Christ on the cross, that is, in His atonement. "If the reconciliation is a work of God from above, then the ministry of reconciliation is also a gift from above, and a ministry given by God."[7] While the Atonement does not need to be repeated, God's reconciliation to humanity through Christ must confront every emerging generation, and so its ministry must be ongoing. Aulén asserts that

> the victory of self-giving love does not mean that the struggle has ceased. The ministry of reconciliation is a ministry of struggle and conflict. As God's act of reconciliation in Christ was carried out in a struggle against the destructive powers, so the messengers of reconciliation are called upon to participate in this struggle. It is carried on . . . in the consciousness that Christ is the victorious Lord and that his messengers go forth under his authority.[8]

The ministry of reconciliation is the fundamental ministry of the church which must be foundational to all other ministries. It is a response to those in need. Without it, any other type of ministry is irrelevant.[9]

THE CHARISMATIC MINISTRIES OF THE BODY

Ministry is the God-given responsibility of all believers. And the Holy Spirit has prepared all of God's people for ministry by

355

giving each one of them a special ministry gift. These gifts (or, special ministry abilities) are many and varied. They are to be given to the members of the fellowship as the Holy Spirit desires (1 Cor. 12:11; Eph. 4:7). Their purpose is that all members of the church should function for the benefit and strengthening of the entire body.

Several passages of Scripture mention the different gifts. The longest list of gifts is found in a detailed discussion Paul had with the Corinthian believers (1 Cor. 12:8-10); nine gifts are listed: the word of wisdom, the word of knowledge, faith, physical healing, miracle working, prophecy, discernment of spirits, tongues, and interpretation of tongues. Other lists are found in 1 Corinthians 12:28, Romans 12:6-8, Ephesians 4:11, and 1 Peter 4:11.[10]

While each believer has at least one ministry gift, some may have more. But no one possesses all the gifts; for "to do so would be attempting to make oneself a little Christ."[11] All believers must accurately assess themselves and their gifts, and use those gifts diligently according to the faith given by the Spirit (Rom. 12:3-8).

There is considerable debate as to whether all the ministry gifts of the New Testament are still operative in the contemporary church. Some claim that all the gifts mentioned are intended to be used in ministry today. Others maintain that some of the gifts—healing, miracles, tongues, interpretation of tongues—were only temporary and have long since ceased. Gary Inrig contends that "the sign gifts were God's confirmation to the second generation of the truth of the message of the apostolic generation."[12] If the purpose of these gifts were the confirmation of the truth of the Gospel, could it not be possible that they are still operative today in those frontier areas where the Gospel is just beginning to make an impact and where there is severe spiritual conflict? Perhaps then in areas where the Christian faith has long been operative, these gifts are rarely used or necessary.[13]

When all is said and done, however, the important thing is that believers minister as the Holy Spirit gives them ability. Authentic ministry must be Spirit-empowered. Only when they know and use the gifts they have received can the church be fully effective in ministry.

SPECIALIZED MINISTRIES IN THE CHURCH

Several Pauline letters mention specialized ministries in the church appointed for purposes of equipping and leadership. In Ephesians 4:11, four ministries were mentioned: apostles, prophets, evangelists, and pastor-teachers. In 1 Timothy 3:1-13, Paul discussed the qualifications for bishops and deacons. Titus 1:5 indicates that Titus was sent to Crete to appoint presbyters, or elders.

Apostles

Apostles are the first of these specialized equipping ministries. Our Lord Himself is described as "the apostle and high priest whom we confess" (Heb. 3:1). It would seem, therefore, that apostles achieve their authority through Him.[14]

The Twelve. The New Testament tells us that Jesus ordained twelve men to be with Him, so that He could send them out to preach and cast out demons (Mark 3:13-15). These men were His constant companions, observing and participating in His ministry. Leon Morris notes:

> In some sense they were leaders among His followers, though the precise sense is nowhere defined. Their functions were two-fold and it is interesting that preaching occupies the primary place. First and foremost they were heralds of glad tidings. Their other function was to expel demons. . . . Interestingly nothing at all is said as to administrative functions, or ordaining. Neither here or anywhere else is it said that they were given Christ's commission for such things.[15]

It is noteworthy that, while the Twelve are prominently featured in the Gospels, they then fade quickly from sight. There are only three mentions of the Twelve in the other books of the New Testament (Acts 6:2; 1 Cor. 15:5; Rev. 21:14), and two mentions of the Eleven (Acts 1:26; 2:14). "Of course," observes Morris, "if we understand the essential function of the Twelve as that of preaching so as to bear the original authoritative witness it is not surprising that they fail to exercise authority. They perform their task, and then vanish from the scene."[16]

357

Other Apostles. As the New Testament writings progress, other apostles beyond the Twelve eventually appear on the scene. Chief among these was Paul. He had an apostolic ministry of note, and he made it plain to all that he was certainly the equal of the Twelve. Of major stature, as well, was James the brother of Christ, who presided over the Jerusalem church. Others mentioned include Barnabas, Silas, Epaphroditus, Andronicus, and Junias. In fact, Paul wrote of the resurrected Christ appearing to the Twelve and afterward to all the apostles (1 Cor. 15:5-8).

Since the root word for apostle is the Greek *apostellō*, "to send," one may ask if the apostle was not one sent, that is, a messenger (sent by a church or group of churches) on a particular mission (as the Twelve were sent by Christ to carry out His mission).[17]

Conclusions. The apostles were sent to set out the saving truths of the Gospel. In so doing, their primary function in ministry appears to have been preaching. While a secondary function was exorcism, they were basically sent by God to proclaim the Good News and to bring people to a saving relationship with Jesus Christ.[18]

Morris suggests that the apostles should be seen as God's gift to a fledgling church. They played a unique role in establishing and building up groups of believers. While this distinctive role gave them a prominent place in the church, there is no evidence to demonstrate that they had received a divine appointment to be its authoritative governors. Any such theory is an assumption unsupported by Scripture. Nor did they exercise any priestly functions. As Eduard Schweizer contends, "We can speak of the apostles' pupils, but not of their successors in office."[19]

Are there present-day apostles? Many scholars (such as Morris) would answer in the negative. If there are parallels to the apostolic office, they would not be bishops in hierarchical churches, but rather pioneer missionaries and church planters (such as William Carey, Mary Slessor, Adoniram Judson, C.T. Studd). There may still be a few in that role today, pushing back the boundaries of darkness as they bring to pagan tribes the light of Christ.

Prophets

There appear to have been an order of prophets as well as a charism of prophecy in New Testament times. The Book of Acts describes both. At the time of Paul's conversion, a Christian at Damascus named Ananias received a vision from God to go to Paul with both healing and instruction. There is no indication that he prophesied on a regular basis; every indication is that he had received a temporary gifting. On the other hand, in Antioch of Syria, Paul encountered a school of prophets, one of whom — Agabus — foretold a coming famine which would spread throughout the world. Later, that same Agabus prophesied that Paul would be bound in Jerusalem and handed over to the Romans. The accounts demonstrate that Paul took both prophecies seriously.[20]

> The epistles which speak of prophets do so somewhat ambiguously. As a consequence, some scholars have concluded that while Paul maintained in theory that all Christians had the potential to prophesy, a goal toward which Paul seemingly exhorted all the Corinthians to move, in reality only a limited number of individuals ever did so, and these few occupied the *office* of prophets.[21]

Some appear to have prophesied only within their local churches while others were itinerant.

Because false prophets existed, prophetic claims were expected to be verified. One means of so doing was by a spiritual gift of spiritual discernment. Additionally, those who prophesy should reflect the nature and character of God. They would encourage a spirit of peace rather than one of confusion. Prophecy should be calculated to build up, or strengthen, the body of Christ.[22]

Modern Prophets? Has prophecy continued into our own time? There is considerable controversy on this question. Luther and Calvin defined prophecy as right exposition of Scripture. Warfield proclaimed that, with the closing of the canon, revelation — and therefore prophecy — ceased. Some charismatics and Vineyard people claim gifts of prophecy, but tend to differentiate such gifts from equivalency to Scripture. They have authority or relevance only for a specific time and place. These "prophecies" are often referred to as "inspired oracles" and are subject to agreement with the biblical authority.[23] Nor do they claim the need for complete accuracy; that is, it is not necessary that the prophecy be fulfilled exactly as given.

If prophecy is equated with preaching, then there are still prophets today. If prophecy consists of sharing a word of inspiration given by God, it certainly is still in operation. But if prophecy consists of bringing a fresh word from God which will come to pass no matter what, the issue is much more doubtful, even to the point of saying—along with Warfield—that it has ceased.

Conclusions. Prophets were given to the church to serve the common good and strengthen the body. They did so by speaking on behalf of God in a particular situation. They spoke for God to His people.[24]

If prophets do not exist in the church today, they should. The church badly needs men and women who can admonish or exhort the body of Christ, helping it steer a safe course through the storms of life. At the same time, Williams gives good advice:

> The church . . . must always be on guard against presumed prophetic messages that claim equal or superior authority to God's written words in Scripture. True prophecy is thoroughly grounded in Scripture and, based upon it, speaks forth God's particular word for the contemporary scene.[25]

There are, as in biblical times, false prophets as well as true. Genuine prophecy will always come to pass, and it will never contradict the written Word of God.

Evangelists

The third special ministry cited by Paul in Ephesians 4:11 was evangelists. An evangelist is one who sets forth the evangel, or Gospel, in such a way that a decision (for or against Christ) is required. Jesus established the pattern for all future evangelists by proclaiming the good news of God and the need for repentance from the beginning of His ministry (Mark 1:14).[26]

It has been said that all believers are called to be evange-lists.[27] While all are expected to be witnesses (a task which may require evangelizing), the office of evangelist is a special calling not given to all. All believers should testify—both actively and passively—to Christ's transforming power in their own lives; sometimes that testimony will necessitate evangelistic follow-up, if the person to whom they are witnessing is obviously under conviction. But an evangelist is involved in active minis-try, continually seeking a positive response from those to whom he or she speaks.

One good biblical example of an evangelist is Philip, one of the original deacons. Philip preached the Gospel to the Samari-tans, won many of them to Christ, and baptized them (Acts 8:5-13). A short time later, at the Spirit's bidding, he went to a desert road south of Jerusalem where he met and evangelized a eunuch of Ethiopia (Acts 8:26-39). We see from this example that the work of an evangelist involves not only exposing people to the Gospel, but leading them to a saving faith in Jesus Christ.

Different from Philip was Timothy. Paul called on him to "do the work of an evangelist" (2 Tim. 4:5). Williams observes, "Unlike Philip, Timothy is not called an evangelist; rather, Paul seems to be speaking of evangelism as one aspect of Timothy's total ministry."[28]

Evangelists Today. Evangelism was a gift much needed in the New Testament era. It is as badly needed in our century. The proclamation of the good news of Jesus Christ is the foundation of the church's mission. The church today has a few evangelists of stature (such as Billy Graham), but—given the great world population—not nearly enough. Additionally, the church needs more evangelists who are capable of doing individual evange-lism. Sadly, this is one office which seems to be in decline in many quarters of the Christian community. Believers should pray that Christ will send more evangelists into the harvest.

Conclusions. While individual believers are called to be wit-nesses (which may involve evangelism), and while pastors will undoubtedly have to do the work of an evangelist from time to time, the special ministry-office of an evangelist is different

361

from both. An evangelist is one who exercises that gift on a regular and on-going basis with a measure of success in leading people to a saving knowledge of Christ Jesus, so that they become a part of His body, the church.

The Pastoral Office

Although some scholars would hold that they are different offices,[29] W.A. Criswell maintains that there are three cogent reasons for believing that pastor (*poimen*), bishop (*episkopos*), and elder (*prebyteros*) are all the same office. "First, other than the names themselves, there is no suggestion in the New Testament that more than one pastoral office ever existed." When Paul told Titus to appoint elders, he made no mention of bishops or pastors; in 1 Timothy 3, he set out qualifications for bishops, but he did not discuss pastors or elders. "Second, the three terms often are used synonymously and are never distinguished from one another." In Acts 20:17-30, for example, Paul used the terms interchangeably. "Third, whenever the officers of the church are listed formally, invariably there are only two, pastors and deacons." Philippians 1:1 addressed the church of that city, "together with the overseers [bishops] and deacons." First Timothy 3:1-13, which is the most exhaustive list of qualifications for church officers, mentions only bishops and deacons. "There is no hint of another office."[30]

The Pastor. The term "pastor" (*poimen*) occurs in the New Testament only in Ephesians 4:11. It is the Greek word for "shepherd" (*pastor* is Latin for "shepherd").

The ancient shepherd had a difficult, but extremely important, task. He took the flock to water and pastureland; he protected them from wild animals; he found them when they strayed. And he did not even own them, but was employed by the owner. "It is not surprising to learn that our Lord Jesus is sometimes described as a shepherd (John 10:1-18; Heb. 13:20; 1 Peter 5:4)."[31]

Like shepherds, pastors are to care for the flock, even though they belong to another (i.e., Christ). They are to see to their feeding and to their protection. They are to go after them when they stray. If necessary, they are to sacrifice themselves on their behalf (John 10:11).

The Elder. The Greek word *presbyteros*, in classical usage, was a term of honor and respect for an older person (generally over 50). In Egypt it became the name for elected agents of village councils who carried out judicial and administrative duties. In Old Testament Hebrew society, it denoted an older man, an envoy or spokesman, and the head of a household or clan. Exodus 12 mentions the "elders of Israel" as men who were representatives of the nation. It would appear that in later Israel the title "elder" was used of the ruling class of the individual tribes and of the nation as a whole. By Jesus' time the elders were drawn from the aristocratic Sadducees, and composed the ruling Sanhedrin.[32]

The first New Testament mention of presbyters (elders) occurs in Acts 11:30, but the office was probably already operational when Paul and Barnabas went to Jerusalem, and may

12.1 On the Pastoral Ministry

> We are agreed as follows on pastors in God's Church: The pastor in God's Church shall, as Paul has prescribed, be one who has a completely good report from those who are outside of the faith. This office shall be for the purpose of reading, admonishing and teaching, warning, disciplining, banning in the Church, leading forth in prayer for the advancement of all the brothers and sisters, lifting up the bread when it is to be broken, and in everything to see to the care of Christ's body, so that it may be built up and developed, and the mouth of the slanderer may be stopped.
>
> This one, furthermore, shall be supported by the Church which has chosen him, wherein he may be in need, in order that he who serves the Gospel may live from the Gospel as the Lord has ordained. But if a pastor should do something requiring discipline, he shall not be dealt with apart from [the presence of] two or three witnesses. And when they sin they shall be disciplined before all so that the others may fear.
>
> But if it should happen that through the cross this pastor should be banished or led to the Lord [as the result of being martyred] another shall be ordained in his place in the same hour so that God's little flock and people may not be destroyed.
>
> **The Schleitheim Confession 5 (1527)**

even have preceded the diaconate. The first official elders were probably appointed by the Hebrew churches and then in those of the Gentiles.[33]

The Bishop. In classical parlance, the *episkopos*, or overseer, was one who gave oversight to a nation and watched over treaties. Homer used the title in regard to men who had a responsible position in state affairs. In cultic groups, *episkopoi* were those people responsible for external relationships, much like trustees.[34]

The Septuagint used the term of those appointed for supervisory purposes (see Num. 27:16). Later, in Israel, the word was used to translate *mebaqqēr*, an overseer in the community. He had administrative and legal responsibilities.[35]

As the disciples' band developed into an institutional church, the need for pastoral oversight—a duty initially shared by all members—became a duty for a specialized ministry office.[36] The bishop, or overseer, was urged to take as his example the Lord Jesus, "the Shepherd and Overseer of your souls" (1 Peter 2:25).

It should be noted here that nowhere in the New Testament is there any hint of a bishop as a monarch or supervisor over other leaders in other churches. The episcopacy as it exists today in churches employing a hierarchical or monarchical form of government was a later, extra-biblical, development.

A Plurality of Elders? Should the church leadership consist of one pastor (elder or overseer) or a plurality of elders? Evangelical churches seem split between the two models. Each model claims to be *the* biblical format for leadership. Can a resolution to this debate be found in Scripture?

Augustus Strong, like Criswell, contends that the three biblical terms used for church leaders—*presbyteros, episkopos,* and *poimen*—are synonymous and so refer to the same office.[37] He asserts that each church ordinarily had only one bishop or elder, although there were cases where some congregations did have a plurality of elders.

In certain of the N.T. churches there appears to have been a plurality of elders (Acts 20:17; Phil. 1:1; Tit. 1:5). There is, however, no evidence that the number of elders was uniform, or that the plurality which frequently existed was due to any other cause than the size of the churches for which these elders cared. The N.T. example, while it permits the multiplication of assistant pastors according to the need, does not require a plural eldership in every case; nor does it render this eldership, where it exists, of coordinate authority with the church. There are indications, moreover, that, at least in certain churches, the pastor was one, while the deacons were more than one, in number.[38]

In addition, James was seemingly the single pastor at Jerusalem.[39]

No single model exists for the number of pastors and elders in a church. The number of pastors and elders will vary from church to church based on the needs of the church and how those needs may be met most efficiently.

Observations. There is no convincing biblical evidence that there was more than one pastoral office in the New Testament church. The terms *pastor*, *elder*, and *bishop* are all aspects of the same leadership role.

The leader of the church must be a shepherd to the flock of God. Leaders must feed God's sheep on the Word and lead them to drink of the water of life. They must protect them from false teachings, false teachers, and other enemies of the Gospel. They must be prepared to search for them and attempt to recover them when they stray from the fold.

Just as ancient Israel held the elder in great respect, so congregations should revere and trust their pastors. Pastors must relate to them as they do to their own families; for they are their family.

Pastors must be overseers of God's people. They must be "set apart for a labor that is unlike any other known to mankind. . . . The spiritual life of [their] people is [their] continual burden and responsibility."[40]

The Diaconate

The word *deacon* is derived from the Greek *diakonos*, or "servant." In classical literature it denoted a servant whose primary

duty was waiting on his master at table and occasionally shop-
ping for him. In the context of the New Testament church, it
often referred to service of many sorts. In 1 Timothy 3:8-13 and
Philippians 1:1, however, the term clearly referred to an office.
One may suppose, therefore, that over the early course of the
church's existence the word evolved from a general meaning of
service to one of specific ministry function.[41]

The Origin of Deacons. A survey of Old Testament history and
of its contemporary Gentile culture does not turn up any ante-
cedents for the office of deacon. It appears that the diaconate
originated with the New Testament church.

As noted in chapter 7, there is some question as to whether
the appointment of the Seven, described in Acts 6:1-6, was the
origin of the office of deacon. Early church tradition from the
time of Irenaeus of Lyons saw it as such. And if it is not the
account of the founding of the diaconate, then no one knows
how it began.[42]

The Duties of the Deacons. If the Seven were the first deacons,
then they may afford insight into the nature of the office. These
were devout individuals who were concerned with the distribution of material goods among those in need. It would also
indicate that "those able to help others" (1 Cor. 12:28) and
"those who work hard among you" (1 Thes. 5:12) may have
referred to deacons. At any rate, the very word *diakonos* suggests one who filled a service role. Yet Hans Küng correctly
observes:

> It is evident that we know nothing very precise about the place
> and circumstances of the founding of the diaconate, and cannot
> be certain about its original function. The only thing we can
> assert with conviction is that deacons existed in the Pauline
> communities, and numbered among their tasks were those of
> caring for the poor and attending to material things.[43]

By the time of the early church, deacons were involved in
practical service. Here, as in the New Testament church, they
assisted the pastor.[44]

Ordination

As demonstrated above, *all* believers share in the ministry of reconciliation. Macquarrie observes that reconciliation "is a ministry which belongs to the clergy as well as the laity, though in any actual situation it may be exercised in different ways, and in some situations the laymen, in others the clergyman, may be better able to minister."[45] This fundamental ministry of reconciliation thus belongs to all the body; yet some within the body are called to the specialized ministries of the evangelist, pastor (or elder or bishop), and the deacon.

What, then, is the difference between the fundamental ministry and the specialized ministry? Macquarrie again responds, "The specific ministry of the clergy then must be thought of as additional to the general ministry. So we come to the thought of grades of fullness in the ministry. It is not the case that the clergy have a ministry and the laity have none, but that the clergy have a fuller ministry."[46]

The Call to Specialized Ministry. While all believers are called to service, those involved in specialized ministry have an additional calling which is twofold, both internal and external.

Some have held the internal call to be of a divine miraculous nature, a special revelation from God. If such "Pauline calls" do come to people today, they are the exception rather than the rule. Berkhof correctly maintains that the internal call consists

> in certain ordinary providential indications given by God, and includes especially three things: (a) the consciousness of being impelled to some special task in the Kingdom of God, by love to God and His cause; (b) the conviction that one is at least in a measure intellectually and spiritually qualified for the office sought; and (c) the experience that God is clearly paving the way to the goal.[47]

Equally, if not more, important is the external call. It comes from the local church. The leadership of the congregation has a vital and guiding role in it, but it is generated by all the members, as seen in Acts 1:15-26; 6:26; and 14:23. The leaders set out the required qualifications for the position, but ultimately the people chose.[48] While the internal call is highly subjective, the external one is objective. Both are important, but the latter should be considered the ultimate affirmation.

The Significance of Ordination. Most denominations single out those involved in specialized ministries by the rite of ordination. While there are some connections to Old Testament practices of the laying on of hands (e.g., Lev. 4:4; Num. 8:10; Josh. 27:23), and to the New Testament practices (e.g., Acts 6:6; 9:17; 13:3; 1 Tim. 4:14; 5:22; Heb. 6:2), they are at best ambiguous. It is difficult to make a biblical case for ordaining pastors and deacons.

One may well ask, then, "what is the significance of ordination?" The answer will depend on the particular tradition surveyed. Fisher Humphreys has distinguished four different views of ordination: (1) ordination as sacrament; (2) ordination as authorization; (3) ordination as installation; and (4) ordination as confirmation and blessing.[49]

The sacramental view is held by the Roman Catholic and Eastern Orthodox churches. "In ordination an individual receives a sacramental grace which is an indelible character, and he enters an order of priests with special rights and duties. God is thus acting upon him through ordination."[50]

Reformed churches hold to the idea of ordination as authorization. The church bestows authority on a person to preach the Word and administer the sacraments, with the stress on the former. Although the power conferred by ordination comes through the church, ultimately it emanates from God; it is His power.[51]

Ordination as installation is undoubtedly the broadest meaning of the term. It involves one who is inaugurated into a new ministry position by a service of consecration which may involve laying hands on the individual. It signals the church's affirmation that God has called the individual to that place and position of ministry.[52]

While rejecting the first two views as biblically untenable, Humphreys accepts the third as both biblically and institutionally adequate, but deems it to fall short of the mark of true ordination. Accordingly, he proposes a fourth view, one that is noninstitutional and communal, namely, ordination as confirmation and blessing. No biblical precedent need be claimed for this view; for it is completely biblical that a church furnish nurture for its members' faith and direction for their lives. This form of ordination affirms the call of both God and the church on the individual for specialized ministry. By laying hands on the individual, the community expresses a communal blessing on the minister's work. "In summary, though ordination as a communal confirmation of a member's call and a communal blessing upon him in his service does not require explicit biblical precedents, in fact it has them . . . a spiritual, religious, theological tie does exist."[53]

Conclusions. Ordination is a means of setting apart those called to specialized ministry. In it, the church confirms the ordinand's call, places its blessing upon that person, and inducts that one into the ministry. It is not sacramental as such, but is rather a recognition of the gifting and call of the Holy Spirit to a particular form of Christian service.

THE MINISTRY OF GOVERNANCE

While Christ is Head and Lord of the universal church, the local expression of His church is a human institution and so must have some type of organization. In looking at the visible church, one finds several kinds of governments.

Some people would argue for one form of church government over others. Other people would contend that "no particular structure of church life is divinely ordained."[54] Just as varying types of civil governments fit various people groups, so different forms of church governments serve different churches. "Support for the freedom of form is sometimes taken from the fact that Christ Himself gave no specific directions concerning the government of the church."[55] At the same time, the majority of interpreters feel that the New Testament sets forth at least some fundamental elements of governance.[56]

The Episcopal Form

The episcopal form of government, which dates back to the patristic period, comes from the Greek *episkopos*, "bishop."

Most churches which employ this type of polity (Roman Catholic, Eastern Orthodox, and Anglican, for example) hold that Jesus gave authority over His church to the apostles, who passed that authority on to their successors, the bishops. Each bishop is head of a church unit (generally geographical) known as a diocese. While each bishop rules the churches within his diocese, matters of national or global concern are decided by a council of bishops.

Roman Catholicism differs slightly from this hierarchical pattern. One of the bishops, the Bishop of Rome, has been raised above all of his brother bishops as supreme pontiff, the "Vicar of Christ" on earth. Even though he relies on bishops who have been elevated to be "princes of the church" in the College of Cardinals, he alone is the final authority, and when he speaks *ex cathedra* on matters of doctrine, he speaks with the voice of Christ (i.e., infallibly).

Below the bishops are the priests. The priest is ordained by the bishops and, through the imposition of the bishop's hands, receives the power to minister the sacraments and the Word of God.

The Presbyterial Form

The presbyterial form of government is related to the Greek word *presbyteros*, "presbyter" or "elder." Churches which employ this model (such as the Presbyterian or Reformed) are controlled by elders. "Like the episcopal model, the presbyterial is rooted in the assumption that reality and unity will be fragmented and distorted if no bodies above local congregations can exercise authority."[57]

One might call the presbyterial pattern a form of representative democracy. The authority of Christ is delegated to the local church, which vests it in a board of elders. The elders are of two kinds, ruling and teaching. The former provide the administrative leadership of the church; the latter, the pastoral leadership. This board is known as the Session (Presbyterian) or Consistory (Reformed). It transacts the church's affairs, including the admission and dismissal of members.

Representatives of each local church in a given geographical area constitute the Presbytery (Presbyterian) or Classis (Reformed), which holds doctrinal and administrative authority over its member churches. These are combined together in regional synods. In the Presbyterian Church, the highest and national level is the General Assembly, which is composed of ruling and teaching elders from each Presbytery.

The Congregational Form

The emphasis of the congregational model is on the membership of the local church (examples of this model include Baptists, Free Churches, and many Mennonites). Authority here is democratic, vested in the congregation as a whole (i.e., those who are members). Strong says:

> While Christ is sole king, therefore, the government of the church, so far as regards the interpretation and execution of his will by the body, is an absolute democracy, in which the whole body of members is intrusted with the duty and responsibility of carrying out the laws of Christ as expressed in his word.[58]

Because authority resides in the congregation as a whole, the officers of the church have only as much power as the church delegates to them. Leaders are always answerable to the congregation.

In this system each church is autonomous. Consequently, "no church or council of churches, no association or convention or society, can relieve any single church of its direct responsibility to Christ, or assume control of its action."[59] At the same time, because every local church is possessed of the Holy Spirit to the same degree, there is a necessary interdependence and mutual sympathy among churches. It is not uncommon, therefore, for congregational churches to band together in cooperative associations and conventions of autonomous churches for more effective service in God's kingdom.

The Unstructured Form

There are some churches which reject any formal pattern of church government (such as the Quakers and some Brethren groups). They hold that the church should have no external

371

shape or form, but each believer should be indwelt and guided by God's Spirit.

In groups which follow such a pattern, membership has little importance and there are few rules for joining. When decisions need to be made, congregational meetings are held, but there are no formal votes. The leadership of the Holy Spirit in the congregation is paramount.[60]

Some Observations

All of these forms of government have arguments both in their favor and against them.

Those favoring the episcopal system will contend that bishops are analogous to the apostles. The latter appointed elders for various churches (cf. Acts 14:23). James, who was in charge of the church in Jerusalem, is seen as the prototype for bishops. And there is the argument of apostolic succession. Those against the system argue that more importance is assigned to the office than to the officeholder, just the opposite to the teaching of Scripture. Nor is the idea of apostolic succession a biblical one; there is nothing to substantiate the notion of perpetuating a particular type of office or government.[61]

Proponents of the presbyterial system point to the rule of the synagogue elders and the imitation of this government by the New Testament church as their basis for operation. Furthermore, the presbyterial system allows for a balanced, representative form of church government, with power being vested in a plurality rather than in a single person. Objection to the system is based on its being a hierarchical pattern which is not found in the New Testament. And "while the presbytery and session are in theory servants and representatives of the individual believers, they may well come to assume a ruling role," usurping the authority they were elected to represent.[62]

Those who promote the congregational form of government make much of the doctrine of the priesthood of all believers fitting well with democratic decision-making. As in the New Testament church, all are equal in status. Such advocates claim that the congregational form may be found in Acts 6, where the church as a whole appointed the first deacons, and again in the report of the Jerusalem Council found in Acts 15. Moreover,

Paul's letters were addressed to the church and not to its bishops or elders. These arguments are countered by assertions that the congregational system denies New Testament evidence for apostolic (and so, episcopal) authority (see Acts 14:23; Titus 1:5). In addition, it is a cumbersome and inefficient form of government.[63]

The unstructured form places heavy emphasis on the direction and action of the Holy Spirit, which is admirable. On the other hand, "the degree of sanctification and sensitivity to the Holy Spirit which they posit of the members of a congregation is an unrealistic ideal."[64]

CONCLUSIONS

Is there a form of church government which is *the* biblical one? If so, which one? Frankly, Scripture provides no definite answers. The New Testament does not set forth a detailed directive on how the church is to be administered. The only passages which speak substantively to the issue — 1 Timothy 3:1-13 and Titus 1:5-9 — are descriptive and not prescriptive, dealing only with character traits regarding positions already established.

When one looks at the New Testament narratives, support may be found for aspects of episcopal, presbyterial, congregational, and unstructured forms of governance. At the same time, any effort to construct the current forms of governance from biblical evidence, would be doomed to failure; for the New Testament church was highly charismatic in its administrative structure and very primitive organizationally. What administrative structure there was seems to have been modeled on existing societal structures.

The New Testament does, however, teach certain principles which should have some bearing on forms of church government. The first of these is the doctrine of the priesthood of all believers. All believers have equal and direct access to God; no mediator other than the Lord Jesus is needed. Additionally, the biblical teaching that the Holy Spirit gifts each believer for a spiritual task demands a structure that employs the gifts of each believer. And the Book of Acts stresses that each believer should participate in decision-making.

Based on the biblical teaching, then, some form of democratic or representative government will best allow the church to function as God intended. As Erickson observes:

> It might be concluded that, since most national democracies today are representative democracies, the presbyterian system would be the most suitable form of church government. But local churches are less like national governments than like the local governments which hold open hearings and town meetings. The value of direct involvement by well-informed people is considerable. And the principle that decisions are best made by those who will be most affected likewise argues for the congregational pattern of local autonomy.[65]

12.2 Church Polities

	Episcopal	Presbyterial	Congregational	Unstructured
View	Jesus gave authority in church to His apostles, who passed it on to their successors, the bishops. Each bishop rules the churches in his diocese; a council of bishops rules nationally or globally.	Christ's authority is vested in the local church elders. Elder representatives of a group of churches form the presbytery which hold doctrinal and ecclesiastical authority over the group.	Every local church is a democratic unity. The power rests in the members of the congregation. Each church is autonomous, with Christ as its Head. Churches may band together in associations and conventions for efficiency but do not thereby give up their autonomy.	There is no formal shape or form. Each believer is indwelt and guided by the Holy Spirit. Membership means little or nothing. Congregational meetings make decisions, but by consensus not vote.
Groups involved	Roman Catholic, Greek Orthodox, Anglican	Presbyterian, Reformed	Baptist, Congregational, Mennonite (some), Pentecostal (some)	Quaker

SUMMARY

The church exists to share the life and ministry of its Lord. The model for Christian ministry must always be the ministry of Jesus as recorded in the Gospels. Just as Jesus came to serve, so Jesus calls His body to serve (Matt. 20:26-28).

The fundamental ministry of the church — one which is incumbent upon every believer — is the ministry of reconciliation. It is characterized by a self-giving love for those in need.

All of God's people are equipped for ministry by the Holy Spirit, who grants to every believer at least one special ability (or, spiritual gift). Romans 12:6-8, 1 Corinthians 12:8-10, Ephesians 4:11, and 1 Peter 4:11 list these ministry gifts. Whether all of the gifts listed in the New Testament are still operative today is a debatable point. But far more important is the obligation of the believer to know and use whatever gift the Spirit has bestowed.

Among God's people are those who are called to specialized ministries: the pastoral office and the diaconate. The first is characterized by three terms: pastor, elder, and bishop. The three are synonymous. The pastor nurtures, protects, and guides the flock on behalf of their Owner, Jesus Christ. The deacon assists the pastor in practical service.

A twofold call sets apart those given specialized ministries. The inward, subjective call is confirmed and recognized by the external, objective call of a local church. Many local churches publicly affirm and seal this call by ordaining the minister, asking the Lord's blessing on the one He has called.

The ministry of governance of the church is an important one. Yet Scripture never sets forth one form of governance as the one, God-ordained model. At most, the Bible advances certain principles that suggest a representative role — principles best served by the congregational form. But nothing prohibits other forms which would work effectively while allowing the members a major voice in the making of decisions.

CHAPTER THIRTEEN

Membership
in the Church

Who may belong to the church? How is membership attained? And how is it maintained?

These questions—questions of church membership—refer to the church universal, the worldwide fellowship of all believers. Institutional requirements for membership in the local church will vary from congregation to congregation. At the same time, the apostles would have found it inconceivable that someone would become a believer and eschew being a part of the local church (i.e., being a member).

REGENERATION: THE PRIME PREREQUISITE

Regeneration is a reversal of the effects of sin (Eph. 2:1-10). The believer is transformed from deadness in trespasses and sins to newness of life in Christ. Regeneration restores human nature to the way it was intended by God to be (i.e., the state before the Fall). At the same time, it is both the birth of a new life and a reversion to the old life and activity.[1]

No one who has not been born again by receiving Jesus Christ as personal Savior and Lord can become a part of the true church. Jesus Himself declared, "I tell you the truth, no one can see the kingdom of God unless he is born again" (John 3:3). Only one who has been animated by the Spirit of Christ may join His body. William Stevens observes, "The work of the church is spiritual, which work can be carried on only by spiritual individuals. How can an unregenerate individual draw

376

lost souls to the regenerating Christ?"[2]

Because the church includes only those who have been born again, church membership is limited to people who are old enough to call on Jesus Christ as their Savior. Thus, no one can be "born" into the church, nor can one profess faith on the part of another. Every person who would become a part of Christ must be convicted by the Holy Spirit, believe the Gospel, repent of sin, and trust Christ. It is a matter of personal, voluntary decision.[3]

BAPTISM: INITIATION INTO THE FELLOWSHIP

Baptism is the external sign of the inward change effected in regeneration. It is the outward manifestation of the Holy Spirit's baptism of the believer into the body of Christ. Jürgen Moltmann observes that

> Christian baptism is eschatology put into practice. It manifests the advent of the coming God through Christ in human life and is the sign of life's conversion to the life of Easter. Like the proclamation of the gospel of the last days, Christian baptism is Christian hope in action.[4]

Baptism, we might say then, is the initiation of the believer into Christian faith and practice.

The Origins of Baptism

The origins of Christian baptism are found in the Judaic milieu rather than the Greek. The baptism of John (the Baptist) is its prototype. While some may wish to link baptism with the atonement immersions of the Qumran community or Jewish proselyte baptism, these baptisms had no eschatological significance. Jesus was baptized by John, thereby affirming the latter's prophetic activity. Jesus Himself followed John's call to repentance and gave it a radical emphasis in His proclamation of the advent of God's rule and in His requirement for all people to submit themselves in faith to God's will. As a result, the church was convinced that Jesus approved this "baptism of repentance for the forgiveness of sins" (Mark 1:4) by His own example.

Moreover, He subsequently confirmed that John's baptism was divinely authorized (cf. Mark 11:27-33) and that its purpose was to seal willing humans for God's new people by symbolizing repentance and forgiveness of sin.[5]

While Jesus evidently appropriated John the Baptist's eschatology, He diverged from John's theme of judgment in favor of the gospel of grace. Whereas John had heralded the kingdom of God as judgment, with a view to repentance, Jesus announced the justice of grace and confirmed it by forgiving sins.[6] Christian baptism arose from Jesus' eschatology and is grounded in the church's eschatological confession of Jesus as God's Messiah. Baptism is fathomable as being a token of the arrival of God in a person's life and in that individual's orientation toward the future. We see, then, that Christian baptism is rooted in the baptism of John the Baptist, but goes well beyond it.

13.1 The Institution of Baptism

> Baptism was instituted and consecrated by God; and the first who baptized was John, who dipped Christ in the water in Jordan. From him it came to the apostles who also baptized with water. The Lord, in plain words, commanded them to preach the Gospel and to baptize "in the name of the Father and of the Son and of the Holy Spirit" (Matt. 28:19). And Peter also, when different ones asked him what they should do, said to them, in the Acts, "Be baptized every one of you in the name of Jesus Christ for the forgiveness of your sins; and you will receive the gift of the Holy Spirit" (Acts 2:38). Thus, baptism is called by some people a sign of initiation for God's people through which God's elect are consecrated unto Him.
> — *The Second Helvetic Confession* 20 (1566)

The Significance of Baptism

In chapter 8, it was pointed out that baptism symbolizes the believer's union with Christ in His death and burial. Consequently, we have died to sin. "The old life of sin has gone; the new life of righteousness has taken its place."[7] As the believer emerges from the water, the world sees a testimony of the believer's participation in Christ's death and the rebirth into regenerate life. Indeed, baptism serves primarily to symbolize the work of the Holy Spirit to regenerate those who have come to the Cross.

Furthermore, baptism is a recognition of the believer's unity with the universal church throughout the whole world. Strong reminds us that, in Ephesians 4:5, it is baptism, not the Lord's Supper, that is mentioned as the symbol of Christian unity.[8] Galatians 3:28 also indicates that those who are baptized are united in a fellowship transcending human distinctions.[9]

Baptism, lastly, symbolizes purification. From the time of Moses on, purification has been associated with washing with water (Ex. 19:10-15). When Paul was converted, Ananias was sent to baptize him; the latter exhorted him, "And now what are you waiting for? Get up, be baptized and wash your sins away, calling on his name" (Acts 22:16). It is not surprising, then, to find three instructive "washing" passages in the Pauline epistles: 1 Corinthians 6:11, Ephesians 5:26, and Titus 3:4-7. The believer is cleansed from sin through regeneration as symbolized by baptism.[10]

13.2 Luther on Baptism

Q. What does baptizing with water signify?

A. It signifies that the old Adam in us, together with all sins and evil lusts, should be drowned by daily sorrow and repentance and be put to death, and that the new man should come forth daily and rise up, cleansed and righteous, to live forever in God's presence.

Q. Where is this written?

A. In Romans 6:4, St. Paul wrote, "We were therefore buried with Him by baptism into death, so that as Christ was raised up from the dead by the glory of the Father, we too might walk in newness of life."

—Luther's *Small Catechism* 4.4 (1529)

The Subjects of Baptism

Because regeneration is the prime prerequisite for inclusion in the body of Christ, only those who can give evidence of having

379

been regenerated by the Spirit of God (Acts 2:38) should be baptized. One may go even further and, on the basis of Matthew 28:19, contend that the appropriate candidates for baptism are those who are willing to, or already have, become disciples of the Lord Jesus. None should be baptized who cannot realize the ravages of sin and their own need for Christ's atoning sacrifice. Therefore, only believers should be baptized; babies and small children are not fitting recipients of the ordinance.

Pedobaptism is not biblical. No instance of infants being baptized can be found in the New Testament. Some might argue that the household baptisms of Acts included children, but this is an argument from silence — there is no proof of such. Louis Berkhof, a Reformed theologian, is absolutely correct in saying that "there is not a single instance in which we are plainly told that children were baptized."[11]

In the absence of biblical examples, some support baptism of infants on the ground that it replaces circumcision of the Abrahamic covenant.[12] Just as all males born to Hebrew parents were circumcised so that they might be included in the covenant, so all children born to Christian parents should be baptized that they may be under the covenant of grace. Strong aptly responds that such a concept "contradicts the New Testament idea of the church, making it a hereditary body, in which fleshly birth, and not the new birth, qualifies for membership."[13] People come to Christ solely on their own faith in Him, not their parents' faith. And while children of believing parents come under the care of the church, they are not yet members of the body of Christ. Faith in Christ fixes them into His body, giving them new identity.

The Mode of Baptism

In Christian churches today three modes of baptism are in common use: immersion (i.e., completely submerging the candidate beneath water), affusion (pouring water on the head), and aspersion (sprinkling water on the head, or making the sign of the cross on the head with water). Are all three forms acceptable? Which were practiced in the New Testament church?

As to the meaning of "baptism" in the New Testament, Trites notes that

380

The Greeks had several words for applying water. These words could refer to the actions of washing, pouring and sprinkling. However, the baptism of Jesus is described by a different word, *baptizo*, which means to submerge, to plunge, to immerse. Similarly, the New Testament writers repeatedly use the word meaning to immerse when they refer to baptism (see Matt. 28:19; Rom. 6:3-4; 1 Cor. 1:14f.).[14]

Scholars of major denominations which do not practice immersion are in agreement with such a position. Joseph Eagan, a Roman Catholic priest, concurs: "When the New Testament writers referred to baptism . . . their experience of baptism was in the context of . . . being baptized through immersion in water in the powerful name of Jesus."[15] Hans Küng, also a Roman Catholic, concedes, "The verb βαπτίζειι (meaning 'to immerse repeatedly' in secular Greek) is used in the New Testament solely in the technical sense of baptism."[16] Karl Barth, a Reformed theologian, asserts that

> The Greek word βαπτιζω and the German word *taufen* (from *Tiefe*, depth) originally and properly describe the process by which a man or an object is completely immersed in water and then withdrawn from it again. Primitive baptism carried out in this manner had as its mode, exactly like the circumcision of the Old Testament, the character of a direct threat to life, succeeded immediately by the corresponding deliverance and preservation, the raising from baptism. One can hardly deny that baptism was carried out as immersion.[17]

During the first century, immersion was the mode practiced. From the second century through the sixth century (the patristic era), immersion was still being practiced, but other modes were in fashion. Affusion and aspersion were becoming increasingly common. In addition, trine immersion (being immersed three times) was popular. One can find none of these latter practices in the New Testament.

Why do many denominations not practice immersion? Stevens informs us that there are three different responses. The first — and smallest — group suggest that the Greek *baptizo* does not mean to immerse, but rather to pour or sprinkle. The second group confess that, while the Greek can mean to immerse, it also can mean to pour. And the largest group by far will admit "that immersion was the original and exclusive mode of baptism but that sprinkling and pouring are justified also. This justification is made on an appeal to the authority of the church or is made simply on the basis of convenience."[18]

How important to baptism is its mode? Much more important, unquestionably, is that the person being baptized should be a believer. But Christian churches should want to follow New Testament practice as much as possible; at least, one would hope so. Jesus has said, "If you love me, you will obey what I command" (John 14:15). His command is to immerse *(baptizo)*. We would not, in the Lord's Supper, substitute cake for the bread and milk for the cup; why would we see fit to make changes in the ordinance of baptism? And, as we have shown earlier (chap. 8), baptism symbolizes burial with Christ; immersion is the only mode which can adequately typify this metaphor. Dean Stanley, a nineteenth-century Angelican cleric, admits that

> It [aspersion] is a greater change than even that which the Roman Catholic Church has made in administering the Sacrament of the Lord's Supper in the bread without the wine. For that was a change which did not affect the thing that was signified: whereas the change from immersion to sprinkling has set aside the larger part of the apostolic language regarding baptism.[19]

Conclusions

Baptism is the rite of initiation into the church. It is the external sign of a regenerated life. The ordinance is rooted in the baptism of John; by participating in that baptism, Jesus affirmed it, but poured new meaning into it by directing it beyond God's judgment to His grace. He went on to command it for all of His followers (Matt. 28:19-20).

Because of what baptism represents, the right subjects of the ordinance are only those who have repented of their sins and have committed their lives to Jesus Christ as personal Savior and Lord; this requirement excludes infants and those who have not yet reached an age of reason. The proper mode of baptism is immersion. No other form is found in the New Testament. Affusion and aspersion were later innovations not compatible with what baptism signifies, namely, union with Christ in His death and burial.

THE LORD'S SUPPER:
CONTINUING FELLOWSHIP IN THE CHURCH

While baptism is a once-for-all ordinance whereby the believer is initiated into the fellowship of the body of Christ, the Lord's Supper is a continuing ordinance (to be observed by believers until the Lord returns) whereby the believer continues in the fellowship of the church. Moltmann tells us that just as baptism eschatologically symbolizes *starting out*, so habitual fellowship at the Lord's Table eschatologically symbolizes *being on the way*. The two ordinances belong together, related to each other in the messianic community:

> In the baptismal event the community is linked to the individual who enters the fellowship of Christ and confesses it publicly. In eating and drinking at the Lord's Table individuals are linked to the community which is visible in these acts. Baptism and the Lord's supper are the signs of the church's life, because they are the signs of the one who *is* their life.[20]

The Institution of the Supper

The Synoptic Gospels and 1 Corinthians all mention the supper on the night the Lord was betrayed. While these accounts are not exactly the same, when taken collectively they depict the institution of the Lord's Supper. G.C. Berkouwer comments that what is described is not a typical meal, but one in which the disciples were called to eat and drink and were also told the significance of these actions. Jesus told them: "this is my body," and "this is my blood of the covenant, which is poured out for many for the forgiveness of sins" (Matt. 26:26, 28). And again one finds Luke relating the same event: "this is my body given for you," and, "this cup is the new covenant in my blood, which is poured out for you" (Luke 22:19-20). And both Luke (22:19) and 1 Corinthians (11:24-25) recount Jesus' command

383

to, "do this in remembrance of me." All these passages have served to set the church's practice and confession in regard to the Lord's Supper.[21]

The Oldest Tradition. The oldest tradition of the Lord's Supper is recorded by Paul in 1 Corinthians 11:23-32. It tells us that Jesus initiated this meal on the night of His betrayal to help His disciples comprehend that in His imminent crucifixion God would be acting to establish His New Covenant. By accompanying what He said with symbolic action—breaking the bread and passing about a common cup—He made His disciples its recipients. "That first Lord's Supper was thus the founding of the Ekklēsia as the fellowship of those who were bound to God and to each other by the death of Jesus."[22]

When Jesus broke the bread and passed the cup around, He commanded His followers, "do this in remembrance of me" (1 Cor. 11:24-25). Paul reminded his readers that "whenever you eat this bread and drink this cup, you proclaim the Lord's death until he comes" (1 Cor. 11:26). Küng asserts, "The Lord's Supper as celebrated after Easter was not a meal looking back in memory of the dead, but a meal which looked forward to the future, full of confidence and hope."[23]

The Old Testament Roots. Among the Hebrews, meals often had a religious and social implication. One meal, the *kiddush*, was held every week as a preparation for the Sabbath. Another, the *chabura*, was an intimate affair between close friends. The most important of all Hebrew meals, however, was the annual Passover meal celebrated by the family. It is undoubtedly this meal which was the occasion for this last supper Jesus celebrated with His band of disciples.[24] Toward its conclusion He instituted the Lord's Supper.

The Passover meal is somewhat analogous to the Lord's Supper. The former was a memorial, an annual reminder to the Jews that God had liberated them from Egyptian enslavement. They were to recall how the angel of death had spared those Hebrew homes which had the blood of a lamb on the lintels and doorposts, but had killed the firstborn son of every Egyptian home (and of any Hebrew home which had failed to use the blood of the lamb!). The Eucharist is a similar memorial, in this case, to the sacrifice of the Lamb of God, who takes away the sin of the world. It is His blood, symbolically sprinkled on the life of the sinner, which saves those who place their trust in Him by acting as a *kiporah* or sin covering. Stevens tells us that, "according to John's gospel Jesus was crucified on the day the paschal lamb was slain, the fourteenth day of Nisan, the day of preparation. Paul's naming Jesus our passover correlates with the Johannine view."[25]

There is one other way in which the Lord's Supper is analogous to the Passover. The latter was not only a memorial, but also an expectation—expectation of a new liberation by the Messiah. The Lord's Supper anticipates an eschatological deliverance—Messiah's return.[26]

The Significance of the Lord's Supper

There are five basic views of the Lord's Supper which have been held throughout the history of the church. Every modern denomination holds to one of these conceptions of the Eucharist (albeit sometimes with some modification).

Transubstantiation. The Council of Trent (1545–1563) set forth Roman Catholic dogma on the Lord's Supper, although the interpretation given—transubstantiation—had been commonly held for several centuries.

The council decreed that the substance of the elements does not persist, but is transformed into Christ's literal body and blood. Two basic interpretations of this decree have emerged (for the council did not specify how the change took place). The first avers that the substance of the bread and wine is destroyed, and the flesh and blood of the Savior are either reproduced or adduced. The second asserts that, while the substance of the elements does cease to exist, it is not annihilated but passes into the preexistent body and blood of Christ. A modern theory is beginning to gain ground; it states that "the entire agglomeration of substances constituting the bread and wine are converted into the body and blood of Christ . . . [although] no modification occurs in such phenomena . . . the bread and wine become the Savior's body and blood without altering their empirical properties."[27]

385

All who take part in the Eucharist, then, literally ingest the physical flesh of the Lord. By this ingestion Christ's atoning sacrifice is carried out anew, just as surely as if He were crucified again. And it has the same effect, propitiating God's wrath and so mediating His salvific grace to the one receiving the sacrament.

Consubstantiation. Martin Luther could not completely escape his Roman Catholic roots when it came to the Lord's Supper. He took very seriously Jesus' words "this is my body." Consequently, he held that the body and blood of Jesus are literally present in the elements. At the same time, there is no change in either their substance or accidents. Rather, Christ's body and blood are literally present "under the form of bread and wine" (*Augsburg Confession*, Art. 10). They coexist with the elements. Though Luther never used the term, his view has been termed *consubstantiation.*

Dynamic Presence. John Calvin held neither to the Roman Catholic view of transubstantiation nor to Luther's concept of consubstantiation. Charles Hodge observes that, while Calvin disavowed the literal presence of Christ's body and blood in the Supper as it was declared by the Romans and Lutherans, he nonetheless maintained that they were dynamically present, that there was something not only transcendent, but indubitably miraculous, in this sacrament.[28] Berkouwer asserts that Calvin "thought of a participation in which body and blood did not occur as isolated substances, but wherein communion was held with Christ himself in his true body and blood, with Christ in his offering."[29] He is fully present; for the Lord's Supper is a genuine communion with Him and His reconciling sacrifice.[30] This view of dynamic presence is held by Presbyterians, the Reformed Church, and many Anglicans.

The Inner Sacrament. There are a few groups—such as the Quakers and Salvation Army—who do not observe the Lord's Supper, claiming that it has been fulfilled in the believer's life through the Lord's death. The Quakers, for example, reject all outward ordinances or sacraments because they fear that such external rites would detract from the believer's reliance on "the inner light" of the Holy Spirit. They want nothing to do with anything which might lead one to idolatry—a reliance on anything other than the inner work of the Holy Spirit.

The Symbolic View. Ulrich Zwingli, father of the Swiss Reformation, strongly opposed Luther's view of consubstantiation. He held that the elements are symbolic of Christ's body and blood offered up for human sin.

This view is multidirectional. It looks back to the crucifixion of Christ, whose death has liberated believers from the bonds of sin. It is connected to the present; for it confesses Christ and His saving grace "till He comes." It is future-oriented; for it looks forward to the Parousia, the consummation of history, and the glad reunion of believers with their God.[31]

The symbolic view does not profess for the Eucharist any sacramental power. It simply symbolizes Christ's death for us, the appropriation of the benefits of His death, and the means of that appropriation which is union with Christ.[32]

Conclusions. Transubstantiation rests upon a false rendering of the account of the Lord's Supper. When Jesus said, "This is my body broken for you," He did not intend for His followers to take the words literally; after all, He was still with them. It is obvious that His usage was metaphorical. Nor should one be expected to believe that, when a priest—regardless of his character—utters a prayer of consecration, the wafer and wine miraculously are transformed into the literal flesh and blood of the Savior. Nor can one accept the idea that Christ is sacrificed afresh every time the Eucharist is observed; such an idea denies the once-for-all view of the Lord's death and questions its sufficiency.

The objections to transubstantiation may be applied equally to consubstantiation. It also violates the doctrine of the priesthood of believers by requiring a priest to consecrate the elements and transform them into the body and blood of Christ.

The dynamic view is more reasonable than the previous two; but it is rather vague. One would not deny that the Lord mediates spiritual power to His people who come to Him in faith, but He does not wait for the Eucharist to do so. Spiritual power is available at any time.

The inner sacrament view is understandable, and the Quaker desire to rely on the interior work of the Holy Spirit is most admirable. Nonetheless, Jesus commanded that His followers are to "do this." Ignoring the Lord's straightforward command on this issue does not encourage the work of the Holy Spirit within one.

The symbolic view of the Lord's Supper seems closest to the biblical intention. The Table represents Jesus Christ's atoning death, calling believers to remember the grace that flows from the Savior's obedience, "even to death on a cross." It symbolizes complete and continuous dependence upon the crucified and risen Lord with whom believers are united by faith. It is emblematic of the coming joy and perfection of God's eternal kingdom.[33] The elements themselves do not bestow these benefits on the believer, but summon His people to mark well what has been received through faith in the Lord Jesus. In this respect, the Lord's Supper serves the same ministry purpose as a sermon: the faithful are called to know the character of their holy God and to remember the great price at which they were reconciled to Him. And while Reformed theology correctly affirms that Christ is present at His table in a very special way, it unwisely goes further and says that the Lord's Supper is a divine sacrament in which grace is mediated in a special way which is unique to the occasion and never repeated at any other occasion.

13.3 On the Lord's Supper

> The Lord's Supper is an ordinance of Jesus Christ to be administered with the elements of bread and wine, and to be observed by His churches until the end of the world. It is in no sense a sacrifice, but is designed to commemorate His death, to confirm the faith and other graces of Christians, and to be a bond, pledge and renewal of their communion with Him, and of their church fellowship.
> — *The Abstract of Principles* 16 (1859)
> **of the Southern Baptist Theological Seminary,**
> **Louisville, Kentucky.**

PREREQUISITES FOR PARTICIPATION

Since the Lord's Supper was intended by Christ only for the church, it follows that there must be certain requirements incumbent on those participating in the ordinance.

A Regenerated Life. Because the Supper is intended for the church alone it is common sense to suppose that a participant should be a member of the true church. There is only one way to belong to that church — by being born again through faith in Jesus Christ. No non-Christian should partake. The admonition that every person "examine himself" before taking the elements infers that spiritual ability — available only to the regenerate — to "recognize the body of the Lord."[34]

A Baptized Believer. The New Testament writings indicate that those participating in the Lord's Supper had been baptized. Jesus selected as His disciples those who had been baptized, probably by John the Baptist (see Matt. 21:25; Acts 1:21-22); following the resurrection He commanded His disciples to "make disciples . . . baptizing them . . . and teaching them to obey everything I have commanded you" (Matt. 28:19). The discipleship process required baptism as the first order of business and then obedience to Jesus' other teachings.

Church Membership. The Lord's Supper is an ordinance for the church, and is to be observed by the gathered church. Church membership, therefore, should be expected of those participating (this is not to suggest "closed communion," that is, that members of other churches should be excluded from participation). Luke writes of the church at Troas, "On the first day of the week we came together to break bread" (Acts 20:7). The Lord's Supper is emblematic primarily of fellowship with Christ, but secondarily of fellowship with other believers in the (local) body: "Because there is one loaf, we, who are many, are one body, for we all partake of the one loaf" (1 Cor. 10:17). Strong declares, "The Lord's Supper is a symbol of the church fellowship. Excommunication implies nothing, if it does not imply exclusion from the communion. If the Supper is simply communion of the individual with Christ, then the church has no right to exclude any from it."[35]

An Obedient Walk. Because disobedience militates against the church fellowship and union with Christ — both of which are integral to the ordinance — no one should participate in it who is not in an obedient walk with Christ. Paul commanded the Thessalonian believers "to keep away from every brother who is idle and does not live according to the teaching you have received from us" (2 Thes. 3:6).

A further form of disobedience is heresy, the acceptance of false doctrine. "Warn a divisive [or, heretical] person once, and then warn him a second time. After that, have nothing to do with him" (Titus 3:10). Strong says, "False doctrine is the chief source of division, and is therefore in itself a disqualification for participation in the Lord's Supper."[36] In the same respect, schism or the promotion of dissension in the church "requires exclusion from church fellowship, and from the Lord's Supper which is its appointed sign."[37] Those who create division in the church are wounding the body of Christ, and so would in effect crucify the Lord anew. How can they take part in that which symbolizes the unity of believers and union with Him?

Conclusions. Admittedly, not everyone is going to agree that all of the above qualifications should necessarily be prerequisites to participation in the Lord's Supper. In our day increasing numbers of people are rejecting both baptism and church membership as an expression of their Christian faith. At the same time, if the Lord's Supper represents the unity of believers in union with Christ (i.e., the unity of the body of Christ), then anything which is fractious of that unity should be ground for exclusion from the Eucharist. Refusal to become a member of a church is surely an attack on the unity of the fellowship of the body. And refusal to be baptized is not only an attack on the body, but also disobedience to the biblical teaching that baptism is a necessary part of the discipling process. It should go without saying that regeneration and obedience are absolute necessities for participation in the Lord's Supper.

Other Considerations

There are several other considerations relative to the Lord's Supper which should be examined. These include its administration, the frequency of its celebration, and the elements used.

The Administration of the Supper. The Lord's Supper is an ordinance for the church, and the church is responsible for continuing its observance and therefore its administration. Because the Lord's Supper is a *koinonia* (or, fellowship) which represents the oneness of the body, the local church is the proper and rightful administrator and locus of the ordinance. The Lord's Supper should not be administered to individuals or groups apart from the context of the gathered church; for example, a wedding or small group (unless it is a constituted house church) is not an appropriate context.

In most evangelical churches, the pastor assisted by the deacons (or elders) administers the Supper. There is nothing in the New Testament teaching which necessitates these leaders as administrators. Any spiritually qualified person may be designated by the church to preside or serve.

The Frequency of Observance. The New Testament is silent on how often the ordinance should be observed. Passover was celebrated annually, but the Pauline account would seem to suggest that the Lord's Supper was celebrated more frequently (1 Cor. 11:26). Present church practice varies widely. Some churches celebrate the ordinance weekly; some, monthly; some, quarterly; and a few, annually. The important thing here is not how often a church observes the Lord's Supper, but rather that it does so on a regular basis.

The Elements. Some churches use regular bread (either in a single loaf or cubed pieces), while others use crackers, and still others unleavened bread (in various forms). Some churches insist on unfermented grape juice while others use wine. If one would be true to the biblical metaphor, the proper elements are unleavened bread in a single loaf and unfermented grape juice in a single cup. Leaven or fermentation is associated by the Bible with sin. "The putting away of all leaven is a picture of the sanctification of the child of God. Cleansed, redeemed by God's lamb, the true believer must put away the sinful leaven of the old life before redemption."[38] The use of these elements is representative of Christ's sinless state.

391

Conclusions

The Lord's Supper or Eucharist is a sign of continuing fellowship in the church. It was instituted by Jesus on the occasion of the Passover immediately prior to His death, and is analogous in many respects to that meal. While there are several views as to the significance of the Supper, the symbolic view propounded by Ulrich Zwingli is probably closest to the intent of Jesus: the Lord's Supper is symbolic of Christ's sacrifice on Calvary, our union with Him, and our union with one another in the fellowship of His church.

The rightful participants in the Lord's Supper are those who have been born from above and who have confessed Christ publicly in the water of baptism. They must also be members in good standing of the local church (i.e., living a pure and obedient Christian life).

While the Eucharist should be observed on a regular basis, the Bible does not specify how often. It should be administered to the gathered church by those who meet the qualifications for participation and who have been appointed by the church to do so.

SUMMARY

No one can be a member of the universal church (and no one should be a member of the local church) who is not a regenerate (born again) person. Such a person is one who has believed the Gospel, repented of sin, and committed to Jesus Christ as personal Savior and Lord.

Baptism is the rite of initiation into the fellowship of the church. It is the external sign of the inward baptism of the believer by the Holy Spirit into the body of Christ. Christian baptism was closely linked to the baptism of John the Baptist and proclaims God's grace in tempering judgment with mercy by providing for the forgiveness of human sin.

The continuing rite of fellowship in the church is the Lord's Supper. It is a memorial supper, symbolic of Christ's broken body and shed blood; it is also a celebration supper which looks ahead to His impending return. It is a rite in which the whole church comes together in unity, recognizing and celebrating its identity as the body of Christ.

CHAPTER FOURTEEN

The Unity
of the Church

From the time of the making of the Constantinopolitan Creed (popularly known as the Nicene Creed) in 381, Christians have affirmed their belief in "the one, holy, catholic and apostolic Church." And yet, there are many churches. How does one reconcile the existence of Eastern Orthodox, Roman Catholic, Lutheran, Anglican, Reformed, Baptist, and a host of other churches with the belief in one church? This question of unity is of utmost importance and deserves careful attention.

THE BASES FOR CHRISTIAN UNITY

The unity of the church has been reiterated from its origination in the mind of Christ. Both the Bible and the church itself have much to say on the matter.

The Bible on Unity

Jesus' high priestly prayer, recorded in John 17, reveals how highly Jesus regarded unity among His people; He prayed for them on the eve of His passion:

> My prayer is not for them alone. I pray also for those who will believe in me through their message, that all of them may be one, Father, just as you are in me and I am in you. May they also be in us so that the world may believe that you have sent me. I have given them the glory that you gave me, that they may be

one as we are one: I in them and you in me. May they be
brought to complete unity to let the world know that you sent
me and have loved them even as you have loved me (17:20-23).

Jesus' prayer for unity had a particular objective, "that the
world may believe that you have sent me" (17:21).

There are varying exegetical and theological interpretations
of Jesus' words. Raymond Brown contends that "these statements do not mean that the world will accept Jesus; rather the
Christian believers will offer to the world the same type of
challenge that Jesus offered—a challenge to recognize God in
Jesus."[1] Barnabas Lindars, on the other hand, argues "that John
thinks of the salvation of the world as a real possibility."[2] Rudolf Schnackenburg concurs that "the unity of all believers is to
lead the unbelieving world to faith in Jesus as the one sent by
God," but observes that "Jesus looks at the community that has
accepted his word and at the same time remembers the world
has rejected it."[3]

Whatever the significance of the challenge to the world of
Christian unity, it is clear that it involves both a vertical and a
horizontal aspect. It concerns the relationship of believers to
the Father and the Son (vertical) as well as their mutual relationship (horizontal) with one another. Thus unity in John's
view is not merely a mystical relationship with God, but neither
is it simply harmonious fellowship among Christians. Since the
model for unity is the relationship of the Father to the Son,
some form of organic unity seems required, namely, the life of
the Father being imparted to the Son and from the Son to
believers.[4]

The Apostle Paul spoke to the issue of unity, as well. He
wrote to the Ephesian Christians:

As a prisoner for the Lord, then, I urge you to live a life worthy
of the calling you have received. Be completely humble and
gentle; be patient, bearing with one another in love. Make every
effort to keep the unity of the Spirit through the bond of peace.
There is one body and one Spirit—just as you were called to one
hope when you were called—one Lord, one faith, one baptism;
one God and Father of all, who is over all and through all and in
all (4:1-6).

Paul called upon believers "to keep the unity of the Spirit." This unity comes through the one truth proclaimed to them and believed by them. Markus Barth observes:

> Obviously, the oneness of the churches spread over the world is (if we follow Ephesians) not a question of better organization, administration, and boards, or of mixing creeds. . . . Such things come and go. The unity of the Church would rest on weak legs, if they, as things, were its support, standard, and means of achievement.[5]

The model for this unity in Paul's mind is the oneness of all spiritual entities: "one Lord, one faith, one baptism." Above all is one God and Father of all.

Theology and Unity

The New Testament not only gives detailed statements and exhortations on Christian unity, but it also contains a number of theological principles which highlight unity in the church.

The Old Testament speaks to the foundation of unity in God's election of one people to bear God's name in the world and so be a blessing to all the nations. Israel's uniqueness was rooted in the unity of God: "Hear, O Israel: The Lord our God, the Lord is one" (Deut. 6:4; cf. Isa. 45:21; Micah 7:18ff). "The whole witness to the unity and incomparability of Israel's God, which implies the uniqueness of Israel as the people gathered by Him, points to an *Einzigartigkeit*, a uniqueness, that leaves no room for the plural."[6] If God had expected His people of the Old Covenant to be one in their relationship to Him and to one another, it should naturally follow that He would expect the same of His people under the New Covenant.

The numerous metaphors used by the apostles are sterling examples of the singularity of the church. Paul likened the church to a bride he was presenting "to one husband, to Christ . . . as a pure virgin to him" (2 Cor. 11:2). He also wrote to Timothy, referring to the church as "God's household" (1 Tim. 3:15). And Peter described the church as "a spiritual house" (1 Peter 2:5). To try to pluralize these images would be absurd. "In the New Testament the outlook on the one Lord of the Church makes it impossible and senseless to replace the singular with a plural for the Church."[7]

Some Observations

The Bible is unequivocal in its stress on Christian unity. And the early New Testament church modeled that oneness: "All the believers were together and had everything in common. . . . They broke bread in their homes and ate together with glad and sincere hearts. . . . And the Lord added to their number daily those who were being saved" (Acts 2:44, 46-47). Here was the most successful church in history, and its success was based in a large measure on its intimate community. The passage cited ties the church's growth to the togetherness of believers in what they did (cf. Acts 4:32). The pagan world looked at this early church and exclaimed in amazement, "See how these Christians love one another!" They were drawn to Christ by the power of that love.

Community attracts unbelievers. Schism or factionalism repels them. This is true especially in lands where Christianity has gotten (or is getting) a bare foothold. Nonbelievers who are unfamiliar with the variety of denominations have difficulty in understanding how different groups, all claiming to be the true church of Jesus Christ, can hurl vitriol at one another. But they are moved by Christians serving together in community.

SCENARIOS FOR CHURCH UNITY

Although the Bible, theology, and the majority of believers agree on the desirability of unity, when faced by the seeming paradox of church plurality, is it still possible to suggest that in some way the church is nevertheless one? Theologians have attempted to posit various scenarios to explain unity amidst plurality.

The Unity of the Invisible Church

As seen above, the church may be viewed in a twofold light: the invisible and the visible church. The former is a spiritual, timeless entity while the latter is an institutional, temporal one.

Emil Brunner has defined the invisible church as "a thoroughly uncultic, unsacred, spiritual brotherhood, which lives in trusting obedience to its Lord Christ and in true love to the brethren which He bestows, and knows itself as the Body of Christ through the Holy Spirit which dwells in it."[8] By virtue of their commitment to the lordship of Jesus Christ, all believers belong to the one invisible church, regardless of what institutional (visible) church they belong to. Thus, the church is a unity, no matter how badly it appears to be divided.

The problem with such an approach is that the unbelieving world does not see the invisible church, but only the visible church rent as it is into a multitude of factions. And one must in all sincerity ask whether Jesus really had in mind a (visible) church which would be divided into different groups and parties, many at war with one another. It just does not seem likely!

Cooperative Unity

John Macquarrie has suggested that a single institutional church is not necessarily a desirable entity. In fact, "the genuine diversity-in-unity of the body of Christ needs to be defended against uniformity just as much as against divisiveness."[9] He sees ecumenism as a possible response to the problem. But it is a path fraught with dangers. One of these is the tendency toward compromise "based on the lowest common denominator of the various groups involved."[10]

Macquarrie recommends the Bible as the most obvious sign of Christian unity. "If indeed the center of the Church's unity is Jesus Christ, as the head of the body, then the Bible is the embodiment of that unity because it is the written word, testifying to the manifestation of the living Word in the flesh."[11] All Christian groups revere the Scriptures. Any ecumenism, therefore, must be firmly grounded in the Bible. But, warns Macquarrie, such an ecumenical theology must avoid being narrowly biblicist, but allow for evolving church tradition.[12]

While such unity may find acceptance among many "mainline" denominations, few evangelical churches would be willing to go along with it, if for no other reason than a fear of human tradition replacing Scripture, as Macquarrie has suggested that it must. Evangelicals wish to remain "narrowly biblicist," and rightly so! For them cooperation rather than ecumenism is more realistic.

Spiritual Harmony

Some Christians have suggested that unity should be primarily a matter of spiritual harmony. John Wesley is representative of such a position.

> I ask not, therefore, of him with whom I would unite in love
> . . . do you receive the supper of the Lord in the same posture
> and manner that I do? nor whether, in the administration of
> baptism you agree with me. . . . My only question is this: "Is
> thine heart right, as my heart is with thy heart?"[13]

The criterion may be a union of heart, or the desire to cooperate with any who acknowledge the lordship of Christ.

While such expressions of fellowship are commendable, they are very much secondary and in need of continual re-forming.[14] Besides, there are very few who would unite on such a basis.

A Confessional Union

A union of those believers with strong confessional similarity has worked well. Martin Marty explains the emergence of confessional denominations.

> When people gather to profess their faith, to unite in proclaiming it, to give substance to its stated and visible life among men, they form confessing churches. Thus the confessing group and its symbols serve to call believers out of isolation and anarchy into the beginnings of coherence and shared life. A confession serves to define and thus to delimit the boundaries of belief and shared life.[15]

Over the last century and a quarter, many confessional groups coalesced on a global level: the Anglicans in 1867, the Methodists in 1881, the Congregationalists in 1891, the Baptists in 1905, and the Lutherans in 1923 and 1947. It was this tendency toward confessional union that gave some impetus to

398

the ecumenical spirit expressed in Edinburgh in 1910 at the World Missionary Conference.[16]

While confessionalism is a natural impulse on the part of Christians which serves to unite them, it is at the same time destructive of Christian unity. Marty observes that "the partiality of the confessing act among the confessions is most evident to those of different confession." One who holds to a particular confession is likely to consider that confession as the ultimate expression of Christian truth. Thus, other confessions are apt to be seen as less than truth. "Each provides a unity for great numbers of Christians; but each divides from others."[17]

Robert Nelson decries these denominational (confessional) divisions in the church. Not only are they unbiblical, he declares, but "it is precisely the separation of these bodies, whether in villages, cities, nations, or the world, which constitutes the problem of division."[18] The New Testament calls into question the right of these confessional groups to exist as separate bodies (cf. John 17:11, 21-23).

14.1 On Christian Unity

It is also taught among us that one holy Christian church will be and remain forever. This is the congregation of all believers among whom the Gospel is proclaimed in its purity and the holy sacraments are administered in accordance with the Gospel. For it is enough for the true unity of the Christian church that the Gospel be proclaimed in accord with an unadulterated understanding of it and that the sacraments be dispensed in conformity to the divine Word. It is unnecessary for the genuine unity of the Christian church that ceremonies instituted by humans should be followed uniformly in all places. It is as Paul says in Ephesians 4:4-5: "There is one body and one Spirit—just as you were called to one hope when you were called—one Lord, one faith, one baptism."

— *The Augsburg Confession* 7 (1530)

A Common Creed and Practice

Many churches have appealed to a common polity and belief as a basis for Christian unity. This has been the attitude particularly of those groups with an episcopal government. The church is made visibly one when its bishops—all representatives of their particular denominations—are in communion with one another and with the early church. The Anglican Lambeth Quadrilateral of 1888 (recast as an "Appeal to All Christians" by the Lambeth Conference of 1920) determined that such unity could be effected by (1) the recognition of the Bible as the rule and ultimate standard of faith, (2) the recognition of the Apostles' Creed and the Nicene Creed as the proper declaration of Christian faith, (3) the use of baptism and communion as instituted by Christ, and (4) the acceptance of the historical episcopate as the basis of governmental unity.[19]

During the last several decades Anglicans and Roman Catholics have held discussions aimed at a closer relationship. And Anglicans have expressed a willingness to acknowledge the pope as supreme among the bishops, as well as infallible *ex cathedra*. But Anglican approval in the last two decades of the twentieth century of the ordination of women has damaged their desired reconciliation with Rome. Nor have all other episcopally governed churches followed the same road. And there are many non-episcopal groups who would never take such a course.

Organic Unity

During the twentieth century there has been a concerted effort on the part of some churches to achieve unity by a literal institutional (or, organic) union. In these cases the identity of each merging denomination has been jettisoned in favor of a new, single identity.

One of the most ambitious church unions took place in Canada in 1925 when the Presbyterian, Congregationalist, and Methodist churches merged into the United Church of Canada. The Anglicans and Baptists were also invited to participate, but declined.[20] Further conversations took place between the United Church, Anglicans, and Disciples of Christ during the 1960s and 1970s (and some local churches from these groups merged), but the proposed union fell through.

A forced union was brought about in Japan by the government of that nation in 1941. Eight major denominations were merged into the Kyodan, or Church of Christ in Japan. Churches, such as the Anglicans, who refused to enter the union, were legally dissolved. After the Second World War, the union continued with largely Methodist, Congregationalist, and Presbyterian elements.[21]

The best known of all unions which have occurred is the Church of South India. This is the only union in church history involving both episcopal and non-episcopal denominations. Anglicans, Methodists, and the South India United Church (Presbyterians and Congregationalists) came together on the basis of the *Appeal to All Christians.* The main difficulty came in regard to professional, ordained ministry. It was finally agreed that all ministers entering the union would be recognized by the new church, but after the union all ministers entering would have to be ordained by bishops together with presbyters (it had been agreed that polity would be episcopal). In 1947 the plan came together and the Church of South India came into being.[22]

In the United States, a group of denominational representatives met together in the late 1960s and early 1970s in the Consultation on Christian Union to plan for a merger of ten denominations into the Church of Christ Uniting. These groups were as widely divergent as the African Methodist Episcopal, Protestant Episcopal, and the Disciples of Christ.[23] Other than some minor mergers, however, these plans never came to fruition. Mergers on a smaller scale included the formation of the United Methodist Church (from the Methodist Church and the Evangelical United Brethren), and the United Church of Christ (from the Congregational Christian Church and the Evangelical and Reformed Church).

The organic union of denominations (unless they have the same theology and polity) requires each of the participating churches to surrender certain distinctives which they have always held of great importance. In the merger of churches to form the United Church of Canada, for example, the Congregationalists had to surrender the very principle which gave them their name—their congregational polity. The Baptists declined the offer of merger because they would have had to give up believer's baptism by immersion, and they were not prepared to make such a compromise. The Anglicans refused the union because they would not surrender their episcopal polity. Too often these unions result in such an overwhelming loss of vital principles that what is left is barely worth having. When organic union of churches of a like confessional stance occurs (such as that creating the Wesleyan Church from the Wesleyan Methodists, the Reformed Baptists of Canada, and the Pilgrim Holiness — all holiness groups), the result is generally more fortuitous.

Conclusions

None of the scenarios explored have really proved to be a satisfactory response to what seems to be a paradox between the unity taught by Jesus and the New Testament church and the plurality of churches that exists. The Reformation emphasis on the invisible church seems simply to ignore the reality of the existing (visible) church, or else it appears to deny that Jesus had in mind the "real" church. Cooperation between churches is laudable, but such cooperation is minimal at best. Organic union — at least between churches with different confessional stands — tends toward an exclusion of vital principles in support of the lowest common denominator. In the end, none of these proposals resolve the paradox.

EFFORTS AT CHURCH UNITY

Attempts at church union have been occurring ever since shortly after the Reformation when Martin Luther and Ulrich Zwingli met at Marburg in an attempt to unite the German and Swiss Reformations. That effort met with failure because they could not agree on the meaning of the Lord's Supper.

Modern efforts at ecumenism began early this century when missionaries realized that denominational divisions were hindering world evangelization. The World Missionary Conference at Edinburgh in 1910 was a first step toward unity, even though it was a strictly Protestant affair — neither Eastern Orthodox nor Roman Catholic representatives were invited.[24] Under the leadership of American Methodist John R. Mott, attending delegates caught a vision of the possibilities for unity. At the conclusion of the conference a unanimous motion was passed to form a Continuation Committee which would confer with the different mission societies and boards toward continuation of the aims and goals of the conference, especially the formation of a permanent International Missionary Committee. The Continuation Committee included native Christians from Japan, India, and China. It was chaired by Mott.[25]

Three organizations resulted from this meeting. In 1921, the International Missionary Council was formed in New York State to effect further cooperation between mission societies; in Stockholm, the Conference on Life and Work in 1925 attempted to harmonize efforts to deal with social, economic, and political problems; the Conference on Faith and Order at Lausanne in 1927 sought a theological foundation for unity. In 1937 the latter two conferences determined that a more inclusive organization was warranted. Though plans were temporarily delayed by the advent of World War II, the World Council of Churches was born in 1948 when delegates from 147 denominations met in Amsterdam. Subsequent assemblies have convened about every seven years since. In 1961 at Delhi, India, the following confessional basis for fellowship was adopted:

> The World Council of Churches is a fellowship of Churches which confess the Lord Jesus Christ as God and Savior according to the Scriptures and therefore seek to fulfil together their common calling to the glory of one God, Father, Son, and Holy Spirit.[26]

Because of its basic theological foundation, the World Council of Churches was comprised largely of "mainline" denominations; it was avoided by conservative and evangelical groups, particularly because of its liberal orientation and its deference to Eastern Bloc churches controlled and directed by Communism. But the latter were not prepared to remain in isolation. In the 1940s American evangelicals established the National Association of Evangelicals and, in 1951 at the global level, the World Evangelical Fellowship. Especially popular in late years have been global emphases on evangelization and missions. In 1966 the World Congress on Evangelism met in West Berlin, followed by the Congress on World Evangelization at Lausanne in 1974 (under the honorary chairmanship of Billy Graham). Lausanne II was convened in 1989 in Manila, with some 3,500

403

delegates from 186 nations; here, strategies were sought for evangelizing the whole earth. "But the emphasis [was] on cooperation for a worldwide task rather than achieving a recognizable Christian unity."[27]

Nor were the fundamentalists idle. Also in the 1940s, a Presbyterian fundamentalist, Carl McIntyre, organized the American Council of Christian Churches and then the International Council of Christian Churches in opposition to the World Council of Churches.

Roman Catholics became open to ecumenism with the advent of the Second Vatican Council under the aegis of Pope John XXIII. The council concluded that non-Roman Catholic Christians were no longer heretics condemned to hell, but rather "separated brethren." As a result of the council's deliberations, in late 1965 Rome and Constantinople mutually repealed the excommunication and anathemas which had separated Roman Catholics and Eastern Orthodox for almost a millennium. The Roman Church also established a special office to foster relationships with other denominations.

Conclusions

While efforts have been made to achieve some type of global Christian unity, it is evident that little progress has been made. Instead of grouping along denominational lines, associations have been formed along theological lines. The old divisions remain: the gulf between liberals and conservatives is as wide as ever. There is even a broad chasm separating evangelicals and fundamentalists. Organic union and close cooperation continue to be elusive. There appears little hope in the foreseeable future of achieving either on a massive scale.

SOME OBSERVATIONS AND SUGGESTIONS

Even a cursory glance at the current state of the church makes it painfully clear that the church is fraught with disunity. While some grouping of denominations has taken place, organic union and close cooperation at meaningful levels among a majority of churches has not occurred. There are simply too many barriers.

Barriers to Achieving Unity

A major barrier to full ecumenicity is theological. Such a conclusion should not surprise us; for theological disagreement has often separated Christians. Modern church history has demonstrated that evangelicals (and fundamentalists, as well) reject cooperation with any denominations or groups which do not hold to certain fundamental doctrines such as the all-sufficiency of Scripture in matters of faith and practice, the deity and lordship of Jesus Christ, His atoning death and bodily resurrection as the only ground for human salvation, and justification by faith. Ecumenism tends to pander to the lowest common factor, and many of the above essentials are jettisoned. Consequently, evangelicals feel that they cannot cooperate with those who do not share their high doctrinal standards.[28]

Nor do most conservatives believe that the ecumenical movement is effective in the task of evangelizing the world. The United Church of Canada is a prime example of this failure. It has been characterized by an increasingly liberal tendency which rejects orthodox Christian doctrine and radicalized biblical interpretation, a trend which has driven off large numbers of conservative members (as in its "New Curriculum" of the 1960s, and its open acceptance of homosexuality in the late 1980s) and left it with a steadily declining membership.

Suggestions for Unity

Christians have an obligation, in view of Christ's desire for the unity of the church, to accept that all who love Christ in sincerity and truth are members of His body and so are brothers and sisters. They therefore must do what they can to cooperate with and love their fellows in Christ. C.S. Lewis, in writing about church unity, quoted Athanasius on the need for purity of faith and emphasized that those who have not kept the faith—having once received and understood it—are apostates and deserters, and should not be included in such concerns for oneness. "They are a warning against the curious assumption that all changes of belief, however brought about, are necessarily exempt from blame."[29] But they are not within our purview either; we are talking here about orthodox Christian groups.

Unity does not necessitate union or even uniformity. All human beings differ, having differing feelings, differing ways of expressing ourselves, and differing emphases. These differences emerge very early in the New Testament accounts of the life of the church.

In spite of these differences, however, there is only one church of Jesus Christ, and that church should present a united front to the world at large. This occurs by cooperating where possible and by zealously avoiding a spirit of competition with one another. An excellent example of such cooperation may be seen in the Evangelical Free Church, which has sent missionaries to the Canadian Arctic to work with Inuit people on Baffin Island in support of the Anglican Church there (and not to establish Free Churches!). Another example is the Anglican Church in Singapore, which supports Assemblies of God churches in the Philippines. This is the sort of cooperative spirit that confounds the world and draws people to Christ.

Another very hopeful sign of the cooperative spirit may be seen in the statement of March 29, 1994: "Evangelicals and Catholics Together: The Christian Mission in the Third Millennium" (ECT). The result of a conference hosted jointly by evangelical activist Charles Colson and Roman Catholic social critic Richard John Neuhaus, this twenty-five page document was signed by forty noted evangelical and Catholic leaders. It suggested cooperation between these two groups on social and cultural issues where both have common goals (such as the fight against abortion). It also emphasized a mutual loyalty to the Apostles' Creed, world evangelism, justification by grace through faith in Christ, and it advocated dialogue over doctrinal differences.[30] While this event has met with some opposition from some conservative evangelicals and from fundamentalists, it is certainly a step in the right direction. One must agree with Charles Colson, who asserted, "If we are to reverse the surging tides of apostasy in Western culture and resist the advancing forces of secularism, then it is absolutely vital that those of us who share conservative, biblically-based views stand together, that we make common cause."[31]

Certainly, the body of Christ should not associate with those who gather in the name of Christ but who are unfaithful to Christ or which are in an apostate condition. But we must make sure that they are truly in such a state. Separation must be based only on genuine biblical teaching and not on fancied shortcomings, cultural observations, or imagined sins. And these problems must be major doctrinal infractions; for example, refusing to cooperate with another group because it has a different eschatological view is sinful behavior, if that is the only reason.

We have a right to disagree with others on the matter of biblical interpretation—but so do others have the right to disagree with us! But such disagreements within the body of Christ must be carried on in love. Insofar as is possible, Christians should major on majors and minor on minors, maximizing agreement and minimizing disagreement. And each church ought always to pray for other churches and seek God's blessing for them. Only in such a spirit can believers promote the unity of the Spirit of Christ.

PART 4

A Practical Theology
of the Church

A Practical Theology
of the Church

As we conclude our theology of the church, the appropriate question to ask is how we may apply the information we have garnered. In other words, how may we practically use what we have learned so that we may better be the church? A number of different vistas present themselves.

BEING THE BODY OF CHRIST

We have observed that one of the most profound—and popular—images of the church is that of the body of Christ. Paul tells us in his epistles that Christ is the head of His body the church (Eph. 5:23; Col. 1:18; cf. Rom. 12:5; 1 Cor. 12:27). Consequently, the church as a body of believers is in Christ, and He is in each member.

Just as Christ came to earth in His physical body to seek and save human beings, so the church as His body exists to carry on His work and ministry to that same end. And just as Christ's first priority was to disciple men and women, so the church's priority must be to disciple people to become mature Christian believers, equipped to live out their faith in every arena of life.[1]

Breaking Down the Barriers

A study of the New Testament church reveals that its outstanding characteristic was its unity. Regardless of their social, economic, racial, or gender standing, all members were equal. Paul expressed it aptly: "There is neither Jew nor Greek, slave nor free, male nor female, for you are all one in Christ Jesus" (Gal. 3:28). Langdon Gilkey exclaims: "What an amazing picture of the church is presented to us through this apostolic symbol of the People of God: the recreation of human community around Christ into a community of love!"[2]

Unfortunately, the church has not maintained this loving harmony, at least in Western society. It is true that many fellowships are very closely knit groups, but only with their own kind of people. Middle class, white collar Christians do not, for the most part, associate lovingly with lower class, "blue collar" people. Like tends to attract like.

If the church is to be the true people of God, if it is to fulfill the Great Commission with effectiveness, then it must regain the New Testament *koinonia* which knows nothing of social, racial, or gender barriers. Only in such a fashion can it become a community of love.[3]

Church leadership must take the initiative—by modeling in their own lives, through preaching, and through exhortation—to open their local churches to all who would come. They must also go even further and act in love toward all church members, accepting and treating everyone alike.

Ministry to the Poor

Both the Old and New Testaments emphasize God's concern for the poor. The former continually points to the Lord's care for the poor, the widow, the orphan, and the oppressed. Jesus declared that He came specifically to preach the Gospel to the poor. He frequently showed partiality to the poor (cf. Matt. 19:21; Luke 12:33; 14:12-14).

As Christ's body on earth, the church must engage in extensive ministry to the poor. And we should be ashamed when we confess—as we must—that this is an area in which evangelical churches have failed miserably. Howard Snyder notes that it is not that they "do not have poor or working-class people in them; of course, many of them do. The point is that there is an almost total lack of awareness of the church's responsibility to *seek out* the poor, to plan for church growth among the poor, rather than to treat them primarily as a social problem."[4]

412

Obviously, the church must engage in a holistic program of evangelizing the poor. This will involve caring for the poor (and the lost and the oppressed), giving them physical and spiritual food, help in finding decent living conditions, and genuine fellowship.[5]

A Kingdom of Priests

Being the body of Christ calls up another image, namely, that believers are called to be a kingdom of priests (1 Peter 2:9). They are called to redemptive mission in the world. They are called to be channels of God's blessing to a fallen and needy society. Findley Edge explains how this comes about.

> There is . . . a basic difference in the priesthood of the Old Testament and the priesthood of the New Testament. In the Old Testament the priest offered the sacrifice. In the New Testament the priest *is* the sacrifice! He offers his life to God in behalf of the world which God is seeking to redeem.[6]

This call to redemptive mission is to every believer and is a ministry which extends beyond the church building and into the marketplace. Churches must move their members out of the "spiritual ghetto" into stores, factories, offices, and homes. They must be trained and exhorted to practice their Christian faith wherever they happen to find themselves.

Such an emphasis is not a new one. For several decades Christian leaders have been calling for the church to get out in mission. Many books have been written as to how to go about doing so. In 1971, Findley Edge wrote *The Greening of the Church*, in which he discussed how a mission group may be formed and energized in reaching out to the world.[7] Gordon Cosby, former pastor of the Church of the Savior in Washington, D.C., wrote a work, entitled *Handbook for Mission Groups*,[8] on how mission was activated in his church. In 1979, Jerry Cook, a pastor at East Hill (Foursquare) Church in Gresham, Oregon, wrote *Love, Acceptance and Forgiveness*,[9] in which he suggested how the church must learn to love people without condition, accept them totally, and assure them of forgiveness when sought. Shortly after, Frank Tillapaugh, then pastor of Bear Valley Baptist

413

Church in Denver, wrote the first of a number of works, *Unleashing the Church*,[10] which described how a church can free its members to move beyond the "fortress church" and into the community with the love and healing of Christ.

Making Disciples

As we have already said, the major priority of the church must be to make disciples. It is not enough to evangelize. Charles Colson rightly comments:

> Though the church must be passionate in its duty to introduce people to Jesus Christ (who came into the world to save the lost), that is only the beginning, only a part of God's commission to us. Evangelism must be fully integrated with discipleship in order for the church to be truly obedient to Scripture.[11]

Certainly, evangelism is essential to the work of the church, but it is only the beginning of conformity to the likeness and image of Jesus Christ. Discipleship is the necessary process to that end.

Training in the Word. Peter tells believers that they should always be prepared to give a reason for the hope they possess (1 Peter 3:15). Disciples must be taught the foundations of biblical and theological truth. Gilkey, however, despairs over the average Christian's knowledge in this area: "The Bible has become a strange and little-used book; the family religion of Scripture readings and prayers has abdicated in favor of what the church can provide on Sunday."[12] And he warns that, if the laity ceases to know the Word, "then Protestantism in its historical form is surely dying or already dead."[13]

Almost three decades ago, Elton Trueblood suggested an answer to the problem: "The congregation must, accordingly, be reconstructed into the pattern of a small theological seminary with the pastor as the professor."[14] While teaching all the members all the necessary things they need to learn is beyond the ability of a single professional, the pastor—as equipper—can take the lead in providing educational opportunities for training believers.

At the elementary level, most churches do a reasonable job with Sunday School and Bible study. There are, however, many parachurch organizations which provide educational and discipling materials at a more advanced level. And few churches are so far removed from seminaries and/or Christian colleges that they cannot take advantage of, or arrange for, continuing education opportunities. Some believers might even wish to take formal ministry training.

Marriage and Family Training. Because the family is the essential building block of society, and because of an ever increasing attack on the institutions of marriage and family, an important part of the discipling process must be a strong emphasis on healthy marriages and families.

Because sex education rightly is the task of parents, the church must train them to explain the basics naturally and frankly to their children. In cooperation with parents, the church must inculcate Christian moral values in children (and, further, in all ages of people). Counseling young people on relationships with the opposite sex should begin early in adolescence, long before marriage. The virtues of chastity should be extolled. As the age for marriage approaches, those couples who are dating steadily should undergo counseling and training more focused on marriage. Following marriage, couples should be invited to a "checkup" counseling session or retreat after nine months, two years, and five years.

Family life education should also be an integral part of discipling. Parents need help in training up children in the way, the nurture, and the admonition of the Lord. Colson observes that "part of that training means equipping parents to be discerning in educational issues. Vigilance is the essential watchword for families whose children attend public schools."[15]

Vocational Training. One of John Calvin's strong convictions was that God called believers to serve Him in all vocations, not just in the pastoral ministry. Accordingly, he founded training schools for his church members and established new modes of employment for them. He and many other Reformation leaders had a high view of work and of the virtues of thrift, effort, and honesty.

415

This form of discipleship training by the church seems to have vanished long ago. It needs badly to be reintroduced. As Colson asks, "If the church doesn't teach a healthy work ethic, who will?"[16] Moreover, the church should provide vocational guidance for its members. And in larger churches—or in cooperation with other churches—opportunities for work should be provided or uncovered.

Evangelism Training. Evangelism is the crucial first step in the discipling process: without evangelism there would be no disciples. All believers should be trained in the basics of evangelism; for all are witnesses. Those who are found to have a spiritual gift of evangelism should be given deeper and more involved training. There are many good programs available (such as Evangelism Explosion) which can help people give an attractive and reasoned explanation of their faith to unbelievers.

Other Ministry Training. Churches need to equip their members for other strategic ministries. Colson tells us that

> if we are to reach out to a world of hurting people with complex needs, we need specialized training in a variety of different areas. (Again, keep in mind that a particular church's ministry will vary depending on location, cultural context, and the unique vision and burdens of its members.) Compassion ministries are tough, front-line work, and many churches have developed great programs for training believers to do them well.[17]

Conclusions

Wherever Jesus went in His ministry, He attracted men and women to Himself. If the church is to be His body in truth as well as in name, then it must also attract people to Christ. It does so in a variety of ways.

By demonstrating its unity, the church attracts people to Christ. What is more inviting than a warm fellowship in which every person is loved no matter what and accepted on a par with every other person regardless of social standing, economic class, or gender?

Again, the church can become the body of Christ only as it

emulates His attitude toward the poor and oppressed. It must seek out the needy and minister to them in their distress.

The church is called, furthermore, to be a kingdom of priests, giving itself in sacrificial service to God and to their fellows. It does so by moving beyond the four walls of its building and into the world to make disciples.

Discipling goes beyond simple evangelism (although it includes it) if the church is to be fully obedient to its Master. Believers must be taught to conform in all ways to the image and likeness of Jesus Christ. This occurs in many fashions: through training in the Word, in marriage and family training, in vocational training, and in other ministries.

As the church increasingly imitates Christ in character and selfless service, it will become more completely His body. And every believer will be equipped to serve Him properly.

THE WORK OF THE CHURCH

The local church has certain basic functions which are the same regardless of when and where it is constituted. These include worship, edification, and outreach.[18]

Worship

Nothing is more important for the church than to worship God. Peter told believers that they are to "declare the praises of him who called you out of darkness into his wonderful light" (1 Peter 2:9). The *ecclēsia*, in short, has been "called out" by God to declare His worth (i.e., to worship Him). Revelation depicts all of creation engaged in God's praises (Rev. 4:8-11; 5:12-14). Worship, we find, is an eternal preoccupation for the people of God.

Unfortunately, worship is not something that is well done by the twentieth century church. One gets the idea from many contemporary services that worship items have just been thrown together with very little thought. Surely God deserves more than haphazard glorification!

Orderliness. In discussing worship with the Corinthian church, Paul wrote, "But everything should be done in a fitting and

417

orderly way" (1 Cor. 14:40). The broader context demonstrates that the Corinthian Christians were rather indiscriminate and chaotic in their worship practices. Consequently, Paul found it necessary to upbraid them: "For God is not a God of disorder but of peace" (1 Cor. 14:33).

Considerable thought and planning need to be put into a worship service. It needs to be structured carefully. No service will seem so spontaneous and smooth flowing as one which has been thoughtfully crafted. Order, after all, is a necessary component of human life; why should it be different in our spiritual life?

Theologically, structured worship is known as liturgy. Charismatic theologian Rodman Williams asserts that

liturgy, to some degree, is invaluable. A printed outline of worship, a book of common prayers, the use of such confessions of faith as the Apostles' Creed and the Nicene Creed—and other traditional forms—help to bring order into the service of worship. Some prescribed forms for such rites as baptism, confirmation, and the Lord's Supper are also helpful. Great hymns of the church have a proper place and should not be neglected. Recall again that Paul speaks of "psalms and hymns" along with "Spirit-inspired songs." Liturgy is important in worshiping the God of order Himself.[19]

Spontaneity. While order is important in worship, it should not be permitted to curtail spontaneity and freedom. Paul reminded believers that "where the Spirit of the Lord is, there is freedom" (2 Cor. 3:17). Thus, if God's Spirit is participating in the service, worship will demonstrate a genuine freedom.

While a service should be ordered, it should be flexible enough to allow for spontaneity in praise, prayer, and thanksgiving. Freedom is particularly important because of the human tendency to lapse into form and ritual. It is vital, therefore, that a service be elastic enough to allow the Holy Spirit to move in worshipers when and as He will.[20]

Full Participation. It is important that believers realize that a worship service is not a time when they are to be entertained. The congregation is not the audience—God is. Everyone is there to worship God, and every person should participate – in such things as singing, prayers, and testimonies. Worship leaders should design services which allow for and encourage maximum congregational participation (in more areas than just singing).

Edification

Williams observes that "the church is not only a worshiping community; it is also a people who are growing in faith and love."[21] Thus, it is vital that members be built up in their Christian faith and life. It is for this very purpose that the Holy Spirit has given special abilities (gifts) to every believer. Sadly, the place and use of the spiritual gifts is a matter of considerable controversy.

Howard Snyder avers that it is the task of the local church

> to expect, identify and awaken the varied gifts that sleep within the community of believers. When all gifts are affirmed under the leadership of the Holy Spirit and in the context of mutual love, each gift is important and no gift becomes an aberration. Whether the Holy Spirit chooses to grant to a particular local congregation all the gifts mentioned in Scripture remains, of course, a divine option. . . . We can be sure, however, that God will give to each local church all the gifts really necessary for its own upbuilding in love.[22]

One effective – and popular – means of utilizing the spiritual gifts for the edification of the body of Christ is the small group. George Webber has described the small group as "a context in which the masks of self-deception and distrust will be maintained only with difficulty and in which men and women will begin to relate to each other at the level of their true humanity in Christ."[23]

Small groups should be structured for service. Areas of mission must be identified and groups should be formed about them. These areas may include study of the Bible, teaching ministries in the local church, music ministries, and so forth. As these groups minister in Jesus' name, exercising their spiritual gifts, the church will be built up.

Outreach

Spiritual giftedness in the context of small groups not only builds up the church but enables it to reach out to non-Christians, fulfilling the Great Commission. For example, one small group might support people who want to witness in their workplace, while another ministers to unwed mothers, and yet another ministers to international students.

Edge suggests that these groups should be formally commissioned by the church and supported in prayer and encouragement (and financially, as well) on a regular basis. Such a commission tells these groups that they are important to the cause of Christ, and it is also "a recognition that though the 'Body' is one, yet when the church is scattered, the various 'parts' (groups) are in the community, each expressing its own particular ministry."[24] He suggests, further, that these outreach missions should be accountable to the church, reporting on a regular basis. In so doing victories may be shared with everyone, and so may difficulties and discouragements. In every instance, the church may help all of those engaged in mission to keep persevering, whether there appear to be tangible results or not.[25]

Conclusions

As the church exercises its necessary functions of worship, edification, and outreach, it is being the body of Christ. It is carrying on the continuing ministry of Christ in this world. It is obediently pursuing the Great Commission. In short, it is exercising its true nature as God created it.

THE UNITY OF THE CHURCH

We have already seen that Scripture holds no aspect of the church to be more important than its unity (see Eph. 4:3-6). We also are well aware that the church as we know it is diverse, fractured, and seemingly many. Fortunately, we realize that the unity of the church is relational rather than organic. But unity in diversity needs some practical suggestions for implementation.

Rex Koivisto declares that we must overcome sectarian attitudes which have invaded us as individuals and have corrupted our thinking.[26] He makes a number of suggestions for transforming our thinking.

First, believers should acquaint themselves with church history.

> It is imperative to understand how diverse and broad the body of Christ really is . . . all Protestants need to realize that there have been, and will continue to be, genuine believers in the Roman Catholic and the Eastern Orthodox confessions. We Protestants may not agree with the biblical legitimacy of their claims, but genuine believers have successfully lived and given their lives for Christ in both of these entities. . . . We simply must know church history, with its warts as well as its beauty spots, recognizing it as the corporate diary of believers, with all their saintly as well as sinful acts.[27]

Familiarity with the history of the church will help Christians to understand the fights that led to the present plurality which exists (and, hopefully, how reconciliation may be attempted!).

Secondly, Christians should learn afresh the history of the church in North America. As we imbibe a keener awareness of denominationalism on this continent, "we can learn the distinctives of denominations different from our own; debate and/or interact with those distinctives, while respecting their right to differ from us; and receive them as family members in the kingdom of God."[28]

Thirdly, believers need to develop a new concept of all the churches within a given community. Koivisto argues that these congregations should be seen as analogous to the house churches which together composed the local city-church of the New Testament era. The leadership of these collective congregations—regardless of their polity or denomination—would comprise the leadership of the church in that community, even if they fail to exercise any oversight beyond their own congregation.[29]

Every effort should be made to encourage the formation of a council of church leaders in the local community, a council which will function effectively. There are many rewards to be

421

gained. It leads believers to strive for unity despite their diversity, to realize that members of other groups in the community are brothers and sisters in Christ no matter what denominational tags they bear. Moreover, such a council would facilitate the complete evangelization of a community, avoiding both duplication of effort and competition. It would also place denominational loyalty in its proper context as secondary to loyalties to the cause of Christ locally. And such a council would allow for the sharing of spiritual giftedness throughout the entire Christian community, rather than each congregation hoarding certain gifts vital to all.[30]

Once a local spirit of cooperation and unity has been achieved, broader efforts may be fostered. A good place to start would be with national networks of evangelicals (in the United States, the National Association of Evangelicals, and in Canada, the Evangelical Fellowship of Canada), and then at the world level (the World Evangelical Fellowship).[31]

Conclusions

The unity of the church must begin with individual believers holding the conviction that Christ desires unity above all else. There must be an open and loving acceptance of believers from other communions, in spite of differences in doctrinal interpretation.

On what is cooperation to be based? Let it begin with the historic basis of unity—the Gospel. Any congregation that truly belongs to the body of Christ will agree on the fundamentals of the good news: its reliability, authority, and recognition of the Person and work of Christ.

Christians who hold a conviction of the need for unity must become aggressively proactive on behalf of their concern, starting by proclaiming the gospel of unity in their own local congregation. Once they have convinced people there, they may make overtures to others.

SOME CONCLUDING OBSERVATIONS

Some of the practical suggestions based on the theology of the church may be seen by some readers as too radical for adoption. But let such dubious souls ask whether the proposals are grounded in Scripture. Does the believer acknowledge the Bible's authority?

While there are many differences between Christian churches and denominations over which we might debate, the most important of all issues is the unity of the church. Nothing so grieves the Savior's heart as schism within His body. It gives His church a bad name before the world. It stifles the evangelistic mission of the church and allows Satan to keep enslaved thousands of souls who might otherwise be won to Christ. Unquestionably, this is a situation our Lord deplores! Do we care enough about His wishes to overcome our prejudices and divisions and seek to heal the wounds of separation that endanger the church's well being? *All God's people* must be one rationally and spiritually if the church is ever to realize the high place God has for it. Our love for Christ demands that we at least make an effort in that direction.

NOTES

Introduction

1. See George Barna, *The Frog in the Kettle, What Christians Need to Know about Life in the Year 2000* (Ventura, Calif.: Regal, 1990), 133–34.

2. Reginald Bibby, *Fragmented Gods: The Poverty and Potential of Religion in Canada* (Toronto: Irwin, 1987), 17.

3. See Barna, *The Frog in the Kettle*, 134 and Arnell Motz, "Who's Growing and Who's Not," in *Reclaiming a Nation: The Challenge of Re-Evangelizing Canada by the Year 2000*, 2nd ed., ed. Arnell Motz (Richmond, B.C.: Church Leadership Library, 1990), 68–70 for respective American and Canadian figures.

4. Motz, *Reclaiming a Nation*, 63–66.

Chapter 1

1. Because the New Testament history of the church will be extensively treated in the section of biblical theology, we shall survey only key elements of that history in this section.

2. F.F. Bruce, *New Testament History* (Garden City, N.Y.: Doubleday/ Anchor, 1972), 216.

3. Christian Frederick Cruse, trans., *The Ecclesiastical History of Eusebius Pamphilius, Bishop of Caesarea, in Palestine* (Grand Rapids: Baker, 1989), 76.

4. Ibid., 75–79.

5. Bruce, *New Testament History*, 391–92.

6. Eusebius, *Ecclesiastical History*, 102–3.

7. Bruce, *New Testament History*, 265.

8. Helmut Koester, *History and Literature of Early Christianity*, vol. 2 of *Introduction to the New Testament* (New York: Walter de Gruyter, 1982), 93. Cf. Raymond E. Brown, *The Community of the Beloved Disciple* (New York: Paulist, 1979), who posits the existence of a separate Johannine Church from a very early period.

9. Eusebius, *Ecclesiastical History*, 100.

10. Those who assume a late date for Revelation place Clement in the same general time period.

11. J.B. Lightfoot and J.R. Harmer, eds., *The Apostolic Fathers*, rev. ed. (London: Macmillan,1891; Grand Rapids: Baker, 1988), 3.

12. Ray C. Petry, ed., *The Early and Medieval Church*, vol. 1 of *A History of Christianity* (Englewood Cliffs, N.J.: Prentice-Hall, 1962; reprint Grand Rapids: Baker, 1981), 4.

13. Clement of Rome, *To the Corinthians*, 1.

14. Ibid., 3.

15. Ibid., 44.

16. Ibid., 64.

17. See Earl D. Radmacher, *The Nature of the Church* (Portland, Ore.: Western Baptist, 1972), 25.

18. Ignatius of Antioch, *Epistle to Ephesians* 4, in *The Ante-Nicene Fathers*, ed. Alexander Roberts and James Donaldson (Grand Rapids: Eerdmans, 1953), 1.50–51.

19. Ibid., 4.

20. Ibid., 6.

21. Ibid., 9.

22. Petry, *The Early and Medieval Church*, 5.

23. Ignatius, *Epistle to the Magnesians* 6, Ante-Nicene Fathers, 1.61.

24. Ignatius, *Epistle to the Smyrnaeans* 8, Ante-Nicene Fathers, 1.89–90.

25. Radmacher, *The Nature of the Church*, 27.

26. Polycarp, *Epistle to the Philippians* 4, Ante-Nicene Fathers, 1.117.

27. Ibid., 5.

28. Ibid., 6.

29. Ibid.

30. Ibid., 11.

31. *Didachē* 7.

32. Ibid., 9.

33. Ibid., 10.

34. Ibid., 11.

35. Ibid.

36. Ibid., 13.

37. Ibid., 14.

38. Ibid., 15.

39. Lightfoot and Harmer, *The Apostolic Fathers*, 293.

40. Hermas, *The Shepherd of Hermas*, vision 3.2, Ante-Nicene Fathers, 2.13.

41. Ibid., 3.5.

42. Ibid., 3.5-6.

43. Hermas, *The Shepherd of Hermas*, mandate 4.3.

44. Ibid.

45. Irenaeus, *Against Heresies* 5.34.1, cited by J.N.D. Kelly, *Early Christian Doctrines*, rev. ed. (San Francisco: Harper and Row, 1978), 192.

46. Irenaeus, *Against Heresies* 3.3.1, in *Understandings of the Church*, trans. and ed. E. Glen Hinson (Philadelphia: Fortress, 1986), 40–41.

47. Irenaeus, *Against Heresies* 4.26.2, in Hinson, *Understandings*, 42.

48. E.H. Klotsche, *The History of Christian Doctrine* (Burlington, Iowa: Lutheran Literary Board, 1945), 103.

49. Ibid.

50. Johannes Quasten, *The Ante-Nicene Literature after Irenaeus*, vol. 2 of *Patrology* (Westminster, Md.: Christian Classics, 1990), 6.

51. Ibid., 24.

52. Clement of Alexandria, *The Instructor* 1.6, *Ante-Nicene Fathers*, 2.216.

53. Clement of Alexandria, *The Stromata*, or *Miscellanies* 7.17, *Ante-Nicene Fathers*, 2.554–55.

54. Ibid.

55. Clement of Alexandria, *The Instructor* 1.6.

56. Quasten, *Patrology*, 2.27.

57. Clement of Alexandria, *The Instructor* 1.6.

58. Ibid.

59. Ibid.

60. Ibid.

61. Justo L. González, *A History of Christian Thought, Volume 1: From the Beginnings to the Council of Chalcedon* (Nashville: Abingdon, 1975), 1.175–77.

62. Tertullian, *Apology* 39.1, cited by Kelly, *Early Christian Doctrines*, 200.

63. Ibid.

64. Ibid.

65. Tertullian, *On Baptism* 1, *Ante-Nicene Fathers*, 3.669.

66. Tertullian, *On Baptism* 17, ibid., 3.677.

67. Kelly, *Early Christian Doctrines*, 209.

68. Ibid.

69. González, *History of Christian Thought: Beginnings*, 1.210–11.

70. Ibid., 213–14.

71. Quasten, *Patrology*, 2.82.

72. Origen, *Against Celsus* 6.48, *Ante-Nicene Fathers*, 4.595.

73. Quasten, *Patrology*, 2.82.

74. Origen, *Against Celsus* 8.72.

75. Origen, *Homilies on Leviticus* 8.3.

76. Origen, *Commentary on Romans* 5.9.

77. Quasten, *Patrology*, 2.82.

78. Origen, *Against Celsus* 8.33.

79. Quasten, *Patrology*, 2.86–87.

80. Ibid., 204–5.

81. Quasten, *Patrology*, 2.374–75.

82. Ibid., 375.

83. Ibid., 376.

84. Kelly, *Early Christian Doctrines*, 206.

85. González, *History of Christian Thought: Beginnings,* 1.251.

86. Cyprian, *Epistles* 63.8, cited by Kelly, *Early Christian Doctrines,* 210.

87. Kelly, *Early Christian Doctrines,* 211.

88. Tertullian, preface to *Ad Fortunatum,* cited by Quasten, *Patrology,* 2.379.

89. Ibid., 2.381.

90. Ibid., 380.

91. Cyprian, *Epistle* 63.14, cited by Kelly, *Early Christian Doctrines,* 215.

92. Kelly, *Early Christian Doctrines,* 215–16.

93. Quasten, *Patrology,* 2.382.

94. Athanasius, *Against Arius* 3.22, cited by Kelly, *Early Christian Doctrines,* 404.

95. Ibid., 3.78–79.

96. Cited by Quasten, *Patrology,* 3.79.

97. Didymus, In *Psalmos* 23.4.

98. Quasten, *Patrology,* 3.97.

99. Ibid.

100. Cyril of Alexandria, *Homilies on 1 Corinthians* 17.21f., as cited by Kelly, *Early Christian Doctrines,* 405.

101. Cyril, *Epistola Dogmatica* 17.11.

102. Bengt Hagglund, *History of Theology,* trans. Gene J. Lund (St. Louis: Concordia, 1968), 91.

103. Quasten, *Patrology,* 3.401–2.

104. Kelly, *Early Christian Doctrines,* 403.

105. Ibid., 420.

106. Ibid., 421.

107. Ibid., 422.

108. Ibid., 422–23.

109. Andrew K. Rule, "Chrysostom, John," *An Encyclopedia of Religion,* ed. Vergilius Ferm (New York: Philosophical Library, 1945), 167–68.

110. Kelly, *Early Christian Doctrines,* 402.

111. Ibid., 430–31.

112. Henry Bettenson, ed. and trans., *The Later Christian Fathers: A Selection from the Writings of the Fathers from St. Cyril of Jerusalem to St. Leo the Great* (Oxford: Oxford Univ. Press, 1970), 173.

113. Ibid., 175.

114. *De sacerdotio* 3.4, in Bettenson, *Later Christian Fathers,* 175–76.

115. Quasten, *Patrology,* 3.479.

116. Bruce A. Demarest, "Jerome," in *Eerdmans' Handbook to the History of Christianity,* ed. Tim Dowley, et al. (Grand Rapids: Eerdmans, 1977), 188.

117. Bettenson, *Later Christian Fathers,* 188.

118. Jerome, *Epistle to Titus* 1.1, 5, in Bettenson, *Later Christian Fathers,* 189.

119. Jerome, *Epistles* 14.8, *Nicene and Post-Nicene Fathers,* 2nd ser.,

ed. Philip Schaff and Henry Wace (Grand Rapids: Eerdmans, 1892), 6.16.

120. Jerome, *Epistles* 14.9, in *Nicene and Post-Nicene Fathers*, 6.17.

121. Jerome, *The Dialogue against the Luciferians* 9, in *Nicene and Post-Nicene Fathers*, 324–25.

122. Ibid., 324.

123. Bettenson, *Later Christian Fathers*, 189.

124. Michael A. Smith, "Ambrose," in *Eerdmans' Handbook to the History of Christianity*, 140.

125. Ambrose, *On the Mysteries* 3.8, *Nicene and Post-Nicene Fathers*, 10.318.

126. Ibid., 4.20, 10.319.

127. Ibid., 3.11, 12, 10.318.

128. Ibid., 6.29, 30, 10.321.

129. Ibid., 9.54, 10.324.

130. David F. Wright, "Augustine of Hippo," in *Eerdmans' Handbook to the History of Christianity*, 198–99.

131. Augustine, *Sermons* 341.12, in Bettenson, *Later Christian Fathers*, 240.

132. Kelly, *Early Christian Doctrines*, 413.

133. Ibid., 414.

134. Ibid., 414–15.

135. Augustine, *Epistles* 49.3, in Bettenson, *Later Christian Fathers*, 240.

136. Klotsche, *History of Christian Doctrine*, 98.

137. For a refutation of this position, see David L. Smith, *With Willful Intent: A Theology of Sin* (Wheaton, Ill.: Victor/BridgePoint, 1994), 358ff.

138. Augustine, *Against Two Letters of the Pelagians* 1.40, in *The Nicene and Post-Nicene Fathers*, ed. Philip Schaff (Grand Rapids: Eerdmans, 1956), 5.390.

139. Ibid., 2.4, 5.238. Cf. Augustine, *On Original Sin* 2.17, 5:242–43.

140. Ibid., 2.11, 5.396.

141. Augustine, *On Baptism, Against the Donatists* 1.1, in *The Nicene and Post-Nicene Fathers*, ed. Philip Schaff (Grand Rapids: Eerdmans, 1956), 4.411–12.

142. Ibid., 1.1, 4.431.

143. Augustine, *Tractate on the Gospel of John* 124.5, cited by Kelly, *Early Christian Doctrines*, 437–38.

144. Augustine, *Enchiridion* 67, cited by Klotsche, *History of Christian Doctrine*, 102.

145. Augustine, *The City of God* 10.5, in Bettenson, *Later Christian Fathers*, 243–44.

146. Ibid., 246.

147. Augustine, *The City of God* 17.20.2, in Kelly, *Early Christian Doctrines*, 454.

148. Ibid., 10.6, 454–55.

149. G.R. Evans, *The Thought of Gregory the Great* (Cambridge: Cambridge Univ. Press, 1986), 4–5.

150. Ibid., 118.

151. Ibid.

152. Ibid., 119.

153. González, *History of Christian Thought: Beginnings*, 1.67–68.

Chapter 2

1. Louis Berkhof, *The History of Christian Doctrines* (London: Banner of Truth, 1969), 227.

2. E.H. Klotsche, *History of Christian Doctrine*, 116.

3. Ibid.

4. Ibid., 116–17.

5. Bernhard Lohse, *A Short History of Christian Doctrine*, trans. F. Ernest Stoeffler (Philadelphia: Fortress, 1966), 141.

6. Ibid., 141–42.

7. William R. Cannon, *History of Christianity in the Middle Ages: From the Fall of Rome to the Fall of Constantinople* (Nashville: Abingdon, 1960), 99.

8. Lohse, *A Short History*, 144.

9. Ibid.

10. Klotsche, *History of Christian Doctrine*, 126.

11. Kenneth S. Latourette, *The Thousand Years of Uncertainty*, vol. 2 of *A History of the Expansion of Christianity* (Grand Rapids: Zondervan, 1966), 412.

12. Nicholas II, "Papal Election Decree," in Petry, *Early and Medieval Church*, 235.

13. Ibid., 235–36.

14. Robert G. Clouse, "Flowering: The Western Church," in *Eerdmans' Handbook to the History of Christianity*, 253.

15. Clyde L. Manschrek, *A History of Christianity in the World: From Persecution to Uncertainty* (Englewood Cliffs, N.J.: Prentice-Hall, 1974), 132.

16. Gregory VII, "The 'Dictates' of the Pope," in Petry, *The Early and Medieval Church*, 236.

17. Staff of the Catholic University of America, *The New Catholic Encyclopedia* (N.Y.: McGraw-Hill, 1967–79), s.v. "Lateran Councils."

18. "(Canon I) The Creed, The Church, The Sacraments, and Transubstantiation," in Petry, *Ancient and Medieval Church*, 322.

19. Ibid., 323.

20. Ibid.

21. "(Canon 21) Confession, Reception of the Eucharist, and Penance," in Petry, *The Early and Medieval Church*, 323.

22. Earle E. Cairns, *Christianity through the Centuries: A History of the Christian Church*, rev. ed. (Grand Rapids: Zondervan/Academie, 1981), 231.

23. Reinhold Seeburg, *The History of Doctrines*, trans. Charles E. Hay (Grand Rapids: Baker, 1977), 2.86.

24. Ibid., 2.87.
25. Hugo of Saint Victor, *On the Sacraments* 1.9.2, cited by Seeburg, ibid., 80.
26. Ibid.
27. Cairns, *Christianity through the Centuries*, 237–38.
28. Thomas Gilby, *St. Thomas Aquinas: Theological Texts* (London: Oxford Univ. Press, 1955), 337–38, cited by Glenn O. Hilburn, "Medieval Views of the Church," in *The People of God: Essays on the Believers' Church*, ed. Paul Basden and David S. Dockery (Nashville: Broadman, 1991), 202.
29. Ibid.
30. Ibid., 203.
31. Walter Farrell, *A Companion to the Summa* (New York: Sheed and Ward, 1947), 4.302.
32. Ibid., 4.307.
33. Ibid., 4.276.
34. Ibid., 4.278.
35. Ibid.
36. Ibid., 4.290.
37. H.D. McDonald, "William of Ockham," in *Eerdmans' Handbook to the History of Christianity*, 341.
38. Seeburg, *The History of Doctrines*, 2.192.
39. William of Ockham, *De Imperatorum et Pontificum Potestate 1-2*, in Petry, *Early and Medieval Church*, 513–15.
40. Ibid., 515.
41. Ibid., 516.
42. Klotsche, *History of Christian Doctrine*, 151.
43. Seeburg, *History of Doctrines*, 2.192.
44. Klotsche, *History of Christian Doctrine*, 147.
45. Cairns, *Christianity through the Centuries*, 259.
46. Tim Dowley, "John Wycliffe," in *Eerdmans' Handbook to the History of Christianity*, 338.
47. John Wycliffe, *The Church and Her Members, 1*, in Petry, *Early and Medieval Church*, 519–20.
48. Ibid., 520.
49. Ibid.
50. Ibid.
51. Ibid., 521.
52. Klotsche, *History of Christian Doctrine*, 161.
53. Caroline T. Marshall, "Jan Hus," in *Eerdmans' Handbook to the History of Christianity*, 330.
54. Ibid.
55. Klotsche, *History of Christian Doctrine*, 161–62.
56. Jan Hus, *On Simony, 4*, in Petry, *Early and Medieval Church*, 531.
57. Ibid., 532.
58. John P. Dolan, ed. and trans., *The Essential Erasmus* (New York: Mentor-Omega, 1964), 207.

59. Erasmus, *An Inquiry Concerning the Faith*, in Dolan, *Essential Erasmus*, 218.
60. Ibid.
61. Ibid.
62. Erasmus, *On Mending the Peace of the Church*, in Dolan, *Essential Erasmus*, 362.
63. Ibid.
64. Ibid., 386.

Chapter 3

1. James Atkinson, "Reform," in *Eerdmans' Handbook to the History of Christianity* (Grand Rapids: Eerdmans, 1977), 360–61.
2. Martin Luther, "On the Papacy in Rome Against the Most Celebrated Romanist in Leipzig," trans. Eric W. and Ruth C. Gritsch, in *Church and Ministry 1*, ed. Eric W. Gritsch, vol. 39 of Luther's Works, ed. Helmut T. Lehmann (Philadelphia: Fortress, 1970), 71.
3. Ibid., 101.
4. Martin Luther, "Answer to the Hyperchristian, Hyperspiritual, and Hyperlearned Book by Goat Emser in Leipzig—Including Some Thoughts Regarding His Companion, the Fool Murner," trans. Eric W. and Ruth C. Gritsch, in *Church and Ministry 1*, 209.
5. Luther, "On the Papacy in Rome," 65.
6. Altman K. Swihart, *Luther and the Lutheran Church, 1483-1960* (New York: Philosophical Library, 1960), 131.
7. Ibid.
8. Martin Luther, "On the Councils and the Church," trans. Charles M. Jacobs, in *Church and Ministry III*, ed. Eric W. Gritsch, vol. 41 of Luther's Works, 145.
9. Martin Luther, *Werke*, Br. 9608, n. 3709 cited by Swihart, *Martin Luther and the Lutheran Church*, 132.
10. Ibid.
11. Ibid., 135.
12. Seeburg, *The History of Doctrines*, 2.293–94.
13. Martin Luther, "That a Christian Assembly or Congregation Has the Right and Power to Judge All Teaching and to Call, Appoint, and Dismiss Teachers, Established and Proved by Scripture," trans. Eric W. and Ruth C. Gritsch, in *Church and Ministry 1*, 312.
14. Swihart, *Martin Luther and the Lutheran Church*, 138.
15. Seeburg, *The History of Doctrines*, 2.280–81.
16. Ibid., 283.
17. Martin Luther, "The Holy and Blessed Sacrament of Baptism," trans. Charles M. Jacobs, in *Word and Sacrament 1*, ed. E. Theodore Bachman, vol. 35 of Luther's *Works*, 29.
18. Ibid., 30.
19. Ibid., 31.
20. Ibid., 32–33.

21. Ibid., 35.

22. Ibid., 37.

23. Martin Luther, "The Blessed Sacrament of the Holy and True Body of Christ, and the Brotherhoods," in *Word and Sacrament 1*, 49–50.

24. Martin Luther, "The Babylonian Captivity of the Church," trans. A.T.W. Steinhauser, in *Word and Sacrament III*, ed. Abdel Ross Wentz, vol. 36 of Luther's *Works*, 23.

25. Luther, "The Blessed Sacrament of the Body of Christ," 51.

26. Ibid., 59–60.

27. Martin Luther, "That These Words of Christ, 'This Is My Body,' etc., Still Stand Firm Against the Fanatics," trans. Robert H. Fischer, in *Word and Sacrament III*, ed. Robert H. Fischer, vol. 37 of Luther's *Works*, 28–29.

28. Seeburg, *The History of Doctrines*, 2.287.

29. Many historians have pointed out that Luther's pilgrimage was, in turn, strongly influenced by the mystics of previous centuries (such as Thomas á Kempis, Meister Eckhart, and Johann Tauler), for Luther tended toward mysticism and the life of devotion they had preached.

30. R. Stupperich, "Philip Melancthon," in *Eerdmans' Handbook to the History of Christianity*, 376.

31. Philip Melancthon, "The Augsburg Confession," in *Creeds of the Churches: A Reader in Christian Doctrine, from the Bible to the Present*, 7, rev. ed., ed. John H. Leith (Richmond, Va.: John Knox, 1973), 70.

32. Seeburg, *History of Doctrines*, 340.

33. Melancthon, "The Augsburg Confession 28," in Leith, *Creeds of the Churches*, 99–100.

34. Melancthon, "The Augsburg Confession 9," in Leith, *Creeds of the Churches*, 71.

35. Melancthon, "The Augsburg Confession 10," in Leith, *Creeds of the Churches*.

36. Melancthon, "The Augsburg Confession 24," in Leith, *Creeds of the Churches*, 86.

37. Seeburg, *History of Christian Doctrines*, 350.

38. St. Amant, "Reformation Views of the Church," in Basden and Dockery, *The People of God*, 211.

39. Ibid., 211–12.

40. Seeburg, *The History of Doctrines*, 363.

41. Timothy George, *Theology of the Reformers* (Nashville: Broadman, 1988), 110.

42. Robert V. Schnucker, "Huldreich Zwingli," in *Eerdmans' Handbook to the History of Christianity*, 379.

43. Ibid.

44. Ibid.

45. Seeburg, *History of Doctrines*, 2.315.

46. Ulrich Zwingli, *An Account of the Faith*, in *Great Voices of the Reformation*, ed. Harry Emerson Fosdick (New York: Random House, 1952), 186.

433

47. George, *Theology of the Reformers*, 136.

48. Ulrich Zwingli, *On True and False Religion*, in *Great Voices of the Reformation*, 165.

49. Zwingli, *An Account of the Faith*, in *Great Voices of the Reformation*, 188.

50. George, *Theology of the Reformers*, 138.

51. Ibid., 139–40.

52. Ibid., 140–42.

53. Ibid., 143–44.

54. Klotsche, *The History of Christian Doctrine*, 190–91.

55. Zwingli, *An Account of the Faith*, in *Great Voices of the Reformation*, 187.

56. John Calvin, *Institutes of the Christian Religion* 4.1.7, trans. Ford L. Battles, ed. John T. McNeill, vol. 21 of The Library of Christian Classics (Philadelphia: Westminster, 1960), 1021.

57. Ibid., 1014.

58. Ibid., 1021–22.

59. Ibid., 1025.

60. Ibid., 1026.

61. Ibid., 1055.

62. Ibid.

63. Ibid., 1056.

64. Ibid., 1061.

65. Ibid.

66. Ibid., 1066.

67. Ibid., 1066–67.

68. Ibid., 1161.

69. Ibid., 1229.

70. Ibid., 1238.

71. Ibid., 1248.

72. Ibid., 1277.

73. Ibid., 1303.

74. Ibid., 1305.

75. Ibid., 1307.

76. Ibid., 1307–8.

77. Ibid., 1320.

78. Ibid., 1323.

79. Ibid., 1326–28.

80. Ibid., 1341.

81. Ibid., 1343.

82. Ibid., 1343–44.

83. Ibid., 1360.

84. Ibid., 1371.

85. Ibid.

86. Klotsche, *History of Christian Doctrine*, 243.

87. Kenneth R. Davis, *Anabaptism and Asceticism: A Study in Intellectual Origins* (Scottdale, Pa.: Herald, 1974), 67–69.

88. Ibid.
89. Ibid., 211.
90. Michael Sattler, "Brotherly Union of a Number of Children of God Concerning Seven Articles," in *The Legacy of Michael Sattler*, trans. and ed. John H. Yoder (Scottdale, Pa.: Herald, 1973), 38.
91. George H. Williams, *The Radical Reformation* (Philadelphia: Westminster, 1962), 183–84.
92. Ibid.
93. Ibid., 36.
94. "The Beginnings of the Anabaptist Reformation: Reminiscenses of George Blaurock," in *Spiritual and Anabaptist Writers: Documents Illustrative of the Radical Reformation*, ed. George H. Williams and Angel M. Mergal, vol. 25 of The Library of Christian Classics (Philadelphia: Westminster, 1957), 42–44.
95. Conrad Grebel, "Letter to Thomas Müntzer," in *Spiritual and Anabaptist Writers*, 80.
96. Ibid., 81.
97. Melchior Hofmann, "The Ordinance of God," in *Spiritual and Anabaptist Writers*, 193.
98. Sattler, "Brotherly Union," 37.
99. Grebel, "Letter to Thomas Müntzer," 76–77.
100. Sattler, "Brotherly Union," 39.
101. Ibid.
102. Ibid., 37.
103. William Klassen and Walter Klassen, ed. and trans., *The Writings of Pilgram Marpeck* (Kitchener, Ont.: Herald, 1978), 34–41.
104. Pilgram Marpeck, "The Children of Christ and of Hagar," in Klassen and Klassen, *Writings of Pilgram Marpeck*, 394.
105. Pilgram Marpeck, "To Helena von Streichen (ca. 1544)," in Klassen and Klassen, *Writings of Pilgram Marpeck*, 385–86.
106. Pilgram Marpeck, "The Admonition of 542," in Klassen and Klassen, *Writings of Pilgram Marpeck*, 299.
107. Ibid., 169.
108. Ibid., 170–71.
109. Ibid., 172.
110. Ibid., 187.
111. Ibid.
112. Ibid., 204.
113. Ibid., 206.
114. Ibid., 239.
115. Ibid., 243.
116. Ibid., 261.
117. Ibid., 263.
118. Ibid.
119. Ibid., 266–67.
120. Ibid., 283–84.
121. Ibid., 291.

122. Pilgram Marpeck, "Judgment and Decision," in Klassen and Klassen, *Writings of Pilgram Marpeck*, 331.

123. Ibid., 361.

124. Pilgram Marpeck, "Another Letter to the Swiss Brethren (1543)," in Klassen and Klassen, *Writings of Pilgram Marpeck*, 367.

125. George, *Theology of the Reformers*, 258.

126. Ibid., 260–61.

127. Ibid., 262.

128. Menno Simons, "Reply to Gellius Faber," in *The Complete Writings of Menno Simons*, trans. Leonard Verduin, ed. Harold S. Bender (Scottdale, Pa.: Herald, 1956), 734.

129. Ibid., 735.

130. Ibid.

131. Ibid., 739–43.

132. Ibid., 747.

133. Menno Simons, "Christian Baptism," in *Writings*, 235.

134. Menno Simons, "The New Birth," in *Writings*, 90–91.

135. Simons, "Christian Baptism," 244.

136. Ibid., 245.

137. Menno Simons, "Foundation of Christian Doctrine," in *Writings*, 123.

138. Ibid., 139.

139. Simons, "Christian Baptism," 249.

140. Ibid.

141. Ibid., 281.

142. Simons, "Foundation of Christian Doctrine," 142–43.

143. Ibid., 143.

144. Ibid., 143–44.

145. Ibid., 145.

146. Ibid., 146–47.

147. Menno Simons, "Instruction on Excommunication," in *Writings*, 969.

148. Ibid., 971.

149. Menno Simons, "Reply to Sylis and Lemke," in *Writings*, 1006.

150. Ibid., 971.

151. Simons, "Foundation of Christian Doctrine," 160.

152. Ibid., 161.

153. Ibid., 170.

154. Ibid., 172.

155. Ibid., 173.

156. Ibid., 176.

157. James Atkinson, "Thomas Cranmer," in *Eerdmans' Handbook to the History of Christianity*, 390.

158. Thomas Cranmer, "Speeches" 1, in *The Works of Thomas Cranmer*, ed. G.E. Duffield (Appleford, U.K.: Sutton Courtenay, 1965), 2.13.

159. Ibid., 14–15.

160. Cranmer, "Speeches" 3, *Works*, 2.21.

161. Cranmer, "Questions and Answers" 9, in *Works*, 2.27.

162. Ibid.

163. Ibid., 11, 28–29.

164. Ibid., 12, 29.

165. Ibid., 16, 29.

166. Ibid., 1f, 25.

167. Ibid., 4f, 26.

168. Ibid., 7, 26–27.

169. Thomas Cranmer, "A Defence of the True and Catholic Doctrine of the Sacrament of the Body and Blood of Our Saviour Christ," 1.4, in *Works*, 2.63.

170. Ibid., 1.5, 64.

171. Ibid., 1.6, 65.

172. Ibid., 5.3, 217.

173. Ibid., 5.16, 229.

174. Cairns, *Christianity through the Centuries*, 335.

175. Ibid., 336.

176. Ibid., 337.

177. Ibid., 360.

178. Klotsche, *History of Christian Doctrine*, 280.

179. John Briggs, "The English Baptists," in *Eerdmans' Handbook to the History of Christianity*, 394.

180. William H. Brackney, ed., *Baptist Life and Thought: 1600-1980*, A Source Book (Valley Forge, Pa.: Judson, 1983), 28.

181. "A Declaration of Faith of English People Remaining at Amsterdam in Holland" 10, in *Baptist Confessions of Faith*, ed. William L. Lumpkin (Philadelphia: Judson, 1959), 119.

182. Ibid., 120.

183. "The Confession of Faith of Those Churches Which Are Commonly (Though Falsely) Called Anabaptist" 47, in *Baptist Confessions of Faith*, 168–69.

184. "A Declaration of Faith," 20–21, 121–22.

185. "The Confession of Faith," 36–38, 166–67.

186. "A Declaration of Faith," 13–14, 120.

187. "The Confession of Faith," 40, 167.

188. "A Declaration of Faith," 15, 120.

189. St. Amant, "Reformation Views of the Church," in Basden and Dockery, *The People of God*, 221–22.

Chapter 4

1. Justo L. González, *History of Christian Thought, Volume 3: From the Protestant Reformation to the Twentieth Century* (Nashville: Abingdon, 1975), 3.374–75.

2. Timothy Ware, *The Orthodox Church* (Baltimore: Penguin, 1963), 103–4.

3. Ibid., 105.

4. Ibid., 106.

5. Herbery Cunliffe-Jones, *Christian Theology Since 1600* (London: Gerald Duckworth, 1970), 8–9.

6. Ibid., 3.

7. Ibid.

8. Ware, *Orthodox Church*, 107.

9. Ibid.

10. Cunliffe-Jones, *Christian Theology Since 1600*, 4.

11. Ibid., 74.

12. Ware, *Orthodox Church*, 136.

13. Alexei Khomiakov, *The Church Is One*, 9, as quoted by Ware, *Orthodox Church*, 243.

14. Ibid., 247.

15. Ibid.

16. Ware, *Orthodox Church*, 254.

17. Cunliffe-Jones, *Christian Theology Since 1600*, 74.

18. Ibid., 74–75.

19. González, *History of Christian Thought: Reformation*, 3.351.

20. Ibid., 3.352–53.

21. Ibid., 3.355–56.

22. Ibid., 3.358.

23. Ibid., 3.358–59.

24. Ibid., 3.359.

25. William J. Bausch, *Pilgrim Church: A Popular History of Catholic Christianity* (Mystic, Conn.: Twenty-third, 1981), 416–17.

26. Ibid., 428–29.

27. Ibid., 430.

28. Ibid., 436.

29. González, *History of Christian Thought: Reformation*, 3.362.

30. Cunliffe-Jones, *Christian Theology Since 1600*, 84.

31. González, *History of Christian Thought: Reformation*, 3.364.

32. John Henry Newman, *Via Media of the Anglican Church*, in Clyde L. Manschrek, ed., *The Church from the Reformation to the Present*, vol. 2 of *A History of Christianity* (Grand Rapids: Baker, 1964), 350.

33. John Henry Newman, *Difficulties of Anglicans*, as cited by Cunliffe-Jones, *Christian Theology Since 1600*, 81–82.

34. Ibid., 82.

35. T. Canby Jones, "A Believing People: Contemporary Relevance," in *The Concept of the Believers' Church*, ed. James Leo Garrett, Jr. (Scottdale, Pa.: Herald, 1969), 75.

36. Barbour and Roberts, *The Quaker Writings 1650–1700* (Grand Rapids, Eerdmans, 1973), 33.

37. Ibid., 37–40.

38. Robert Barclay, "Catechism and Confession of Faith" in *Early Quaker Writings 1650–1700*, 333.

39. Ibid., 334–37.

40. George Fox and James Naler, "Saul's Errand to Damascus," in

Early Quaker Writings 1650-1700, 258.

41. Ibid.

42. Ibid.

43. Jones, "A Believing People," 78.

44. Dale W. Brown, *Understanding Pietism* (Grand Rapids: Eerdmans, 1978), 21–23.

45. González, *History of Christian Thought: Reformation*, 3.275.

46. Ibid., 3.276.

47. Brown, *Understanding Pietism*, 38–39.

48. Ibid., 45–46.

49. Philipp Spener, *Wenn du Kånntest Glauben*, 75–76, as quoted by Brown, *Understanding Pietism*, 46.

50. Ibid., 49.

51. Ibid., 50–51.

52. Philipp Spener, *Pia Desideria*, 47, as quoted by Brown, *Understanding Pietism*, 55.

53. Brown, *Understanding Pietism*, 55.

54. Ibid., 58.

55. Ibid., 59–60.

56. Ibid., 60.

57. A. Skevington Wood, "Awakening," in *Eerdmans' Handbook to the History of Christianity*, 444–45.

58. González, *History of Christian Thought: Reformation*, 3.280.

59. Ibid., 3.286–87.

60. Cunliffe-Jones, *Christian Theology Since 1600*, 72.

61. Rudolf Otto, Introduction to Friedrich Schleiermacher, *On Religion: Speeches to Its Cultured Despisers*, trans. John Oman (New York: Harper, 1958), ix.

62. Friedrich Schleiermacher, *The Christian Faith*, ed. H.R. Mackintosh and J.S. Stewart (Edinburgh: T and T Clark, 1968), 3.

63. Ibid., 5.

64. Ibid., 68.

65. Ibid., 526.

66. Ibid., 533.

67. Ibid., 677.

68. Ibid., 678.

69. Ibid., 682.

70. Ibid., 690–91.

71. Ibid.

72. Ibid., 624.

73. Ibid., 635.

74. Ibid., 636.

75. Ibid., 638.

76. Ibid., 638–39.

77. Ibid., 641.

78. Ibid.

79. Ibid., 649.

80. Ibid., 651.
81. Ibid., 652.

Chapter 5

1. For a simple overview of neo-orthodoxy and its prime movers, see David L. Smith, *A Handbook of Contemporary Theology* (Wheaton, Ill.: Victor/BridgePoint, 1992).

2. Emil Brunner, *The Misunderstanding of the Church*, trans. Harold Knight (Philadelphia: Westminster, 1952), 9.

3. Ibid., 11.

4. Ibid., 12.

5. Emil Brunner, *The Christian Doctrine of the Church, Faith, and the Consummation*, vol. 3 of *Dogmatics* (Philadelphia: Westminster, 1962), 21–22.

6. Brunner, *Misunderstanding of the Church*, 17.

7. Brunner, *Christian Doctrine of the Church, Faith, and the Consummation*, 3.29.

8. Brunner, *Misunderstanding of the Church*, 117.

9. Emil Brunner, *The Word of God and Modern Man*, trans. David Cairns (Richmond, Va.: John Knox, 1964), 80.

10. Brunner, *Dogmatics*, 3.53.

11. Brunner, *Word of God and Modern Man*, 80.

12. Brunner, *Dogmatics*, 3.57.

13. Ibid.

14. Ibid., 3.62.

15. Ibid., 3.61.

16. Brunner, *Word of God and Modern Man*, 81.

17. Ibid., 82.

18. Brunner, *Misunderstanding of the Church*, 50.

19. Ibid., 51.

20. For further information on Pentecostalism, see Smith, *Handbook of Contemporary Theology*, 41–57.

21. Matthew S. Clark, Henry I. Lederle, et al., *What Is Distinctive about Pentecostal Theology?* (Pretoria: Univ. of South Africa, 1989), 67.

22. Ibid.

23. Walter J. Hollenweger, *The Pentecostals*, trans. R.A. Wilson (Peabody, Mass.: Hendrickson, 1972), 430.

24. Ibid. Some Pentecostal groups have even joined the World Council of Churches.

25. Clark and Lederle, *Pentecostal Theology*, 76.

26. Ibid., 76–77.

27. Gloria Grace Kulbeck, *What God Hath Wrought: A History of the Pentecostal Assemblies of Canada*, ed. W.E. McAlister and George R. Upton (Toronto: Pentecostal Assemblies of Canada, 1958), 355.

28. Hollenweger, *Pentecostals*, 392.

29. Kulbeck, *What God Hath Wrought*, 355.

30. For further information on the charismatic movement, see Smith, *Handbook of Contemporary Theology*, 117–32.

31. James W. Jones, *Filled with New Wine: The Charismatic Renewal of the Church* (New York: Harper and Row, 1974), 92–93.

32. Peter D. Hocken, "Church, Theology of the" in *Dictionary of Pentecostal and Charismatic Movements*, ed. Stanley M. Burgess and Gary B. McGee (Grand Rapids: Zondervan, 1988), 215.

33. Ibid.

34. Ibid.

35. Ibid., 95.

36. For further information on evangelism, see Smith, *Handbook of Contemporary Theology*, 58–71.

37. Millard J. Erickson, *Christian Theology* (Grand Rapids: Baker, 1983–1985), 1027.

38. Ibid., 1049.

39. Ibid., 1052–59.

40. Ibid., 1063.

41. Ibid., 1068.

42. Ibid., 1099.

43. Ibid., 1104.

44. Ibid., 1108.

45. Ibid., 1123.

46. Donald G. Bloesch, *Essentials of Evangelical Theology* (San Francisco: Harper and Row, 1979), 2.xi.

47. Donald G. Bloesch, *The Invaded Church* (Waco, Texas: Word, 1975), 15.

48. Ibid., 16.

49. Ibid., 96.

50. Ibid., 97.

51. Ibid., 98.

52. Bloesch, *Essentials*, 2.171.

53. Donald G. Bloesch, *The Future of Evangelical Christianity: A Call for Unity amid Diversity* (Garden City, N.Y.: Doubleday, 1983), 64.

54. Ibid., 65.

55. Ibid.

56. Bloesch, *Essentials*, 2.171.

57. Ibid., 83.

58. Ibid., 97.

59. Ibid., 107.

60. Ibid.

61. Ibid., 108.

62. Ibid., 109.

63. Charles Colson and Ellen Santilli Vaughn, *The Body: Being Light in Darkness* (Dallas: Word, 1992).

64. Ibid., 43.

65. Ibid., 45–46.

66. Ibid., 66.

67. Ibid., 103.
68. Ibid., 106.
69. Ibid., 137.
70. Ibid., 139.
71. Demetrius J. Constantelos, *The Greek Orthodox Church: Faith, History and Practice* (New York: Seabury, 1967), 30.
72. Ibid., 63.
73. Ibid., 65.
74. Vladimir Lossky, *The Mystical Theology of the Eastern Church* (1944; reprint, London: James Clarke, 1957), 179.
75. Ibid., 197.
76. Ibid., 187.
77. Ernst Benz, *The Eastern Orthodox Church: Its Thought and Life*, trans. Richard and Clara Winston (Garden City, N.Y.: Anchor, 1963), 32.
78. Ibid., 33.
79. Lossky, *Mystical Theology*, 170.
80. Lawrence Cross, *Eastern Christianity* (Philadelphia: E.J. Dwyer, 1988), 58.
81. Ibid.
82. Ibid., 59.
83. Constantelos, *The Greek Orthodox Church*, 86.
84. Ibid., 87.
85. Ibid., 88.
86. Ibid., 89.
87. Smith, *Handbook of Contemporary Theology*, 87.
88. Ibid., 87–88.
89. Avery Dulles, "The Church," in *The Documents of Vatican II*, ed. Walter M. Abbott and Joseph Gallagher (Piscataway, N.Y.: New Century, 1966), 9.
90. Ibid., 12.
91. *Lumen Gentium* 1.6-7, in *The Documents of Vatican II*, 18–21.
92. *Lumen Gentium* 1.8, 22.
93. Ibid., 23.
94. *Lumen Gentium* 2.9, 26.
95. *Lumen Gentium* 2.14, 26.
96. *Lumen Gentium* 2.15, 34.
97. *Lumen Gentium* 2.17, 36.
98. *Lumen Gentium* 3.18, 37–38.
99. *Lumen Gentium* 3.20, 40.
100. *Lumen Gentium* 3.22, 42–43.
101. *Lumen Gentium* 3.25, 47–49.
102. *Lumen Gentium* 3.32, 58–59.
103. *Lumen Gentium* 3.37, 64–65.
104. Karl Rahner, *The Church and the Sacraments*, trans. W.J. O'Hara (New York: Herder and Herder, 1963), 13.
105. Karl Rahner, *Foundations of the Christian Faith*, trans. William V. Dych (New York: Seabury, 1978), 176.

106. Rahner, *Church and the Sacraments*, 13.
107. Ibid., 20.
108. Karl Rahner, *The Dynamic Element of the Church* (London: Burns and Oates, 1964), 45.
109. Karl Rahner, *Theological Investigations* 2.290–91 in *A Rahner Reader*, ed. Gerald A. McCool (New York: Seabury, 1975), 296–97.
110. Rahner, *Church and the Sacraments*, 76–77.
111. Ibid., 82.
112. Ibid., 89–90.
113. Ibid., 90–91.
114. Ibid., 93.
115. Ibid., 95.
116. Hans Küng, *The Church* (Garden City, N.Y.: Image, 1976).
117. Ibid., 169–70.
118. Ibid., 172.
119. Ibid., 173.
120. Ibid., 174.
121. Ibid., 239–40.
122. Ibid., 247.
123. Ibid.
124. Ibid., 270.
125. Ibid., 271.
126. Ibid., 273–74.
127. Ibid., 274.
128. Ibid., 280.
129. Ibid., 286–87.
130. Ibid., 288.
131. Ibid., 291.
132. Hans Küng, *Signposts for the Future: Contemporary Issues Facing the Church* (Garden City, N.Y.: Doubleday, 1978), 120.
133. Ibid., 121.
134. Ibid., 124.
135. Ibid., 129.
136. Ibid., 130–31.
137. Ibid., 155.
138. Ibid., 156.
139. Ibid., 159.

Chapter 6

1. Charles C. Ryrie, *Basic Theology* (Wheaton, Ill.: Victor, 1986), 399.
2. James I. Packer, "The Nature of the Church," *Basic Christian Doctrines*, ed. Carl F.H. Henry (Grand Rapids: Baker, 1962), 242.
3. George E. Ladd, "Israel and the Church," *Evangelical Quarterly*, 36 (Oct.-Dec. 1964): 207.
4. George E. Ladd, *The Gospel of the Kingdom: Scriptural Studies in the Kingdom of God* (Grand Rapids: Eerdmans, 1959), 117.

5. F.F. Bruce, *The Epistle of Paul to the Romans*, Tyndale New Testament Commentaries (Grand Rapids: Eerdmans, 1963), 196.

6. Ibid., 207.

7. C.E.B. Cranfield, *The Epistle to the Romans*, The International Critical Commentary (Edinburgh: T & T Clark, 1979), 2.542.

8. Ibid., 2.545.

9. Ladd, "Israel and the Church," 204.

10. Walter C. Kaiser, Jr., "Israel and the People of God," in Basden and Dockery, *The People of God*, 105.

11. Ladd, "Israel and the Church," 211.

12. For a brief summary of those arguments see Cranfield, *Epistle to the Romans*, 565–66 or Bruce, *Epistle of Paul to the Romans*, 217–18.

13. Cranfield, *Epistle to the Romans*, 570–71.

14. See Bruce, *Epistle of Paul to the Romans*, 222.

15. Markus Barth, *The Broken Wall: A Study of the Epistle to the Ephesians* (Philadelphia: Judson, 1959), 133.

16. Walther Eichrodt, *Theology of the Old Testament*, trans. J.A. Baker, The Old Testament Library (Philadelphia: Westminster, 1961), 36.

17. M. Weinfeld, "berit," *Theological Dictionary of the Old Testament*, 1975, 2.253–55. For a fuller treatment of the concept of covenant, especially in its etymological roots, see Dennis J. McCarthy, *Old Testament Covenant, A Survey of Current Opinions* (Atlanta: John Knox, 1972).

18. It should be noted that the idea of covenants (e.g., for business, marital, and other purposes) between two human parties was a normal way of life in the ancient Near East, including Israel.

19. Ibid., 255–56.

20. Thomas Edward McComiskey, *The Covenant of Promise: A Theology of the Old Testament Covenants* (Grand Rapids: Baker, 1985), 140.

21. J. Barton Payne, *The Theology of the Older Testament* (Grand Rapids: Zondervan, 1962), 393.

22. For a review of many of these theories on Egypt's "reproach," see Trent C. Butler, *Joshua*, vol. 7 of Word Biblical Commentary (Waco, Texas: Word, 1983), 59; and J. Alberto Soggin, *Joshua, A Commentary*, The Old Testament Library (Philadelphia: Westminster, 1972), 72.

23. McComiskey, *Covenants of Promise*, 145.

24. Ibid.

25. Ibid.

26. Brevard S. Childs, *The Book of Exodus, A Critical Theological Commentary*, Old Testament Library (Philadelphia: Westminster, 1974), 367.

27. Eichrodt, *Theology of the Old Testament*, 43.

28. The Hebrew word translated "husband" in Jer. 31:32 is ba'al, which also is rendered "Lord." J.A. Thompson, *The Book of Jeremiah*, The New International Commentary on the Old Testament (Grand Rapids: Eerdmans, 1980), 581n. suggests that the latter meaning, given the context, is a better translation than the former.

29. McComiskey, *Covenants of Promise*, 84.

30. Thompson, *Book of Jeremiah*, 581.

31. McComiskey, *Covenants of Promise*, 87.

32. Ibid., 88–89.

33. R.N. Whybray, *Isaiah 40–66*, The New Century Bible Commentary (Grand Rapids: Eerdmans, 1975), 75.

34. Payne, *Theology of the Older Testament*, 81.

35. Eichrodt, *Theology of the Old Testament*, 2.37.

36. G. Ernest Wright, *The Old Testament Against Its Environment* (Chicago: Alec R. Allenson, 1955), 71.

37. Charles E. Van Engen, *The Growth of the True Church: An Analysis of the Ecclesiology of Church Growth Theory* (Amsterdam: Editions Rodopi, 1981), 120.

38. Eichrodt, *Theology of the Old Testament*, 2.190.

39. W.J. Dumbrell, *Covenant and Creation: A Theology of Old Testament Covenants* (Nashville: Thomas Nelson, 1984), 84.

40. Eichrodt, *Theology of the Old Testament*, 2.211.

41. Ibid., 231.

42. This thought is developed by E.A. Speiser, *Genesis*, The Anchor Bible (Garden City, N.Y.: Doubleday, 1964), 87.

43. James Muilenburg, "The Book of Isaiah, Chapters 40–66," *The Interpreter's Bible* (Nashville: Abingdon, 1956), 5.569.

44. Eichrodt, *Theology of the Old Testament*, 38.

45. Ibid.

46. Elmer A. Martens, *God's Design: A Focus on Old Testament Theology* (Grand Rapids: Baker, 1981), 79.

47. Eichrodt, *Theology of the Old Testament*, 39.

48. Van Engen, *The Growth of the True Church*, 132.

49. Trent C. Butler, *Joshua*, vol. 5 of Word Biblical Commentary (Waco, Texas: Word, 1983), 276.

50. H. Strathmann, *Theological Dictionary of the New Testament*, ed. Gerhard Kittel, ed. and trans. Geoffrey W. Bromiley (Grand Rapids: Eerdmans, 1967), 4.36.

51. Van Engen, *Growth of the True Church*, 133.

52. Eichrodt, *Theology of the Old Testament*, 289ff, 392ff.

53. See Yehezkel Kaufmann, *The Religion of Israel*, trans. and abr. Moshe Greenberg (New York: Schocken, 1960), 225.

54. Ibid.

55. Eichrodt, *Theology of the Old Testament*, 291.

56. See Gary V. Smith, "Prophet," *The International Standard Bible Encyclopedia*, ed. Geoffrey W. Bromiley (Grand Rapids: Eerdmans, 1986), 3.987.

57. Ibid.

58. Eichrodt, *Theology of the Old Testament*, 306.

59. John Bright, *A History of Israel*, 2nd ed. (Philadelphia: Westminster, 1972), 171.

60. Bernhard W. Anderson, *Understanding the Old Testament*, 2nd

ed. (Englewood Cliffs, N.J.: Prentice-Hall, 1966), 110.

61. Ibid., 111.

62. James M. Ward, *Thus Says the Lord: The Message of the Prophets* (Nashville: Abingdon, 1991), 13.

63. Anderson, *Understanding the Old Testament*, 190.

64. Ibid., 192.

65. Ibid.

66. Ward, *Thus Says the Lord*, 23.

67. Earl S. Kalland, "Priest, Priesthood," *Wycliffe Bible Encyclopedia* (Chicago: Moody, 1975), 2.1395.

68. Ibid., 2.1396.

69. Gerhard von Rad, *Old Testament Theology*, trans. D.M.G. Stalker (New York: Harper and Row, 1962), 1.244.

70. Eichrodt, *Theology of the Old Testament*, 438.

71. David Noel Freedman, "Divine Commitment and Human Obligation," *Interpretation* 18 (1964): 421.

72. J.A. Thompson, *Deuteronomy*, Tyndale Old Testament Commentaries (Downers Grove, Ill.: InterVarsity, 1974), 269.

73. Freedman, "Divine Commitment and Human Obligation," 421.

74. Ibid., 428.

75. Ibid., 429.

76. Eichrodt, *Theology of the Old Testament*, 466.

77. Freedman, "Divine Commitment and Human Obligation," 430.

78. Ibid., 431.

79. John Bright, *The Kingdom of God: The Biblical Concept and Its Meaning for the Church* (Nashville: Abingdon, 1953), 159.

80. Bright, *History of Israel*, 458.

81. Ibid., 459.

82. Bright, *Kingdom of God*, 170.

83. Eichrodt, *Theology of the Old Testament*, 473.

84. Timothy R. Ashley, *The Book of Numbers*, The New International Commentary on the Old Testament (Grand Rapids: Eerdmans, 1993), 469–92.

85. Ibid., 503.

86. John J. Davis, *Paradise to Prison: Studies in Genesis* (Grand Rapids: Baker, 1975), 297.

87. Gerhard von Rad, *Genesis*, rev. ed., trans. John H. Marks, The Old Testament Library (Philadelphia: Westminster, 1972), 426.

88. Eichrodt, *Theology of the Old Testament*, 476.

89. Ibid., 477.

90. Derek Kidner, *Psalms 1-72*, The Tyndale Old Testament Commentaries (Downers Grove, Ill.: InterVarsity, 1973), 19.

91. Eichrodt, *Theology of the Old Testament*, 479.

92. Some interpreters reject the Day of the Lord as eschatological in nature. For a summary of scholarly interpretations, see Gerhard F. Hasel, *Understanding the Book of Amos: Basic Issues in Current Interpretations* (Grand Rapids: Baker, 1991), 105ff.

93. Ernst Jenni, "Day of the Lord," *The Interpreter's Dictionary of the Bible*, ed. George A. Buttrick (Nashville: Abingdon, 1962), 1.784.
94. Page H. Kelley, "Doing It God's Way: Introduction to Isaiah 40-55," *The Review and Expositor* 88 (Spring 1991): 172.
95. Eichrodt, *Theology of the Old Testament*, 482–83.
96. Ibid., 485.

Chapter 7
1. Frank Stagg, *New Testament Theology* (Nashville: Broadman, 1962), 171.
2. Hans Küng, *The Church* (Garden City, N.Y.: Doubleday/Image, 1976), 157.
3. Alfred Loisy, *L'Evangile et l'Eglise* (1902), 111, cited by Küng, *The Church*, 69.
4. Friedrich Nietzsche, *The Complete Works of Friedrich Nietzsche* (1909), 14.138 cited by Leonhard Goppelt, *Theology of the New Testament* (Grand Rapids: Eerdmans, 1981), 1.207n.
5. H.E.W. Turner, *Jesus, Master and Lord: A Study in the Historical Truth of the Gospels* (London: A.R. Mowbray, 1970), 262. Cf. Joachim Jeremias, *New Testament Theology*, trans. John Bowden (London: SCM, 1971), 1.167–68.
6. Goppelt, *Theology of the New Testament*, 1.208.
7. E.P. Sanders, *Jesus and Judaism* (Philadelphia: Fortress, 1985), 231–32.
8. Goppelt, *Theology of the New Testament*, 1.209.
9. Dietrich Bonhoeffer, *The Cost of Discipleship*, rev. ed., trans. R.H. Fuller (New York: Macmillan, 1959), 49.
10. See J. Dwight Pentecost, *Design for Discipleship* (Grand Rapids: Zondervan, 1971), 14.
11. To make such a statement does not imply that the person trusting in Christ must at all times be in perfect obedience to His will. But one must be progressively moving to that state (complete only in the next life). A willingness to obedience is absolutely necessary.
12. Goppelt, *Theology of the New Testament*, 1.210.
13. Jeremias, *New Testament Theology*, 173.
14. Stagg, *New Testament Theology*, 173.
15. Ibid.
16. D.A. Carson, *The Gospel According to John* (Grand Rapids: Eerdmans, 1991), 513.
17. Rudolf Schnackenburg, *The Church in the New Testament*, trans. W.J. O'Hara (New York: Seabury, 1965), 110.
18. Ben F. Meyer, *The Aims of Jesus* (London: SCM, 1979), 154.
19. Jeremias, *New Testament Theology*, 1.235.
20. Goppelt, *Theology of the New Testament*, 1.212.
21. George R. Beasely-Murray, "John 13-17: The Community of True Life," *The Review and Expositor* 85 (Summer 1988): 473–74.

22. Ibid., 481.

23. Ray Summers, *Behold the Lamb: An Exposition of the Theological Themes in the Gospel of John* (Nashville: Broadman Press, 1979), 212.

24. Merrill C. Tenney, *John: The Gospel of Belief* (Grand Rapids: Eerdmans, 1976), 246.

25. Summer, *Behold the Lamb*, 213.

26. See Beasley-Murray, "John 13-17: The Community of True Life," 481–82. Cf. Barnabas Lindars, *The Gospel of John* (London: Oliphants, 1972), 524.

27. See Carson, *Gospel According to John*, 562. Cf. Rudolf Bultmann, *The Gospel of John: A Commentary*, trans. George R. Beasley-Murray, R.W.N. Hoare, and J.K. Riches (London: Blackwell, 1971), 503.

28. Tenney, *John: The Gospel of Belief*, 247.

29. George E. Ladd, *A Theology of the New Testament*, rev. ed., ed. Donald A. Hagner (Grand Rapids: Eerdmans, 1993), 305.

30. Summers, *Behold the Lamb*, 221.

31. Tenney, *John*, 249.

32. Summers, *Behold the Lamb*, 222.

33. Beasley-Murray, "John 13-17: The Community of True Life," 483.

34. Stagg, *New Testament Theology*, 186.

35. Ladd, *Theology of the New Testament*, 390.

36. Küng, *The Church*, 454.

37. Stagg, *New Testament Theology*, 188.

38. Ladd, *A Theology of the New Testament*, 115.

39. George R. Beasley-Murray, *Jesus and the Kingdom of God* (Grand Rapids: Eerdmans, 1986), 182.

40. Stagg, *New Testament Theology*, 188.

41. Ibid., 191–92.

42. Jeremias, *New Testament Theology*, 1.96–97.

43. Ladd, *Theology of the New Testament*, 109–17.

44. Ibid., 110–11.

45. Donald Guthrie, *New Testament Theology* (Downers Grove, Ill.: InterVarsity, 1981), 704.

46. Ladd, *Theology of the New Testament*, 114–15.

47. Schnackenburg, *Church in the New Testament*, 191.

48. Ladd, *Theology of the New Testament*, 114–15.

49. Ibid., 115.

50. For a brief overview of these different views of the kingdom's significance see Küng, *The Church*, 84ff.

Chapter 8

1. Guthrie, *New Testament Theology*, 731.

2. Leonhard Goppelt, *Apostolic and Post-Apostolic Times*, trans. Robert A. Guelich (Grand Rapids: Baker, 1970), 8.

3. Küng, *The Church*, 115.

4. Guthrie, *New Testament Theology*, 733.

5. Schnackenburg, *Church in the New Testament*, 65.
6. T.C. Smith, *Studies in Acts* (Greenville, S.C.: Smyth and Helwys, 1991), 18.
7. F.F. Bruce, *The Acts of the Apostles* (London: Tyndale, 1951), 102.
8. David S. Dockery, "Acts 6-12: The Christian Mission Beyond Jerusalem," *The Review and Expositor* 87 (Summer 1990): 427.
9. Ibid., 426–27.
10. C.H. Dodd, *The Apostolic Preaching and Its Developments* (New York: Harper and Row, 1964), 30–31.
11. Ibid., 21.
12. Ibid., 21–22.
13. Ibid., 22.
14. Ibid., 23.
15. Ibid.
16. Ibid.
17. Küng, *The Church*, 269–70.
18. Goppelt, *Apostolic and Post-Apostolic Times*, 42.
19. Ibid., 26.
20. Guthrie, *New Testament Theology*, 739.
21. Ibid.
22. Ladd, *Theology of the New Testament*, 389.
23. Küng, *The Church*, 517.
24. Ibid.
25. Radmacher, *Nature of the Church*, 328.
26. Guthrie, *New Testament Theology*, 743.
27. Schnackenburg, *Church in the New Testament*, 149.
28. Goppelt, *Theology of the New Testament*, 1.149.
29. Ladd, *Theology of the New Testament*, 591.
30. Radmacher, *Nature of the Church*, 240.
31. Ibid., 248.
32. Guthrie, *New Testament Theology*, 748.
33. Jonathan H. Gerstner, *The Epistle to the Ephesians: A Study Manual* (Grand Rapids: Baker, 1958), 39.
34. C.F.D. Moule, *Worship in the New Testament* (Richmond, Va.: John Knox, 1961), 9–10.
35. Ferdinand Hahn, *The Worship of the Early Church*, trans. David E. Green (Philadelphia: Fortress, 1973), 35.
36. Gerald L. Borchert, "The Lord of Form & Freedom: A New Testament Perspective on Worship," *Review & Expositor 80* (Winter 1983): 7.
37. Charles C. Ryrie, "Lord's Day," *Wycliffe Bible Encyclopedia* (Chicago: Moody, 1975), 2.1049.
38. Leon Morris, *The First Epistle of Paul to the Corinthians: An Introduction and Commentary*, Tyndale New Testament Commentaries (Grand Rapids: Eerdmans, 1958), 238.
39. Ralph P. Martin, *Worship in the Early Church* (Grand Rapids: Eerdmans, 1964), 40–41.

40. Andrew T. Lincoln, *Ephesians*, vol. 42 of Word Biblical Commentary (Dallas: Word Books, 1990), 345.

41. Francis Foulkes, *The Epistle of Paul to the Ephesians: An Introduction and Commentary*, Tyndale New Testament Commentaries (Grand Rapids: Eerdmans, 1963), 148.

42. Ralph P. Martin, *Philippians*, The New Century Bible Commentary (Grand Rapids: Eerdmans, 1976), 101.

43. Martin, *Worship in the Early Church*, 51.

44. Leith, *Creeds of the Churches*, 12.

45. Martin, *Worship in the Early Church*, 54.

46. Borchert, "The Lord of Form and Freedom," 10.

47. Martin, *Worship in the Early Church*, 60.

48. Ibid., 49.

49. Borchert, "The Lord of Form and Freedom," 15.

50. Goppelt, *Apostolic and Post-Apostolic Times*, 48.

51. Martin, *Worship in the Early Church*, 35.

52. Ibid., 37.

53. C.K. Barrett, *A Commentary on the Second Epistle to the Corinthians*, Harper's New Testament Commentaries (New York: Harper & Row, 1973), 78.

54. William Barclay, *The Letters to the Corinthians*, The Daily Study Bible (Edinburgh: Saint Andrew Press, 1954), 180.

55. Ibid., 181–82.

56. Morris, *The First Epistle of Paul to the Corinthians*, 239.

57. George R. Beasley-Murray, "Baptism in the Epistles of Paul," *Christian Baptism*, ed. A. Gilmore (Philadelphia: Judson, 1959), 130–31 surveys various scholarly views.

58. Ibid., 131.

59. George R. Beasley-Murray, *Baptism in the New Testament* (Grand Rapids: Eerdmans, 1962), 132.

60. Anders Nygren, *Commentary on Romans* (Philadelphia: Fortress, 1949), 233–34.

61. G.R. Beasley-Murray, "βαπτιζο," *The New International Dictionary of New Testament Theology*, ed. Colin Brown (Grand Rapids: Zondervan, 1975), 1.144.

62. See William H. Willimon, *Word, Water, Wine and Bread* (Valley Forge, Pa.: Judson, 1980), 28.

63. Beasley-Murray, "Baptism in the Epistles of Paul," 138.

64. Murray J. Harris, *Colossians and Philemon* (Grand Rapids: Eerdmans, 1991), 103.

65. Ibid., 141. For a contrary view, see Moule, *Worship in the New Testament*, 52.

66. Morris, *First Epistle of Paul to the Corinthians*, 98.

67. Ibid., 174.

68. Beasley-Murray, *Baptism in the New Testament*, 200.

69. Markus Barth, *The Broken Wall*, 178.

70. Beasley-Murray, "Baptism in the Epistles of Paul," 143.

Notes

71. Moule, *Worship in the New Testament*, 21.

72. Ibid., 21–22.

73. William Barclay, *The Lord's Supper* (London: SCM, 1967), 57.

74. A.J.B. Higgins, *The Lord's Supper in the New Testament* (London: SCM, 1952), 67–68.

75. Gunther Bornkamm, *Paul*, trans. D.M.G. Stalker (New York: Harper & Row, 1971), 192.

76. Higgins, *The Lord's Supper in the New Testament*, 65.

77. Harold S. Songer, "Problems Arising from the Worship of Idols: 1 Corinthians 8:1-11:1," *The Review and Expositor* 80 (Summer 1983): 372.

78. Higgins, *The Lord's Supper in the New Testament*, 72. Cf. Morris, *First Epistle of Paul to the Corinthians*, 164.

79. Higgins, *The Lord's Supper in the New Testament*, 72–73. Cf. Fred D. Howard, *1 Corinthians: Guidelines for God's People* (Nashville: Convention, 1983), 102.

80. Geoffrey Wainwright, *Eucharist and Eschatology* (New York: Oxford Univ. Press, 1981), 185.

81. Bornkamm, *Paul*, 193.

82. Charles H. Talbert, *Reading Corinthians: A Literary and Theological Commentary on 1 and 2 Corinthians* (New York: Crossroad, 1987), 79.

83. Guthrie, *New Testament Theology*, 760.

84. Robert J. Banks, "Church Order and Governments," *Dictionary of Paul and His Letters*, ed. Gerald F. Hawthorne and Ralph P. Martin (Downers Grove, Ill.: InterVarsity, 1993), 134.

85. There is considerable debate over whether the Pastoral Epistles are truly Pauline or Deutero-Pauline. I am assuming here that they are Pauline in authorship.

86. Martin Dibelius and Hans Conzelmann, *The Pastoral Epistles*, trans. Philip Buttolph and Adela Yarbro, ed. Helmut Koester, Hermeneia (Philadelphia: Fortress Press, 1972), 54–55.

87. Ronald A. Ward, *Commentary on 1 and 2 Timothy and Titus* (Waco, Texas: Word, 1974), 55.

88. Robert L. Saucy, *The Church in God's Program* (Chicago: Moody, 1972), 147.

89. C.K. Barrett, *The Pastoral Epistles in the New English Bible* (Oxford: Clarendon, 1963), 59.

90. Ward, *Commentary on 1 and 2 Timothy and Titus*, 57.

91. Saucy, *Church in God's Program*, 147.

92. Guthrie, *New Testament Theology*, 763.

93. For a summary of both sides, see Saucy, *Church in God's Program*, 154–55.

94. Ward, *1 and 2 Timothy and Titus*, 59.

95. For a summary of both views (wives or deaconesses), see Barrett, *Pastoral Epistles*, 61–62.

96. Ibid., 62.

97. Dibelius and Conzelmann, *Pastoral Epistles*, 59.

98. George B. Caird, *The Apostolic Age* (London: Duckworth, 1955), 57.

99. Gary Inrig, *Life in His Body: Discovering Purpose, Form, and Freedom in His Church* (Wheaton, Ill.: Harold Shaw, 1975), 51.

100. Ibid., 52. For alternative classifications, see William Baird, *The Corinthian Church: A Biblical Approach to Urban Culture* (New York: Abingdon, 1964) or Jack W. MacGorman, *The Gifts of the Spirit: An Exposition of 1 Corinthians 12–14* (Nashville: Broadman Press, 1974).

101. Ralph P. Martin, *The Spirit and the Congregation: Studies in 1 Corinthians 12-14* (Grand Rapids: Eerdmans, 1984), 14.

102. John Eadie, *Commentary on the Epistle of Paul to the Colossians*, 122, as cited by Saucy, *Church in God's Program*, 99.

103. J.W. MacGorman, "The Discipline of the Church," in Basden and Dockery, *The People of God*, 77.

104. Martin, *Spirit and the Congregation*, 82.

105. However, for an interesting view of Luke's view of women, see Mary Rose d'Angelo, "Women in Luke-Acts: A Redactional View," *Journal of Biblical Literature* 109/3 (1990): 441–61.

106. Guthrie, *New Testament Theology*, 774.

107. For a more detailed exposition, see the section on "Baptism," above.

108. Mary J. Evans, *Women in the Bible: An Overview of All Crucial Passages on Women's Roles* (Downers Grove, Ill.: InterVarsity, 1983), 82.

109. E. Margaret Howe, *Women and Church Leadership* (Grand Rapids: Zondervan, 1982), 58.

110. Talbert, *Reading Corinthians*, 68–69.

111. F.F. Bruce, *1 and 2 Corinthians*, New Century Bible Commentary (London: Oliphants, 1971), 103.

112. Evans, *Women in the Bible*, 95.

113. Talbert, *Reading Corinthians*, 91. Cf. Evans, *Women in the Bible*, 99.

114. Talbert, *Reading Corinthians*, 91–92.

115. David W. Odell-Scott, "Let the Women Speak in Church," *Biblical Theology Bulletin* 13 (July 1983): 90–91.

116. For a readable discussion of authorship from this viewpoint, see William Barclay, *The Letters to Timothy, Titus, and Philemon*, The Daily Study Bible (Edinburgh: Saint Andrew, 1956), 11–17.

117. Mary Hayter, *The New Eve in Christ: The Use and Abuse of the Bible in the Debate About Women in the Church* (Grand Rapids: Eerdmans, 1987), 132.

118. Roger L. Omanson, "The Role of Women in the New Testament Church," *The Review and Expositor* 83 (Winter 1986): 23.

119. See Donald Guthrie, *The Pastoral Epistles*, Tyndale New Testament Commentaries (Grand Rapids: Eerdmans, 1957), 77.

120. Evans, *Women in the Bible*, 102.

121. Aída B. Spencer, *Beyond the Curse: Women Called to Ministry* (Nashville: Thomas Nelson, 1985), 86–87.

122. Catherine C. Kroeger, "Ancient Heresies and a Strange Greek Verb," *The Reformed Journal* 29 (March 1979): 14.

123. Evans, *Women in the Bible*, 104.

124. Barrett, *Pastoral Epistles*, 56.

125. Guthrie, *Pastoral Epistles*, 78.

126. Evans, *Women in the Bible*, 108.

127. Ibid.

128. See Dale Moody, "A New Chronology for the New Testament," *The Review and Expositor* 78 (Spring 1981): 227.

129. Goppelt, *Theology of the New Testament*, 2.238. Cf. William Barclay, *The Letter to the Hebrews*, The Daily Study Bible (Edinburgh: Saint Andrew, 1955), xvii.

130. Barclay, *The Letter to the Hebrews*, xix-xx. Cf. Goppelt, *Theology of the New Testament*, 238–39.

131. Ray C. Stedman, *What More Can God Say? A Fresh Look at Hebrews* (Glendale, Calif.: Regal, 1974), 41.

132. Barclay, *Letter to the Hebrews*, 26.

133. Stedman, *What More Can God Say?* 223.

134. Guthrie, *New Testament Theology*, 779.

135. Philip E. Hughes, *A Commentary on the Epistle to the Hebrews* (Grand Rapids: Eerdmans, 1977), 415.

136. Barclay, *Letter to the Hebrews*, 226–27.

137. James B. Polhill, "Prejudice, Partiality, and Faith: James 2," *The Review and Expositor* 83 (Summer 1986): 397.

138. Guthrie, *New Testament Theology*, 782.

139. Roger L. Omanson, "The Certainty of Judgment and the Power of Prayer," *The Review and Expositor* 83 (1986): 433.

140. For a summary of arguments for and against Petrine authorship, see James L. Blevins, "Introduction to 1 Peter," *The Review and Expositor* 79 (Summer 1982): 401–3.

141. For a fuller discussion of these matters, see Michael Green, *The Second Epistle General of Peter and the General Epistle of Jude: An Introduction and Commentary*, Tyndale New Testament Commentaries (Grand Rapids: Eerdmans, 1968), 13–17.

142. Blevins, "Introduction to 1 Peter," 410–11.

143. Green, *The Second Epistle of Peter*, 20.

144. Peter H. Davids, *The First Epistle of Peter*, The New International Commentary on the New Testament (Grand Rapids: Eerdmans, 1990), 85.

145. Bo I. Reicke, *The Epistles of James, Peter, and Jude*, vol. 37 of The Anchor Bible (Garden City, N.Y.: Doubleday, 1964), 91.

146. Alan M. Stibbs, *The First Epistle General of Peter*, Tyndale New Testament Commentaries (Grand Rapids: Eerdmans, 1959), 104.

147. Ibid.

148. Reicke, *Epistles of James, Peter, and Jude*, 93.

149. Davids, *First Epistle of Peter*, 143.
150. Roger L. Omanson, "Suffering for Righteousness' Sake (3:13–4:11)," *The Review and Expositor* 79 (Summer 1982): 444.
151. Marty L. Reid, "Images of the Church in the General Epistles," in Basden and Dockery, *The People of God*, 171.
152. Gerald L. Borchert, "The Conduct of Christians in the Face of the 'Fiery Ordeal' (4:12-5:11)," *The Review and Expositor* 79 (Summer 1982): 456–57.
153. Ibid., 457.
154. Guthrie, *New Testament Theology*, 730–31.
155. See John R.W. Stott, *The Epistles of John*, Tyndale New Testament Commentaries (Grand Rapids: Eerdmans, 1964), 200–201.
156. Richard L. Niswonger, *New Testament History* (Grand Rapids: Zondervan/Academie, 1988), 278.
157. Guthrie, *New Testament Theology*, 785–86.
158. George E. Ladd, *A Commentary on the Revelation of John* (Grand Rapids: Eerdmans, 1972), 248.
159. Ibid., 295.

Chapter 9

1. John Macquarrie, *Principles of Christian Theology*, 2nd ed. (New York: Scribner's, 1977), 386–87.
2. Louis Berkhof, *Systematic Theology*, 4th ed. rev. (Grand Rapids: Eerdmans, 1941), 570.
3. Guthrie, *New Testament Theology*, 702.
4. Erickson, *Christian Theology*, 1048.
5. See Ethelbert Bullinger, *The Mystery* (London: Eyrie and Spottiswoode, n.d.), 40, as cited by Saucy, *Church in God's Program*, 57.
6. L. Coenen, "εκκλησια," *New International Dictionary of New Testament Theology* (Grand Rapids: Zondervan, 1975), 1.293–94.
7. Saucy, *Church in God's Program*, 13.
8. Coenen, "ἐκκλησία," 1.294.
9. See Radmacher, *Nature of the Church*, 121.
10. Coenen, "εκκλησια," 1.295.
11. Radmacher, *Nature of the Church*, 123.
12. Ladd, *Gospel of the Kingdom*, 107.
13. Edmund P. Clowney, *The Doctrine of the Church* (Philadelphia: Presbyterian and Reformed, 1974), 29.
14. Gustaf Aulén, *The Faith of the Christian Church*, trans. Eric Wahlstrom and G.B. Everett Arden (London: SCM, 1954), 330.
15. Clowney, *Doctrine of the Church*, 30.
16. Aulén, *Faith of the Christian Church*, 330–31.
17. Küng, *The Church*, 107.
18. Though one might term it a "proto-church."
19. Aulén, *Faith of the Christian Church*, 333.
20. Dale Moody, *The Word of Truth: A Summary of Christian*

Doctrine Based on Biblical Revelation (Grand Rapids: Eerdmans, 1981), 447.

21. Macquarrie, *Principles of Christian Theology*, 460.
22. Saucy, *The Church in God's Program*, 65.
23. Ibid.
24. William Hendriksen, *New Testament Commentary: Exposition of Colossians and Philemon*, New Testament Commentary (Grand Rapids: Baker, 1964), 51, cited by Saucy, *Church in God's Program*, 68.
25. Emil Brunner, *Misunderstanding of the Church*, 20.

Chapter 10

1. Macquarrie, *Principles of Christian Theology*, 386.
2. Moody, *Word of Truth*, 440.
3. L. Coenen, "εκκλησια," *New International Dictionary of New Testament Theology*, ed. Colin Brown (Grand Rapids: Zondervan, 1975), 1.297.
4. Saucy, *Church in God's Program*, 16.
5. Moody, *Word of Truth*, 442.
6. Macquarrie, *Principles of Christian Theology*, 387.
7. Harold S. Bender, *These Are My People: The New Testament Church and Its People According to the New Testament* (Scottdale, Pa.: Herald, 1962), 7.
8. Ibid., 10–11.
9. Ibid., 13.
10. Ibid., 14.
11. Ibid., 15.
12. Ibid., 17.
13. Aulén, *Faith of the Christian Church*, 331.
14. Ibid., 331.
15. Ibid., 332.
16. Ibid.
17. Moody, *Word of Truth*, 444.
18. Ibid.
19. Erickson, *Christian Theology*, 1037.
20. Moody, *Word of Truth*, 444.
21. Ibid.
22. Saucy, *Church in God's Program*, 45.
23. Ibid., 46.
24. Ibid., 47.
25. William W. Stevens, *Doctrines of the Christian Religion* (Grand Rapids: Eerdmans, 1967), 304.
26. Brunner, *Misunderstanding of the Church*, 49.
27. Hans Küng, *The Church*, 228.
28. Moody, *Word of Truth*, 447.
29. Inrig, *Life in His Body*, 49.
30. Ibid.

31. Moody, *Word of Truth*, 448.
32. Ibid.
33. Edgar Y. Mullins, *The Christian Religion in Its Doctrinal Expression* (Philadelphia: Judson, 1917), 91.
34. Rudolf Bultmann, *Theology of the New Testament*, trans. Kendrick Grobel (New York: Scribner's, 1951), 1.4.
35. C.H. Dodd, *The Parables of the Kingdom* (New York: Scribner's, 1935), 35.
36. Ladd, *Theology of the New Testament*, 60–61.
37. Stevens, *Doctrines of the Christian Religion*, 291.
38. Ibid., 292.
39. Ladd, *Theology of the New Testament*, 66–67.
40. Brunner, *Christian Doctrine of the Church, Faith, and the Consummation*, 363–64.
41. Bright, *Kingdom of God*, 236.
42. Stevens, *Doctrines of the Christian Religion*, 296.
43. Küng, *The Church*, 59.
44. Erickson, *Christian Theology*, 1044–45.
45. Ibid., 1045.
46. *The New Catholic Encyclopedia*, s.v. "Visibility of the Church."
47. Erickson, *Christian Theology*, 1045.
48. Ibid., 1046.
49. John T. Mueller, *Christian Dogmatics: A Handbook of Doctrinal Theology for Pastors, Teachers, and Laymen* (St. Louis: Concordia, 1934), 541.
50. Ibid., 542.
51. Ibid.
52. Berkhof, *Systematic Theology*, 566.
53. Ibid.
54. Ibid.

Chapter 11

1. W.A. Criswell, *The Doctrine of the Church* (Nashville: Convention, 1980), 55.
2. Moody, *Word of Truth*, 429.
3. Ibid.
4. Bender, *These Are My People*, 91.
5. Ibid., 92.
6. George S. Hendry, *The Gospel of the Incarnation*, 170, as cited by Bender, *These Are My People*, 92.
7. Moody, *Word of Truth*, 430.
8. Ibid.
9. Ibid.
10. Ibid., 431.
11. Ibid.
12. Bender, *These Are My People*, 93.

13. Ibid., 94.

14. Erickson, *Christian Theology*, 1059.

15. Thomas N. Finger, *Christian Theology: An Eschatological Approach* (Scottdale, Pa.: Herald, 1987), 2.249.

16. Ibid., 250.

17. Bender, *These Are My People*, 50.

18. Ibid., 53.

19. Ibid.

20. Gustavo Gutiérrez, *A Theology of Liberation*, rev. ed., trans. and ed. Sister Karidad Inda and John Eagleson (Maryknoll, N.Y.: Orbis Books, 1988), 265.

21. Finger, *Christian Theology*, 2.322.

22. Jürgen Moltmann, *The Church in the Power of the Holy Spirit*, trans. Margaret Kohl (London: SCM, 1977), 261–62.

23. Finger, *Christian Theology*, 2.325–26.

24. John Macquarrie, *Christian Theology*, 2nd ed. (New York: Chas. Scribner's Sons, 1977), 493.

25. Ibid., 494.

26. Aulén, *The Faith of the Christian Church*, 403.

27. Ibid., 406.

28. Finger, *Christian Theology*, 2.327.

29. Ibid., 2.328.

30. Karl Barth, *The Doctrine of Reconciliation*, vol. 4, part 3 of *Church Dogmatics*, trans. Geoffrey W. Bromiley (Edinburgh: T and T Clark, 1961), 772.

31. G.C. Berkouwer, *The Church*, trans. James E. Davison (Grand Rapids: Eerdmans, 1976), 393.

32. Ibid., 394–95.

33. Criswell, *Doctrine of the Church*, 60.

Chapter 12

1. Franklin M. Segler, *A Theology of Church and Ministry* (Nashville: Broadman, 1960), 23.

2. James D. Smart, *The Rebirth of Ministry* (Philadelphia: Westminster, 1960), 18–19.

3. J. Rodman Williams, *Renewal Theology* (Grand Rapids: Zondervan, 1992), 3.160.

4. Ibid.

5. See Elton Trueblood, *The Company of the Committed* (New York: Harper & Row, 1961), or *The Incendiary Fellowship* (New York: Harper & Row, 1967).

6. Macquarrie, *Principles of Christian Theology*, 421.

7. Aulén, *Faith of the Christian Church*, 411.

8. Ibid., 411–12.

9. Macquarrie, *Principles of Christian Theology*, 423.

10. For a description of these gifts and what each entailed, see chapter 8.

11. Saucy, *Church in God's Program*, 133.
12. Gary Inrig, *Life in His Body*, 59.
13. It is not my intent to "put the Holy Spirit in a box," which is why I say "rarely" rather than "never" used. I have always accepted that the Spirit moves where and as He wills.
14. Williams, *Renewal Theology*, 3.165.
15. Leon Morris, *Ministers of God* (London: Inter-Varsity, 1964), 41.
16. Ibid., 42.
17. Williams, *Renewal Theology*, 3.168–69.
18. Ibid., 55.
19. Cited by Morris, ibid., 61.
20. C.M. Robeck, Jr., "Prophecy, Prophesying," in *Dictionary of Paul and His Letters*, ed. Gerald F. Hawthorne and Ralph P. Martin (Downers Grove, Ill.: InterVarsity, 1993), 756.
21. Ibid., 757.
22. Ibid., 760–61.
23. Ibid., 761–62.
24. Williams, *Renewal Theology*, 3.173.
25. Ibid., 3.174.
26. Ibid.
27. D. James Kennedy, *Evangelism Explosion*, 3rd ed. (Wheaton, Ill.: Tyndale, 1983), 3.
28. Williams, *Renewal Theology*, 3.176.
29. See Moody, *Word of Truth*, 456–57.
30. Criswell, *Doctrine of the Church*, 69–70.
31. Ibid., 70.
32. L. Coenen, "πρεσβύτερος," *The New International Dictionary of New Testament Theology*, ed. Colin Brown (Grand Rapids: Zondervan, 1975), 1.192–96.
33. Berkhof, *Systematic Theology*, 586.
34. L. Coenen, "επισκοπος," *The New International Dictionary of New Testament Theology*, 1.188–89.
35. Ibid., 1.190.
36. Ibid., 1.191.
37. Augustus H. Strong, *Systematic Theology* (Valley Forge, Pa.: Judson, 1907), 914–15.
38. Ibid., 915–16.
39. Ibid., 916.
40. Criswell, *Doctrine of the Church*, 75.
41. Saucy, *Church in God's Program*, 153.
42. Ibid., 154.
43. Küng, *The Church*, 512.
44. Saucy, *Church in God's Program*, 156.
45. Macquarrie, *Principles of Christian Theology*, 427.
46. Ibid.
47. Berkhof, *Systematic Theology*, 587.
48. Ibid., 587–88.

49. Fisher Humphreys, "Ordination in the Church," in Basden and Dockery, *The People of God*, 291.

50. Ibid.

51. Ibid., 292.

52. Ibid., 292–93.

53. Ibid., 294–95.

54. Donald G. Miller, *The Nature and Mission of the Church* (Richmond: John Knox, 1957), 82, as cited in Saucy, *Church in God's Program*, 105.

55. Saucy, *Church in God's Program*, 105.

56. Ibid., 106.

57. Finger, *Christian Theology: An Eschatological Approach*, 2.363.

58. Strong, *Systematic Theology*, 903.

59. Ibid., 926.

60. Erickson, *Christian Theology*, 1085.

61. Ibid., 1074.

62. Ibid., 1078.

63. Ibid., 1082.

64. Ibid., 1083.

65. Ibid., 1086.

Chapter 13

1. Erickson, *Christian Theology*, 944.

2. Stevens, *Doctrines of the Christian Religion*, 308.

3. Ibid., 309.

4. Moltmann, *Church in the Power of the Holy Spirit*, 235.

5. Küng, *The Church*, 269.

6. Moltmann, *Church in the Power of the Holy Spirit*, 234.

7. George R. Beasley-Murray, "Baptism in the Epistles of Paul," 132.

8. Strong, *Systematic Theology*, 942.

9. Allison A. Trites, "Baptism," 4, cited in Ronald F. Watts, *The Ordinances and Ministry of the Church: A Baptist View* (Toronto: Canadian Baptist Federation, 1986), 7.

10. Dale Moody, "Baptism in Theology and Practice," in Basden and Dockery, *The People of God*, 41–43.

11. Berkhof, *Systematic Theology*, 632.

12. Ibid., 632ff.

13. Strong, *Systematic Theology*, 954.

14. Trites, "Baptism," 7.

15. Joseph F. Eagan, "The Authority and Justification for Infant Baptism," *The Review and Expositor* 77 (Winter 1980): 49.

16. Küng, *The Church*, 269.

17. Karl Barth, *The Teaching of the Church Regarding Baptism*, trans. Ernest A. Payne (London: SCM, 1948), 9.

18. Stevens, *Doctrines of the Christian Religion*, 331.

19. Dean Stanley, "Article on Baptism," in *Nineteenth Century* (Oct.

1879), cited by H.S. Burrage, "Immersion Essential to Baptism," in *Baptist Doctrines*, ed. Charles A. Jenkens (St. Louis: Chancy R. Barnes, 1881), 165.

20. Moltmann, *The Church in the Power of the Holy Spirit*, 243.

21. G.C. Berkouwer, *The Sacraments*, trans. Hugo Bekker (Grand Rapids: Eerdmans, 1969), 190.

22. Brunner, *Christian Doctrine of the Church, Faith, and the Consummation*, 61.

23. Küng, *The Church*, 284.

24. Moody, *Word of Truth*, 468.

25. Stevens, *Doctrines of the Christian Religion*, 343.

26. Ibid.

27. *The New Catholic Encyclopedia*, s.v. "Transubstantiation."

28. Charles Hodge, *Systematic Theology* (Grand Rapids: Eerdmans, 1977), 3.628.

29. Berkouwer, *The Sacraments*, 231.

30. Ibid., 239.

31. Stevens, *Doctrines of the Christian Religion*, 347.

32. Ibid., 348–49.

33. Strong, *Systematic Theology*, 963.

34. Ibid., 971.

35. Ibid., 973.

36. Ibid., 974.

37. Ibid., 975.

38. Ceil and Moishe Rosen, *Christ in the Passover: Why Is This Night Different?* (Chicago: Moody, 1978), 29.

Chapter 14

1. Raymond E. Brown, *The Gospel According to John*, vol. 29A of The Anchor Bible (Garden City, N.Y.: Doubleday, 1970), 778.

2. Lindars, *The Gospel of John*, 530.

3. Rudolf Schnackenburg, *The Gospel According to John*, trans. David Smith and G.A. Kon (New York: Crossroad, 1990), 3.191.

4. Brown, *Gospel According to John*, 776.

5. Barth, *Broken Wall*, 108.

6. Berkouwer, *The Church*, 41.

7. Ibid.

8. Brunner, *Christian Doctrine of the Church, Faith, and the Consummation*, 33.

9. Macquarrie, *Principles of Christian Theology*, 403.

10. Ibid., 404.

11. Ibid.

12. Ibid., 405.

13. Michael Kinnamon, *Truth and Community: Diversity and Its Limits in the Ecumenical Movement* (Grand Rapids: Eerdmans, 1988), 75–76.

14. Ibid.

Notes

15. Martin E. Marty, *Church Unity and Church Mission* (Grand Rapids: Eerdmans, 1964), 62.

16. Ibid., 64.

17. Ibid., 65.

18. J. Robert Nelson, *One Lord, One Church* (New York: Association, 1958), 23.

19. Kinnamon, *Truth and Community*, 76–77.

20. For more detailed information on the church union, see John Webster Grant, *The Church in the Canadian Era* (Burlington, Ont.: Welch, 1988), 124–30 and H.H. Walsh, *The Christian Church in Canada* (Toronto: Ryerson, 1956), 294–304.

21. Nelson, *One Lord, One Church*, 77–78.

22. Ibid., 79–81.

23. Sydney E. Ahlstrom, *A Religious History of the American People* (New Haven: Yale Univ. Press, 1972), 1083.

24. George H. Tavard, *Two Centuries of Ecumenism* (London: Burns and Oates, 1960), 95–96.

25. Stephen Neill, *Men of Unity* (London: SCM, 1960), 24–25.

26. T.R. Weber, "Ecumenism," in *Evangelical Dictionary of Theology*, ed. Walter A. Elwell (Grand Rapids: Baker, 1984), 341.

27. Williams, *Renewal Theology*, 3.46.

28. Erickson, *Christian Theology*, 1143.

29. C.S. Lewis, "On the Reading of Old Books," in *Undeceptions: Essays in Theology and Ethics*, ed. Walter Hooper (London: Geoffrey Bles, 1971), 165.

30. Joe Maxwell, "Evangelicals Clarify Accord with Catholics," *Christianity Today*, 6 March 1995, 52.

31. Doug Koop, "Evangelicals and Catholics Together: Convergence and Controversy," *Christian Week*, 19 September 1995, 8–9.

Conclusion

1. Colson and Vaughn, *The Body*, 282.

2. Langdon Gilkey, *How the Church Can Minister to the World without Losing Itself* (New York: Harper & Row, 1964), 64.

3. Ibid., 71.

4. Howard A. Snyder, *The Problem of Wineskins: Church Structure in a Technological Age* (Downers Grove, Ill.: InterVarsity, 1975), 41.

5. Ibid., 43.

6. Findley B. Edge, *The Greening of the Church* (Waco, Texas: Word, 1971), 42.

7. Ibid., 136ff.

8. Gordon Cosby, *Handbook for Mission Groups* (Waco, Texas: Word, 1975).

9. Jerry Cook and Stanley C. Baldwin, *Love, Acceptance, and Forgiveness* (Ventura, Calif.: Regal, 1979).

10. Frank R. Tillapaugh, *Unleashing the Church: Getting People Out of*

the Fortress and into Ministry (Ventura, Calif.: Regal, 1982).

11. Colson and Vaughn, *The Body*, 291.
12. Gilkey, *How the Church Can Minister*, 111–12.
13. Ibid., 91.
14. Trueblood, *The Incendiary Fellowship*, 45.
15. Colson and Vaughn, *The Body*, 291.
16. Ibid., 292.
17. Ibid., 295.
18. Williams, *Renewal Theology*, 3.85.
19. Ibid., 3.106.
20. Ibid., 3.104–5.
21. Ibid., 3.109.
22. Snyder, *Problem of Wineskins*, 135.
23. George W. Webber, *The Congregation in Mission* (New York: Abingdon, 1964), 121.
24. Edge, *Greening of the Church*, 171.
25. Ibid., 173–74.
26. Rex A. Koivisto, *One Lord, One Faith: A Theology for Cross-Cultural Renewal* (Wheaton, Ill.: Victor/BridgePoint, 1993), 274.
27. Ibid.
28. Ibid., 275.
29. Ibid., 276.
30. Ibid., 277.
31. Ibid., 284–85.

SELECT NAME AND SUBJECT INDEX

A

Abraham   *200, 203, 205, 209, 215, 228, 323–25, 333*
Affusion   *27, 36, 46, 64, 77, 90, 113, 119, 380–82*
Ambrose   *55–57, 67*
Anabaptists   *95, 98, 108–23, 127, 138, 149, 374*
Anglicans   *11, 124–28, 132–33, 138, 151, 336, 369, 374, 393, 398,*
    400–401, 406
"Anonymous Christian"   *184*
Apostles   *22, 28–29, 31–32, 41, 55, 58, 65, 147, 183, 233, 237–38,*
    243, 245–46, 250–51, 253, 257–58, 265, 286, 315, 318, 335, 357–58,
    369, 372, 376
Apostolic Succession   *32, 53–55, 62, 65, 73, 183, 335, 369–70, 372*
Assemblies of God   *162*
Assembly   *320–21*
Arians   *45–46, 57, 63*
Arius   *45*
Aspersion See *Sprinkling*
Athanasius   *45, 48, 405*
Augsburg Confession   *399*
Augustine   *39, 47, 56–64, 67, 79, 92, 99, 103, 180*
Aulén, Gustaf   *325, 348, 355*
Authentein   *295*

B

Ban *115–16, 120–21, 123, 245, 363*
Baptism *13, 18, 25, 27, 31, 35–38, 41–44, 46–52, 54–56, 58–61, 65,*
  76–77, 80, 84, 89–91, 97–98, 103–5, 107, 110, 113–14, 118–19, 123,
  126–27, 131, 147, 149, 153–54, 160–61, 164, 169, 175–76, 178, 182,
  186, 188–89, 192–93, 256–57, 268, 270, 273–78, 303, 307, 316, 337,
  361, 374, 377–84, 389, 392, 401
Baptism, Infant *38–39, 42–44, 58–59, 62, 90, 98, 104–5, 107, 110,*
  114, 117, 119, 123, 131, 147, 149, 154, 161, 164, 169, 380
Baptists *11, 130–33, 138, 147, 194, 336, 371, 393, 398, 400*
Barclay, Robert *146–47*
Barclay, William *297–99*
Barrett, C.K. *272*
Barth, Karl *158, 350, 381*
Barth, Markus *206, 395*
Beasley-Murray, George R. *241, 274, 276*
Bender, Harold *324, 341–42*
Bennett, Dennis *165*
Berengar of Tours *68–69, 79*
Berkhof, Louis *311, 367, 380*
Berkouwer, G.C. *350, 383*
Bernard of Clairvaux *78*
Bishops *23–24, 31–32, 34, 36–37, 41–42, 53, 55, 61–62, 93, 121,*
  125–26, 141, 178, 183, 282–83, 357–58, 362, 364, 367, 369–70, 372,
  375
Bloesch, Donald *170–73, 194*
Bonhoeffer, Dietrich *234*
Borchert, Gerald L. *270, 304*
Bornkamm, Gunther *281*
Brausch, William *143–44*
Bright, John *227–28, 334*
Browne, Robert *129*
Bruce, F.F. *202, 253*
Brunner, Emil *158–62, 194, 334*
Bucer, Martin *101*
Bultmann, Rudolf *331*

C

Dockery, David S. *254*
Dodd, C.H. *255, 331*
Donatism *57–58*
Drozdov, Philaret *139–40*
DuPlessis, David *163*
Durandus *69*
Dynamic Presence *386–87*

E

Eagan, Joseph *381*
Ebionites *20, 64*
Ecclesia *88, 159–61*
Edge, Findley *413, 420*
Edification *168, 419–20*
Education *13*
Edward VI *123, 125*
Eichrodt, Walther *214, 216, 221, 223, 230*
Ekklēsia *23, 232–33, 236, 242–45, 247, 259, 311–13, 321–23, 417*
Elders See *Presbyters*
Elect, election *100, 160, 171, 187, 232, 314, 318, 324, 331, 378, 395*
Elizabeth I *124*
Episcopalians *11, 401*
Erasmus, Desiderius *83–84*
Erickson, Millard J. *167–70, 194, 311, 344, 373–74*
Eucharist See *Lord's Supper*
Eusebius (of Caesarea) *19, 300–301*
Evangelicals *167–76, 192, 194, 364, 405, 422*
Evangelism *13, 168, 173, 413–14, 416–17, 422*
Evangelists *147, 192, 287, 357, 360–61, 367, 397–98*
Excommunication *41, 71, 73, 86, 112, 186, 245, 389*

F

Faith *26, 57, 88, 92, 97, 99, 105, 114, 118, 139, 154, 176, 202, 277, 299, 300–301, 303, 325, 337, 342, 344–45, 361, 377–78, 405, 419*
Father See *God*
Febronianism *142*

N

Nazarites *220–21*
Neitzsche, Friedrich *233*
Nelson, Robert *399*
Neo-orthodoxy *158–62, 192*
Neo-Pentecostalism *162, 165–67*
Nestorius *49*
Neuhaus, Richard John *406*
Newman, John Henry *144–45*
Nicholas II *69–70*
Niebuhr, Reinhold *158*
Norden, Edward *269*
Nygren, Anders *274*

O

Obedience *303, 307, 346, 352, 389–90*
Ockham, William *77–79, 92*
Oecolampadius, Johannes *98*
Offering *272, 348–49*
Omanson, Roger *294*
Ordinances *25, 35–36, 39, 75, 78–79, 83-84, 90, 94, 97, 106, 126–27, 130, 140, 147, 149, 160–61, 169, 177–79, 181, 185, 192–93, 337–38*
Ordination *13, 41, 88, 102, 178, 357, 366–69*
Origen *30, 38–40, 45, 48, 52, 296*
Orthodoxy, Eastern *45, 51, 63, 65–67, 88, 135–40, 156, 176–80, 193, 336, 368–69, 374, 393, 402*
Overseers See *Bishops*

P

Pastors *88, 92, 101–2, 111, 120–21, 131, 147–49, 172, 192, 287, 357, 362–63, 365–66, 375, 391, 414*
Paul *19–21, 26, 28, 32, 65, 202–3, 255, 260–63, 265, 271–73, 275–76, 278–81, 285, 289–91, 293–95, 316, 318, 322, 328, 330, 354, 358–60, 363, 379, 385, 394–95, 411–12, 417*
Payne, Barton *208, 213*
Pelagius *58*

Pellican, Francis Conrad *83*
Penance *43, 50–52, 59–60, 65, 80, 85, 126, 186*
Pentecost *18, 235, 240, 252–53, 255, 264, 307, 311, 315–19, 325, 329–30, 346–47*
Pentescostals *162–65, 192, 374*
Pentecostal Assemblies *162*
Peter *18, 32, 41–42, 45, 53, 54, 65, 124–25, 201, 242–43, 245, 254–55, 257, 300, 302, 315, 317, 323, 355, 378, 395, 414*
Petry, Ray *22*
Philips, Obbe *117*
Pietism *147–51, 157*
Pius IX *143–44*
Polycarp *25–27, 30, 32*
Prayer *271–72, 300, 330, 347–48, 350–51, 387, 393–94, 420*
Preaching *171–72, 342*
Presbyterians *133, 336, 370–72, 374, 386, 400–401*
Presbyters *22, 25–27, 32, 36–37, 53, 61–62, 101, 131, 178, 258–59, 282, 300, 303–4, 362–66, 375, 391, 401*
Presbytery *24, 34*
Priesthood of Believers *85, 167, 172, 343, 354, 372*
Priests *51–52, 60, 62, 73, 92, 125–26, 182, 222–23, 282, 302, 344, 387, 413, 417*
  Celibacy of *70*
Prophets *28–29, 221–22, 265, 286, 357, 359–60*
Puritans *128–29, 132*

Q

Quakers *138, 146–47, 157, 371, 374, 386*

R

Radbertus, Paschasius *67–68, 79*
Radical Reformation *108–23, 146, 163*
Radmacher, Earl *25, 264*
Rahner, Karl *184–87, 193*
Ratramnus *79*
Real Presence *51, 61–62, 105, 127, 155, 194*
Reconciliation *43, 159, 178, 186, 212, 354–55*
Reformation *77, 84, 86–134, 190, 337, 354, 402, 415*

SCRIPTURE INDEX

Mark

1:4 *377*
1:14f. *331, 360*
1:15 *246, 333*
1:17-20 *234*
2:14 *234*
2:23–3:6 *267*
2:27 *267*
3:13-15 *357*
3:13-19 *236*
4:30-32 *247*
10:14 *119*
10:44 *344*
10:45 *284*
11:27-33 *378*
14:36 *271*

Luke

4:18-19 *333, 340*
4:21 *333*
4:43 *246*
6:1-11 *267*
6:13-16 *237*
8:1 *246*
9:2 *246*
9:60 *246*
10:16 *237*
10:27-37 *344*
11:20 *246*
11:52 *243*
12:32 *235*
14:26 *234*
18:15-17 *98*
18:16 *114, 119*
19:10 *333, 340*
22:19 *383*
22:19-20 *383*

John

3:3 *376*
3:16 *351*
4:42 *351*
5:24 *171*
8:39 *324*
10:1-18 *236*
10:11 *362*
10:14-15 *236*
13:34 *241*
13:34-35 *343*
14:15 *382*
15:1 *236*
15:1-8 *236*
17 *393*
17:1-5 *238–39*
17:2 *239*
17:3 *239*
17:5 *239, 241*
17:6-19 *238–40*
17:11 *239, 399*
17:15 *240*
17:17 *239–40*
17:19 *240*
17:20 *240*
17:20-23 *238, 394, 399*
17:21 *241, 394*
17:24 *241*
17:24-26 *238*
17:25-26 *241*
17:26 *241*
20:27 *172*
21:15 *236*
21:16 *236*
21:17 *236*

Acts

1:1-26 *257*
1:4-5 *17, 317*

481

482

485

James

1:1 *299*
1:27 *344*
2:2 *321*
2:5 *299*
2:14 *299*
2:26 *344*
5:14-16 *300*

1 Peter

1:1 *300*
1:10-11 *206*
2:4-8 *301*
2:5 *31, 343, 348, 395*
2:9 *201, 323, 417*
2:25 *364*
3:18-21 *303*
4:11 *356, 375*
5:1-4 *303*
5:2 *236*
5:5 *362*

1 John

1:3 *316*
3:2 *333*
3:18 *344*
4:19 *328*

2 John

1 *305*
9-10 *305*
10-11 *305*
11 *305*

Revelation

1:6 *344*
1:9 *305*
2–3 305
2:2 *306*
2:13-16 *306*
2:20 *306*
3:8-9 *306*
4:8 *306*
4:8-11 *306*
4:11 *306*
5:9-10 *306*
5:12-13 *306*
5:12-14 *417*
7:10 *306*
7:12 *306*
11:15 *306*
11:17-18 *306*
12:10-12 *306*
20:10 *284*
21:14 *357*
22:17 *306, 332*
22:20 *352*

- FOUR VIEWS ON DIVORCE
  BY H. WAYNE HOUSE

- SMALL GROUPS MINISTRY IN THE 21ST CENTURY
  GROUP. com (ENCYLOPEDIA OF PRACTICAL IDEAS)